ONLY TO GOD

The Extraordinary Life of
Godfrey Lowell Cabot

LEON HARRIS

ONLY TO GOD

The Extraordinary Life of
Godfrey Lowell Cabot

Atheneum   *New York*
1967

The author wishes to thank the following for permission to quote from copyright works: Beacon Press, for *The Right to Read: The Battle Against Censorship* by Paul Blanshard. Dr. L. Cabot Briggs and Goodspeed's Book Shop, Inc., for *History and Genealogy of the Cabot Family* by L. Vernon Briggs. Curtis Brown, Ltd., for *The Oxford History of the American People* by Samuel Eliot Morison. The Bruce Publishing Company and Walter Kerr, for *Criticism and Censorship* by Walter Kerr. Coward-McCann, Inc., for *Peabody of Groton* by Frank D. Ashburn, copyright 1944 by Frank D. Ashburn. E. P. Dutton & Co., Inc., for *The Fine Art of Political Wit* by Leon A. Harris, copyright © 1964 by Leon A. Harris, Jr.; *New England: Indian Summer* by Van Wyck Brooks, copyright 1940, 1950 by Van Wyck Brooks; *The Proper Bostonians* by Cleveland Amory, copyright 1947 by Cleveland Amory. Farrar, Straus & Giroux, Inc., for *A View of My Own* by Elizabeth Hardwick, copyright © 1959 by Elizabeth Hardwick. Harcourt, Brace & World, Inc., for *The Robber Barons* by Matthew Josephson. Houghton Mifflin Company, for *The Affluent Society* by John Kenneth Galbraith; *One Boy's Boston* by Samuel Eliot Morison. Thomas H. Johnson, for *The Puritans* by Perry Miller. Alfred A. Knopf, Inc., for *Prejudices: A Selection* by H. L. Mencken (Vintage Books); *The Spirit of Liberty* by Learned Hand. Little, Brown and Company—The Atlantic Monthly Press for *The Adams Family* by James Truslow Adams; *Memoir of Colonel Henry Lee* by John T. Morse, Jr. Macfadden-Bartell Corporation, for *The Wicked and the Banned* by John Roeburt, copyright © 1963 by Macfadden-Bartell Corporation. Massachusetts Historical Society, for "A City on a Hill, 1630" by John Winthrop, in *American Principles and Issues: The National Purpose,* edited by Oscar Handlin, published by Holt, Rinehart and Winston, Inc. Oxford University Press, for *The Uses of the Past* by Herbert J. Muller. Random House, Inc., for the Modern Library edition of *The Education of Henry Adams* by Henry Adams and the Introduction by James Truslow Adams, copyright 1918 by The Massachusetts Historical Society, copyright 1946 by Charles Francis Adams, copyright 1931 by The Modern Library, Inc. Charles Scribner's Sons, for *The Last Puritan* by George Santayana and the Introduction by Irwin Edman. The Viking Press, Inc., for *Black Cargoes* by Daniel P. Mannix with Malcolm Cowley. The University of Chicago Press, for *Puritanism in Old and New England* by Alan Simpson, copyright © 1961 by Alan Simpson.

68-311

THIS BOOK IS FOR

Lucile Harris

TO WHOM WORDS SUCH AS *duty, integrity,* AND *character*

HAVE MEANING

Acknowledgments

To all the members of the Cabot family I am grateful beyond expression. In our first discussions, I was told to write whatever I wanted, "warts and all." I was given not only all the correspondence and papers available, but also all the interviews I asked for, and the assurance that there would be no effort on their part to influence, to edit, or to change anything I wrote. No member of the Cabot family has read this book in advance of publication and none has any responsibility for its content.

I will not list all the members of the family, their relatives, connections, business associates, and friends, some eighty in number, who have helped me, but I am grateful to each of them. I am also particularly grateful to Dr. L. Cabot Briggs for his permission to use letters and research found in the two-volume work *History and Genealogy of the Cabot Family, 1475–1927* by his father, L. Vernon Briggs.

Others who have been most kind and helpful are Sam Acheson, John Quincy Adams, Wilbur J. Bender, Dr. Carl Binger, Dr. Sam Bojar, Lyman Butterfield, Mary Anne Caldwell, Margaret Cousins, Paul Crume, Frank Freidel, Lon L. Fuller, William Garrett, John George, Oscar Handlin, Yvette Hartman, Howard Mumford Jones, Victor O. Jones, John E. Kilgore, Jr., Albert Outler, Ruth Spence, Marina Svetlova, Lon Tinkle, Decherd Turner, Victor White, Walter Muir Whitehill. I wish here to acknowledge my debt to each of them for whatever is right in this book and to absolve them from any responsibility for what may be wrong.

My thanks, too, to the Massachusetts Historical Society, the Widener Library, the Houghton Library, the Boston Public Library, the New York Public Library, the Dallas Public Library, the Boston Athenaeum, the Boston *Globe,* and the Boston *Herald.*

My special thanks also to Simon Michael Bessie, Mrs. Joan Hardin, and my wife for all their help. But, first and last, I am grateful to the Cabot family for knowing the difference between "image" and truth; unlike some other prominent families, they understand and respect the difference between public relations and history.

Foreword

And this is good old Boston,
  The home of the bean and the cod
Where the Lowells talk only to Cabots
  And the Cabots talk only to God.

All three participants in this famous dialogue are found in the name of Godfrey Lowell Cabot. He was born in "Cold Roast Boston" on February 26, 1861, before the Civil War, and died there on November 2, 1962, well into the atomic age. His 101 years covered the entire period of America's coming of age as an industrial power and as a world leader in science and in politics; Cabot played a not insignificant role in this growth.

The turbulent and far-reaching life of this vigorous Victorian offers some useful views of the growth of big business in America and of the decline and renaissance of Boston in the last hundred years. If we are now sufficiently past the Victorian age, we may at last be able to learn from its virtues as well as laugh at its fatuity. We may begin to understand it instead of merely continuing a revolution which has long since been won and in which, as in all revolutions, much good was thrown out with the bad.

It would not be difficult to find a more charming subject to illustrate these points, for Godfrey Lowell Cabot was, even for his time, extraordinarily selfish, irascible, and tyrannical, and his contempt for what "is done" confirms the old Boston saying which today's Cabots still enjoy quoting, "The Cabots are a Massachu-

setts tribe known to have many customs but no manners." A
product of America's closest approximation to aristocracy, Godfrey Lowell Cabot had to an exaggerated degree its particular
combination of arrogance and naiveté and the social security
which enabled him to be both consciously and unconsciously eccentric. He was afire with the "Yankee passion for self-improvement"
and a terrible compulsion to cleanse the Augean stables of life, a
man of the sort who often, in Chesterton's phrase, "pours righteous indignation into the wrong things."

But as it is perhaps helpful now to be reminded that the
Victorian age was a combination of good and ill, so it is perhaps
useful in our age, which so values conformity, comfort, and the
avoidance of controversy at almost any cost, to see how much real
benefit, both public and private, can come from a prickly, conten-
tious, and unpsychoanalyzed eccentric. Cabot typified that puritanism which is an unnatural reaction against nature. His Journal
throughout his life reflects his terrible battles against temptation,
but never in his life did he even, in Santayana's words, "suspect
that it would have required much more heroism for him to yield to
temptation than ever for St. Anthony to resist it." His was not
quite the early New England puritanism, but he had aspects of it
which Santayana described. "It's a popular error to suppose that
puritanism has anything to do with purity. The old Puritans were
legally strict, they were righteous, but they were not particularly
chaste. They had the virtues and vices of old age. An old man may
be lecherous: but that vice in him, like avarice, gluttony, despot-
ism, or the love of strong drink, soon becomes monotonous, and
sordid, and is easy to cover up hypocritically under his daily routine. The Bolshies have the one element of puritanism which was
the most important . . . integrity of purpose and scorn of all
compromises, practical or theoretical." And yet if he was compulsively energetic, exaggeratedly competitive, chronically suspi-
cious, and demanding, he was at the same time often inventive, generous, visionary, and, above all, courageous, to a degree which
enabled him to attack and often defeat not only external enemies
but also psychological problems within himself of which he had
no real understanding.

I decided to devote myself to this book only after considerable reflection. I chose to write a biography of Cabot because I believed his was not only an interesting story but also one which provided an opportunity to write a microcosmic history of America and Boston for the last hundred years. In fact, Cabot's story must go back further than his birth, to the arrival in Massachusetts of his ancestors at the very beginnings of America, for he was partially a product of their strengths and their flaws, their principles and their prejudices. This is not, however, a full history of the Cabot clan in America prior to Godfrey's time and does not even touch on the work of several distinguished contemporaneous Cabots, such as the Doctors Richard and Hugh Cabot.

It seemed to me useful to ask ourselves today the still unanswered questions about men of this type and epoch, who left so enormous a mark on our national life, who occupied so remarkable a place in their own society, local and national. Men like Cabot had a sense of station, and if they fulfilled the duties of that station, they were satisfied. This attitude contrasts interestingly with that of many today who have no sense of station or role but only a rather general and flabby view that intentions, however vague and quixotic, to promote the greatest good for the greatest number are enough.

Although Cabot was dogmatic about his beliefs and absolute in his standards, one wonders whether today's amoralists are any less so in their absolute relativism, and which dogmatism is worse for society. His problems would more than qualify him for membership in that vast group presently styled "alienated." However, those problems led him to an avid but unembarrassed pursuit of duty and decency, and such is not always the case with today's "alienated."

Uncompromising as he may seem at first glance, Cabot did at least adjust to his time and environment sufficiently to attain considerable power and recognition, unlike Henry Adams, who simply withdrew, observed, and condemned. Godfrey had many of the doubts of Henry Adams, which were well expressed by James Truslow Adams: "We are no longer sure that we are to achieve social and economic democracy by giving everyone except minors and idiots the vote; that wealth will create a satisfying scale of values for us; that by losing our individuality so that every want can be satisfied under a national brand we shall somehow attain to a higher standard of living." But Cabot was an activist rather than merely a critic like Henry Adams, who "never got to the point of playing the game at all; he lost himself in the study of it, watching the errors of the players."

While making fun of Cabot and his kind, it is wise not to forget that they brought us to the highest level of creature comfort yet enjoyed by man, a position where we have both the time and the opportunity to make fun. In criticizing his awful self-righteousness we should consider the possibility that in half a century or so it may compare not too unfavorably with our own pious impiety.

Cabot's years are a part of our past, and Cabot was a single individual who summed up an important slice of that past. I discovered in Cabot a kind of surrogate for recollection, and I believe you will find that in a significant way he belongs to your past too, and that his story is relevant to your present and your future. Cabot's sense of *noblesse oblige* came in no small part from the Hebraic feeling of his Puritan ancestors that they were a chosen people with extra obligations, but it is surely no more archaic than a recent Bostonian's suggestion, ". . . ask not what your country can do for you—ask what you can do for your country."

Today, when crimes are so often explained away as evidence of mental illness, when individual responsibility so often hides behind group thinking and committee decision, it may be well to observe a man often in error, often misguided, but never avoiding responsibility or the opportunity to lead. At the important moments in its history, America has always had leaders willing to lead. If willingness to accept the lonely responsibility to lead disappears, if our politicians follow polls instead of principles, our future will be less fortunate than was our past.

New England in the three centuries from the settlement of the Massachusetts Bay Colony had an exceptional role in producing men and families of steady habits. Of these, Cabot was one of the most interesting because, far from being the least successful and significant scion of a burnt-out line, he was the climax of a long, long line—a rare phenomenon anywhere, but especially in America.

This is a biography, and everything Cabot and others say or do in it is based on diaries, letters, newspaper reports, or the recollections of witnesses to the events. To the best of my ability whatever opinions are expressed are so labeled, and nothing factual has been assumed or invented. Some of Cabot's idiosyncrasies of grammar, spelling, paragraphing, punctuation, abbreviation, use of ampersands, and the like have been changed slightly for easier reading and with care to avoid the slightest change in sense; but enough of these have been left to give the feeling of his style. There are Notes at the end of the book for quoted material other than Godfrey's own words, excepting quotes identified in the text or taken from Cabot papers and genealogy.

The reader is warned that in the course of learning about Cabot and writing this book, my own feelings about him changed from initial interest to outraged anger and finally to reluctant admiration for this remarkable example of the human enterprise. I hope to show that he was a tragicomic hero—with clay feet surely up to his hips and perhaps up to his eyeballs, but nevertheless a hero; that is to say, a man who struggled, often outrageously and sometimes ridiculously but always valorously, to do his duty as he saw it and to make the world a better place. I hope, too, that I have avoided becoming one of those historians who, in Henry Adams' words, are "not exempt from the passion of baiting their bears."

Half of his life was funny, half was ennobling, and another half was tragic; and if that makes three halves, that's part of what I mean. He was a man willing to risk the whole damn show to win or lose on a single moral issue—a rare gamble for a Boston Brahmin or, indeed, for anyone, at any time, in any place.

He was a comic hero turned tragic; a hero not in the Greek sense, but in the only sense in which we have heroes left: a man who performs over and above his duty by normal standards, who marches to his own drums and is willing to take risks in doing so;

who is dedicated in the literal sense of self-placement without stint, not driven to a position but self-given, and whose life is ordered by such presently démodé words as *duty, probity, integrity,* and *character.*

Godfrey Cabot was an extraordinary mixture of strength and energy and sense of duty with intolerance and literary voyeurism and lust for power. He held himself accountable only to one strict and rigorous master, himself. He practiced what Henry James called "the art of being completely whatever it was that one happened to be." It is at the least interesting, and perhaps something more in this time of conformity and moral laissez-faire, to see such a free man, who, except as he was constrained by psychological bonds he did not understand, lived his long, useful, and exciting life exactly as he chose.

Leon Harris

June 20, 1967

Contents

Illustrations

ONLY TO GOD

The Extraordinary Life of
Godfrey Lowell Cabot

CHAPTER I

Earlier Cabots

My Fathers and Brethren, this is never to be forgotten, that New England is originally a plantation of religion, not a plantation of trade. JOHN HIGGINSON, *Election Sermon,* May 27, 1663

It would puzzle a convocation of casuists to resolve their degrees of consanguinity. CERVANTES, *Don Quixote,* Pt. i, ch. 8

The Cabots made their money in trade, in slaves, rum, and opium, in piracy, and by marriage. The founder of the family in America was John Cabot, who came to Salem, Massachusetts, from his native Island of Jersey about 1700.

The Cabots, of course, have ancestors going further back than 1700—presumably, like all of us, all the way to the tree of the knowledge of good and evil, or perhaps even earlier. Some later Cabots, convinced of their relationship to the noble French families of Rohan Chabot and Chabot du Perche, assumed their coat of arms, including three catfish, which in the language of English heraldry are called bullheads and in French *chabots.* Pretensions to noble, or at the very least aristocratic, ancestry are common to many of Boston's First Families. However, with the exception of the Saltonstalls and Winthrops, most were Puritan yeomen or merchants, and some came to the New World as prisoners or indentured servants.

3

Some few American Cabots have further assumed a relationship to the great Genoese explorer John Cabot, who sailed to North America in 1497, and have chosen to honor him and his equally famous son, Sebastian, by naming their sons for them. There is even a story that one of the Cabots paid an impoverished historian to seek out his antecedents and that when the industrious historian traced the family further back than anyone ever had before, to some tenth-century Lombardy Jews, his employer paid him to forget his research.

Aside from such tales there are fascinating facts about pre-American Cabots. The earliest mention of a Cabot in Jersey is in 1274, when one Peter Cabot was condemned "to be hanged at the gibbet for a larceny committed by another person, and when he refused to acknowledge himself a thief they remanded him to prison whence a fair trial freed him." This book, however, is arbitrarily limited to American Cabots, beginning with John Cabot, baptized in St. Helier's Church on April 7, 1680, who emigrated to Salem about eight years after the famous witchcraft trials of 1692. He provided two examples followed by most of his descendants: he set up as a merchant, importing and exporting, and he married into a prosperous family. (No Cabot to date, however, has quite matched the record of Governor John Winthrop, who married four wealthy wives.) John so flourished that he was able to build a house which nearly a hundred years later, in 1798, was appraised for taxes at $5,250, the tenth most valuable property in Salem, where the average value of all 932 houses was $1,425.

John Cabot set another example followed by many of his descendants by producing a large family numbering nine children. When he died, John Cabot's estate included a warehouse and wharf; Mansion House and land; horse; cow; two schooners, the *Diamond* and the *John;* a pew in the Great Meeting House; and various bonds, mortgages, merchandise, and other assets totaling in value £15,740.12.1 and including 410 gallons of rum.

John Cabot's oldest son and namesake, the first of more than a hundred of his descendants to attend Harvard College, became a physician "by private study," there being no medical school in

America at that time. The Cabot family has produced very few politicians, clergymen, teachers, lawyers, poets, or artists. Most of the Cabots who did not choose to be merchants became medical doctors, and several of these were quite distinguished. The first Dr. Cabot married Sarah Higginson, who died with no issue on June 14, 1746. Not quite a year later he married Hannah Clark, the granddaughter of one of the witchcraft judges of Salem. When Dr. Cabot and Hannah died, both left sizable estates, including a number of Negro slaves. The two other sons of the first American John Cabot, Joseph and Francis, inherited their father's prosperous mercantile business and as partners continued and expanded their trade with Great Britain and the West Indies.

Three of Joseph's sons—John, Andrew, and George—continued the merchant tradition, but in Beverly, which now had equaled or surpassed Salem in importance as a seaport. In addition to their regular commercial business, they undertook piracy on a large scale. In November of 1775 an act was passed by the Massachusetts Legislature "empowering the Council to commission with letters of marque and reprisal any person or persons within the colony, to fit out and equip at their own expense for the defense of America, any vessel, with general authority to take all vessels of the enemy. The master of a private armed vessel was required to give bonds as principal, with two good names as securities, in order to satisfy any claim that might be made for illegal capture. The bond was $5,000 for vessels under 100 tons, and $10,000 for vessels of 100 tons and over. Later it was found that deserters from the Continental Army often enlisted on private armed vessels, and such vessels were put under bond not to take any soldier from the Continental Army or any man not a citizen of Massachusetts. Bonds were also required that the crews of any vessels captured should be brought as prisoners into the state and not, as often was done, set free on some worthless prize to avoid expense." The first such vessels were privateers, as distinguished from others bearing letters of marque. Privateers were not merchantmen armed to resist attack, but ships whose chief purpose was to capture prizes. Letters of marque covered armed merchant ships that sailed with cargo but had the right to take prizes during the cruise.

In their own view, the Cabots did not practice piracy, but their activities were often so regarded by the British, Spanish, Portuguese, and others whose ships they captured. Conversely, French, Spanish, and British letter-of-marque vessels and privateers were often viewed by American ship owners as no better than pirates. There was considerable confusion and controversy because any enterprising ship captain could almost always find some country to give him letters of marque to prey on ships of her enemies. It is even thought by some that Captain Kidd, who sailed out of New York in 1696 and was later hanged for piracy, was not a pirate but a legal privateer, and such was emphatically his own view.

The Cabots provided America with more privateers than any other family. The first privateer commissioned out of Beverly in 1778, the *Terrible Creature,* was owned by George and Andrew Cabot. Larger than most, she carried 16 six-pounders. In the same year the Cabots, with other merchants of Beverly and Salem, commissioned William Swett of Salisbury to build what they intended to be "the largest, fastest, and most heavily armed privateer ever launched from our Massachusetts shipyards," the *Black Prince,* ship-rigged, 220 tons, with 18 guns and a crew of 130.

In addition to these two ships, the Cabots had the most successful Beverly privateer during the Revolution, the *Pilgrim,* whose first master was the *beau idéal* of a privateer captain, Hugh Hill. Born in Carrickfergus, Ireland, Hill was handsome, "courageous almost to rashness, courteous to the fair sex, and not burdened with scruples." He was a cousin of Andrew Jackson, and under Hill and subsequent captains the *Pilgrim* captured over fifty prizes, probably a record for any Beverly privateer.

In a perilous business the Cabots did exceedingly well even after the war, by which time privateering had proved unprofitable for many. Few families had the means or courage to risk new ventures in 1781, but the Cabots began that year by commissioning on the same day two new vessels with letters of marque. Only a few days out of Beverly on her first voyage, the *Commerce* was taken by an English cruiser and was, therefore, a total loss.

(George Cabot once said that if an owner could save one out of every three ships, he made a handsome profit on the lot.) The *Cicero,* on the other hand, in her first five months of cruising under Hugh Hill captured various prizes, including the *Mercury* running as a packet to Cadiz and containing besides a valuable cargo £15,000 in gold.

By this time, only eighty years after the first Cabot had come to America, his grandchildren had acquired fortunes large enough to inspire considerable comment and envy, not the least from old Salem families who had bet on the wrong horse, becoming Royalists and returning to Britain during the Revolution. One of these, Samuel Curwen, born in Salem in 1715 and living in exile in Bristol, England, wrote in a letter on February 10, 1780: "It is a melancholy truth that while some are *wallowing* in undeserved wealth that plunder and rapine have thrown into their hands, the wisest, most peaceable and most deserving are now suffering want. . . . The Cabots of Beverly, who, you know, had but five years ago a very moderate share of property, are now said to be by far the most wealthy in New England. . . ."

A traveler, Colonel John Trumbull, wrote in his *Reminiscences* that he took passage from Bilbao for Beverly in 1781 in the *Cicero,* a fine letter-of-marque ship belonging to the house of Cabot, and that on his arrival at Beverly he saw lying in the harbor eleven privateers, all finer than the *Cicero* and all belonging to the Cabots.

Chastellux, in his *Travels in North America* (translated from the French, London, 1787), wrote: "The town of Beverly began to flourish greatly towards the conclusion of the war, the extraordinary spirit of enterprise and great success of the Messrs. Cabot, gentlemen of strong understandings and the most liberal minds, [being] well-adapted to the most enlarged commercial undertakings and the business of government. . . . Two of their privateers had the good fortune to capture in the European seas, a few weeks previous to the peace, several West-Indiamen, to the value of at least £100,000 sterling."

That the reports of increasing Cabot wealth were true was proven each time a family member died. It also became evident that, besides their own mercantile and shipping business, the Cabots were increasingly investing in various enterprises and developing new ones. When John Cabot died on August 28, 1821, his estate included shares in "Boston, State, Manufacturers' and Mechanics', Suffolk and Marine Banks, all of Boston; the Essex and Marine Banks of Salem; the Salem Iron Factory, Amesbury Nail Company, Salem Turnpike, etc."

Andrew also followed the family tradition. Not only did he marry Lydia Dodge, whose father was one of the wealthiest merchants in Salem, leaving an estate of $282,000; he also made enough money as a merchant to be able with his brother John in 1781 to buy for £354,470 the famous confiscated estate of the Royalist Governor Wentworth at Wolfeborough, New Hampshire.

But the most successful and best known of this third American generation of Cabot brothers was George, who left Harvard at sixteen in 1767 and went to sea as a cabin boy. He so impressed his older brothers that before he was of age he was given command of a ship. He made several long voyages and in the process learned French and Spanish. George Cabot became a strong Federalist, a friend of Alexander Hamilton, and was an exception to the rule that Cabots are not politicians. Then as now, special legislation for special business interests was most helpful, and among other pieces of legislation, George Cabot was able to get through the Congress a bounty of five cents on every quintal of dried fish or barrel of pickled fish exported; a government refund of duties collected on goods imported and sent out of the country within a year; a much higher tax on goods brought into port in foreign ships than that laid on cargoes brought into port in American ships; and permission for American captains to sail into every Atlantic Coast port on the payment of a single fee, whereas foreign masters were required to pay port fees at each port entered.

George Cabot in 1791 was chosen as a United States Senator from Massachusetts, but he so disliked the rough and tumble of politics that he resigned in the fifth year of his term. He was appointed the first Secretary of the Navy by John Adams on May 3, 1798, but refused to serve.

A Massachusetts shipping man and a Federalist, he opposed Jefferson's Embargo in 1807 and even more the entry of the United States into the War of 1812. So opposed to the national policy was he that he served as President of the Hartford Convention in 1814.

The New England conservatives had opposed the government's policy since the 1807 Embargo Act, and even though isolation had actually brought them wealth in manufacturing and smuggling, they nevertheless opposed "Mr. Madison's War." The Federalists who had led the Essex Junto were reluctant to release their militia to national service and, despite their prosperity, refused to support the Federal loan of 1814. After the Embargo Act of 1813, talk of secession and a separate peace with Great Britain was common. John Adams even said that what George Cabot really wanted was to be President of New England. Jackson's victory at New Orleans and the Treaty of Ghent ended the particular problems, but in the light of later Cabot outrage at the southern view of state rights, it is interesting to note that state rights and secession were fully discussed and defended at the secret meetings in Hartford at which George Cabot served as president. The most important effect of the Convention, however, was the discrediting and destruction of the Federalist Party.

In 1774 George Cabot had married his double first cousin Elizabeth Higginson, setting a pattern frequently followed in the Cabot family. With such large families and such frequent intermarriage of its members and connections, Cabot genealogy became tremendously confusing. Mary C. Wheelright, whose mother was a Cabot, once remarked, "It sometimes happened that a Cabot girl would be a great-aunt before she was born."

One of the ventures of George Cabot and his brothers outside of shipping was their establishment in 1788 of the first cotton mill in America at North Beverly. The Cabots and their associates petitioned the Massachusetts Legislature, listing among many reasons in favor of building up a cotton industry that it would "find employment and support for a great number of persons, and among others, for infirm women and children, who for want of employ are often burdensome to the Public." Cabot wrote to Alexander Hamilton asking for aid from Congress by means of a national lottery.

On October 30, 1789, George Washington noted in his diary that he breakfasted with George Cabot and then described at considerable length his visit to the remarkable new cotton mill. Eventually, however, the mill proved uneconomic, the Cabots finding that there was much more profit to be made in importing cheap cotton goods from India. Nevertheless, the mill marked the first effort to establish an industry which was to become one of the most important in New England.

Besides these three sons of Joseph, there were five others. The youngest of these, Samuel, was the great-grandfather of Godfrey Lowell Cabot. Born in Salem in 1759, he early engaged in commerce and privateering in Beverly. But in 1784 he moved to Boston, and in 1796 he was appointed, at a salary of $2,500 a year, Secretary to the United States Commissioners on British Spoliation Claims in London. He served twice in this capacity, returning from London permanently in 1803 and living for the rest of his life in Boston, where he became a large shareholder and later president and a director of the Boston Marine Insurance Company.

Samuel Cabot was painted by John Singleton Copley, who was related by marriage to the Cabots and who caused them great embarrassment. He accused Samuel Cabot of cheating him while acting as his agent in the sale of some land Copley owned in Boston. A group of Boston merchants, including Harrison Gray Otis, bought Copley's Beacon Hill estate at a very cheap price, allegedly with advance information that the new State House would be built on the site. So upset was Cabot by Copley's accusations of dishonesty, which endangered his and his family's honor and credit, that he went to great lengths to get Copley to withdraw his words. Copley finally did so reluctantly.

Samuel Cabot married Sally (or Sarah) Barrett, who was a descendant of Mary Chilton, "the first white woman to set foot on New England shores," having come to Plymouth on the *Mayflower* with her parents. This circumstance gives her descendants the inestimable advantage of having three *Mayflower* passengers as ancestors—a considerable advantage over those with only one, or none at all.

Samuel Cabot's marriage to Mary Chilton's descendant, however greatly it enhanced the social prestige of his heirs, cannot be compared in good fortune to the marriage of his oldest son, Samuel. This son engaged in business in the best family tradition, working when he was only nineteen as a merchant in the Isle of France (Mauritius). In the same Cabot family tradition, he traveled widely, becoming a Master Mason in Paris at the age of twenty. He formed a partnership in 1806 in Philadelphia, where he worked hard as a merchant to increase his wealth. But it was by his marriage to Eliza, the oldest daughter of Colonel Thomas Handasyd Perkins, that Samuel brought to the Cabot family the greatest fortune until the time of his grandson, Godfrey Lowell Cabot, who would outdo even this feat many times over.

Of all the Massachusetts men who made fortunes in the mercantile trade, Thomas Handasyd Perkins has always been held up as the greatest example. Not only because his fortune may have been the largest, but because his attitude, his actions, and his stance reflected the very best of what this particular group of early Americans contributed to the country's traditions. Perhaps the story which best indicates this position concerns the time a Boston jeweler approached Perkins, who always wore his watch on a leather thong, and said, "Colonel Perkins, a man of your position should wear his watch on a gold chain." "A man of my position," replied Perkins, "can wear his watch on a leather thong." What might mistakenly be regarded only as arrogance was, in fact, the real social security of a man who had made his own fortune and who was spending it on himself, his family, and his town as he believed was proper.

This was a man who believed he understood the world and his proper place in it, who with vigor and often with joy addressed himself to his business, his pleasures, and his duties. His was a mental posture reflected then and now in varying degrees in the best men and institutions Boston has produced.

In the eighteenth century, Americans such as Perkins and

Elias Hasket Derby, were still the largest fleet owners in the world. Boston First Familydom, much of which was based on shipping, seems to have closed its membership about 1878 with the death of John Lowell Gardner, the last East India merchant. Fortunes made subsequently, no matter how, have not gained admittance. There is an unofficial pecking order even within the First Families. First place goes to those families whose fortunes were made in the China trade. Therefore, although the Cabots have had to appropriate a coat-of-arms, at least they did not need to invent sailor ancestors, as did some of Boston's First Families whose ancestors made their money in textiles or railroads. Intermarriage, however, has now happily provided most of them with a suitable number of sailors.

Perkins was born in Boston on December 15, 1764. Instead of going to college, he became an apprentice in a counting room and later worked in Santo Domingo. In 1788 he married Sally, the only daughter of Major-General Simon Elliot, and a year later he sailed on his first trip to China as supercargo on the *Astrea*. The ship's officer in charge of all the commercial concerns and decisions of the voyage, the supercargo was often allowed to trade on his own account as well as for the ship's owners.

On September 18, 1789, Perkins arrived at Canton, where he learned much of what was to make him the most successful merchant in Boston. He learned, for example, about sea-otter pelts from the chief mate of the *Columbia*, which on her next voyage would claim the whole Northwest Coast for the United States, naming its great river the Columbia and subsequently carrying the American flag around the world for the first time.

In Paris in 1795, Perkins was advised by the United States Minister, James Monroe, that it was the desire of George Washington to obtain the escape from revolution-ridden France of his godson, George Washington Lafayette. Perkins arranged to smuggle young Lafayette out of France and send him to the United States in one of his own ships. The boy stayed first with Perkins' family in Boston and then at Mount Vernon. Perkins also loaned money to the Marquise de Lafayette in order that she might join her husband in Austria.

The following summer Perkins spent the night at Mount Vernon, where George Washington expressed his gratitude and personally lit his visitor's way to bed. (At the end of that same year, Perkins was billed $1,740.82 by another Revolutionary hero, Paul Revere, for bells and other hardware furnished to Perkins' ships.)

As did virtually all the shipping merchants of his day, Perkins traded in slaves, rum, and opium. For generations the Cabots attended church, sent their sons to Harvard College, and made fortunes in the slave trade, which, according to a slaver turned clergyman, John Newton, "renders most of those who are engaged in it too indifferent to the sufferings of their fellow creatures" and "gradually brings a numbness upon the heart." This was "the distinguishing feature of the trade: not its dangers, not the loss of life it involved, not even the cruelties it inflicted on millions, but rather the numbness of the traders and their loss of human sympathies. . . . From beginning to end the trade was a denial of any standards except those of profit and loss. . . . White sailors before the mast were also treated as mere items in the ledger. Because they had less value than the slaves, they were often given less food and more floggings . . . the rate of mortality among seamen on the Guinea voyage was higher, on the average, than among slaves packed in the hold."

There were profits to the countries involved in the slave trade as well as to the individual traders. America—as well as Britain, France, and Holland—not only increased its merchant fleet and found markets for its growing industries, but also accumulated capital which was invested in the factories of the industrial revolution and in railroads and mines at home and abroad. Especially in America, slave labor made possible the large-scale production of cotton, tobacco, sugar, and rice, which were the country's greatest sources of wealth for many years.

The profits, direct and indirect, of slavery were irresistible, and it is difficult today to understand the attitude which existed then. It is often forgotten that perhaps half the early settlers of North America were themselves white slaves—that is, indentured servants, convicted criminals, and Scottish and Irish prisoners of war, who were sold as slaves for periods ranging from five years to life. There were some distinct advantages to these white slaves. They already spoke English and could therefore be more easily trained; if their indentures ran only five or ten years, their masters could work them harder and not worry about their health or usefulness in later years; and there was no need to provide for them in old age.

If Biblical text was needed to justify slavery, there was Leviticus xxv:44: "Both thy bondmen and bondmaids, which thou shalt have, shall be of the heathen that are round about you; of them shall ye buy bondmen and bondmaids." And black slaves also happily fell under Noah's curse on his second son, Ham, and Ham's son Canaan: "And he said, Cursed be Canaan; a servant of servants shall he be unto his brethren" (Genesis ix:25). As advanced and Christian a scholar as Bishop Berkeley maintained that Negroes were "creatures of another species who had no right to be included or admitted to the sacraments." Compared to this view, Massachusetts' own Cotton Mather, not generally remembered for the softness of his heart, sounds almost loving when he chastises those who treat their slaves as "domestic animals" and reminds himself concerning his own slaves, "I will remember that they are in some sense my children."

Although black slaves existed in Spanish Florida as early as 1565, the first Negroes sold in the English colonies in the north came in a Dutch ship to Jamestown in 1619, a year before the *Mayflower* landed at Plymouth. It was considerably later in the seventeenth century, however, before black slaves became substantially important to America.

First, sugar in the West Indies, which could be produced profitably only on large plantations with much hand labor, created a need for Negroes. "England had formerly depended for sweetening almost entirely on honey and on what little sugar she could purchase from Spain, the sugar being so precious that it was sold by the ounce. But with the acquisition of West Indian colonies and an unlimited supply of cheap labor, sugar could be produced by the ton and molasses by the hogshead." Molasses was easily converted into rum, a product then tremendously in demand. "By 1750 there were sixty-three distilleries in Massachusetts alone and each year they turned 15,000 hogsheads of molasses into about 12,500 hogsheads of rum. Even with the help of perhaps thirty distilleries in Rhode Island, they were unable to supply the demand."

Next cotton created a demand for Negroes, especially after the invention in 1793 of the cotton gin. "Before that time it had taken a Negro woman all day to clean the seeds from a single pound of cotton staple. Eli Whitney's original invention, a hand turned gin, made it possible for one person to clean fifty pounds of cotton a day, and the first power-driven gins cleaned a thousand pounds."

Before making moral judgments on the social and political attitudes of that time, it is useful to remember some of the economic facts; by 1850 King Cotton used about 60 per cent of the hundreds of thousands of Negroes in America; this single crop accounted for two thirds of the total value of all American exports.

In 1714 the total slave population in British North America had only been 59,000, with 2,000 in Boston. By 1754 the total had risen to 298,000, and the census of 1790 showed a slave population just short of 700,000.

There were economic perils, of course, in the slave trade, including the fact that there was much spoilage. It has been estimated that over half of perhaps thirty or forty million Negroes captured in Africa died before reaching the Americas. "The interior is drained of all its working men. . . . Africa is bleeding out her life's blood at every pore . . . the slave trade will die a natural death from the total destruction of the population."

The trade was so profitable, however, that anti-slavery advocates offended many in high places. In 1766 Boston petitioned against the further importation of slaves, as did Salem in 1775. Indeed, by 1770 there had been so many such petitions that George III's government instructed the colonial legislatures "upon pain of the highest displeasure to assent to no law by which the importation of slaves should be in any respect prohibited or obstructed."

In spite of the fact that he was himself a slave owner, Thomas Jefferson tried to throw the onus of the existence of slavery on George III; he wrote in the first draft of the Declaration of Independence: "He has waged cruel war against human nature itself, violating its most sacred rights of life and liberty in the persons of a distant people who never offended him, captivating and carrying them into slavery in another hemisphere or to incur miserable death in their transportation thither. This piratical warfare, the opprobrium of INFIDEL powers, is the warfare of the CHRISTIAN king of Great Britain. Determined to keep open a market where MEN should be bought and sold, he has prostituted his negative for suppressing every legislative attempt to prohibit or restrain this execrable commerce." This statement was later deleted, according to Jefferson, "in complaisance to South Carolina and Georgia, who had never attempted to restrain the importation of slaves, and who, on the contrary, still wished to continue it. Our northern brethren also, felt a little tender under these censures; for though their people had very few slaves themselves, yet they had been pretty considerable carriers of them to others."

Like Jefferson, most Revolutionary heroes, including George Washington, were slave owners. Patrick Henry admitted, "I am drawn along by the general inconvenience of living without them [but] I will not, I cannot justify it." Only the righteous and crusty John Adams refused to own slaves but complained, "It cost me thousands to employ free labor." Not until 1827 was slavery abolished in New York State, and it lasted until 1836 in Massachusetts.

In 1806 the British government finally passed its first law against slavery and slaving, and through 1833 it continued to pass others and to try to enforce them by use of the Navy. The result of this prohibition was an increase in the value of slaves and in the dangers and profits of slaving. Thomas Handasyd Perkins' ship captains, like those of other Massachusetts merchants, carried the flags and papers of many countries and became as adept at the smuggling of slaves as they did at the smuggling of opium.

Perkins' letter books, present a picture of world trade in the eighteenth century. Some of these letters to and from his captains, customers, and agents show the sources of the Cabot fortunes and philanthropies. They also illustrate a business morality and attitudes of business toward government not unknown today.

Cape, Oct 7, 1788

To Messrs. Sam'l & Jno. Smith, Balt.:

. . . You mentioned something of a small Cargo of negroes. . . . Petiton will land them for 1 Joe per head: he will give, for prime negroes from 13 to 20 yrs. of age, 25 Joes. . . . He has all the Fishermen & indeed officers at the Fort subservient to him . . .

A Joe was a Portuguese or Brazilian gold doubloon worth eight or nine dollars. The subservience mentioned was necessitated by the fact that in many ports, both American and Caribbean, the bribing of port officials was mandatory, especially when local laws prohibiting the importation of slaves were passed, as happened in Maryland in 1783.

Wars and natural disasters have always provided excellent opportunities for profit.

1 Dec. 1791

To Messrs. S. & J. Smith, Zacharis Coopman & Co., David Stewart, Commercial Committee of Baltimore:

Yesterday Eve' we received Advices from Pt. au Prince which have given a General Alarm in this quarter. Twenty-seven squares in this City have been destroy'd by the Mulattoes, (at least one-half the Town). We are uncertain how the people of Color in this place may be affected by the example of their brethren, & whether we are to expect the same fate. . . . We are raising prices gradually, but dare not refuse to sell at or near the late value. Should flour be withheld, or the prices suddenly enhanced, it might become a prey to the Mob. . . . The little balance due from Chacon is lost forever; he had his throat cut by the Negroes some weeks since, & has left nothing. Molines Estate at Laid is totally destroyed. The Mulattoes have been the authors of the evil there: the Blacks are still quiet. . . . A

Frigate arrived yesterday from France, announcing the most formidable preparations for our relief. In Addition to this we have had repeated supplication from the Blacks for Pardon; their terms are a general amnesty & an emancipation of 50 of their Chiefs; their deputies have been sent back with disdain; they acknowledge a want of provisions . . . and we expect their surrender will soon be unconditional; the number of troops for this Island is said to be 1300; when the troops arrive Flour must become Brisk. . . .

In a letter to Captain Robert Adamson, master of the ship *Willing Quaker* bound for the Coast for slaves in 1792, Dan. McNiel wrote that he should "take care that they are young & healthy, without any defects in their Limbs, Teeth & Eyes, & as few females as possible. Every attention is to be paid them that they are well fed, well used, kept clean & dry. For if they once get disheartened they will die like Sheep. Suffer no person to strike them on any account, & always keep your men Slaves in Irons, & see the Gratings Locked at Sunset . . . proceed to Surinam & there dispose of your Women Slaves . . . if you can get $50 a head you may dispose of the whole."

Perkins expressed strong opinions on politics both national and international, and his views were not totally unrelated to his business.

July 10, 1804

To Eph. Bumstead:

. . . Skin teas are getting into general use in this Country. It is not that the Rich have abandoned Hyson & substituted Hyson Skins, but that the Farmers have given up Bohea & other inferior teas & taken to Skin teas. As population & its handmaiden luxury are increasing, we expect that Bohea will be out of use in a few years, until we again see Europe settled down into a state of Peace, when the means of acquiring property will be much more difficult for us all than at present, & we shall be as a people obliged to resort to our former

economical habits, & the inferior teas may come into
use. . . .

Nov, 1804

Capt. Harvey, Schr. Williams

. . . at the Havanna you must let y'r vessell have
the appearance of being in distress, by springing her
boom, bow-sprit, &c. & by putting some fishes on y'r
main mast just below the hounds. Y'r water must be
nearly out & y'r logbook must appear as if you had
experienc'd bad weather & had stove y'r water. You will
be told to heave to at the Moro & will appear to obey the
order, but continue to drift up the harbour a considerable way. . . . We shall calculate upon y'r keeping the
whole transaction a perfect secret, to whatever port you
may go, as no good and great mischief may result from
its being known that we have proceeded with the intention of smuggling. . . . Let y'r men suppose it is for the
purpose of selling y'r onions & pears, & not for smuggling valuable goods. . . .

Nov. 26, 1804

To E. Bumstead:

. . . We are very desirous of taking advantage of
all the openings there are during the European
War:—when Peace comes again it will in all probability be on a broader basis than the last, & be durable . . .
"make hay while the sun shines" sh'd be our
motto. . . .

Calcutta, 1804

To Capt. Charles Cabot:

. . . Notice your having purchased for our a/c the
ship *Dutchess of York* & taken on board a cargo for
trading to the Eastward. . . . Such voyages are like
Lotteries, & may prove blank or prize. . . . Our flag
will be preferable to the British, even if you had a
Country built ship, unless for an object to wh. none but
the British is permitted. . . .

Such use of false colors and forged papers was common to almost all ships.

In 1799 China forbade the importation of opium (it was relegalized for a few months only in 1837), but this act merely encouraged smuggling, since profits were increased. The letters between Perkins and his captains deal with giving aid to Captains Lewis and Clark, how to do business with the King of Siam, the pirate prows which abounded in the China seas, the Indians of the Northwest, and how and where bribes would be most effective. There are also various letters to and from a New York merchant whose name and descendants have achieved a certain fame in America and Great Britain.

New York, Oct. 6, 1809

Messrs. J. & T. H. Perkins
Gentlemen:
        . . . I thank you for the information as to Insurance on the *Beaver,* if you can get me $50,000 wish you would get it done, say our cargo, $35,000 and one-half the ship $15,000. I will value the ship at $30,000 only she is worth $40,000 and more.

        I am gentlemen, respectfully your humble servant,

John Jacob Astor

March 18, 1816

Prime, Ward & Sands:
        We observe the draft on **J. J. Astor** is expressed "Spanish dollars":—we shall not accept paper, tho' we have no doubt he will attempt to pay in that.

Apr. 18, 1816

J. J. Astor:
        The proposition you make us is to take $10,000 in Bank bills, as they will command specie at our Banks when presented. As this is a sacrifice of 6% in the present state of Dollars, we cannot accept it. Congress may

pass laws for the non-exportation of specie, but we do not think they can prevent it from going out.

Insurance on slave cargoes became increasingly difficult and finally impossible to place, even when a premium of 25 per cent of the value of the cargo was offered. The illegality of slaving was not the only reason for this. It was not unknown, if the slaves were ill and looked as though they would not bring a good price, for the ship's captain to jettison them, throwing them overboard on the excuse that there was not enough food or water, and their value was then claimed against the insurance.

March 24, 1818

F. W. Paine, Leghorn:
From the intention of the Chinese to be very strict about Opium, the competition you fear we think will not exist. We know of no one but Astor we fear. It is our intention to push it as far as we can. We have sent pr Boxes, direct from New York, about 60,000 Sables from the No. West, of superior quality, such as have been sold at Smyrna for 2½ Span. Dols each. We bought them low, say $1¼ so there is a large margin. . . . Situated as we are we do not attach much conse- quence to the introduction of Opium in China, as it may be kept on board until an opportunity offers to sell it deliverable alongside. Persons with a limited time for their vessels to stay, will not adventure, we think. . . . There was a parcel of opium from the Gulf of Persia last year & purchased by Astor, for about $3 & sent to China where it was pronounced to be without value, & returned. It is stated that last year's produce of opium was only 150,000 lbs. of which the wants of Europe will demand at least 50,000, & leave for China 100,000. We think by keeping a vessel on the spot, even this large a quantity might be disposed of to advantage.

The correctness of this prediction is demonstrated by entries in Colonel Perkins' memorandum books showing shipments of opium in his vessels from January 1824 to July 1825 of 177,837 pounds and the comment, "opium should be moderately soft, of a reddish brown when broken, without leaves and other impurities in the cakes. It is sometimes adulterated with stones, sand, etc." So large were Perkins' opium operations that by January 28, 1827, he was writing, "We know of none in the United States except what we hold." An idea of the value and profit of a single cargo may be seen from a letter of December 10, 1829: ". . . The Cargo of the *Bashaw* (including 1000 chests of opium) will amount to something like 570,000 to 600,000 dollars . . . [and] it cannot fail under the most unfavorable circumstances to give a gain of 150,000 to 250,000 dollars. . . ."

That the United States government condoned the opium trade is made clear by the papers issued to Perkins' brig *Nile*, which also give a further example of the wide variety of merchandise in which he dealt.

> Permission is given to Robert Edes, Commander of the Brig *Nile*, 193 tons, lying at Boston bound for Manilla to depart on said voyage. Cargo contains Candles, Copper, Glassware, Duck, Iron, Opium, Saffron, Shell, Flour, Signed by James Monroe, President of the United States, John Quincy Adams, Sec. of State and countersigned by Henry A. Dearborn, collector of the Port of Boston, Feb. 12, 1824. S. Blagge, Notary Public.

That Cabots were viewed as pirates is clearly indicated in a letter from Stephen Cabot to his brother, Samuel:

> Port au Prince, 2 Nov. 1830.
>
> *Dear Sam:*
>
> . . . I am now and ever shall, go where I may be considered as a Pirate, except by my private acquaintances. . . . I am now under bonds to this Government not to commit piracy while I remain in the country. I have been openly insulted in the street and called "You Damned Pirate! Why did you come here?" This I have had to bear and, go where I will, I shall have to bear,

unless I can return to St. Thomas, . . . and stand a
trial and the consequences of it. . . . For God's sake do
what you can for your unhappy

Bro.
Stephen Cabot

The list of men made rich by their association with Thomas
Handasyd Perkins is long and includes the financial founding
fathers of many of the First Families of today's Boston. There
was, for example, John P. Cushing, a nephew of Perkins, for whom
his cousin Eliza Perkins was sorry when her father sent him to
Canton, "because he was a person of great literary and artistic
taste, with no desire to become a merchant." Such frustrations as
this sensitive young man endured were perhaps of more concern to
him than to his descendants, for he acquired before his death in
1862 a fortune of over $7 million. Less fortunate was Perkins'
grandson, Thomas Handasyd Cabot, a young man of considerable
talent who was not permitted to follow the career of artist but was
sent out to Canton, where he died, probably of bubonic fever, at
the age of twenty-one. Among others more fortunate in their
relationship with Perkins was this boy's father, Perkins' son-
in-law Samuel Cabot, who was Godfrey's grandfather. A trial
balance of his estate, which he drew up on December 31, 1834,
revealed a total value of $340,879.18, well diversified in insur-
ance-company, bank, and manufacturing stocks, as well as shares
in turnpikes, canals, land, railroads, and mills.

In 1838 the firm of Perkins & Company was dissolved, and
Samuel Cabot thereafter made his business "the conservation and
continued augmentation of his fortune by judicious investments"—a Boston pastime, if not profession, pursued by many of
his descendants to this day.

Both Samuel Cabot and his father-in-law were far removed
from any early Puritan asceticism, enjoying many and various
luxuries. Indeed, the whole concept of American Puritans living a
Spartan life has been rather overemphasized. The Pilgrim fathers, for example, divided among themselves captured Indians as
slaves and separated parents and children with a noteworthy

Christian impartiality. Nor was there much prejudice against good food and alcohol, when available.

At his estate in Brookline, Perkins built one of the two earliest greenhouses in America, to which were sent rare and exotic plants by various of his ship captains and agents all over the world. One horticultural experiment brought forth a letter from the second President of the United States:

Quincy, 16 Sept. 1825.

Honorable Thomas H. Perkins.
Dear Sir:

I am deeply indebted to you for a polite and friendly letter and for a noble basket of Grapes, which were the more delicious for the fair hand by which they were presented. Such clusters and varieties of Grapes I have never seen, since I lived some part of the day in Boileau's garden in Auteuil in France. They are perfectly delicious. You have merited the thanks of the Country, by giving proof, by experiment that such fruits may be raised in our climate and in our soil. Accept my sincere thanks for this splendid and kind rememberance of me, which I shall never forget. I have the honour to be your obliged friend and Hble Servt.

John Adams

Perkins' trips to Europe reflect the curiosity, pleasures, and perils of the wealthy tourist. "At the Ascot races . . . the King and Dukes of York & Wellington were in the Royal Lodge. . . . While pressing to get a near sight at Royalty, some of the light fingered gentry relieved me of my watch. I gave out that I would give 15 guineas to get it back and the next day it came back."

Although he had his wife's portrait and his own painted by Gilbert Stuart, as well as his own by Thomas Sully, in his travels he refused to buy originals, preferring to spend a good deal of money having whatever sculpture and paintings he admired copied by local artists—a practice not uncommon in his day but depressing to his descendants. Perkins, however, did collect certain objects of historic interest. One of his captains brought from St. Helena a chair of Napoleon's. Perkins had had an interview with Bonaparte in 1812, writing to his wife on June 2 of that year on paper bearing as a watermark a picture of the Emperor, "I saw the original of the personage whose face is in the water lines on this paper for a couple of hours at my leisure." Perkins had been given by Captain Isaac Hull some of the original oak from the frigate *Constitution*. When Perkins gave his house on Pearl Street to be a school for the blind (which was to become the Perkins Institute for the Blind) and built a new house on Temple Place, this wood was made into the front door. When the Temple Place house was sold to the Provident Savings Bank, the wood was made into an acutely uncomfortable and hideous corner chair. Heirlooms more pleasing to present-day tastes are the sets of china brought home by Perkins' ships, including dolls' tea sets for the girls.

Perkins made many large charitable gifts and was very active in obtaining financial support from others for causes he thought worthwhile, two occupations vigorously pursued by his descendants. The first meeting of the trustees of Massachusetts General Hospital was held on February 13, 1813, at his house. He made numerous gifts to the Athenaeum and helped it to raise funds to buy a part of George Washington's library and Gilbert Stuart's "original portraits of Washington and his Lady, painted at Philadelphia in 1796." When it was proposed in 1826 to raise $30,000 for the Athenaeum, Perkins and his nephew each gave $8,000 on condition that another $16,000 be raised by the public. In the same way, when he gave his $50,000 house to found the Perkins Institute, it was on condition that another $50,000 be raised for its support.

Although no Puritan and not anti-European, Perkins could be shocked, as in 1835: "Aug. 23 at Chiltenham. . . . I am sorry to see the waltz patronized here, as I think it ill suited to the deportment of a delicate female, and from the eternal turning around should think it injurious to the health."

Perkins enjoyed being referred to as "Colonel," perhaps because he never saw any real military service, active or otherwise, but he was a Colonel of Boston's company of Independent Cadets.

He was not averse to joining prominent politicians in speculations.

Quincy, 3 October, 1827.

Col. T. H. Perkins,
Brookline
My dear Sir:

. . . Mr. Thorndike said that there would be 10 or 15 shares in the new factory stock which I might have. . . . The large investment he informed me that you had made was a strong inducement to me to accept his proposal. . . .

Your sincere old friend,
J. Q. Adams

Washington, May 16, 1836

Messrs. Perkins & Co.,
Gentlemen:

I have entered into a speculation which will call for $20,000, within the next month and have authorized Mr. [Daniel] Webster, on the best terms he can to draw that amount, which I beg you to honor. If you have difficulty in procuring the money sell such of my Lowell bank stock or R. R. stock as may be needful. . . .

Your friend,
T. H. Perkins

It is not clear to which railroad Colonel Perkins is here referring, but he had seen railroads in operation in Great Britain and in 1826 had built the first railroad in America. Its cars were horse-drawn and its initial purpose was to haul stone from the Quincy quarries to build the Bunker Hill monument. Before building, Perkins carefully calculated the amount of stone per day which horses and cattle could draw, as well as the expense of keeping animals and men as compared with his projected railroad. At this same time Perkins sent 437 trees and plants to Quincy to beautify the town where he was making money.

In a very real sense he was also responsible for the major railroad building in the West done by his nephew John Murray Forbes, who made the great fortune which he later expanded in railroads while working in Canton for Perkins. This same Perkins-launched money of Forbes was, through Forbes' son William, used to help a Scottish teacher interested in deafness, Alexander Graham Bell, to launch the American Bell Telephone Company. Neither Perkins' nor Forbes' railroad ventures suffered from the scandals common to nearly all the other railroad ventures, such as the Ames brothers' Union Pacific or as perhaps best typified by the machinations of Daniel Drew, Jim Fisk, Jay Gould, and Cornelius Vanderbilt in connection with the infamous Erie.

On January 11, 1854, at the age of ninety, following an operation by his grandson Dr. Samuel Cabot, Thomas Handasyd Perkins died. To the end he continued to express the independence which had characterized his whole life. Asked if he would not please go to bed, he replied, "Certainly not. I have always proposed to die dressed and sitting in my chair." Within an hour he was dead. Only Perkins' own son, the younger Colonel Perkins, had a more Bostonian exit line. Asked as he was dying whether he repented his sins and hoped for heaven, he replied, "I am about as good as Gus Thorndike, Jim Otis, or Charlie Hammond, and almost as good as Frank Codman. I shall go where they go, and there is where I wish to go."

CHAPTER II

Godfrey's Parents

The end is to improve our lives to do more service to the Lord . . . that ourselves and posterity may be the better preserved from the common corruptions of this evil world. . . . For we must consider that we shall be as a city upon a hill, the eyes of all people are upon us. JOHN WINTHROP

How shall a man escape from his ancestors, or draw off from his veins the black drop which he drew from his father's or his mother's life? It often appears in a family, as if all the qualities of the progenitors were potted in several jars—some ruling quality in each son or daughter of the house,—and sometimes the unmixed temperament, the rank unmitigated elixir, the family vice, is drawn off in a separate individual, and the others are proportionally relieved. EMERSON, *Conduct of Life: Fate*

On garde toujours la marque des ses origines. [We always retain the traces of our origin.] ERNEST RENAN, *La Vie de Jésus*

Godfrey Lowell Cabot's father, Samuel, the son of Perkins' son-in-law Samuel, was born in Boston on September 20, 1815. He attended the Boston Latin School, Harvard College, and Harvard Medical School. At the College he was very popular and was elected to the most exclusive "final" club, The Porcellian.

For four years he was the undergraduate boxing and quarter-sticks champion of Harvard, although he was only five feet nine inches tall and very slight of build. His spread from fingertip to fingertip, however, was six feet, and he was extraordinarily quick and agile. When Godfrey, his seventh child, was old enough to spar well, he reported that even though his father was smaller than he and no longer young, so long was his reach, so fast his movement, and so accurate his blows, that he could never touch him. Already as an undergraduate at Harvard, Samuel Cabot was interested in ornithology, which was to be his lifelong passion.

After receiving his M.D. degree in 1839, Samuel Cabot studied in Paris at various hospitals for a year before returning to Boston. On July 15, 1841, his mother, Eliza Perkins Cabot, wrote, "Sam is busy in Broad Street where he is the Dispensary doctor."

The following year he went as doctor and ornithologist on the archaeological trip to Yucatan headed by John Lloyd Stephens; there he discovered and took specimens of many new species of tropical birds. His work in ornithology attracted the attention of Alexander von Humboldt, and Cabot's proudest possession was an engraving of the German scientist and explorer inscribed "To my friend Samuel Cabot." (When he died, Dr. Cabot left his collection of three thousand birds, most of which he had stuffed with his own hands, to the Boston Society of Natural History, of which he had been the curator of birds for ten years.) Cabot used to tell his children the story of chasing through the jungle a new variety of parakeet which he had wounded and stumbling on the massive walls of an unknown Indian city. He enjoyed too telling a tale of becoming ill with fever on this same Stephens-Catherwood expedition and falling behind the rest of the party. To rejoin them later, he had to be carried in a hammock slung between two natives armed with machetes to cut their way through the jungle. Cabot had arranged the price of this transportation before starting, but halfway to the goal the natives struck for more money. Unarmed and too weak to walk, Cabot nevertheless swore that he would pay them no more than he had originally agreed, and such was his authority that the natives meekly shouldered him in their hammock and carried him the rest of the way.

The young Dr. Cabot also tried to exert authority over his

parents from time to time, as evidenced by a sentence in a letter written by his mother on April 26, 1842, to her son Elliott: "I expect Sam will be mad with us when he returns and finds we are all advocates of homeopathic remedies."

In 1844 Dr. Cabot established himself as a physician and surgeon in Boston, where he was in active practice for forty years. As a surgeon at Massachusetts General Hospital he was well regarded by his fellows, though he was hardly the medical pioneer sometimes pictured by his children and grandchildren. He was seven years Pasteur's senior and cannot have practiced scientific medicine as it is known today. He seems to have had, however, a good deal of imagination and courage for his time. The story is told of his going with a barely intelligible drunk to help the man's wife, who, he found, was choking to death with diphtheria. Having no ether with him and no time to send for it, Dr. Cabot stepped out into the yard on this bitter winter's night, collected enough snow and ice to freeze the woman's neck, and performed a tracheotomy, saving the woman's life. In Paris Dr. Cabot had also learned the operation to correct crossed eyes, which he performed in Massachusetts to improve the appearance of female relatives, among others.

In 1844 he married his double first cousin, Hannah Lowell Jackson. Both were great-grandchildren of John Cabot and of Captain John Higginson. (Sam and Hannah's son Godfrey also married a cousin, Maria Buckminster Moors.) The Cabots had a princely disdain for the usual arguments against consanguinity, intermarrying with Lowells, Lees, Higginsons, and Jacksons. According to Colonel Henry Lee, this was because they "knew each other well . . . and had a satisfying belief that New England morality and intellectuality had produced nothing better than they were; so they very contentedly made a little clique of themselves, and intermarried very much, with a sure and cheerful faith that in such alliances there could be no blunder." This interrelation and small-town atmosphere has been noted in verse:

> Oh! to be born in Boston, in the chill of a winter day.
> To the family tree of a social grandee, and the tap of a
>   pap-frappé;

With a cousin at every corner, and on every street an
    aunt;
To be known "who you are" on the Little Green Car,
    And your family seat at Nahant
With your "old man" strong in the market, and in
    mourning "Mamma so missed";
A hunter or two, and a Trinity pew, and a vanishing
    visiting list.
Ah yes, to be born in Boston, introduced by a spectacled
    stork;
In our great social spawn 'tis the place to be born—
But, ye gods, let me live in New York!

Hannah Lowell Jackson was descended from or connected
with the Quincys, the Lowells, Governor Thomas Dudley, Governor Simon Bradstreet, and the Reverend John Cotton, the father-in-law of Increase Mather and the man in whose honor Boston was named, because his parish in Lincolnshire had been at
Boston. Her father, Patrick Tracy Jackson, had in 1813 joined
his brother-in-law Francis Cabot Lowell in establishing at Wal-
tham, Massachusetts, the first power-loom cotton mill in America.
In 1822 Patrick Tracy Jackson and others founded the town of
Lowell, Massachusetts, when they secured control of the falls of
the Merrimack River. From 1830 to 1835 Mr. Jackson organized
and built the Boston and Lowell Railroad, the first passenger
steam railroad in America. Jackson, however, chose to use stone
ties, which proved to be impracticable, had to be removed, and
may still be seen in fences along the right of way. This setback
enabled the Baltimore & Ohio Railroad to be the first to run
scheduled passenger trains in the United States.

    The histories of all the distinguished Lowells would take too
long to recount, but a few family members were: John Lowell,
the founder of the Lowell Institute; James Russell Lowell, the
poet; Percival Lowell, the astronomer; Abbott Lawrence Lowell,
President of Harvard College; Amy Lowell, the cigar-smoking
poetess; and Pulitzer Prize poet Robert Lowell. Although some
present-day Lowells tend to minimize the importance of money
making and to stress the family's accomplishments in poetry,

architecture, education, and astronomy, one was more frank. Harvard President Abbott Lawrence Lowell understood well that money was the basis of position in Boston as elsewhere in America, and a few days before his death he told his friend George Cabot, "I'm getting rather worried about the Lowell Family, George. There's nobody in it making money any more." Since the day he had been given them by his grandfather, Lowell always wore as cuff buttons two twenty-dollar gold pieces.

In all societies social position has resulted from power, and in societies where money is power, it has resulted from money. Until recently most members of Boston society have merely been more frank and unembarrassed about the relationship than many members of other social aristocracies. In 1846 a pamphlet titled *Our First Men, A Calendar of Wealth, Fashion and Gentility* announced, "It is no derogation, then, to the Boston aristocracy, that it rests upon money. Money is something substantial. Everybody knows that and feels it. Birth is a mere idea which grows every day more and more intangible."

Hannah Lowell Jackson had experienced severe trials before her marriage to Dr. Samuel Cabot. She had been brought up as a rich young lady, but her older sister, Anna Cabot Jackson, had married Charles Russell Lowell, who had subsequently run off with another woman, taking with him much of the family fortune. As a result, Hannah at eighteen had had to take over the care of her younger brothers and sisters. A far greater sacrifice, however, was one she imposed on herself by her decision that she must break off her tacit engagement to Charles' brother, the poet James Russell Lowell. Many of Lowell's poems were addressed to the beautiful, petite Hannah, who was graced with dimples, wavy red-brown hair, and very blue eyes—"the blue unclouded heaven of her eyes," as Lowell described them. He did not describe, however, another characteristic of Hannah's which her son Godfrey inherited as well as her blue eyes: a whim of iron.

Although Dr. Samuel Cabot was hot-tempered and sometimes, according to his oldest daughter, Lilla, "tended to favor an implicit military obedience" from his children, he was also "quick to acknowledge a fault" and "kept his boyishness and unconventional tastes to the end." His wife, however, was "conventional in her tastes, unlike her husband," and brought up all eight of her surviving children "on the maxim of 'simple living and high thinking.'"

She told Lilla, "There is nothing wrong in taking a glass of wine and no harm in it in the company of your parents' friends, but just remember in the company of friends of your own age, that your refusing a glass of wine may make things easier for some young man in need of help."

According to Mrs. Ralph Bradley, Godfrey Lowell Cabot's daughter, "Grandmother had first-hand knowledge of the evils of drink, as her Cabot uncles—her mother's brothers—had been victims of drink. The youngest one, realizing his danger, had not touched liquor until he was twenty-five years old, when he was taken sick and the doctor prescribed wine. He became a victim of the habit and, rather than fill a drunkard's grave, he shot himself on the Lynn marshes."

Godfrey's obsessive views on sex may also have been partially the result of his mother's views on the subject, as well as of his idolization of her and some unfortunate experiences he had as a young boy. Again according to Mrs. Bradley, "My grandmother also asked her daughter, Lilla, to cooperate with her in striving to minimize the temptations which her brothers were bound to face by keeping the house filled with young girls and boys of the right ages for her brothers and giving them so much wholesome fun that her brothers would not wish to get their pleasure from women of a more undesirable stamp. They were apparently successful because my father and his brothers each have told their wives that they had no sexual intercourse before their marriage.

"I might add that my three brothers have each told me the same. This information was volunteered in every case, and though cynics may doubt, I know their integrity is beyond question."

Besides her strong views on drink and sex, Hannah Cabot and her husband were passionate abolitionists, a fact perhaps not totally unrelated to the fortunes their ancestors had in large measure made in the slave trade. Their house was a way station on the underground railway by which runaway slaves reached freedom, and Dr. Samuel Cabot was a friend of John Brown, though disapproving of his acts at Harpers Ferry. That he was politically somewhat naive is indicated by his plans to leave the Whig Party for the Know-Nothings. When he learned more about the group, however, he balked and joined the rising Republican Party, becoming a staunch supporter of Lincoln.

He and his wife sent money and guns and anti-slavery emigrants to "bleeding Kansas," and their household as a result was occasionally short of money for necessities. Other reasons for this were Dr. Cabot's insistence on living half the year in Canton, Massachusetts, where there were fewer patients who could pay their bills, and the fact that so much of his work even in Boston was charitable.

As so often has proved to be the case with New England morality, the moral thing to do often also turned out to be the profitable thing. After the Civil War on Black Friday, when Jay Gould and James Fisk tried to corner the gold market, government bonds had fallen to thirty cents, and according to a story in Dr. Cabot's family, he went to his wife and said, "Hannah, the government needs every cent they can get, and with your permission I want to put all our money into government bonds." Allegedly his wife gave her permission, and when the bonds went back to par, the Cabot fortune tripled.

The family tell a similar tale: that Alexander Agassiz came to Dr. Cabot for money to build the Calumet and Hecla mine; Dr. Cabot bought shares at $24 from a feeling of duty, because Agassiz, the stepson of his cousin Elizabeth Cary Agassiz (later the first president of Radcliffe), could not get money from the Boston banks. Whether Cabot and all the other Boston families who invested with Agassiz—the Higginsons, Paines, Russells, Gardners, Coolidges, and Shaws—did so out of duty or because they recognized a bright young man and a great investment opportunity, all were rewarded when the stock rose to over $1,000. In any event, Dr. Cabot inherited, made, and kept enough money to educate his children in both America and Europe and to leave an estate of half a million dollars. More importantly, he gave them all an intense sense of probity and a consuming curiosity and willingness to experiment. He frequently told his son Godfrey, "Honesty is certainly the best policy, but I should hate to have my sons adopt it merely as a matter of policy."

Dr. Cabot had a mania for prescribing fresh air for all his patients as well as for his family. According to his daughter Lilla, he said, "Tuberculosis is considered inherited and not contagious, but I think it is not inherited and is contagious." He sent a man with tuberculosis to live in a tent in the Maine mountains, saying, "If you don't die in the first fortnight, I think you have a fighting chance of winning out." The man was cured after three years, as was a poor tubercular woman to whom Cabot, knowing she could not go away, recommended living in a tent on the roof of her tenement in order to get fresh air.

Dr. Cabot had great curiosity and a speculative turn of mind. He told one of his daughters he had an idea that malaria was somehow associated with mosquitoes, though he had no idea how. He also speculated with all his children on various possibilities of human flight. He was unafraid to expound and to practice unorthodox medical theories, having early in his career angered many prominent physicians—including the dean of Boston medicine of that day, his wife's uncle James Jackson—by opposing the bleeding of patients and later by supporting the admission of women to the medical profession.

He had the Cabot predilection for living by his own beliefs, and he constantly preached this practice to his children. In lectures to his medical students he described a case in which he had followed the usual operative procedure only to have the patient die. Cabot then admitted that he had wanted to depart from the usual procedure and now felt that, had he done so, he might have saved the patient. "I am telling this to you young men," he said, "so that you will never have the sorrow of losing your patient's life because you neglected to follow your own better judgment."

CHAPTER III

A Bumptious Boyhood

> . . . all helped him to attain good and avoid evil. . . . The bath, the bottle, the change of linen . . . seemed to have been decreed by the Medes and Persians. Experience, duty, and science left little to chance. And life, at least physical life, in the model infant responded perfectly to each appointed stimulus. It was seldom necessary to cry; it was never appropriate to laugh.
>
> Breakfast, with its solemnity, ill-humour, and unappetizing profusion of food, seemed to cast a moralizing and steadying influence over the whole day: it was the improved Unitarian substitute for morning prayers. It incapacitated you, during the day, for doing anything unconventional. SANTAYANA, *The Last Puritan*, 76, 27

All of his life Godfrey Lowell Cabot was a fighter, and he began early. As a little boy under the elms and chestnut trees on Boston Common, he took part in the brutal snowball fights between the sons of Boston Brahmins like himself and the "micks," the sons of the Irish who were coming to Boston in ever increasing numbers after the great potato famines of the late 1840's. The "toughs" often enhanced the effectiveness of their snowballs with rocks.

Henry Adams, describing his own boyhood part in one of these bloody affairs, wrote: ". . . the boy Henry had passed through as much terror as though he were Turenne or Henri IV, and ten or twelve years afterwards when these same boys were

36

fighting and falling on all the battle-fields of Virginia and Maryland, he wondered whether their education on Boston Common
had taught . . . [them] how to die." In his Journal, Godfrey
noted his early battles—for example, a run-in with "a mick
[who] had the cheek to lie down on my sled and [when] I collared
him he got off."

Godfrey was born only a block from the Common, in his
father's house at 11 Park Square, on February 26, 1861. Six
days later, in his First Inaugural Address, Abraham Lincoln
tried in vain to avoid what was to be the Republic's most bitter
fight. Addressing himself only to those matters about which there
was "special anxiety or excitement," he pleaded with his fellow
citizens of the thirty-four United States to avoid violence. "There
has never been any reasonable cause for such apprehension. . . .
I have no purpose, directly or indirectly, to interfere with the
institution of slavery in the States where it exists. I believe I have
no lawful right to do so, and I have no inclination to do so . . .
the ills you fly from have no real substance."

This appeal to reason was not believed in the South, and in
rabidly abolitionist Boston, which had hated Clay and considered
even Daniel Webster a Judas Iscariot, President Lincoln was as
vilified as he was in South Carolina for these words. Little more
than a month later, on April 12, Fort Sumter was fired on, and
the fighting began which was to end one era of American history
and to begin another.

The war greatly influenced Godfrey's boyhood. He listened
to his parents discuss its bloody battles, in which a number of
relatives and friends were killed or wounded. He heard their
anti-Southern views and their abolitionist condemnation of the
terrible suffering of the Negroes. The result was that when he
played on the Common, he wore a blue soldier's cap and insisted
that boys smaller than he, if he could find any, be the Rebs. At the
age of ninety-five Godfrey wrote: "My childhood was passed in
the atmosphere of the Civil War. I grew up in a nursery on the
walls of which hung pictures of cousins of mine that fell in the
Civil War fighting on the side of the North against slavery. The
youngest of them was Cabot Russell who fell leading a negro

company at Fort Wagner a few days before he became nineteen years of age. Then came James Lowell . . . and then Charles Russell Lowell with regard to whom his uncle, James Russell Lowell wrote . . .

> Wut's words to them whose faith an' truth
> On War's red techstone rang true metal,
> Who ventered life an' love an' youth
>   For the gret prize o' death in battle?
> To him who deadly hurt, agen
>   Flashed on afore the charge's thunder,
> Tippin' with fire the bolt of men
>   Thet rived the Rebel line asunder?

He was the nephew of James Russell Lowell and was mortally wounded by a bullet through his chest. He fell off his horse and insisted on being put back on to it and riding in pursuit of the rebels; was wounded again by a bullet through his medulla ablongata which paralyzed him from his neck down. He lay upon his back and gave the needful orders for the disposition of the troops the next day and with the dawn he died. . . .

"My father was twice at the front serving as a doctor and a surgeon and . . . my mother found time amidst the cares of a family of eight children to fulfill the duties of an important position with the United States Sanitary Commission; the precursor of the Red Cross. . . .

"I learned to read at the age of four and among my earliest books I read 'My Days and Nights on the Battlefield' and 'Following the Flag' by Charles C. Coffin, 'The Youths History of the Rebellion,' 'Grant and Sherman, their Campaigns and Generals.'. . .

"The first recollection to which I can put a date was the return of the soldiers to be mustered out at the Readville Parade Ground near where we spent the summer on a farm bought that very year, 1865."

The Boston of Godfrey's youth was a Currier-and-Ives town. In 1860 the population was only 177,840 compared to New

York's 805,658, and it continued to fall further behind New York every year. If the total number of inhabitants was small, Cabot's world of old Boston families was the size of a village. To two senses other than sight—the sense of smell and the sense of hearing—the Boston of a hundred years ago was very different from today's city. There was neither the sound nor the odor of the internal-combustion engine. The sweet smell of horse manure was everywhere, as was the sound of horses' hoofs on cobblestones or sleigh runners on snow. Individual noises seemed louder then because they were not drowned in the constant drone of mechanical sound. When the blacksmith was trimming a horse's hoof for shoeing, the dogs barking for a delicious sliver of hoof could be heard a long way.

Park Square today is surrounded by bus terminals, a commercial hotel, and rather seedy night clubs. Even in 1861 it was one of Boston's least attractive neighborhoods, but with the *je m'en foutisme* typical of the Cabots, Dr. Samuel Cabot continued to live there because it was where his house was and he saw no reason why he should move.

Besides playing soldier on the Common, in winter Godfrey coasted there and on Beacon Hill as Boston boys had since colonial times. During the Revolution the boys of Boston had appealed to General Haldimand for the restoration of their coasting rights, which had been temporarily forbidden by the "lobster-backs." A primitive toboggan of two sleds connected by swivels with a long board, called a "double runner," provided extra winter excitement. Skiing, however, had to await the sophisticated youth of the twentieth century.

If little Godfrey could run fast enough to jump on the runner of a passing sleigh and hold tight, he got a thrillingly fast and dangerous ride. If he could not catch the sleigh, he shouted, "Cut, cut behind!" as a plea to the driver to wrap his whip around the would-be passenger to pull him. But, like skating on Back Bay, this was a dangerous and forbidden sport, never reported to his strict and serious mother.

Hannah Lowell Jackson Cabot was not a Puritan by earlier standards. She would have been furious if she or her children were called "miserable sinners," and she did not live "more in the dread of damnation than in the hope of glory." The Cabots' religion was Boston Unitarianism, "with nothing in it either to discourage a believer or to annoy an unbeliever." But the point of view drilled into Godfrey and his brothers and sisters had the characteristic weaknesses of Puritanism, most especially its want of proportion and its special demands which come with being among the elect. This Puritan sense of being especially chosen was reinforced with the generations of Cabot and Lowell wealth and the resultant necessity for *noblesse oblige*. It required the diligent searching out of duty and obligation, and especially it required discipline.

"My parents on both sides taught me by precept and by example that the main object of life should be service to others. When my Father died the office was full of former patients of his weeping as if they had lost a parent."

The other Boston Cabots said that "Hannah loved causes, not graces, and she neglected the graces." They said she lived too rigidly, with too little money and too many children, and when her daughters visited their grandmother and the old woman saw that there was no trimming on their pantalettes, she sewed on some Hamburg edging so they would be a bit less unfashionable.

Like Henry Adams, Godfrey as a child was too small, too sickly, too unsure of himself to allow himself the luxury of cowardice. Like Adams, who was twenty-one years older than he, Godfrey lived in an atmosphere of the Stamp Act, the Tea Tax, and the Boston Massacre. "Don't tread on me," "I have not yet begun to fight," and "Don't give up the ship" were not vague slogans from a distant past but current commands to courageous action.

Brown-haired, blue-eyed Godfrey, the runt of the family, was often ill. Skinny, short, underweight, and pale, he dared not show it when his ears smarted with pain from the penetrating January winds or complain when his hands were red from the winter cold. He could not be bothered with a cap, so he often felt his scalp stiffen from the cold. When he tripped on the rutted mud frozen solid in the Boston streets, he had to jump up as fast or faster than the bigger boys. Since the Cabots had never been noted for good looks, their absence was no shock, but to be little, small, *undersized*—that was almost unbearable!

Despite his problems of size and health, or perhaps because of them, Godfrey was so bumptious and energetic that his six older brothers and sisters were required by their parents daily to take turns "sitting on Godfrey." His older brothers and sisters teased Godfrey not only about his small size but also about his big feet. "It isn't that Godfrey is really so short. The trouble is too much is turned up at the bottom."

The effect of early illness and restraint was to make him more ambitious, more self-assertive, and more energetic than any of the older children or any of his contemporaries. He recorded each fraction of an inch he grew and every game he played— High-Low-Jack, whist, Jack Straws, Sancho Pedro, or Old Maid. With every victory, the entry in his Journal reflected pride; with every defeat, anger at himself or chagrin. The same was true in sports. Each effort at cricket, football, bowls, apple fights, fishing, or swimming was always reported in terms of the competition. And even the chores assigned him at the family's summer house in Cherry Hill— haying, splitting kindling, or picking peas, apples, or chestnuts—were for him a measure of his worth compared to that of his brothers and sisters.

Cabot's oldest sister, Lilla, was thirteen years older than he and assisted in "sitting on Godfrey" until he was thirteen years old, when she married. Lilla remembered that the first time she played Fox and Goose, Ralph Waldo Emerson was the fox and Louisa May Alcott the goose.

His oldest brother, Samuel, eleven years older, set the scientific pattern Godfrey was to follow. He went from the Boston Latin School to the Massachusetts Institute of Technology in 1866, only five years after its founding, and then to the Zurich Polytechnicum.

Godfrey's next brother, Arthur, after graduating from Harvard College and Harvard Medical School, studied medicine in Europe. He came back to Boston, where he became one of the most distinguished surgeons of his day. He was a well-known bon vivant, famous for having won a bet at an early hour of the morning after a night of considerable gaiety at the Dedham Club, during which he had sampled every wine in the club's ample cellar, by mounting a polo pony and driving a ball around Dedham Common. This feat is remarkable only because it demonstrates that the same heredity and the same environment produced both one of Boston's gayest blades and its most famous Puritan since the Mathers.

The fourth child, James Jackson Cabot, died on June 13, 1875.

Godfrey's next sister, Elizabeth, whom he called Nellie, was five years older and always the closest to him of all his relatives. After Lilla married in 1874, Nellie took over the raising of Godfrey, and the family felt that she spoiled him, never correcting him because she wanted him to love her; Lilla had felt he was too bumptious and needed correction because it was more important that people be able to love him. Lilla said that Godfrey felt too superior to his brother Guy.

Nearly two years older, Guy was mentally retarded and he remained Sam's ward for all of his adult life.

A younger brother, Russell, died before the age of two.

The greatest influence on young Godfrey was not his hot-tempered but easy-going father, nor his older brothers and sisters, but his duty-ridden mother. She could say, with William M. Evarts, "I pride myself on my success in doing not the things I like to do, but the things I don't like to do." Unfortunately she was not able, like Benét's Mary Lou Wingate, "to hate the sin and to love the sinner," but instead, like Macaulay's Puritan, she "hated bear-baiting, not because it gave pain to the bear, but because it gave pleasure to the spectators."

John Quincy Adams wrote, "A Letter Book, a Diary, a Book of receipts and expenses—these three Books, kept without intermission, should be the rule of duty of every man who can read and write. But to keep them perseveringly requires a character given to very few of the Sons of men. Above all it requires a character to which toil is a pleasure, and of which untiring Patience is an essential Element." Patience was never Cabot's most conspicuous trait, but in its place he developed a superabundance of self-discipline, and all of his life he found toil a pleasure.

Godfrey's Journal, which he kept off and on for forty years, started on November 7, 1872, in Canton. The entries for the first day show an intensity of interest in things scientific and mathematical rather beyond that of the average eleven-year-old. He spent the morning studying geology by himself. "In the afternoon I calculated the average increase per cent of all the cities of over 20 thousand inhabitants now, from 1860 to 1870, having the last census in my geography. When father came from the depot I had a short run in the fields with him. . . . After supper father and I played 2 games of High-Low-Jack. Father beat the first and I the second game."

Almost every day Godfrey reported some form of competition—tennis, bean picking, Constantinople, chess, wood chopping, wrestling, croquet, or Logomachy with his brothers, cousins, and friends, and always he recorded who "beat." The runt's competitiveness never left him; indeed, it increased with the years, along with his concern about his small size.

Until he was almost nine years old, Godfrey's instruction had come from governesses, who began his Latin and French at seven. In the winter of 1869 he went to the Brimmer School at the time Mr. Bates was principal. For the next four years he was at the Boston Latin School under the stern eye of Dr. Gardner and the next two years at Mr. Hopkinson's School.

At fourteen he noted, "I am 4 ft. 10 in. and weigh 85 lbs. I am smaller for my age than any of my cousins on Father's side." A year later, although intelligent and hard-working enough to have passed his examinations for entrance to Harvard College, he was still well below average in size. "I weigh 94 pounds. I am about 5 feet and $\frac{1}{13}$ of an inch." His size hurt him in that area in which he most tried to prove himself, sports. At sixteen and a half he wrote, "Played football. . . . I really begin to feel as if I might sometime become a tolerably good player. I have grown an inch since August I am a little over 5 feet 3 now an inch over the average height of women. . . ." His parents, too, worried about Godfrey. "Father engaged a boxing master for me last Saturday he is to come on Monday Wednesday and Friday. . . . Father and mother made a rule two or 3 weeks ago that I should be out 2 hours every afternoon I have not kept it very strictly but I average over 2 hours."

Humiliation was more effective than parental fiat. On June 2, 1877, he noted, "A gentleman named Dr. Richardson came out today. . . . I was quite flattered when he told me that I swam very well . . . but it took down my pride somewhat when he guessed my age at 12 and told me that I was about the size of his little brother of 12 and swam about as well."

On November 10, 1872, three days after he began the Journal, Godfrey reported seeing clouds of smoke rising from what would become known as the Great Fire in Boston. He noted that his father lost at least $2000 in the fire. He had a predilection for numbers, and the Journal is full of them—inches of rainfall, daily changes of temperature and barometric pressure, the number of miles he walked. There were horse cars all over Boston and a railroad to the North Shore, but Godfrey usually walked wherever he went, noting in the Journal when he took "the cars."

His days were full and varied. "I chopped kindling in the morning. In the afternoon I was reading from Science Monthly. . . . After breakfast Nellie heard me recite *Mère Michel* which I finished and then I studied Latin with Nellie to teach me to prepare me to go into the Latin School another winter. . . . Willie [William Putnam, Cabot's distant cousin, his only lifelong friend and the future grandfather of McGeorge and William Putnam Bundy] came to dinner in the afternoon and he and I buried ourselves in the driest leaves used for winter bedding . . . for 5 horses and five cows all but Bessie (father's town horse) and told stories. Willie stayed to tea and I beat him 2 games of High-Low-Jack and he beat me one of that and 2 of Casino."

After keeping his Journal for a month, Godfrey misplaced it and did not begin another until Friday, June 12, 1874, when he noted that he was "aged 13 years, 3 months, 14 days." He now began analyzing and criticizing people and situations. His first analysis was rather more charitable than the many which succeeded it: "Got a new master on Thursday. Tall, black eyes, black hair, whiskers and moustache. Dark complexion. Very quiet but I guess he will do what he says." He was now going to school six days a week and noted on Saturday, June 27, "Hurrah, vacation's begun!!!!"

His summer vacations from 1865 were spent with relatives on the North Shore and at his father's summer house in Canton; they were full of discovery and adventure. "I went to Houghton's pond. I took a dive, two scoots and a jump, sounded once, jolly fun, played cricket and ate cherries in the forenoon. . . . Saturday [July] 4th Jim had bought 5 papers of fire-crackers . . . in the afternoon one paper caught fire at Willie's elbow and began to go off at a great rate another one lay close by after the smoke began to clear away I saw it and rushed in and slung it far away . . . once I heard a sharp crackling about ten yards off a small circle of dead grass about a foot across was blazing up 6 inches. . . . I stamped it out right off . . . sailed down Salem harbour . . . I noticed that a kind of seaweed reflects a beautiful blue light when under the water in the shade . . . got some sea-anemones on the rocks. . . . We had a spattering fight all of us against George Lee he ducked Ted 3 times and me once. . . . Willie and Guy plugged me with apples I made Willie sing 3 times and Guy once one apple bounced fully 8 feet from Guy and several broke on Willie . . . walked nearly 19 miles.

"Took a bath and went wading on the seal flats. We got within 60 feet of a seal . . . they are funny looking objects with old-man-ish faces and pug noses . . ."

But vacations always ended. "We have a new master in Algebra strict small man with black hair black eyebrows and a short black beard and a funny nose [Here Godfrey drew a sketch of the master. The Journal is full of sketches of things described.] . . . Greek comes very hard."

Much learning came outside the classroom. "Friday. I had a skirmish with a fellow in school to-day, we were on bad terms last year he was in the habit of kicking me in a crowd or from behind a corner. . . . I took it pleasantly for some time but once I hit him in return and we had a skirmish . . . the other day we were playing prisoners base and he was caught but said he was not I was on his side but nevertheless persisted in saying that he was caught. he slapped my face and got out of reach of my hand so I kicked him, today he came up behind the corner where I was standing and kicked me I went after him and hit him on the shoulder. he backed me up against the wall we had a skirmish I cut my finger on his jaw then Smith came in and dragged Frost away he is 16 years old and a good deal stouter but a little shorter he is more than my match in wrestling. he slapped my face after recess and just then the master came in and I could not retaliate . . . Saturday. Father told me to slap his face 'hard' the next time I saw him I saw him today standing on the steps he looked so unsuspecting that I only slapped it very gently he backed me up against the wall and punched my face. Smith then separated us we fought after school he gave me a slight black eye and a hard blow on the jaw I backed out like a coward I barked his chin and cheek-bone. I fought wild and kept following him up and I was so flurried I couldn't hit straight which gave him a great advantage."

Some months later Godfrey noted in his Journal, "Frost has been expelled. He had been in the habit of occasionally punching and bothering smaller boys (though he never meddled with me since we had a fight)."

Throughout the Journal, Cabot never hesitated to give very definite appraisals of people or events. He wrote at thirteen: "the Master we have in Greek is Mr. Fiske I like him very much. . . . Mr. Davenport teaches us history and geography he is a crossgrained old gent with a worried look and a peaked face we call him Nilsy he's the only master we raise and yet he marks more than any other master we have. . . . Our drawing master Mr. Hitchings is a short fat man . . . the boys call him Cudjo and think him a great fool. . . . In recess time we raised old Nilsy like fury."

Resistance to schoolmasters has never been unique to Boston, but, as Henry Adams pointed out, it had a special flavor there. "Resistance to something was the law of New England nature; the boy looked out on the world with the instinct of resistance; for numberless generations his predecessors had viewed the world chiefly as a thing to be reformed, filled with evil forces to be abolished, and they saw no reason to suppose that they had wholly succeeded in the abolition; the duty was unchanged. The duty implied not only resistance to evil, but hatred of it. Boys naturally look on all force as an enemy, and generally find it so, but the New Englander, whether boy or man, in his long struggle with a stingy or hostile universe, had learned to love the pleasure of hating; his joys were few.

"Politics as a practice, whatever its professions, had always been the systematic organization of hatreds, and Massachusetts politics had been as harsh as the climate. The chief charm of New England was harshness of contrasts and extremes of sensibility—a cold that froze the blood, and a heat that boiled it—so that the pleasure of hating—one's self if no better victim offered—was not its rarest amusement; . . ."

Adams, with surprising passion and considerably greater style than ever Godfrey achieved, went on to describe the Boston boy's love of summer and escape to nature which was so evident in Cabot. "Town was winter confinement, school, rule, discipline; straight, gloomy streets, piled with six feet of snow in the middle; frosts that made the snow sing under the wheels or runners; thaws when the streets became dangerous to cross; society of uncles, aunts, and cousins who expected children to behave themselves, and who were not always gratified; above all else, winter represented the desire to escape and go free. Town was restraint, law, unity. Country, only seven miles away, was liberty, diversity, outlawry, the endless delight of mere sense impressions given by nature for nothing, and breathed by the boys without knowing it. . . . Winter and summer then were two hostile lives, and bred two hostile natures. Winter was always the effort to live; summer was tropical license. Whether the children rolled in the grass, or waded in the brook, or swam in the salt ocean, or sailed in the bay, or fished for smelts in the creeks, or netted minnows in the salt marshes, or took to the pine-woods and the granite quarries, or chased muskrats and hunted snapping-turtles in the swamps, or mushrooms or nuts on the autumn hills, summer and country were always sensual living, while winter was always compulsory learning. Summer was multiplicity of nature; winter was school."

Like Adams, Godfrey could not be unaware of his ancestors. On a trip to Lowell to visit his brother Sam's new factory he noted in his Journal that he saw a portrait of his grandfather Jackson, one of the city's founders. He noted the various manufacturing processes in great detail and also the fact that Sam "and other manufacturers own whole streets of houses which they let to the operatives at extremely low rents."

Whether on cold winter nights in Boston before a thriftily laid fire or on relaxed, starry, summer evenings on the comfortable piazza at Canton, young Godfrey, listening to his father's tales of adventure in the wild jungles of Yucatan or to his mother's accounts of the heroism of various uncles and cousins on the battlefields of the Civil War, viewed life as an adventure to be lived fully, intensely, and nobly. His reaction to the challenge of his ancestry was quite the opposite of Henry Adams'. Godfrey came quite unconsciously but quite automatically to the belief which Justice Oliver Wendell Holmes expressed that "Life is action and passion . . . it is required of a man that he should share the action and passion of his time at peril of being judged not to have lived." But as young Godfrey studied the variety of the lives of his ancestors—China merchants, manufacturers, doctors, founders of cities and of institutions—it was difficult for the boy to decide which of the many exciting paths to adventure and duty he should follow.

Like most nineteenth-century American boys, Godfrey was intensely and chauvinistically patriotic. He was proud of the part his forbears had played, but his Puritan conscience told him that pride was not enough, that he was obligated to serve his country as they had. His idea of what role women should play was likewise formed early. He learned about Thomas Handasyd Perkins' mother, herself a Universalist, who had heard that the Roman Catholics in Salem had no place to worship because prejudice against them was so strong no one dared rent them a hall and they were too poor to buy one. She had thereupon scandalized her friends by giving the Catholics her large coach house as a place of worship. Godfrey learned, too, of his own mother's work in the underground railway, helping escaped slaves. He thus came to believe that women—at least Cabot women—must actively do good as well as be good. Women who ate the bread of idleness or craved the pomps and vanity of this world were simply not good women.

There were few of this world's frivolities in young Godfrey's life. Even Christmas and birthday presents were few and useful. Baths were taken in cold water, and the tub was not to be over a quarter full. The plumbing in Godfrey's youth was simpler than today's, as were his pleasures, but the joys were nonetheless many and real.

"Nellie took Guy and me to Barnum's Circus. We saw a Japanese balancer and a little negro girl perform. There were lots of gorgeous chariots with men in tin armor and women dressed up swell, and men with masks on to represent negros. Some had smooched faces to represent Chineese. Then a man dressed up in a 3 tiered crown to represent the pope with a lot of bishops . . . there was a man dressed in brown linen with long tow hair . . . and a young man below kept pulling the lappel of his coat he whacked at him.

"We all went up to see the king of the Sandwich Islands. He was a very large fat man with a large head with little brain in it. . . . He had hair like a negro but on the whole he was pretty goodlooking. . . . When he came in and when he went out Mr. Gardiner made us all stand up . . . and we were dismissed an hour earlier than usual."

In May 1876 Godfrey went to the Centennial in New York with other members of his family. For many pages in the Journal he listed the multitude of educational and worthy sights he saw, but he particularly remembered "a pair of boots made of human skin" and "the learned fleas one of them drew what the man said was 1200 times his own weight it was a horsecar another drew an elephant another drew a phaeton very rapidly . . . there was a large orchestra of fleas . . . one flea was reading a newspaper 4 playing whist. They had a little box divided into a hundred partitions to sleep in."

Much of Godfrey's entertainment was of his own making. At

fourteen he noted: "The white mice will climb the mast of a toy ship for a piece of bread.

"Father caught a large rat in the same hole in which he had caught 5 woodchucks and I tried to dissect her with my jacknife, but before I had her skinned I had to bury her and go into supper." He was more successful a few days later. "When we got home father told us that he had caught a sable which father told us was extremely rare and almost extinct in Massachusetts. . . . I immediately had my knife sharpened and commenced to skin him with Willie's help. . . . Last night I got his leg partly out and skinned most of his body, today I got his right hind leg out to the ankle and cut it off I then stripped the foot to the last joint of the toes where I cut it off and when father came down to breakfast (I had set to work at 6:10 A.M.) I told him how far I had got he told me I ought to have left the leg adhering to the skin and stripped all the flesh of its bones I did this with the remaining hind leg . . . in the afternoon I stripped the flesh off of the fore-legs and neck and head as far as the nose and took out the eyes . . . and cleaned out the brains by means of some cotton wool and a stick then I pasted skin all over and inside as well as outside of the skull with arsenic after previously removing the body which Willie and I had dissected in the morning."

Nearly a century later, in 1956, Godfrey wrote to Dr. James R. Killian, President of the Massachusetts Institute of Technology: ". . . when I was about six years old I saw him [his father] siphoning wine from its dregs in a bottle and I could not understand how the wine could flow up hill and he explained to me the effect of the atmosphere, qualitative and quantitative. I went out onto the Public Gardens and picked dandelion stems and made a siphon with dandelion stems and used it to siphon water from a tumbler into the basin of a sink in my nursery."

Some of these practical experiments with nature were dangerous and painful, but even these were described dispassionately and with clinical interest: "On my way back I picked up a queer brown ant with black eyes. It stung me on my wrist which caused quite sharp pain for a few minutes. It could stick out its sting for nearly half the length of its body. It made gritting noise by rubbing together two of the rings which encircled its abdomen."

It is nearly impossible to exaggerate Godfrey's need as a child to prove his courage and strength. Once when he and Guy found a skunk caught in one of his father's traps, Godfrey noticed that the animal was gnawing off its broken leg in an effort to escape. Godfrey sent Guy to fetch his father and, in order to prevent the animal's escape, held it by the tail until his father arrived and shot it. His father laughed at Godfrey and made him bury his clothes, apparently aware only of the ludicrousness of the boy's act and not of the incredible tenacity.

Other boyhood pleasures were varied and many, but for any Boston boy, and particularly for a Cabot, ships were the most exciting. "Went down to the wharves with Johnnie Reynolds went aboard several vessels some they were loading with cotton some they were unloading bricks from."

One of his greatest joys as a boy was reading. "Mother has bought a new edition of the encyclopedias and I spend most of my time reading them." Scientific books and journals occupied most of his reading time, but he read some fiction. "I like Scott's style very much it is so simple and gentlemanly." His favorite fiction consisted of fairytales; he not only read them himself and read them aloud to others, but he also made up new ones for anyone who would listen.

Unitarianism in Godfrey's time had lost much of the beauty and poetry of its predecessor Christian religions, as well as all the mystery and magic. This perhaps explains his penchant for fairytales, where his taste for magic could be satisfied. Although he attended Unitarian church services, Godfrey's passion for the struggle between good and evil in fairytales, with their perfect heroes and absolute villains, was as close to any strong religious feeling as he ever got. At fourteen he noted in his Journal in describing a schoolboy trial held to determine which boy had made a disturbance, "Some boys would not take their oath (as if it made any difference whether the hand was on the Bible or not when they lied)."

Godfrey was given no money for toys. At fifteen his yearly

allowance was $25 "to buy boots and mittens." The only permissible tomfoolery was on April Fool's day, when he pinned as many papers on people's backs as possible while trying to avoid having them pinned on his own.

There are in Godfrey's Journal a number of examples of presence of mind remarkable in a boy of fourteen. "After dinner I had a snow fight with Donald and Perin, they stood on the pile of snow in our yard and I stood in their yard so that they could dodge down behind the wooden wall. Then the woman called them to come in and get ready for a party. Perin in getting over the wall, fell and his wrist struck one of the clothes hooks, which are very sharp, and he got a horrid gash. I immediately seized his wrist holding the flap of flesh down with one hand and squeezing the arm just above to prevent it from bleeding and led him into the house yelling for Dr. White. By the time Donald (who is only 11) collected his wits enough to go after his father, Dr. White came into the back entry. . . . [Arthur] then came back and called father who sewed up the wound."

Despite Godfrey's increasing abilities, the youthful Journal entries contain examples of self-doubt, self-examination, and self-criticism which later disappeared entirely. "My chief trouble in shooting is indecision. . . . I fear Mr. Mudge would not have given such high marks to another boy for the same work for he is very partial and I think he likes me because I have always behaved myself and not 'raised' like the other fellows. I hope I have outgrown raising but I'm afraid that my good behavior was only due to the fact that there were no fellows there that I liked well enough to join in with them."

Godfrey was particularly critical of his shyness. On April 18, 1875, at the Centennial Celebration at Concord and Lexington, he noted that he was afraid to go up and shake hands with President Ulysses S. Grant.

"November 9 [1877]. I joined a dancing school got up by Aunt Lillie and Mrs. Coolidge I dreaded going the first time and I felt very uneasy when I got there but I felt sure I should have a good time and I did. . . . I have improved a great deal since I began to go I can get along pretty well with almost all the girls that I have danced with at all now. . . . If I can't dance well with a girl I take her out and dance with her as much as I can till I can dance with her."

This attitude of toughing it out—of doing whatever was difficult again and again until he was satisfied that he could do it as well or better than anyone else—was frequently reflected in the Journal. In matters social it earned him a reputation as an intense, humorless boor. The heroes of Godfrey's fairytales tried and tried and tried again until they had climbed the topless mountain and bested the invincible witch; but girls, even Boston girls, resent being treated like mountains and witches, and Godfrey's reputation as a stubborn and eccentric young man was soon well established. A bad case of acne, which lasted for years, did little to increase his self-confidence or his popularity. He was sometimes left alone "in the middle of the floor feeling like a cat in a strange garret and not knowing where to go or what to do."

Uncomfortable himself, he was sometimes sensitive to the problems of others, and the knight errantry of helping damsels in distress on the dance floor not only appealed to his sense of gallantry but was also less dangerous than competing for the belles of the balls. "Maggie Cabot who was at the same party was scarcely taken out at all except by me. She is small and pudgy and does not dance well. I tried to persuade Size [a cousin] to dance with her, but he would not; then I asked Harry and he danced with her once then I asked George and he said he would but did not. I suppose he forgot it. Size only dances with a few girls and always goes in for the belles. . . . Miss Burnett . . . I like better than any 'belle' that I know, but then my experience is very limited."

Cabot's contacts with members of the opposite sex of his own class were proper and superficial, for, as Henry Adams pointed out speaking of himself, "From women the boy got the domestic virtues and nothing else. He might not even catch the idea that women had more to give. The garden of Eden was hardly more primitive." Even boys of Brahmin society, however, could not remain untouched by the abundance of vice which existed at other levels of society. "To balance this virtue, the Puritan city had always hidden a darker side . . . only too educational, and to most boys much the more interesting . . . no boy escaped some contact with vice of a very low form . . . and [it] had the charm of force and freedom and superiority to culture or decency. One might fear it, but no one honestly despised it."

Cabot's most important boyhood experience with the opposite sex did not take place at the well-chaperoned and proper private dances he mentions in his Journal. Indeed, it was never mentioned in his Journal at all; he kept it secret for over eighty years. Only when Cabot was ninety-six years old and his thoughts wandered back to his childhood, did he finally relate to his son Jack and to several of his trained nurses the most awful experience of his youth. He told them that the house on Carver Street which backed up to the back fence of his father's house at 11 Park Square was a brothel. He admitted watching the girls in the house and as they washed their hair and dried it in the back yard. The girls had made obscene gestures and indecent proposals and tempted him to come over the fence, and when he had not, they had laughed at him.

When the old man was asked why he had never told his mother about these incidents, he became outraged. "My God! Tell my mother! My mother never knew that such things existed. She was a saint. I would never, never have spoken to her of such a thing." He described his response as anger. "They were not like the women I knew. They were bedraggled and bad. I thought that God should punish them, and I wished that I had the money to buy the house and turn them out."

CHAPTER IV

Harvard College

His senses, his reactions, his memory did everything perfectly for him if he only let them alone. All the routine liturgy of knowledge, dates and conjugations, and demonstrations, registered itself early in the passionless upper regions of his brain, to be rehearsed on occasion almost unerringly. Meantime the heart within was asleep or dreaming of something else. It remained immature even in his manhood.
SANTAYANA, *The Last Puritan*, 94

The summer he was sixteen, Godfrey went on his first trip without his family, a two weeks' walking tour with his friend Willie Putnam. In his Journal he reported in great detail his first odyssey.

". . . lodging for the night with supper and breakfast for $1.50 apiece . . . it took us more than four times as long to climb Mt. Monadnock as it did to climb up Wachusett; it took 2 hours and 20 minutes. . . . Monadnock is 3186 feet high . . . we could see 33 lakes from the top. . . . I noticed that all the bridges over the Connecticut were roofed over and it was forbidden to drive over them faster than a walk. The toll for foot passengers was 2 cents.

"In the evening a man who worked in the hotel took me up to see Jim Fiske's grave it was in a pretty country cemetery over looking the river, it had quite a handsome monument over it which the man told me had cost $30,000. What a waste of money thought I. The monument had four female figures representing his investments at its four corners . . . we passed several manufactories some of which were worked by water brought from a distance in wooden pipes. . . .

"In this fortnights tramp, I ascended 7 or 8 higher hills, and mountains than I had ever seen before. I went further north than I had ever been before. I was in two states which I had never been in before, I saw a longer tunnel than any I had ever seen before and saw a great many trees and woods such as I had never seen before. July 24 Willie and I walked 18½ miles most of the way along a public road without meeting a team or a vehicle of any description. . . . What pleased me as much as anything was that we met so many pleasant kind hearty people. . . . We were two or three times mistaken for peddlers and once were asked if we were in search of employment."

The rest of the summer Godfrey spent at Canton and with his cousins on the North Shore having "a bully time" hunting, "bathing," sailing, shooting, and playing croquet, chess, vingt-et-un, and robbers-and-policemen.

His father considered Godfrey too young and too small to enter Harvard at sixteen (he was still only five feet three and a half inches tall and weighed 108 pounds), so he was sent to the Massachusetts Institute of Technology for a year. There he studied only Mechanical and Free-hand Drawing, leaving him time to go discovering. He visited his older brother Sam's factory, which produced lampblack and roofing oil and which was just beginning to show a profit.

"I have an allowance for every-thing now 240 dollars a year I am also getting some money by collecting bills for father at 6% commission. It is a pretty disagreeable business. The first time I went out I had 7 bills to collect. I only collected $3.00 and that was from a woman so poor that father afterwards sent me to refund the money."

Although Godfrey was not an overwhelming success as a bill collector, he was very thrifty with his allowance. "I saved $17.00 out of an allowance of $20 last month."

There was plenty of time to act in plays in the theater in his grandmother Cabot's house and to play "Hide the slipper, and King George and his troops and fox and geese (I was fox) and going to Jerusalem."

On Tuesday, February 26, 1878, he noted that he was that day seventeen years old and that after learning his lessons he had gone down to the wharves. There was, as usual, no mention of birthday gifts. The day before, he noted, "I am nearly 5 ft 4 in in height and I weigh over 110 pounds I have gained eleven pounds and about 2¾ inches in the last year."

His strongly expressed opinions and his self-righteousness did not help his popularity at Technology: ". . . when I got to my desk today I found it flooded with water. My things were a good many of them injured and most of them were hung by a string in a long festoon to the hot water pipes. My instrument case was locked and the key inside (as it afterwards turned out) and various damage was done such as breaking my ink dirtying my triangles and curves, wetting my paints, stealing my knife, etc."

No amount of hazing, however, could budge him from his strict views of right and wrong and particularly from his strong feeling against drinking. When he was hit in the cheek by a baseball bat thrown by his retarded brother, Guy, he was sufficiently injured to be put to bed. "Then Dr. Richardson came and ordered a little brandy and water to be given to me, the brandy and water tasted like slops and made me vomit."

In the fall of 1878 Godfrey went to Harvard College. In his freshman year he roomed in 24 Matthews with his friend Willie Putnam, and his yearly allowance was raised to $300. His Journal began to reflect Cantabrigian influences, including some college slang and references to "micks," "niggers," and "cheesits."

"Willie and I went to see the Harvard-Yale football match. . . . It was the first match I have ever seen . . . the Yales played a very rough game. . . . The Harvards thoroughly deserve to get beaten the eleven don't practice enough. . . . I rode to dancing-school in the horse-car with Miss Long, I notice the Highland horse-cars are a great deal sweller than the Cambridge horse-cars though the fare is not so much.

"I was highly complimented in Elocution today for my reading, modesty compels me however to declare that it was not because I read well but because the rest of the class read so wretchedly, abominably. It's torture to one of my 'delicate sensibilities' to hear fellows get up and murder the best passages of Shakespeare the way they do. . . . I did not get our thermometer above 50 once today, although I kept a roaring fire all day. . . . Dabney and I made quite a circus in my room last night he came over to study and after we had done studying we set to work to wrestle and after a bout or two we upset the lamp smashing the lampshade and chimney all to pieces and bending the lamp out of shape."

By the time Godfrey arrived at Harvard, his aesthetics, too, were already greatly influenced by a hyperactive sense of morality. "I forgot to say that I went to the Art Museum last Sunday just before dinner. Some of the casts of Greek statues interested me very much. I noticed that the busts of the Roman Emperors made them out about as homely a set of men as you could find anywhere. . . . I remember the bust of Nero looked like the sensual cowardly scoundrel that he was. . . . Don Juan I thought a most absurdly unnatural drama; the idea of his being allowed to run riot through society one week seemed to me absurd. If Pierrot had been any kind of a man he'd have punched his head for him. . . .

"I have also read Notre Dame de Paris . . . I came near throwing down the book in disgust when I came to the scene between Phoebus Claude Frollo and Esmeralda, it is simply revolting. . . . I think of Tennyson's Idylls of the King, Queen Guinevere is the finest. . . . I read a very sensational book of Mayne Reids at Joe Gardner's some time ago called 'Run Away to Sea.' It's about the poorest trash I ever had the pleasure of reading except a Dime Novel I once endeavored to struggle through   When I was a small child my chief incentive was that it was a forbidden 'sweet' but it was so weak that I had to give it up. . . . What I long for now-a-days is a novel in which the characters of the hero and heroine are perfectly pure and unselfish and not one by one remove from the common place as is almost always the case in novels now. . . . I have also read and had read to me all the stories that I had not read in a volume of Hans Andersen. I think his works are the best medecine for me that I ever got hold of, when I'm all sharpset and blue and 'off my base' and generally unhappy they soothe me down in no time. There is something so sweet and pure and simple in his stories that it acts like a balm."

Godfrey read a great deal besides what was required for his college courses, and many of his reactions pointed toward the course his life was to take. "Mother and I have finished 'The life of Charles Bianconi' by his daughter it is very interesting in some ways, he was a man who was very parsimonious in his business habits and yet very liberal in private life, he struck me as a man who meant to do the fair thing by everybody, but he did not mean to do more than the fair thing without getting the credit for it. He always considered lending money as giving the interest on it without getting the credit for it, at least so I interpret his exacting 5% int. on money he lent his daughter. . . . With all his faults Charles Bianconi was . . . really of a great deal of benevolence. . . . His large charities and the instance in which he came forward during famine times bear witness to his benevolence; . . . All together he is a character well worth studying especially by me who have some of his bad qualities though I think in a lesser degree. There is one trait in his character well worth imitating and that is his tireless 'go' or energy which continued unimpaired to the end of his long and useful life. . . .

". . . [I read] a life of my great grandfather, T. H. Perkins which I found very interesting. . . . The thing that impresses you is his great humaneness and benevolence . . . the most dauntless personal courage. He was a man of extra ordinary business capacity . . . of the most earnest and improtruding charity, and possessed of the greatest veneration of anything good and great. . . .

"I have just finished a book called 'Janoof the Windmill.' . . . One sentence in the book, which is put into the mouth of a rich man, [says:] 'the chief luxury in having riches is the luxury of giving.'

"I read also a short memoir of my grandfather Jackson   I

never realized before what a very large place he filled in the community for years he was the leading businessman in Boston he founded Lowell and built the Boston and Lowell railroad. I inherit from him my passion for dancing. After a hard days work he used to dance till late at night. He was a man of undaunted courage, tireless energy, endless perseverence and a patient steadfastness which carried him triumphantly through the reverses which overtook him late in life. His unrivalled business ability seems to me to have been the result of moral strength rather than intellectual skill. He loved business and threw himself into it heart and soul and forced the gates of success by enterprise, judgement, foresight, and above all by constant care close attention to detail and hard unremitting labor. He was most emphatically a worker he was never happy but when he was busy and this more than any other thing led to the enormous results he accomplished."

Although there had been little in Godfrey's Journal about his mother prior to March 28, 1878, thereafter there were an increasing number of entries, almost all relating to her health. "Mother had a severe attack of asthma last night, the first one for two weeks. I read to her 2 or 3 hours every day.

"I took a walk with father in the afternoon. Father has been growing old very fast lately . . . mother's asthma is beginning to tell on her I hate to think of it but I can't help noticing it.

". . . this confounded cough has been tormenting me for the past week. Mother has been having a still worse time than I, poor old darling, she gets more peaked every day. I thought of something today that seemed to me very true, a man is between two telescopes one with the big end and the other with the little end towards him   through the former he looks at his own pleasures and his neighbor's troubles   through the other he sees his own troubles and his neighbor's pleasures.

"Mother is getting slowly weaker. . . . Sunday and most of Monday I spent in town taking care of mother. . . . I am at present the happy possessor of $124 I am going to get a bicycle as soon as I can persuade mother to let me have one. . . . Mother is very weak indeed and growing weaker I am afraid the poor darling can not last another year she suffers all the time and gets very little sleep.

"Monday, June 30 [1879], At about twenty minutes past 11 I was called up to mother's room and told that she had not long to live she was lying very pale and scarcely breathing. She died about noon after a short struggle. Father, Nellie, Arthur, Sam and I were in her room when she died; Father 'lifted' up his voice and gave thanks to God that the poor darling was at last released from her sufferings. Her body was laid flat upon the bed for the first time for over a year and a quarter. We had all been expecting and for my part I may almost say hoping for it for a month or two but yet it was a terrible shock when it came. I felt as if I would give a great deal to be able to tell her once more how much I loved her."

Not the least affecting of Godfrey's problems as a child, and one which continued throughout his life, was his difficulty in expressing affection and his feeling of doubt about his ability to love.

"Tuesday, July 1. I have set to work in good earnest on my Rhetoric. Mother was 59 years and 26 days old when she died and had been married thirty-five years 11 days. June was an eventful month for her, she was born the 3rd, married the 19th and died the 30th.

"Wednesday, July 2. The funeral took place today; I suppose all felt as blue as razors after it, I know I did and in the afternoon I went out and took a long ride on my bicycle and came in feeling much better. I went out to Chestnut Hill Reservoir rode round there a little while rode a mile in 4½ minutes and rode in from the further side of the reservoir to Arlington street church 5¼ miles in 31 minutes the best I have done yet."

Although he was by now five feet eight and a half inches tall, Godfrey was still much concerned with his size and strength and abilities. "I have been instigated by a book called 'How to get strong and how to stay there' by William Blaikie to begin a regular course of exercises to develop my arms, my legs and my chest. I trust to wrestling rowing and chopping for my loins and back. I run from quarter to half a mile every day; rise on my toes 160 times both morning and evening; clench my fists an equal number of times; raise a pail of water to my chest 16 times and to my shoulder 8 times with each arm. . . . I have brought up my calf from 12¾ to 13¾ in 2 weeks . . . all small measurments for a fellow of my height, and I think I may add strength."

Day after day Godfrey measured himself in every possible way. "Wednesday, Mar 12, I had another wrestling match with Willie Dunbar today. I got him on his back once. Thursday, Mar 13, I played three games of chess with a fellow named Bradley and beat him all three. Friday, Mar 14, Rainy. Beat a fellow named Allen a game of chess."

Perhaps not totally unrelated to his self-criticism and self-doubt were his frequent judgments on his Harvard classmates. "There are two awfully conceited chaps in our class. One is Fred Prince who is rather pompous and who has a very peculiar air of gracious condescension to everyone he meets; the other one is a fellow named Bache . . . he throws enough dignified condescension into the way in which he greets you in the yard to sink a 74 gun boat. . . . I was rather disgusted by a fellow's coming in and relating how he cleaned out a fellow gambling at poker. . . . I can't make out Dunlevy he's a queer kind of cus who seems to know a good many fast fellows but doesn't seem to care for them and I don't think he does anything worse than going into the theatre all the time. He seems to me a fellow with plenty of money and more time than he very well knows how to use too lazy to use it well and too much of a gentleman to use it very ill. . . . Charley Sturgis's room is just papered with pictures and photographs (too many photographs of actresses for my taste)."

The Journal contains criticisms of classmates whom Godfrey knew but slightly—a cox who cursed his crew too much and various classmates who, in his view, drank excessively. It also contains rather pious appraisals even of his few close friends. "I went to pay Joe Gardner a visit. He lives with his uncle . . . and aunt Mr. and Mrs. Jack Gardner. . . . His aunt is a pleasant woman with the remains of former beauty. She has the most perfect manners of anyone I ever saw. This is as it should be for she is an able woman and a great society leader in Boston. I have but one fault to find with her, she evidently considers that the two things best worth having in this life are intellectual ability and accomplishments and courteous manners. She is a dangerous leader for Joe; he is the most thorough gentleman that ever walked this earth but alas he is comparatively rich and what temptations does that not imply. I am sure he will never do anything unworthy of a gentleman but whether he will ever take the high stand and fill the great place in the world for which his conscientiousness and talent fit him I know not; who knows."

Godfrey was also critical of day laborers on his sister Lilla's place at Kingston, "the lazy shift-less way in which the men were working most of the time. More than half of them were idle and meanwhile they were being paid 2 dollars a day; more than double what you would pay for much better labor in Boston." His Journals also contain moral judgments of servants in his father's house, gardeners, seamstresses, and washerwomen.

One result of Godfrey's critical attitude at college and his prickly self-righteous morality was that although he was elected to the Hasty Pudding, he never made a "final" club, let alone The Porcellian. This omission was particularly extraordinary because his father had been a member and he was related to two of the club's first members, Francis Cabot Lowell and Robert Treat Paine (who had named the club originally the Pig Club because of their love for roast pork). If he was upset at all by the slight, he never indicated as much.

As early as his Harvard days, J. P. Morgan had shown how different he was from Godfrey. Like Godfrey, he had not been selected by a "final" club, but instead of accepting or ignoring it as Cabot had, Morgan founded his own. He called it The Delphic Club, but it has always been known as the "Gas" because the club steward was instructed to keep the lights burning all night to prove what a jolly time was being had by the members.

Because he was so small, Godfrey played the part of a maid in one of the Hasty Pudding theatricals. "All through the play fellows kept throwing kisses to me and after rehearsal was over I was regularly beseiged." Even though he had not been one of the first elected himself, he enjoyed in his junior year sitting up late at the Pudding, electing the first nine members of the class of '83, which included a large percentage of Lowell, Cabot, and Lee cousins. There was comparatively little class or race prejudice reflected in his Journal, although he recorded chess victories over "Menke, an English (Jew?)" and "Ludwig Lieberman a dark clear-complected German Jew from New York." He was never an anti-Semite as Henry Adams was.

While not a success in club circles at Harvard, Godfrey, in spite of his small size, was more successful and happier in his athletic career. An active and faithful member of the Harvard Athletic Association, he broke his collarbone playing football. Thereafter he concentrated on crew, lacrosse, and wrestling and in the country on shooting and swimming. Very proud of his father's record as a boxer at Harvard, Godfrey became a first rate wrestler, making up for his small size with a terrierlike determination and winning the prize for light-weight wrestling on March 12, 1881. He took part in the activities of the Harvard Bicycle Club as well as going off on long rides by himself.

A month after his mother's death, Godfrey learned how to play tennis from his friend Willie Putnam, and for the rest of his life tennis was Cabot's favorite sport.

Godfrey's Harvard was substantially different from today's College. It was still, with few exceptions, a school for New England and New York gentlemen's sons, and not yet invaded by foreigners from the dim reaches of the Middle West and from Boston's Irish wards. Students still walked beneath great elm trees which would also soon be destroyed by another foreign invader, the European gypsy moth.

Godfrey was very successful in his studies; his Journal reflected the confidence in this area which he lacked in others. ". . . we have begun Trigonometry which seems rather queer at first but I know it is going to be easy. I got 90% in Geometry and am in the advanced section in German. We shan't hear from the Literature examinations for a long time but I have no doubt I passed fast enough. . . . I got 80 on Rhetoric   I like Chemistry very much. Freshman Advanced Analytics and Greek 3 are soft so far. . . . I have been working pretty hard all winter I got 88 in Chem 4, 84 in Chem 3, 80 in Physics. . . ." At least part of his scholastic success was due to his father's strictness. "Father does not want me to play chess any more in college," and limitations were also put on bicycle riding and shooting.

But Godfrey still managed to have some typical undergraduate fun. In the winter of 1879 there was a fire in Stoughton Hall, which he reported with glee. "The most amusing incidents were the careful wetting down of the crowd and the way in which a thundermug was carefully lowered to the ground while furniture etc. was thrown out the window." Although Harvard had no inside plumbing, Cabot noted with pleasure the new steam heat in the entries and the building of brick walks.

Godfrey loved dancing. In his junior year, in 1880, he went to a "Leap Year German. I got more favors than usual but not nearly as much dancing. I came to the conclusion that much as I liked being a lady, I greatly prefer being a gentleman." He was by now five feet nine inches tall and weighed 135 pounds, but his acne was still active and he had never shaved; he apparently did better when he was asking young ladies to dance than when the situation was reversed. When he could "privateer" all he wanted, and especially with young ladies who were not belles and were often cousins, he usually had a "galuptious time." Then, as today, Boston dances were strictly supervised and disciplined affairs, more like a well-regulated coeducational sports event than a romantic rapprochement. First under the watchful eyes of Italian Lorenzo Papanti and later under those of his son, Boston dances were proper and energetic but not romantically exciting.

In February 1880 Cabot developed mumps; apparently unaware of this, he went "to a German at the Nobles. The next day I woke up suffering from severe pain in the veins above the left testicle. . . . Father put me right to bed. I grew steadily worse till Wednesday and also suffered from orcitis (I don't know whether this is the way to spell it) on Wednesday I was leeched and was immediately relieved." Whether his mind was relieved when the swelling passed is more doubtful, for boys with less inclination to doubt and to measure themselves than Cabot have worried about the permanent effects of orchitis.

At this same time Godfrey read *Paul et Virginie* (in French) and *Henry Esmond* and confessed in his Journal a strong preference for the former. It was typical that Godfrey preferred the innocent Virginie to the naughty Beatrix, whose author wrote of her, "she was flighty, she was false. She had no reverence for character and she was very, very beautiful." A month later Cabot confided to his Journal, "I began to write a fairy story to amuse myself when I was sick and write a little in it every Sunday."

The beardless Godfrey by his senior year at Harvard was still unsure of himself. He was, however, slowly approaching that Cabot tradition which enables the members of that clan to view their faults and idiosyncrasies as virtues and commendable marks of uniqueness. At the Thanksgiving gathering at Godfrey's grandmother's in 1881, the members of the family sang their own version of *Patience:*

"We are the Cabot clan, just count us if you can,
That slightly iniquitous rather ubiquitous
Brookline and Beverly clan.
When playing upon the shore, we drown the ocean's roar.
Whatever the weather, we're always together
The same as we were before.

"Then we each came forward and in turn gag songs were sung for each of us. . . . Mine was
A Chemistry four young man. A put in your oar young man.
A rather statistical slightly sophistical
'There's where you're wrong' young man.

Most of my girl friends who have heard it ask me to repeat it and when I get thro say 'how good' or make some other mark of approval. And then I grin and say 'Yes, and it's true too' and then they look disconcerted and usually try to back out of it which, as Guy would say, 'warms the very cockles of my heart' with secret joy."

Godfrey was unable to accept the fact that his brother Guy was mentally deficient. He seemed to feel that with enough discipline and effort he could make Guy normal. "I spent most of the morning trying to teach Guy how to play the games of chess in Morphy's book. I am also trying to teach him to stand up straight. . . . The poor fellow was all the time troubled by apprehensions of different people trying to injure him in different ways and also he had mild hypochondria and was troubled by the idea that he had injured me or done something wrong. It was always possible to temporarily rouse him and make him acknowledge the foolishness of his fears but in a moment he was back again as bad as ever, it was like the task of Sisyphus, rolling a rock up hill to have it fall back again."

"On my 21st birthday I was a little over 5′ 10¾″ in height and weighed 155 pounds with my ordinary clothes on. I made the acquaintance during the winter of a daughter of Uncle William Russel, Ellen by name. I was charmed by the naivete with which she called me by my first name on first acquaintance, she is no blood relation whatever to me. . . . I made up my mind to get my best marks on my Senior annuals and I did. Chem 2, 72%, Chem 5, 89%, Chem 6, 92%, I led the section of five. N H 4, 87% Forensics 84. I wrote a Commencement Part on Free Trade but was not requested to speak it. Average just under 85%. . . . Will got a magna in Mathematics. [Godfrey graduated *magna cum laude* in Chemistry.] I thought we did credit to W 17 [room 17 in Weld Hall], dear old room many a quiet hour have I passed therein. Will graduated 17th, I graduated 34th in a class of 177. G. L. Kittredge got four 100's his senior year. . . . I much enjoyed Charley Copeland's Commencement Part."

In summing up his analysis of himself and his family, Godfrey wrote, "Indeed I have been very fortunate in my brothers and sisters each and every one of them has been most earnestly desirous that I should profit by his or her experience and improve to the utmost the golden hours of youth. The result is, I think, that my character partakes somewhat of the characteristics of each of the others. Two virtues I think I may claim as especially noticeable in all of us. Love of purity, self-reliance. Our enemies would say we were conceited and prudish."

CHAPTER V

Wanderjahr

He wasn't one of those romantic cads who want to experience everything. He kept himself for what was best. That's
why he was a true puritan after all. SANTAYANA, *The Last
Puritan*, 7

After Commencement Godfrey went to work for his brother Sam.
The work mainly consisted of chemical experiments, particularly
the burning of crude petroleum to make lampblack. Godfrey also
did chemical analyses, including two on shoeblacking, for which
he was paid $38. In June 1882 he came into an inheritance of
nearly $5000 and began investing in the stock market.

In December, Godfrey was still making experiments for his
brother, this time burning both kerosene and gas to make black.
Black—or "soot," as Godfrey was to call it all his life—was
carbon deposited on a surface by incomplete combustion as, for
example, the lampblack which is deposited on the inside of a
hurricane lamp by the incomplete combustion of candle tallow or
kerosene. This black was used mainly in ink, but also in stove
polish, in shoe polish, in patent leather, and as pigment in paints
and varnishes. Sam Cabot was interested in finding new and
cheaper ways of making blacker black.

In 1859 Edwin Laurentine Drake had drilled the first oil
well in America at Titusville, in northeast Pennsylvania, and in
the oil-field area and to the south there was a great surplus of

natural gas. Although a little of it could be used locally for heating and lighting and minor manufacturing if anyone could be found who was willing to lay pipelines, most of the gas that was found by drillers seeking oil was useless and therefore cheap. Most of it, in fact, was burned uselessly night and day into the sky or simply vented into the air without regard for safety.

In December 1882 Sam Cabot went for a second time to Pennsylvania because he was interested in the possibilities of converting this cheap gas into carbon black. He left Godfrey in charge of his factory. When Sam returned, he was disappointed in Godfrey's performance. Godfrey confided to his Journal: "I had no competent assistant my directions were repeatedly neglected or disobeyed I was much pressed by other business. . . . Sam thought I was densely stupid and inefficient but he was mistaken. I undoubtedly showed lack of experience, but not uncommon stupidity."

This was hardly an auspicious beginning for a career in business. Sam had offered eventually to take Godfrey into the business as a partner, and his father had urged Godfrey to accept, offering to lend him money from time to time so that he could obtain an equal footing with his older brother. Godfrey had preferred to wait and see, and now he was glad he had not committed himself. He preferred being a hired hand at $500 a year but with time to make up his mind what he really wanted to do, and he planned to study abroad for two or three years before making up his mind.

In January 1883 Godfrey took a trip "South," to the oil and gas fields of Pennsylvania. This was his first real business trip. The summer before his senior year at college he had made a trip "out West" to Chicago, Cincinnati, Detroit, Cleveland, St. Paul, Pittsburgh, and Kansas City. He had seen and described and sketched in his Journal rolling mills, a cracker bakery, a broom factory, a brick kiln, and a sawmill. He had contracted diarrhea in Kansas City, where he had looked after some property of his father's, and he had gone to Duluth and to the Calumet and Hecla mine, which had made so much money for his family and their friends in Boston.

He had been delighted with that trip, noting in his Journal: "I had travelled about 5000 miles in thirty-four days and been about half-across the continent. . . . For the first time in my life I had not seen a Cabot face for over a month."

On his first business trip in 1883 Godfrey was too busy to notice the absence of Cabot faces. He went to the Pennsylvania village of Worthington "and put up according to Sam's advice at the little village hotel. He had instructed me to make myself as comfortable as money could make me so I occupied the parlor which enjoyed the inestimable advantage of an open stove in which there was a fire day and night.

". . . Worthington is reached from Pittsburg by running up to Kittanning 44 miles. Northeast along the Allegheny Valley road and then driving a little north by west across a hilly but mostly cultivated country for about six miles. . . . Kittanning is a town of about 2000 inhabitants, containing some large iron works to which the heat is mostly supplied from a natural gas well which is probably not as large as Sam's. The Reynolds House, the best hotel in the town, is an unusually comfortable second-class hotel. They give you plenty of water, clean towels and bed linen and a fire for a small extra charge. . . . A dirty but industrious German tailor named Seligman keeps the hotel at which I am staying. His wife is a most excellent woman and makes me as comfortable as one could expect to be at $5 a week. My greatest privation is lack of reading of which I am very fond. . . . The post man appears to be the most intellectual man in the town and he has never had a good education. . . . Walked the whole length of the [gas] line I found it leaked about every second joint."

He was a compulsively hard worker and soon noted, "I have recently developed a faculty for getting along with only 7 or 8 hours sleep instead of nine or ten. I go to bed between 10:30 and half-past twelve and get up between six and seven, or on Sundays, eight or thereabouts." He usually walked twenty or more miles a day, often in the snow and mud, preferring walking to horseback riding and finding it usually both faster and surer. Nor was he unaware that his walking greatly impressed the local inhabitants.

He spent days experimenting with new ways to make black from gas. "I tried all day, unsuccessfully to get enough black, by burning gas in chlorine, to test its quality. Sam sends me each week the Weekly Transcript which is a great boon. . . . Seeing by the Weekly Transcript that Bell Telephone was selling at what appeared to me more than it was worth, I wrote to Jackson and Curtis to sell my eight shares. . . . Counting the increased value of my bond, I have made over a thousand dollars on my investment in Bell Telephone. . . . Went to Pittsburg [to get] a first-rate bath and dinner at the Monongahela House."

Even his graduation with honors from Harvard and being out West working on his own had not relieved Godfrey of his concern about being a runt. "Monday, Feb 26 [1883] I was twenty-two years old. I weigh about 160 lbs. stand over 5 ft 11 in my stockings. Hitherto I have increased in height and weight each year, but I don't suppose I shall ever be quite a six footer except when I put my shoes or slippers on. I have acquired quite a reputation in this neighborhood for fast walking. I can cover about five miles in an hour, up hill and down when the roads are in decent condition. I have not shaved but expect to before long. I have just enough moustache and whiskers to look dirty and my chin is getting a little downy. I usually pass for eighteen or nineteen."

Day after day he made experiments to increase and improve his production of black. "Saturday, Feb 24, I had an explosion. . . . Friday, March 16, Tried enriching gas with acid oil. . . . Wednesday, Mar 21, Y [Young, an employee] was terribly burned today by carelessly stooping down in front of the exhaust from the blower while carrying something lighted. . . . Friday, March 23, Black packed 226 lbs. . . . Sunday, March 25 . . . I finished today a book on etiquette called 'Decorum' it is on the whole an excellent book but I remember one remark that I must take exception to. It intimates that a suitor can usually tell, by his lady's deportment toward him, whether she will favor his suit or not and thus perhaps save himself the humiliation of a refusal. I believe that, in nine cases out of ten, if a man is thoroughly in love his safest course is to learn his fate at all costs from the lips of the woman he loves, nor it is always wise to take a refusal as final. . . .

"Saturday, March 31, I got to bed at five minutes of one last night and was up 5:55 this A.M. . . . Friday, April 27, . . . In the neighborhood of Millerstown I saw a number of oil wells the first I have ever seen. In some places I could count a dozen or more derricks. Some were being pumped and the heavy walking beams were often counterbalanced with stone."

Godfrey made up his mind while working in Pennsylvania to go to Europe as he had planned. On May 28, 1883, he returned to Boston to enjoy the Commencement festivities before sailing. Throughout his life Cabot was often away from Boston on Christmas or on his own or his wife's birthday, but he rarely missed a Commencement. Another momentous occasion of that June came on the third, when for the first time in his life Godfrey shaved.

In 1883 Boston was still of sufficient importance to have direct sailings to Europe, and on June 30 of that year "I got the last of a number of letters of introduction which Sam has written or procured for me . . . said good-bye to father just after dinner and took a cab to the Cunard wharf in East Boston." He took with him £30 in cash [the pound in 1883 was worth $4.83], a letter of credit on Baring's Bank for £1000, two small bags, a greatcoat with some books in the pockets, and nineteen pounds of samples of lampblack.

Once on board he wrote in his Journal. "Today was the close of the fiscal year at the beginning of which I came into possession of $4764.06. At the present market value my stocks . . . are worth about $6267.00 and my bank balance is somewhat larger than last year on May 29 so I am over 1500 dollars richer. My allowance has been $300. Salary and fees $331.67. The balance is due to dividends and net profits on stock, minus what I have spent for myself during the year. I do not expect soon to make another hit as good as that in Bell Telephone but I think the stocks I now own will be higher at this time next year. My principle in owning stocks is to try to get a pretty just idea of their real value; when I buy to buy those which I think are really the cheapest at their market value, not to sell and buy unless I think I can see a profit of about fifteen per cent in the transaction nor to hold for profits much higher than this unless I feel pretty sure of my ground.

"I expect to get bitten once in a while but as I shall try to keep clear of enterprises in dishonest hands I do not think I shall run unreasonable risks. This I consider legitimate speculation and I shall engage in no other till I take leave of my senses, both common sense and sense of honor and justice. I intend never to own stock while I am owing any considerable sum of money nor to borrow one cent to invest in stock. In my own business I may, some time, throw good money after bad, but not, I trust, in other peoples."

During much of the passage Godfrey was seasick and spent most of the time in his cabin reading. As often happened, when he found nothing reprehensible in a book, he also found it uninteresting. "I finished a novel Gaston lent me written by Holme Lee, 'Sylvan Holt's daughter' I thought it unobjectionable but rather dull and commonplace."

When on July 10 he arrived in Liverpool, Godfrey compared England and the English to his own country and people and sensed "a desire to entrap your pennies. Give me an ounce of civility rather than a pound of servility." He did, however, prefer the English countryside to that of New England: ". . . everywhere hawthorne hedges instead of stone walls or unsightly fences."

Not infrequently Godfrey recorded his dreams in his Journal. He had had a number "of there being great wild places in different parts of Boston." He had been eighteen years old before he ever went to South Boston on an errand to the Kearney Hospital. "I had no idea South Boston was such a pleasant place . . . the main street is lined with trees . . . and in many places linger most alluring gardens with fruit trees in them. . . . Such gardens have always had a peculiar and somewhat uncanny charm for me and I have often dream't about them."

When he visited Chester, "A guide pointed us out the remains of a Roman wall near 1800 (?) years old. . . . I was strangely reminded by the queer little silent gardens and bits of green tucked away among the houses of many dreams I have had. City gardens have always had a peculiar charm for me. They represent the old among the new, silence amid hubbub, peace amid the hubbub of trade, solitude amidst a multitude."

From Chester, Godfrey proceeded to Manchester and then to London, where he found that "London streets are spacious London cabs are cheap but London cabmen are truculent beggars. I hate English begging I hate English snobbishness and I hate English brutality."

His hatred of things foreign was somewhat diminished when he and his traveling companion, Harry Cabot, found more things which reminded them of home. "The next day the whole gang of us had a row up the Thames from Maidenhead to Henley and a more delightful day one could hardly wish." Henry Bromfield Cabot, a first cousin, had been Godfrey's great friend at Harvard and their wandering amid the alien corn so strengthened their friendship that Harry would be Godfrey's best man. Godfrey made very few friends in his life, but those he cherished, and, unlike Schulberg's Sammy, he knew that you can't have your friends and eat them too. "It is against my policy," Godfrey wrote, "to lose any friends except by death."

Godfrey, a great deal more worried about expenses than Harry, soon found his way to digs. "The Pultney House is a very comfortable quiet unpretending shanty for a man to stay in who is worth a million a minute but as my income lacks a few cents of that sum I prudently withdrew on Monday morning to Mrs. Vincent Yardley's, No. 20 Bloomsbury St., where they were proportionately exhorbitant but on a somewhat smaller scale. Harry still stayed at the Pultney."

Godfrey, who had already proven himself exceptionally critical of what he read, was no less critical of what he saw in Europe. "I must say I did not enthuse over the Elgin marbles. The sculpture is certainly wonderful but my imagination was not sufficiently active to fill in the gaps. . . . I went one day to St. Pauls and very much enjoyed it. The church is in some ways a type of the English people large, handsome, cold and respectable (I think the English respectability is rather superficial however) . . .

paid a visit to Eton rambled over the queer battered and foot
worn buildings . . . meeting any number of boys in their queer
precocious uniforms . . . went to Oxford. . . . Most of the colleges have a strangely battered look . . . the students rooms . . .
appeared to us much smaller than Harvard rooms. . . . I visited
the Tower. . . . The crown jewels are beautiful and interesting
but I can't help thinking that 15,000,000. is a great deal to lock
up in such trumpery. . . . I remember noticing that the Kohinoor
was not there. . . .

"One day we all went to Hyde Park to see the riding and got
a good idea of the English method of riding. . . . English women
of fashion look like hour glasses it gives me the stomach ache to
see them." Nor was Cabot favorably impressed with the royal heir
apparent, whom he saw at the theater. "In a word he behaved in a
way which would earn him the epithet of fatted swine were he not
the Prince of Wales."

At the National Gallery, Cabot admired some of Turner's
paintings, "but some of his pictures mean little more to me than if
he had sat down on his palette and stretched the seat of his
breeches across a picture frame." He was rather more favorably
impressed by Madame Tussaud's waxwork museum and especially
by the Crystal Palace and the electric lights that were being
installed in the great hall of the Knights of the Garter at Wind-
sor.

Godfrey also did some business in London for Sam and for
his cousin G. E. Cabot and "did a great deal of shopping and had
three or four suits of clothes made. Good clothes are from a half to
2/3 as much in England as in America but I did not think under
clothing was any cheaper." Godfrey was happiest in Britain when
he went with other Boston tourists—Morisons, Denistons, or Ly-
mans—to a tennis match.

He also felt at home when he called on his cousin Minister
Lowell. "Mrs. Lowell removed a spot from her husband's coat. I
am inclined to think Mr. Lowell finds it hard to keep up the
dignity of an American minister in the sumptuous fashion of his
predecessors altho' it is said his cousin Augustus Lowell supplies
him with money. In my inexperience I can't help thinking it is a

great mistake to consider expensive entertainments and that sort
of thing a necessity of diplomatic and court life. The great world
says otherwise but the great world is often wrong, and my very
stomach rises at the thought of yielding my opinion to that of any
or all. This peculiarity of mine has gained for me a reputation for
self-assertion and arrogance, but, like most bears, I am humored
and very often if people don't want to hear my ideas they must
get out of ear-shot for I am capable of being very obstinate not to
say bumptious."

On July 27, 1883, Godfrey and Harry started their visit to
the Continent. Godfrey later wrote in his Journal a further analysis of his own character in connection with that trip. "Harry and
I started on a trip in Europe which was in many respects one of
the pleasantest trips I ever took or ever expect to take. I wish I
thought I had contributed as much to Harry's enjoyment of it, as
he did to mine, but indeed, I can not think so. In the first place the
society of another is not so necessary to him for the enjoyment of
anything as it is to me. In the second place Harry is a very much
pleasanter fellow than I am. He is less annoyed by the petty
discomforts of travelling, his enjoyment is more placid is free
from that constant impatience and restless desire to get forward
which prevents my ever long enjoying the role of a placid spectator. The only dark spots I have to look back upon in that little
trip are one or two cases in which, I fear, I sacrificed Harry's
pleasure to my own wishes. I feel sure however that I have been
readily forgiven for I believe that Harry's regard for me is not
inferior to mine for him.

". . . We reached Antwerp somewhere between nine and ten
and immediately went to a swell hotel where we had a bath and a
first class feed. . . . I was glad I had Harry with me to sling the
French. I felt as helpless as a new born babe among the
Dutch-men. To keep my reputation for knowledge I criticised
Harry's French, talked wise about exact definitions and was immensely pleased when he tried to persuade me that 'ombrelle'
(which he inadvertently used) was the French for parapluie. We
went to the Antwerp cathedral and there, with my usual pighead-
edness I positively refused to enthuse over Rubens paintings.

Rubens madonnas are capital Dutch women and would look first-rate in their proper place, properly dressed; mutatis mutandis. . . .

". . . We visited the [Cologne] cathedral both morning and afternoon and I was more impressed by it than by any other building I have ever seen. . . . I remember in the cathedral an old ragged woman tottering up with a great basket on her arm and dropping some coin in a box for Peter's pence. I did not know whether more to admire a religion that could prompt such self-sacrifice from one so poor or to hate a religion that could thus cheat the poor to feed the rich. . . .

". . . This part of the [Rhine] river reminded me very much of the Mississippi. . . . I then paid a visit to the [Munich] Pinakotek a big picture gallery. . . . He [Rubens] has put such a swinish look into some of the faces as I should scarcely think possible in the human face." Just as he had been in college, Godfrey was still more interested in the morality of the subject than in the quality of the painting. In a list of paintings he liked in a Swiss exhibition he included "The Berlin Congress. I was particularly interested by Disraeli and Bismarck's faces. I imagine there is no other man in Europe who has done so much mischief as either of them in the last ten years."

Whether visiting galleries or mountain climbing, "I always carried a stylographic pen and paper and envelopes with me and thus improved many odd moments." Godfrey had also decided to improve his education and, as had Sam, to attend the Zurich Polytechnicum that winter and perhaps longer. Until then, however, he continued his trip with Harry. His Journal contains crude sketches of a wide variety of subjects from their Alpine guide to the Gotthard tunnel.

His pleasure in Harry's company continued. "When we went to bed we had a scrimmage to which Harry gave the provocation by treading upon me while I was going thro my nightly exercise (Dipping 26 times between my hands on the floor). Alarmed by the noise one of the servants rushed upstairs and attempted to enter the room, evidently thinking that we were slaughtering each other. We had a good haw! haw! at his expense and turned in."

Godfrey continued to note the differences between Harry and himself, for example in dealing with "two miserable old women [who] sat wailing a doleful song to extract a few centimes. I'm afraid Harry was weak enough to give them something. I never give money to beggars tho' it sometimes makes my heart pretty sore to refuse. . . .

"The only expensive pleasure which has ever taken much of a hold upon my fancy is that of climbing among Swiss glaciers. . . . All of us with the exception of Arthur Lyman who was suffering from a lame knee . . . crossed over the Mer de Glace without a guide and came down by the Mauvaise Pas which presents no kind of difficulty except perhaps to women invalids and fat men. . . . The Matterhorn stood majestically out, sharply outlined against a deep blue sky. It seemed to say 'Pshaw, you think you have seen mountains look at me, climb me if you dare' and I was possessed with an earnest desire to accept the invitation but concluded that the game wasn't worth the candle."

After a short visit to Glasgow, Godfrey went to Paris. "I had a long talk with a Frenchman who held forth about the moral rottenness in England. There is certainly a great deal of moral rottenness in what is called the best society in England. I think however that the great mass of the English people will compare favorably in this respect with the people of France. My chief ground for this opinion is that there is a very large demand for a high order of fiction in England whereas French fiction is a byword. If I went into a Paris bookstore and bought a dozen cheap novels at random I should not expect to find more than one or two which I should be willing to read to a girl out loud. In a London bookstore on the other hand in a like number I should not expect to find more than four or five which I shouldn't.

"On the other hand London is the only city I have ever been in where I am afraid not only of being addressed but of being assaulted by shameless women. I myself have never been interfered with but one or two of my friends have been struck in passing such in Piccadilly at an early hour in the evening. I should not like to escort a lady in any part of London after nightfall. I have it from two sources that there are certain parks in London where no decent person is safe after nightfall. If a man is assaulted and applies to the police-courts the presumption always is that he went thither for the purposes of prostitution."

Cabot himself seems to have escaped the corruption of London and Paris which he considered so dangerous for others. On September 16, 1883, he returned safely to Zurich, where he immediately hired a young schoolmaster named Leidle to read scientific German to him. After one session Godfrey determined that his comprehension was adequate and discontinued the lessons.

He settled at a pension run by Frau Direktor Weber, the widow of a member of the Swiss parliament, and set about to improve his German, reading a German translation of Turgenev's *Fathers and Sons* and 1,700 pages of scientific German before the term began on October 23. He also made friends with a number of other young men in the pension, but he was no less critical of these new friends than he had been of his classmates at Harvard. "Herr Escales . . . heavy black moustache, black hair, fat face and square-shaped fat body, waxy unhealthy looking skin . . . talks and laughs loudly. . . . He looks like a caricature of Napoleon Bonaparte without the imperial. He is a German Jew from Zweibrucken in the Pfalz. . . . Perhaps there may have been better things in some of the corners of his heart that he did not let me into than in that part which he showed me. He was often intensely annoying to me, and yet I have a warm feeling for him. . . . Perhaps this was because he liked me."

Godfrey's Journal entries reflect his enormous concern with whether or not he was liked. "Mrs. Kelly . . . thinks everything is as it should be . . . and has a good word to say for almost everyone. This universal optimism gets tedious once in a while but it is comfortable to know that when one has left the room she will say what a very nice young man Mr. Cabot is."

Cabot's concern with what was said about him when he left the room may not be totally unrelated to his own criticism of others. He was also aware that he was not relaxed in society. "Miss Kelly is studying jurisprudence in the University. Her profil is most violently Irish, but when she looks straight at you

she is pretty good looking. She has a certain 'savoir faire' which
leads me to think she has seen something of society . . . and her
conversational efforts are by no means confined to small talk.
Apropos of 'small talk,' it always tires me in a little while & I use
it myself chiefly as a means of opening a conversation on serious
subjects. Very small talk I try never to indulge in (See an article
in Argosy 1865(?) on 'Small Talk and Very Small
Talk'). . . .

      "One curious thing about the daughter [of his landlady] is
that her eyebrows are black and her hair is brown. The only other
person I ever noticed this in is myself. My moustache has not yet
made up its mind which color it will be, there is scarcely enough of
it to swear by. I think a beard would be becoming to me if I could
raise a respectable one but don't think I could."

      In Zurich Cabot took five courses in chemistry and geology,
but with only a few exceptions, he was unimpressed by his professors, his fellow students, and, indeed, by the university and the
country. "There is a good deal mythical about the tremendous
work done at these German Universities. Holidays are very frequent, cutting is more or less prevalent, term never begins when it
is supposed to and every lecture is a quarter of an hour or more
late. I don't think the men average nearly as much work here as at
Harvard. . . . I enjoy Schiller on an average as much as I do
Shakespeare but haven't read anything I liked as much as Ham-
let. . . . In all I think I read about 5000 pages of German before
the Christmas vacation. . . . I think the greatest curse to the land
is the habitual use of wine or beer. . . . The preaching seems to
me pretty good, altho' I didn't understand it very well, and the
doctrine about the same as Unitarian. . . . I felt drawn toward
him [another man at the *pension*] from the beginning because he
doesn't smoke and doesn't drink and has American ideas about
morality."

      It is hard today, 1914 and 1939 having intervened, to realize
the exaggerated admiration in which Germany and German culture were held at a time when, as Henry Adams wrote, "Goethe
was raised to the rank of Shakespeare—Kant ranked as a law-
giver above Plato," and when, according to Santayana, "Emerson

served up Goethe's philosophy in ice-water."

Even away from home Godfrey did not forget his much-drilled sense of duty to others. "Toward the end of November I sent word to Sam to give Mr. Clark a check for $50. as a present from me to the negro schools."

For his Christmas holiday Godfrey took a trip alone through Germany and Italy. "I am very fond of being out alone at night. Every thing is usually cool & still, I feel a conscious loneliness & freedom from observation, I can meditate. Then I think the presence of imaginary dangers which nevertheless do not frighten me adds a certain pleasure, perhaps by flattering my self-vanity. By self-vanity I mean a feeling of ones own superiority quite independent of the opinions of others. For the same reason I enjoy all danger which is merely apparent. I have too much common sense, & natural timidity to court the real thing."

Despite his professed enjoyment of loneliness, Godfrey did not much enjoy being alone, and on his travels he tended to pick up other young men. "Sunday ev'g I was accosted by a young man, well-dressed, rather small, with a rather large head and an expression of thoughtful almost grim earnestness that is very rare I think outside of England and America. He said he noticed I seemed alone and thought perhaps I would like to drop into his room for a while and smoke a cigar. I replied that I never smoked and had some writing to do just then, but should be very glad if he would permit me to avail myself of his courtesy a little. He acquiesced and an hour later I found myself comfortably seated in a large pleasant room. . . .

"One of my new friend's first remarks was 'You're an American are you not?' 'Yes' 'Indeed I took particular pains to ascertain that you were before seeking your acquaintance. I should have feared a rebuff from an Englishman, I'm an Englishman myself but I think we are the most surly people in the world, I always avoid my countrymen in travelling.' To which I replied that I thought he did his countrymen injustice. . . . We wandered off onto other subjects and talked into the small hours of the night. I never had a man so open his heart to me on so short acquaintance. . . . His heart seemed as tender and pure as a woman's and he spoke with deep feeling of different friends he had had."

The day after Christmas in 1883 Godfrey described his visit to the Berlin zoo, where he saw "a number of snakes some of which I think are eight feet long. They gave the snakes rabbits and guinea-pigs to eat while I was there and they ran fearlessly about over the piles of snakes as unconcernedly as if they were so many turnips. I think the stories about fascination are all bosh. The rabbits would often fool around the same snake's head half a dozen times within an hour, apparently from mere curiosity. If he were struck at he would squeak and run off for a little while. No rabbit was eaten while I was there and only one guinea pig."

His very personal view of art continued to express itself. "I wish nine tenths of the out-door statuary were at the moon and most of the rest were put under cover. Naked or even bare-headed statues look to me out of place when exposed to the frosts of a northern winter."

After Germany, Godfrey went to Italy. "We visited the [Milan] Cathedral. . . . It made me sad to see the faces of the priests and other officials. Such besotted absolutely unintelligent faces I have seldom seen, never so many together. The Catholic religion may be a good thing for the people of Italy many of them could appreciate nothing higher, but I am sure that its usual effect upon its ministers and immediate connections is most deadly. I have now seen hundreds of such and do not remember a really noble face among them. The predominent impression, among the grown men at least, was either that of servile hypocrisy or of a rayless stupidity that betokens a torpid soul."

In Genoa his anti-Catholic feelings were again stimulated. "We saw pretty nearly all the churches in Genoa . . . priestly mummery was going on in one or two. I deeply pity the poor superstitious priestridden people. My pity is mingled with admiration of their devotion and disgust with the objects of it. Truly here is a great field for work." A Puritan such as Cabot would have been shocked had he been told how close he was to Augustine's belief that "this world must be used, not enjoyed."

In Pisa a beggar presented Godfrey with a moral problem: "a pretty girl with a weeping baby in her arms begged alms. I saw her pinch the child to make it cry. I thought of scolding her but it occurred to me that she would then conceal her cruelty more adroitly and the next person would be more likely to give and thus encourage the fraud."

Like most Boston Puritans, Godfrey had been brought up to believe in charity, but, also like them, even stronger in his background was his fear and horror of being had. It was less painful to be thought stingy than to be thought a sucker, and like Benjamin Franklin, another Boston boy, Godfrey did not want to pay too much for a whistle.

In Florence, Godfrey attended two farces, "the first I couldn't understand, the second was short, simple and smutty. . . . Judging by the faces of the people and their comic papers, morality as regards women must be almost unknown in Italy."

Godfrey's morality was such that he felt he must explain and justify even his traveling. "I do not for a moment beguile myself into the belief that I am seeing & enjoying Europe as it might be seen & enjoyed. Were I travelling for pleasure I should go slower see less and see it more thoroughly. I am travelling to increase my stock of recollections and experiences, to exercise my powers of observation & memory. My time is short, the field is limitless, my aim is to use my faculties to the utmost. A picture gallery is to me a deep pleasure & a study, a days walk is a task to be got thro', a fine view a picture to be intently studied & remembered. . . . Alas thro' all runs the feeling, I must not wait here too long, & I cannot come here again to-morrow, perhaps never. It is an ever making of friends both animate & inanimate & making only to lose them again, a perpetual parting, & yet I feel that my whole being is continually enriched & strengthened by the process."

Godfrey did not spend much time appraising himself or philosophizing about life, however. Soon he was again criticizing the drinking habits of the Europeans. "During the winter I very often took walks with Edward Meyer and his friends but they walked very slowly seldom seemed to get anywhere in particular and a public house was always the prospective point so I cannot say that I enjoyed these excursions very much. One time I asked Edward M. if it was impossible for a German to have a good time without going to a public-house. Yes, said he, it is impossible otherwise to thoroughly enjoy anything. What a humiliating confession, and yet I think Edward Meyer is a very nice fellow for a German."

On February 26, 1884, Godfrey noted, "I was 23 years old. I think I have increased in mental, moral and physical strength in the last year and hope to do the like in the next."

In all matters, great and small, Godfrey tried so punctiliously to be absolutely honest and correct that he not infrequently appeared ridiculous to his contemporaries. In describing George Washington at a reception, "I damned him with faint praise. Miss Kelly told me afterwards she was glad I should never speak her funeral oration. 'I would try at least to tell no lies about you' I replied."

Traveling north from Rome by express train, "My travelling companions were a young French woman and her child, an Italian officer and two other Italians. My three male companions took a great deal of interest in the French girl who was decidedly pretty. . . . Under the influence of frequent potations the officer waxed confidential and tried to persuade me to go off on a spree with him, promising me 'buono vino e belle donne.' My answer was so frigid that it froze up the fountains of his eloquence and he soon afterward went to sleep. . . .

"The amount of beer & wine consumed in Europe is perfectly disgusting. I have never been urged by an elderly person in America to take beer or wine   I have been pressed by every body whom I have really known in Europe to take one or both but have steadfastly refused. . . . I have had some long arguments with Harry on the subject & I am always ready to take up the cudgels with anyone on the subject, it is one of my crusades. I believe that alcohol drinking in one form or another is the most palpable social evil in every country which I have ever visited."

From America, Sam had once again offered his younger brother a partnership in his growing stain-and-varnish business, but he suggested that Godfrey must make up his mind, since his place could not be held open indefinitely. In his long reply God-frey made very clear the firmness of his youthful views. "I am well aware that I shall probably never again have a pecuniary oppor-tunity so good as that which your kindness opens to me, but I must not embrace it till I have opened my heart to you, and come to a distinct agreement on certain points which I shall now men-tion.

"While I was in your employ I made, in a desire to conceal the details of your business, statements, which, while verbally true, were calculated to mislead. I do not wish ever to do this again. I do not wish, ever, for my own or any one else's pecuniary advantage, to utter a single word calculated to convey other than the exact fact with regard to that of which I speak, a single word calculated to conceal my thoughts. If I join hands with you I shall wish a veto power on anything which goes against my con-science in the transactions of the firm.

"I am not willing that black should be sent out by us labelled 'Put up by F. W. Devoe & Co.'

"I should, of course, expect you to decide all other questions relating to the firm.

"Should you decide to admit me on these terms I shall be ready to start for home on twenty-four hours notice; and, much as I should regret leaving Europe prematurely, should count myself very lucky to have such good reason for doing so."

Godfrey, not unaware that his older brother might not choose to allow him to be his moral censor, confided to his Journal: "I consider this the most important letter I ever wrote, it may close to me the opportunity of entering upon a profitable business with an honorable man, and one who will try to be to me, not merely just, but kind and generous; yet I could not rightly do otherwise."

Four weeks later he noted, "I received a letter from Sam today in answer to mine of May 20 (?) in which he says among other things . . . 'if you do become my partner you will always have the right to protest against anything you do not like. . . . I consider certain secrets of my business entirely my own property and I might feel justified in deceiving any shark who should try to steal them. . . . Deception is in my opinion wrong because of its injury to others, not intrinsically.' I answered as follows . . . 'From what you say I judge you would never be willing to give me the veto power which I wished and without which I do not think it would be right for me to go into partnership. For this reason I cannot promise to shorten my stay in Europe in case you should wish to take me again into your employ. I should like to know, as soon as it is convenient to you what if anything, I may expect from you in future as it may influence my occupations here. . . .' "

In the last months of his *wanderjahr* Godfrey traveled and read as much as possible and noted in his Journal what he learned. "I have been so used to a country where the towns are largely the creation of the railroads that a land where the towns not only do not owe their existence to the railroad but are usually inaccessible to it, makes a curious impression on me. . . . Today I finished 'I Promessi Sposi' a terribly long (638p) tedious novel by Mansoni . . . it shows highmindedness and a delicate sense of right and wrong. Slow as it is I read it with more pleasure than a cartload of smutty French trash could have afforded me. If there is anything that makes me wrathy down to the very soles of my shoes it is that false sentiment one meets with in French novels."

In Venice, Godfrey met his first cousin George Lee, who showed him the busts of Sebastian and John Cabot in the Doge's palace. In his Journal Godfrey passed judgment on his wealthy cousin: "I regret to say his morals are by no means what they should be. So far as I know he alone among Grandmother Cabot's grandchildren is guilty of fornication."

Wherever he went Godfrey saw people and things through Puritan glasses. ". . . the queer old Ponte Vecchio which reminds me in some unaccountable manner of the Castle of giant Despair in the 'Pilgrims Progress' of my childhood. . . . A kindly gentle child-like people is the Italian but, I fear, weak, cowardly, unreliable in every respect."

In Switzerland, Godfrey began a lifelong career of writing letters to newspapers. "I wrote two articles in German for the Zurich Tagblatt correcting some figures they had given with

regard to our national debt. The other a longer article in answer
to a letter in the Basler Nachrichten from a Mr. Allen in Boston
containing the absurd statement that the Yankee race was growing thinner and paler and dying out. I gave the actual facts. . . .
I sent last Autumn an open letter on Evolution to the Century
which was not printed. I think they showed their sense in not
printing it for the subject is a pretty well worn one and I contributed no new raw material moreover there was no earthly occasion
for the article except a maggot in my brain. I must say however
that I think the Century prints some very stupid 'Open
Letters.' "

Godfrey alternated visits to cultural establishments with visits to factories. "I think the Venus of Milo is overrated I do not
think it by any means so beautiful as the Apollo Belvedere in
Rome. . . . Apropos of statues I notice the French have the good
sense to shun the use of what might be called the indecent fig-leaf
which the Italians stick onto their statues every winter in defer-
ence to supposed foreign prudery. If it is right to have naked
statues it is right to have them naked. I must say however that I
think that the French artists of today offend against propriety
and common sense on the side of too much nudity in their painting
and sculptures. I should consider it as absurd and annoying to see
a picture of our house of representatives taken (a la David) in a
state of nature as to see a statue of Apollo represented in full
evening dress. . . .

"I like the French people less than any other European
people that I know but must allow that my knowledge of them is
wholly local & superficial. I think they are as immoral & menda-
cious as the Italians, as selfish in little things as the Germans &
have not the kindliness of the Italians nor the sterling industry &
honesty of the Germans. Moreover I think they are still the most
self-conceited people I know. I went to the Theatre Francois . . .
& thoroughly enjoyed the acting altho' the plays were a little too
Frenchy for my taste. . . . I can stand almost anything in the
way of a play or novel if there is one chief character that is
thoroughly upright and honorable. Without such a one I don't
want to read or see a novel or a play even where there are no very

objectionable features. Above all such a composition must teach a good moral lesson, otherwise when I am thro' with it I feel as if I should like to corner the author and say, you dirty scalawag why do you turn such rotten trash loose on the public to pollute the social atmosphere."

In Edinburgh, Godfrey got into a lively argument with an old Tory gentleman who characterized Godfrey's views of morality in business as sentimental trash and advised him that business was business and a man should do what he was paid to do. "I reiterated my objections [to dishonest newspaper reporting] still more emphatically stating that if it were business it was a dirty business, that I knew sensible men who would not so act, that indeed I could never call a man honorable who systematically falsified his own utterances and I trusted I numbered many honorable men among my acquaintance. My audience looked unutterable contempt at my youth and inexperience and the subject was dropped by mutual consent. The assumption that all the world is corrupt is to my mind a sure sign of vulgarity. The man who cries 'all men are thieves' convicts one."

Godfrey had not stayed two or three years in Europe as he had originally planned, nor had he taken a degree, as Sam had done. Unlike Sargent or Whistler or Henry James, who had preceded him there, or many Americans who would follow, he was consistent in his disdain for Europeans and for most of what he saw in Europe. All his life he would remain unwaveringly content with most things American and chauvinistic about his country's future. He had seen a great deal in Europe, but wherever he had gone and whatever he had seen, he had remained, as he would remain all his life, a man who, in the words of Henry Adams, "carries his own inch rule of taste, and amuses himself by applying it triumphantly, wherever he travels."

On October 29, 1884, sixteen months after leaving Boston, Godfrey Cabot, uncorrupted by the manifold iniquities he had seen and catalogued in Europe, boarded the *Cephalonia* to return to Boston and make a career.

CHAPTER VI

Cabot in Love

I don't believe Oliver was ever really in love. . . . He
regarded all women as ladies, more or less beautiful, kind,
privileged, and troublesome. He never discovered that all
ladies are women . . . many of the ladies . . . suffered from
the same impediment as himself: it comes from being over-
protected in one region and over-developed in another. Sex
for them becomes simply a nuisance, and they can't connect
it pleasantly with their feelings for the people they love.
Therefore sensuality for them remains disgusting, and tenderness incomplete. SANTAYANA, *The Last Puritan*, 8–9

Even before Godfrey could address himself to the question of his
business career, he became aware that he was also somewhat behind in what he viewed as one of life's many races. "I got my
things thro' the custom house. In the afternoon I called on the
Reynolds where I learned among other things that Jack Reynolds
had just married. It makes me feel quite superannuated to have a
friend two years younger than I married."

Once home, he first discussed his business future with his
father. "I showed father Sam's letters to me while I was abroad.
Father concurred with Sam in thinking my best course would be
to go into some independent business on my own hook with the
idea of later incorporating it into Sam's if successful. . . . I must
freely confess that I look with considerable trepidation on the
prospect of risking my own money and probably some of father's

89

in any business without a previous course of practical training."

He now plunged into the Boston social season with his usual vigor, and as a temporary job, he went to work for Sam at a salary of $2 a day doing chemical analyses.

"I have been making calculations for Sam on the costs of manufacturing Soda. He is thinking of going into the Soda business in Pa. I hope he will not engage in this or any new business in Pa. till he has made his black business there successful of which there doesn't seem to be much immediate prospect. Mismanagement may spoil any business and I doubt if he can ensure good management at that distance."

After Christmas, Sam asked Godfrey to take his wife, Helen, down to Point Comfort, and then to investigate the chrome-iron-ore regions of Pennsylvania, where Sam was considering going into the manufacture of chromates. Godfrey's notes on Richmond reflect a prejudice against the South natural to a boy who grew up in an abolitionist household—a prejudice which was to last his whole life and was much like Henry Adams' view that from Southerners "one could learn nothing but bad temper, bad manners, poker, and treason." Godfrey was exceptional in holding this view, because most Boston aristocrats at Harvard, both before the Civil War and after, found it easier to understand their counterparts from the South than to understand Westerners. They used the same words to mean the same things—for example, "gentleman."

From Richmond, Godfrey went to Washington, where "I regret to say . . . I have seen smoking in the House of Representatives, altho' contrary to the rules, and I have seen a member put his feet on his desk. Both practices are however unusual."

On his twenty-fourth birthday Godfrey was back in Boston sledding and tobogganing with his cousins. He began revising the long fairytale he had begun five years earlier, and he decided to finish and publish it. He continued his omnivorous reading. "I recently finished [Henry Cabot] Lodge's life of Alexander Hamilton, which I thought very interesting, not least so on account of the sidelights it throws on Washington's character and also on

Lodge himself. I do not believe Lodge is a high-minded man but I have a better opinion of his character than Sam or father has." (The first Senator Henry Cabot Lodge, eleven years older than Godfrey, was his double third cousin.)

Godfrey began practicing bookkeeping by working on Sam's books during the day, but he spent more and more time with his father. "Father is apt to play his high cards out too quickly [at whist]. I often keep mine in too long." Godfrey took turns with his brothers and sisters sitting up with their father, and the household was further disturbed by their unhappy cook, Sarah. "I don't know of a more accomplished hypocrite, always excepting the president of Harvard college."

At six in the morning on April 13, 1885, Dr. Cabot died after having suffered long and painfully from Bright's disease. In his Journal, Godfrey wrote at length about his father. "It is a sad fact that one rarely realizes the value of anything until one has lost it. We all knew that many people owed much to father, but I for one never realized how many people and how much. To many people whom the rest of us knew but slightly he was the best friend they had. The quality which I think above all others won him the first place in so many hearts was his persistent disregard of self. Only two or three weeks ago when urged to give up his practice and go south he said 'I won't give in. I am going to go till I can't go any longer and then I shall go to bed and stay there.'

"The last intelligent words he ever spoke to me were about a week ago. He was probably laboring for a moment under the hallucination his disease was contagious. I stopped and kissed him, an expression of pain passed over his face, the tears started to his eyes and he exclaimed in a broken voice, 'But;—but don't you know dear, didn't I tell you dear you mustn't kiss me.' . . . He raised his hand tapping my chin caressingly and said 'It isn't every old man that has three such nice boys to look after him as I have. And dear Guidie would be a fourth if he knew how.' . . . Again and again . . . he urged us not to—'stay fussing about an old fellow like him' but go and attend to our duties nor could he be satisfied until convinced that no important duty would be neglected on his account. Good God, thought I, my duty is not far to seek. . . . In the afternoon a cast was taken of father's head, for use in making the bust which Dan French is at work on."

Since his childhood Godfrey had worried about not being loving enough and about his inability to show affection. When his mother died, he had worried about not having showed how much he loved her, and with the death of his father he again worried about the same problem. Godfrey was not the only young Massachusetts man who worried because he was not loving. Just before his nineteenth birthday, Emerson wrote, "I have not the kind affections of a pigeon. Ungenerous and selfish, cautious and cold, I yet wish to be romantic; have not sufficient feeling to speak a natural, hearty welcome to a friend or stranger," and a year later he wrote, "there is not in the whole Universe of God one being to whom I am attached with warm and ideal devotion." Both boys were painfully shy and unsure of themselves, and if Godrey never developed the extraordinarily loving heart of the "Sage of Concord," still his heart did grow and in his own awkward way he learned to try to show affection more often.

A few weeks prior to Dr. Cabot's death Godfrey's grandmother had also died. His Journal in the weeks following his father's funeral, therefore, contains all the details typical of the settlement of a Boston Brahmin estate. The steps of such a settlement are as formal and as punctiliously carried out as those of a Kabuki dance. Most Boston aristocrats keep all correspondence sent to them, and at their death the correspondence is carefully gone through and sent back to the writers or their heirs. In Dr. Cabot's case certain letters relating to natural history were given to the Natural Historical Society. Others, relating to medicine, were given to his son Dr. Arthur Cabot for his use or to be offered to the Massachusetts General Hospital. The rest were returned to the senders.

All the personal effects—clothing, furniture, rugs, photographs, and books—had first to be independently appraised. "In the afternoon we had a family meeting to transact various business among other things the distribution of personal effects. We drew lots for the order of choice and I had first choice. Guy came last and then the choices were repeated in reverse order, Guy choosing first and I last. Sam, who is to be Guy's guardian, representing him and using a list which Guy had made out at my suggestion. Uncle Edward is sole executor, Uncle Eliot having declined to serve. We went nine times up and down the list." Godfrey's first choice was the engraving of Alexander von Humboldt autographed and inscribed to Dr. Cabot and valued at $2. Other of his selections ranged from eighteen soup spoons appraised at $34.65 to a large photograph of the Roman forum valued at $.50. Such personal effects as no one wanted could be sold and added to the estate, excepting "the office clock, a few bronzes etc. that we couldn't sell as they were presents [which] were auctioned for among ourselves a week ago last Friday. I got the barometer in the office at $11."

Not the least important of those activities occasioned by a death is the interpretation of the will, and in Puritan families the careful balancing of duty, love, self-interest, and generosity are not infrequently interesting to observe. "In father's will the property is divided equally among us, then there are a few letters of instructions. Articles in them will be appraised and taken at the appraised value by those for whom they are intended. An account of expenditures for each of us from 16 to 26 has been kept to date of father's death for Guy and me.

"Lilla spent the most and the balance due to make up the expenditure of each of the others to that of Lilla was paid each of the elder ones as he or she reached the age of 26. No provision for the payment of the balance due Guy or me is made in the will. My account up to date of father's death was 8300 dollars and there would probably have been a pretty large balance due me in two years from now. The seeming inequality is however probably much more than made up by the natural increase of the property. That is to say Guy and I have cost father less but receiving at an earlier age a nearly equal property we have received a much greater pecuniary assistance in life than Lilla or Sam for instance. Thus if to Lilla had been allotted at my age a sum equal to my present inheritance minus all previous excess over expenditures at like ages with compound interest; [and] if this sum had been put at compound interest 6% and from it deducted whatever sums were from time to time paid to Lilla, it would in my opinion at this time amount to more than the share she will actually receive. There is one clause by which I shall receive $3800 before the provision is made on the ground that each of the elder ones received this sum at marriage.

"Another codicil was drawn up providing that from Lilla's portion should be deducted certain sums that have been advanced to her during the last two years. This codicil was brought to father to sign while he was sick but I believe there didn't happen to be a pen handy and he didn't feel like writing and so the business was deferred till he should recover. This might be supposed an instance of the danger of putting things off on account of the uncertainty of human affairs but in my opinion father was fully prepared for what actually happened, and was glad of an excuse for evading what must have been intensely repugnant to him altho' in his opinion a duty.

"For the reasons above given I think that his idea of giving his children equal advantages has been in the end more nearly carried out by the omission of this codicil than it would have been in its execution. It was decided not to let Lilla know of this codicil, and, I think, rightly so decided. I don't see how any one of us could have conscientiously consented to its going into execution and remaining, as it must, a dead letter, it could only make Lilla feel uncomfortable to know of it without, I think, any corresponding advantage."

Not the least unpleasant duty which fell to Godfrey concerned his father's old dog: ". . . it was decided at the last meeting that Dan should be killed, as he had become completely blind and it's enough to make one sad to look at him. I shot him yesterday. It was not so simple a matter as I had supposed for he would not stand still. He did not however have the slightest inkling of impending harm nor did he utter a sound after I fired."

It was determined to sell the house in Park Square and the country place as well; Godfrey therefore temporarily moved in with his favorite sister, Nellie, and her family. The death of his father and the breaking up of his home were a great shock to Godfrey and caused the only philosophical or psychological speculation he ever committed to writing. "A curious speculation came into my head last night. Is sleep a torpor of the soul or is it a temporary death that is separation of the soul from the body. Memory, as we are conscious of it, I take to be a physical phenomenon i.e. an impression upon the brain, if this be the case any activity of the soul apart from the body would leave no impression upon the memory. Truly Life and Death are mysteries. God grant they be some time satisfactorily explained to every human soul."

Godfrey now made a will himself for the first time, but he was not given to long philosophical thoughts and, as always, his sovereign remedy for all ills was physical exercise and competition. "Sam and Tom and I played 124 games of tennis 13 sets in the course of the day. We took turns one playing against the other two. I was but once on the losing side in a set. . . . I did not lose my serve once. . . . I played checkers with Mr. Pushaw [Guy's male companion] and beat him 14 . . . games to 10. I succeeded in felling a large dead elm tree . . . and cut down some more trees in the grove."

Long walks, dances, and youth also distracted him from his sorrow. "Quite a party of us walked up over Fisher's Hill in the afternoon. . . . Our walk was interrupted in a most unpleasant manner. We surprised a man and woman 'in coitu.' Luckily some of us saw what was up when still a good way off and Harry had the presence of mind to direct the party off to the side. . . . Perhaps none of the girls suspected what was the matter but I'm afraid one or two did. . . . In the evening Ruth [Cabot] sang to us and Elise [Cabot] and Miss Lyman played a little. I have just noticed for the first time that Elise bids fair to become a very beautiful woman . . . she holds herself like a queen. . . . It is quite possible that some other person than myself may read this page and might fancy that I am in love with Elise, I am not. . . . The Parkmans gave a tea-nic. We had beautiful moonlight."

Godfrey's main activity after his father's death, however, was undertaking his own business as an analyzing chemist. Since he had inherited over $80,000 from his father, he could afford to wait for success. Trained as a chemist, he could now practice that trade without worrying about its profits while he waited for an opportunity for something bigger. He had no greed for money nor the lust to add house to house and field to field and trample on the faces of the widows, but he had a great need to find an opportunity to prove himself. When that opportunity came, he would now have the capital to try to seize it.

In order to solicit business, Godfrey sent out advertising circulars of his venture. "I directed a lot of envelopes. I have got my addresses first from my bundle of correspondence since last November (I keep most of the letters I get). Secondly my immediate relatives and friends. Then I have looked thro' my list of classmates in the last class report; have copied the addresses of all the architects and paperhangers in Boston and have looked thro' the list of physicians and have sent to such of my acquaintances as I have thought would be likely to want a job done in analysis of water or paper. In all 350 addresses so far."

Business was slow in coming. Godfrey sent out a second circular, proposing to test wallpaper for arsenic, to everyone who had taken out a building permit for a brick dwelling in Boston in the past two years.

Late in October a new customer wanted Cabot to duplicate a depilatory powder used on corpses and an essence used to scent embalming fluids. Two weeks later he noted in the Journal, "I have succeeded in making the depilatory which C. E. Bemison ordered. This is my best job yet. I shall get $25."

By Thanksgiving his business was picking up. "I finished today a lot of 14 wall-papers making the best day's earnings $22. and the best weeks earnings $29. that I have made yet. . . . Mr. Austin is going to give up his present laboratory next Jan and Sam asked me if I would take it and said he would give me the business he had been giving Austin. I accepted his offer. He says he has been paying Austin $300 to $400 a year which will make a considerable difference in my earnings if I get as much. . . . Monday, November 30 [1885], I finished a water analysis for Joe Gardner today, this makes $93 that I have earned this month. In August I earned $5 in Sept $13 in Oct $9. Total since I hung out my shingle $120."

In addition to building his business, Godfrey continued to read avidly, and he began making himself a more active member of that society into which he had been born by joining the various men's clubs and charitable organizations which typify Brahmin Boston. "I finished Sense and Sensibility by Mrs. Austin not long since. I thought it very dull. Most of the characters are insufferably vulgar and they talk endlessly. . . . I began visiting [the poor] for the Ass. Charities. . . . I read a little while ago a book called Profit-sharing which gives a brief account of some of the best known experiments in that line [also] a detective story. . . . I guessed who the murderer was when I reached the 10th page (there are 600) nor did I once falter in my belief."

"There was a small party at Lyceum Hall, given by the gentlemen of the Monday club of which I have become a member. . . . I went to a small party at the Curtises and spent the night at the Puritan Club. . . . I finished today a very interesting German novel. . . . I much admired both the hero and the heroine. It is a good old fashioned romance where the characters act not perhaps as they probably would act but as they ought to act."

But no amount of work, reading, charitable visiting, or society life quenched the loneliness which Godfrey had felt since his parents died. He determined to find himself a good old-fashioned romance in which the characters would act as they ought to act. His approach was typical of him—rapid, vigorous, and intense.

Since he was twenty he had known a girl named Ellen Russell. He had seen her at dances and spoken to her casually but had never given any indication that he had any more interest in her than in any of a hundred other young women in the same social circle. Once he had selected the object of his suit, however, he set about to accomplish his purpose with a frightening energy.

"Sunday, Nov 15 [1885]. . . . Yesterday afternoon I called on the Russells who have taken 294 Beacon St. for the winter. . . . Sunday, Nov 22 . . . I called at the Russell's. . . . Monday, Nov 23. I went to Aunt Ellen's to lunch and met Ellen Russell Uncle Williams daughter [although he called Mr. Russell "Uncle," they were not related]. . . . Friday, Dec 11 . . . I took dinner with Aunt Ellen and afterward called on the Russells. Ellen was out. . . .

"Thursday, Dec 17. I called on the Russells today for the purpose of offering myself to Ellen Russell, she was out. Last week I made up my mind to make this offer if I got a good chance and the spirit moved me. Yesterday I made up my mind that I would call today. Today when I found her not in I got impatient and as soon as I got back to my office I sat down and wrote asking her to name a time when I could call and speak with her alone. I took the letter up to the central office and mailed it with a special delivery stamp hoping I might get an answer this aft. No such luck.

"Friday, Dec 18. Found a note stating that Ellen would be in from eleven till eleven forty. I called on time and was refused.

"She was seated at the piano in the dining-room and playing some tunes from the Mikado. We bid each other good morning, she suggested I should close the door which I did and then began talking about the tune she was playing. I could as soon have discussed Sanskrit roots.

" 'Ellen' said I 'My errand is short and simple I have come to ask you to be my wife.' I meant at least to have told her I loved her but I swear I hadn't breath enough in my body. My voice was husky my heart beat as though it would choke me.

" 'I'm sorry Godfrey that I can't accept your offer' said she, then she went on to say that we weren't suited to each other that some one else would make me happier, hoped that we should still be good friends, 'certainly' said I, begged that I would sit down, I replied that I found it more comfortable to stand. I was simply standing round till my heart subsided a little and a sufficient time had elapsed to obviate notice by the servants of the suddenness of my departure.

"Ellen did not trust herself to look at me after I made my declaration. In a few minutes I left. I omitted to mention that I attended last night the first meeting of a new club at the Houghtons. That is the house of young Mr. Houghton right on this same place. The club was named the Nomads and arranged to meet once a fortnight on Thursdays. Then we played Dumbo Crambo. This Friday evening I went round to see the H. P. C. [Hasty Pudding Club] act Robin Hood which was quite good. . . . That night before I went to bed I vowed I would lay seige to the fortress I had failed to carry by assault.

"Saturday, Dec 19. . . . This morning I wrote Ellen a letter. I began by telling her that I had never for a moment thought that any act of hers had given me the right to expect a different answer. I ended with 'Perhaps I may fall in love with some other girl one of these days but meanwhile if I can find the road to your heart I intend to travel it at any sacrifice save that of duty.' What else I said shall not be given here the more so that my memory is likely in this instance to serve me in good stead. I signed myself

'*Your lover*
Godfrey Lowell Cabot'

"Sunday, Dec 21 [sic]. . . . I went home with Will [Putnam] and confided to him my little love affair. 'I shouldn't think anything of that' said he 'you can't expect a girl to fall in love with you at short notice and without any courting in particular.' There was a good deal of truth in this. I have never made love to any girl, I have indeed studiously avoided giving any girl a right to think I was in love with her. I have for instance never told Ellen either directly or implicitly that I loved her except in my letter and except in so far as any offer of marriage implies love.

"Well, I am not sorry that I asked her when I did. Anything was better than suspense. I am so constituted that when I have once made up my mind to do a thing I am never quite easy till it's done. If the thing is very important and I dread it, this uneasiness is no longer a slight impatience to erase something from the tablets of my memory and the pages of my memorandum book, a moderate wish to have a job done and behind me, it is a strong desire to escape from a mental pressure to get rid of a worry.

"In the present instance I found I couldn't properly attend to what I was about, which is always hard enough for one of my absent-minded turn. It is a good solid satisfaction to me that

Ellen knows that I love her. I feel that it has put me on a more definite footing. I do not think she dislikes me or thinks there is anything against me. It is an old saying that hate may change to love, indifference never, and I fear that Ellens feelings toward me are those of comparative indifference. I am however certain that there is no human feeling that one human being ever entertained toward another that may not and has not sometimes changed to that of love but it does sometimes make my heart sink to think how long the siege may be and that some one may come along, in every way more attractive than I, and snatch the prize for which I am struggling.

"Well, I can stand it if a good man and a true win her, but if some second rate sort of chap ever wheedles her into loving him or thinking that she does, I shall gnash my teeth.

"Tuesday, Dec 29. I got estimates on having some fountains cast and wrote to the water-board for further information. I intend to erect half a dozen to a dozen cheap public fountains erected in different parts of the city. . . .

"Sunday, Jan 3 [1886]. . . . I moved [his office] on Dec 31 and Jan 1 from 15 Congress to 82 Water St. I have been getting some estimates and getting advice with regard to a scheme I have for laying out about a thousand dollars on public fountains for man, horse and dog. I intend that the fountains shall be as service-able as possible and as cheap as is compatible with such service-ableness . . ."

In a society as small as his, Godfrey was bound to see Ellen Russell often. He pursued every possible opportunity to dance, sit, or sup with her, noting in his Journal, "I should hate to have her feel that I was persecuting her. . . . At the same time I don't mean that she shall forget me."

"Thursday, Jan 7. Went to the Harvard Assembly at Berkeley Hall. Ellen was there. I danced once with her and walked a few minutes with her. She was very brief almost curt in her answers to my remarks. Perhaps it is vanity but I can hardly think she actually dislikes me. I am more inclined to attribute her conduct to a conscientious wish to make my agony shorter if sharper by convincing me of the hopelessness of my suit. I don't somehow notice that it has the desired effect. . . .

"Monday, Jan 25. Went to a Cotillion at Berkeley Hall. These Cotillions are the most expensive parties I have ever been to. The regular price is $15 for four and I had to pay this to go to two. . . . Ordinarily I should consider this an unwarrantable extravagance but I thought Ellen might be there nor was I disappointed. . . .

"Tuesday, Jan 26. Went to a dinner at the Lothrops. . . . Mr. Lothrop took Ellen Russell in. She studiously avoided my eye and didn't take the smallest notice of me in the whole course of the evening. N. B. None of the Russell family are models as regards manners. . . .

"Friday, Jan 29. Game Club met at Ellen Coolidge's. Ellen Russell was at another table but after supper I got a chance to have a few words with her, monosyllabic as ever. If she doesn't thaw out a little I think it will excite remark sooner or later, the very thing which I suppose she wishes to avoid. As for me I care little if it does except for her sake. . . .

"Wednesday, Feb 3. Three people today spoke of seeing my fountain project editorially mentioned in the Daily Advertiser."

Continually rebuffed by Ellen, Godfrey tried to find comfort in work. Many nights he worked in his laboratory until midnight. But he always attended any party or dance where he thought there was a possibility of running into Ellen. He increased his charitable work and his exercise. "I visit now three families every Sunday. In the afternoon Will and I walked to Longwood to call on the Codmans and then I walked to Brookline. . . . I walked home. I must have walked over 17 miles in the course of the day.

"Monday, Feb 15. Went to a party at the Lothrops. Ellen was if anything more repellent than ever and declined to dance with me on the score of feeling too warm, she was wearing a shawl at the time. I can't quite understand her conduct. It is to me entirely incredible that she should feel offended by the very slight and inconspicuous attentions which I pay to her. I attribute her conduct rather to a conscientious wish to convince me of the utter hopelessness of my suit.

"After each rebuff my spirits are at low ebb and I often feel as if the most attractive prospect would be some way of getting honorably out of the world. After a while my courage rises again and my reason tells me that even a ghost of a chance of success is well worth living for. At the same time I force myself to face the probability of failure in attaining the first and only thing in the way of earthly happiness I have ever set my heart on.

"Ever since mother's death I have felt lonely and this sense of loneliness has increased as one after another of the family have left home. At the time of his death father was the chief immediate object of my life and filled the first place in my heart. For years I have prayed God that I might fall in love with some good woman. He has granted my prayer, and I am thankful for it, altho it has made a sad and lonely life sadder and much lonelier. . . . Success in my suit or in any other undertaking I have never prayed for. . . . I do not think it is reasonable to pray for that which may perhaps after all not be wholesome and proper for me. Perhaps God has some work for me which can be done better by one whose heart has been sorely tried. . . .

"Friday, Feb 26. Twenty-five years old today. It has been the saddest and the most eventful year of my life. I feel more than a year older than I did a year ago. Sad as it has been I can look back on it with a good deal of solid satisfaction. I have tried pretty hard to do my duty and I think on the whole I have succeeded pretty well. I think I was a real comfort to father last winter and in my love affair of this winter I have so conducted myself that if all the world were to say you have done wrong I could reply you are all wrong. I have acted rightly in every particular.

"At the same time I am not blind to the fact that I have very great short-comings, particularly that I am not modest and considerate enough in my manners and conversation and that I am a very inefficient bread-winner. Still I can say that since I began business last August not one single customer has expressed himself dissatisfied with my work and many have thanked me for my promptness. One other thing I must notice. I have contracted a contemptible petulant habit of mind which manifests itself by my cursing when things go wrong in the laboratory and (inwardly) when a carriage or person gets in my way in the street or any other trifling vexation occurs. I think this is partly due to fatigue and worry as I don't always get enough sleep and am in rather a high-strung state of mind.

"Wednesday, March 10. I made up my mind today that, in spite of all my talk I have been unwarrantably inconsiderate in my attentions to Ellen for altho' in themselves most trivial and inconspicuous they were obviously very annoying to her and I had no right to ignore this annoyance because I thought it was unwarranted so I sat down and wrote her as follows:

> *Dear Ellen*
> I have been wrong in ignoring the annoyance my attentions have caused you and ask your pardon. I shall be more considerate in future.
>
> *Yours truly etc"*

Once resolved to put Ellen from his mind, Godfrey addressed himself to his fortune and his work. He studied everything he could find on the Bell Telephone Company and became convinced that it was a worthwhile business in which to invest much of the money distributed to him from his father's and grandmother's estates. In his youth Godfrey had been taught that the most important thing in life is "being of service." He later preached to his children so often that they became tired of hearing it, that a man must be of service and that if he is, he will surely be rewarded monetarily. Seeing that the telephone was such a service, he invested in it, most profitably. This Poor Richard philosophy is incarnated in almost every page of his Journal and his letters. Without mentioning them, he lived the maxims in the *Almanac*, and they paid off.

He began again to rewrite the long fairytale begun in his sophmore year, changing the title from "Everard of the Eaglestone" to "Ralph of the Rock." He went to hear lectures by Oliver Wendell Holmes and James Russell Lowell, and he increased his reading.

Just as Ellen's rebuffs were making Boston completely intolerable, Godfrey had the good fortune to be sent back to Pennsylvania by his brother. "Wednesday, April 7. Took the 11 A.M. train to N.Y. I am bound for Penn to look over the ground with a view to going into the manufacture there of Iron pigments with Sam if the outlook is satisfactory. It is like pulling teeth to leave Boston even for a short time just at this stage of the game but it would be folly to throw away such a chance. . . .

"I reached Pittsburgh an hour late this A.M. and spent the morning visiting some salt and bromine works. I took the afternoon train for Kittanning. We were delayed by a landslide. I finished 'Phineas Finn' by Anthony Trollope today. I think it quite clever and interesting. Novels naturally possess a peculiar and vital interest for me just now.

". . . I walked up to Monticello to see Mr. Acheson's property there. Monticello is about three miles up the track from Kittanning. I walked most of the way up and back on the rails themselves, at one time walking over two miles in this way without losing my balance. I find I can usually walk faster in this way than on the sleepers but it is more fatiguing. Late in the afternoon I walked out to Worthington. The roads were execrable and it took me two hours and a half.

". . . All of Worthington Buffalo and Craigsville is now supplied with Sam's gas. He used it instead of steam in a little engine that runs his plates. He has now eight plates going all under one roof but they only make 2200 to 2300 lbs of black a week. The plates are stationary and the system of gas burners, brush and box for black revolve beneath them. The box dumps itself automatically into a longer box along which the black is carried by a revolving screw to the receptacle. The black is also sifted by machinery. The whole thing works automatically and one man can attend to the whole. The business has not hitherto been profitable giving very small returns on the capital invested.

"Tuesday, April 13. Anniversary of father's death. . . . I had a chat at the store with Ed Graff this evening. Later in the evening Mrs. Young came down to the office, where I sleep, to see if I wouldn't come up to a little social gathering at the house so up

I went. The sitting room was thronged with young men and young women most of the young men had girls in their laps, there being a deficiency of seating accomodation. N.B. I incline to think the houses most popular for these impromptu gatherings are those in which there is a deficiency of sitting accomodations.

"I was plumped down on a sofa between two men and the game explained to me. In the middle sat a girl alone upon a chair. Another girl armed with a towel made the round striking each man in turn with the towel and asking him if he was satisfied with his neighbor. The usual reply was no. Who will you have? was the next question and then the young man addressed called the name of the girl he wanted or indicated his choice in some other way such as winking, beckoning or grabbing her hand if she were near enough. The two girls then changed places unless the dunce was quick enough to get the place of one of them in which case she took the dunce-stool. If any young man were audacious enough to profess himself satisfied with his partner he was called upon to prove it which was done by kissing her. Moreover there was a great outcry made if he didn't kiss her on the lips.

"The next game they played was known as stealing partners and in this game the men sat in the girl's laps when there was not room for them to sit side by side. There was one girl over and she called for any man she wished then the girl she had robbed did the same and so on. Presently one of the girls called upon me. I was somewhat relieved to find she only expected me to come and stand by her at the door but presently another summoned me and I went and sat in her lap with the best grace possible. I was soon called by still a third girl and I remember sitting in her lap was like sitting on the slope of a roof with your heels hanging over. Most of the young men steadied themselves by embracing the damsels who supported them, but my modesty forbade my thus presuming on a first acquaintance. I couldn't help laughing to think what some of my young lady acquaintances who have never seen me except in full dress would say to see me clad in a rather dirty coat and trousers and very dusty pair of very large heavy shoes sitting in the lap of a village girl and sort of chuckling all over at the absurdity of my position.

"After a while it was proposed to shift and let the men have a turn at stealing partners. So two girls were retired and I could hardly do less than ask my partner to sit in my lap which I think was more comfortable for both of us. When she was stolen however I suddenly discovered that it was about time to go to bed and quietly skipped. . . . I have been writing a good deal on Ralph of the Eagles Rock since I have been here."

On April 16, 1886, Godfrey returned to Boston. There he was offered by Sam the absolute control of the iron chromate business Sam had sent him to Pennsylvania to consider starting. "I gave Sam a definite No thanking him, at the same time for the confidence he had shown in me in making it."

Godfrey then computed his expenses in the first twelve months after his return from Europe on November 10, 1884. They amounted to $1,433.49: $41.90 for clothing, $474.83 for sundries (including everything bought from his father's estate), $77.67 for Christmas gifts and charitable gifts, $478.96 spent in his business, and $360.14 for board. He estimated that in 1886 the total would be about $2,700: $300 for clothes, $300 for sundries, $400 for board, $1,000 for gifts, and $700 for business. He had not yet come into his full inheritance, but he noted, "I have much confidence in the future of Bell Tel and if I had control of all my property I should put about a third of it into Bell Tel."

He continued to note in his Journal each encounter with Ellen Russell, but his eye had fallen on a new prospect. "Tuesday, May 4. Called on Miss Frona Brooks from whom I received an invitation for last Wednesday which I had to refuse. She is very attractive and clever. Speaks German and French, sings, acts and so forth. . . .

"Wednesday, June 9. I went to a very pretty garden party given at the Kennedy's on Highland St. in aid of the Avon Place home. I escorted Miss Frona Brooks home from the party."

Every day or two thereafter his Journal contains "Called on Miss Brooks later in the evening" or "I stopped in and called on Miss Brooks on my way home," interspersed with "I went to a party at Associates' Hall, Milton. Ellen Russell was there" and "lovely garden party, E.R. was there." Godfrey took Frona Brooks to all his Harvard Class Day activities on June 25—not the least important occasion of the year to him. There he saw Ellen Russell, as he noted in his Journal.

His chemical analyses did not occupy his time fully, but he kept himself dutifully busy "visiting my paupers," recopying his Journal, and investigating new ways in which he hoped to make his fortune.

In July he followed Frona Brooks and her mother to Maine, where they were taking their vacation. "I took up my quarters at Kimballs Hotel [Northeast Harbor] at which Mrs. and Miss Brooks (Frona Brooks and her mother) and Franklin H. Brooks are staying. . . .

". . . Monday, July 5. Hired a boat for a week I took a row with Miss Brooks in the morning and then went with her and her mother by sail-boat to Southwest Harbor. . . . In the evening Miss Brooks initiated me in the mysteries of Russian backgammon. . . .

". . . I see on looking back that I have omitted to mention the fact that I finished a week or two ago 'Spain and the Spaniards' by De Anicis. It is a very charming book. He is the most poetical writer of travels that I know of. I am bound to say however that his poetry (i.e. poetical prose) is often voluptuous. . . .

"Tuesday, July 6. . . . In the afternoon Mrs. and Miss Brooks and I rowed out to Bakers Island. Miss Brooks pulls a very good oar at which I was rather surprised as she looks like rather a delicate girl. We ate a little lunch at the Island and then rowed back to supper, about twelve miles in all as we didn't go the shortest way. Miss Brooks sang most of the way back, she sings most exquisitely. We had a lovely sunset.

"Thursday, July 8 . . . Before I record what follows it will be well to go back a little way and mention in chronological order certain pertinent facts.

"I had intended both the Wednesday and the Thursday ev'g before class-day to relate to Miss Brooks my love affair with Ellen Russell and then ask her to be my wife. Had any one told me a year ago that I should live to ask two girls to marry me within the space of seven months I should have said they didn't know me. Yet, I have done it. The following circumstances combined to bring this about.

"Firstly, I am alone and my nature most imperatively demands love, something more than the love of sisters, brothers or friends. My loneliness gives a sombre tint to my whole life and has paroxysms of great acuteness.

"Secondly the opportunities I have had to know and fall in love first with Ellen F. Russell then with Frona Marie Brooks. Their natures are very different but have in common, absolute truthfulness, unselfishness. To compare them here would be not merely odious it would be, for me, sacrilege.

"Could I have been sure of another opportunity I would not, at any rate, from mere impatience have broached the subject of love to any girl within a year of having made an offer to another.

"It made me sick at heart when Miss Brooks told me she should leave Cambridge for good in June, that she should be away from the vicinity of Boston all summer, then perhaps go abroad for a long and indefinite time and then 'Quien sabe'. I made up my mind that however small my hopes were I would seize the opportunity and in any case not fail for lack of trying. . . .

"To return to Thursday, July 8, as soon as we came to a cool shady spot we sat down. I cannot remember word for word what followed but I will recall the gist of it. I promised that I wished to tell her now what I had wished to say on class-day and had followed her to Mt. Desert to say to her and hoped she would hear me thro'.

"I then spoke of Ellen Russell and told her that I had made her an offer last December and been refused. I was going on to give her some details of this love-affair which I thought were more or less pertinent to the matter in hand when she cut me off. 'Don't pain yourself by giving me the details,' said she, 'pray go on' I did so when I got thro' she said she did not know what to say. She hated to refuse me, her heart was perfectly free, she esteemed me, she had much in common with me but she didn't think she cared enough for me to give up everything for my sake, she didn't think she loved me well enough to be my wife. What should she say wouldn't I tell what she should say. No I wouldn't ('The wealth of Ormus and of Ind' wouldn't have tempted me to incline the scales one way or the other if I could have done so with a breath), she must decide. We walked up and down, we returned, I stood and waited. 'O for some one to tell me I must do this or that,' she said, 'O for a revelation from heaven' and she raised her hands toward the sunny sky.

"She asked me if I had been encouraged to ask her by her behaviour toward me, if I should have asked her if she had held aloof a little more when I came here to Northeast Harbor. I should, said I, little enough encouragement did Miss Russell ever give me.

" 'I'm so glad,' said she 'You wont think I have treated you unfairly then' 'Miss Brooks' said I 'never in my inmost heart shall I blame you in the smallest degree for your treatment of me, far less hint such a thing to any living creature.' Apropos, I think, of the last question I said to her that there was one thing that was intolerable to me and that was an uncertain relation with any one, there must be a distinct understanding.

"She recurred to this later in the conversation when I told her she might defer her decision and, if she wished ask her mother's advice. No said she I can not put it off and yet I cannot answer you and finally we dropped the subject with a sort of a half-understanding that I should have a more definite answer before I left."

Some days later Godfrey again asked Miss Brooks to marry him. "Then I took her hand and said 'What's the word?' 'Just what I told you the other day. I do not love you well enough to be your wife. I told you that I cared for you as much or more than for any man, I do not know that that is so I have some very dear friends. . . . You will excuse me if I am frank with you. How can you dare ask me such a question as you did yesterday, you don't know me, I don't know you well enough to be willing to be your wife. I cannot see how you can ask me to be your wife six months after you have asked another girl I suppose you were perfectly sincere in your offer to her. Certainly said I.

"How can I tell you may not change again in six months.

"She couldn't, it would have been folly for her to have accepted me, 'Very well' said I 'then let [it] be understood between us we are both as free as air' and I went out for a lovely stroll in the moonlight (we had reached the house by that time). This is of course not a verbatim report of what passed between us but it gives the gist of it. I must mention one thing that I said the day before. In answer to some expression of anxiety for me I said 'Whatever happens Miss Brooks you may be sure I shall not break my heart on your account.'

"According to all the laws of novel-writing a young lady would have been piqued almost insulted by such a remark but I venture to think she took it as it was meant in all simplicity and truth. I wished simply to ease her conscience, to lighten the load of responsibility which seemed more than she could stagger under."

His offer of marriage rejected by two different women in less than a year, Godfrey's old feelings of inadequacy came back in force. As before, his answer was intense activity in business, in sports, in good works, and again he sought to storm the citadel of love.

He had earlier expressed his intention to rewrite his long fairytale, but now he actually went to work on it. "Began rewriting 'Ralph of the Eagles rock.' Intend to carry this thro' now." After two months' work he noted in the Journal, "I finished my revisal of Ralph of the Eagles Rock today."

The hero of Godfrey's 20,000-word fairytale, Everard (whom he sometimes called Ralph), was descended from "a poor woodcutter" who had "disappeared one day and returned after some years rich and powerful, bringing with him a wife [who was] enormously rich . . . a powerful enchantress and there was also a mystery about her hands, which were always concealed in a muff when she appeared in public, which was seldom. [He] built a castle on one of the promontories which jutted out at irregular intervals along the coast the family had a weakness for this sort of situation . . . paid liberally for service and treated his servants kindly . . . he was known to be a good master, and, in spite of the poorness of the soil, his vassals were more comfortable and contented than any in the neighborhood. . . . [He was blessed] with a magic haystack. However much was taken from it, it always remained as large as ever."

Of Everard himself, Godfrey wrote: "the first thing he could remember was . . . picking up a poor little eaglet which had fallen from its nest and broken its leg, and taking it to his father who set its leg with a small piece of wood for a splint and returned it to its parents. . . .

"On his 14th birthday his father presented him with a stout javelin; it was too heavy to be easily wielded even by a man but his father foresaw that however difficult it would be for him to use it at first the time would come when he would wield it with utmost ease." Everard was "tall straight and well proportioned; humanity and courage shone from his calm blue eyes" and on his shield were inscribed both "Constancy" and the motto "I strike, but spare." He drank only "cold water."

Everard saved the life of a "rich old Jew" who had a beautiful daughter because he "was not overfond of Jews, but his sense of justice prevented his sending even a Jew, unheard, to almost certain death." As Everard "gained much in size and strength and endurance," he vanquished a long list of evil enemies including a king who "was ever generous with other people's property" and "an enormous Afrite."

A bit of Godfrey's poetry got Everard some shining armor:

> Light light
> Flash bright
> Give sight
> To the stranger wight
> When the charm is finished quite
> He shall be in armor light

but Everard was reluctant to take the armor because "it is unworthy of a brave man to take an unfair advantage of his antagonist by calling magic to his assistance." Finally Everard accepted the armor after being assured that it was not itself magic, "only magic proof." (Interestingly, Everard had no qualms about the magic haystack he had inherited from his father.)

He defeated a great assortment of black hats with such dreadful names as Mordato the Witch of the Lybyan Desert, Haornor Farfager the Black Baron, and a dwarf with the name of Orgin. Everard always succeeded because "the thought of possible failure was agony to him." Not the least of his achievements was flying, "sailing thro' the air at a prodigeous speed while plains, rivers, forests and mountains passed rapidly beneath."

But this effort, too, was for nothing. The manuscript was rejected by both *St. Nicholas* Magazine and Houghton Mifflin and Co.

In an effort to prove himself in business, having failed in love, Godfrey made what was for him a tremendous investment —$14,500—in a new company called LeGay Heel Co., which had a patent on a new heel for ladies' shoes. Five weeks later he wrote in his Journal, "Thursday, Oct 7. Sam said something to me today about this LeGay Heel business that had more effect upon my feeling about it than all possible arguments against its financial success could have. He said he believed I had said I never cared to make money out of any thing that wasn't a benefit to the community. I said yes. 'Well why is this any more benefit to the community than a corset company or a patent medecine?'

"I hope we shall ultimately make more low heels than high ones but I cannot conceal from myself the fact that there is no warrant for thinking that this will be the case. I believe our heel will be better than those now sold and insomuch we shall be benefitting the public but it is a great question whether, on the whole, the public would be better off for having any high heel cheaper and better. I wish I were well out of the whole business and I think if I get a good chance I shall get out of it. For the present however I am more likely to get further in than to get out of it, and must content myself with trying to see that it is managed in the best manner possible. I had thought of the general moral question in a vague sort of way before but had never had it set before me in so strong a light."

He was depressed by the suicide of his college chum Joe Gardner, the nephew of Mrs. Jack. But he kept up his health by great doses of physical exercise. "I have got myself in good condition by walking out to Cambridge every night and I believe I could dance or walk all night."

His intensified other activities did not preclude his search for love. He went to all the many parties to which he was invited. "Ellen is getting to be more at her ease with me now she perceives that I no longer seek her society. There is something to me inexpressibly sad in the expression of her face. Sometimes when she is talking, full of warmth and animation her expression suddenly changes and becomes almost hard. It is as if a pool rippling beneath a summer breeze should suddenly grow still and veil itself in a thick layer of ice."

He determined to renew his attack on the citadel of Miss Frona Brooks. Profiting somewhat from his failure with Ellen Russell, he resolved this time not only to tell the lady he loved her, but to woo her family as well.

"Monday, August 16. . . . Last night I had a most whimsical dream. I thought I was on West Beach and somehow became aware that Miss Brooks was on Misery Island and was wishing, or at least willing, to see me. I flew thither, which was accomplished by swimming thro' the air. As I approached she was standing on the beach with Will Putnam, he raised her, set her on his left shoulder and ran up the bank. 'Hallo Will' I cried jestingly 'whose girl are you running off with.' She heard me and turned her head. In a moment I was at her side, took her right hand in mine, passed my left round her waist, pressed without resistance a long, a fervid kiss upon her lips, then I asked (and somehow it seemed to me that I was ten years older, but she unchanged) 'Can you love me, will you be mine after this long waiting?' I never heard a human voice more plainly than I heard hers in that dream. Clear as bell, soft and sweet it came, passionless but kind and gentle. 'That can never be' she explained to me that I had hesitated, or had not come quick enough when she summoned me.

"Somehow there was suddenly a door between us and from without her voice sounded merrily, 'What rhymes with "nein." ' I strove to answer 'Ein,' in some occult way referring to myself. 'Ei . . . n . . .' I groaned and my soul passed from my body and somehow I became aware of what was passing in Will's mind, as my lifeless body fell into his arms. He was in a state of wrath and indignation that I should have died for love of any woman. 'Ah' said Miss Brooks sadly 'I would that I were dead too, that I might meet him in the water as he comes from the dark river.' At this I struggled desperately to come to life again, a sort of a spiral disk seemed to spin before my eyes and curl up, (I remember similar phenomena attending a frightful dream some twenty years ago). Something whirred and buzzed within my head and I woke up. It has flashed across me, while I have been writing this, that stripped of its fantastic accessories, this dream presents a most marvelous epitome of Miss Brooks' character, as I conceive it."

In early September, Godfrey determined to renew his suit in person, and followed the Brooks family to Lake George. "In the evening I took a stroll with Miss Frona by moon-light. She intends to come back to the Annex [now Radcliffe College] for another year if she can find a comfortable boarding place; it shan't be my fault if she doesn't. . . . In the course of our stroll I told Miss Frona something that I have never told to any human soul or recorded in these pages namely that although I did believe in a cold and theoretical sort of way in God and the immortality of the soul, and had an intense inclination and longing toward a personal God, it was without the power of conceiving in any way of either the one or the other and of having an undoubting and satisfactory faith in either. That I felt as if to get such a faith I could bring my mind to sacrificing absolutely everything I had on earth.

". . . I said if I didn't believe in God as well as might be I most certainly did in goodness and she asked me what I considered was the motive for goodness and I said unselfishness and she asked what I considered the motive of unselfishness and I said, love. I also recited the lines 'Who God doth late and early pray, More of his grace than goods to lend,' and said that I didn't remember ever to have prayed for anything I wanted although I had prayed for things for others. (How often have I prayed for happiness for her) That it seemed to me a sort of sacrilege to pray for anything for ones' self except advice or assistance."

In the area of religion, as in most areas, Godfrey's reaction differed from that of Henry Adams, who wrote: "The boy went to church twice every Sunday; he was taught to read his Bible, and he learned religious poetry by heart; he believed in a mild deism; he prayed; he went through all the forms; but neither to him nor to his brothers or sisters was religion real. Even the mild discipline of the Unitarian Church was so irksome that they all threw it off at the first possible moment, and never afterwards entered a church. . . . That the most powerful emotion of man, next to the sexual, should disappear, might be a personal defect of his own; but that the most intelligent society, led by the most intelligent clergy, in the most moral conditions he ever knew, should have solved all the problems of the universe so thoroughly as to have quite ceased making itself anxious about past or future, and should have persuaded itself that all the problems which had convulsed human thought from earliest recorded time, were not worth discussing, seemed to him the most curious social phenomenon." Godfrey took his religion more seriously and was, if it is not a contradiction, a devout Unitarian. Nor would he have been amused at the saying, common then, that "The Universalists believe that God is too good to damn anyone, but the Unitarians believe they are too good for God to damn."

Discouraged by his lack of success with Miss Brooks, Godfrey determined to try to make his own fortune in addition to the $102,000 he had by inheritance from his father and grandmother.

His brother Sam had invented a new gas regulator and hoped to manufacture and sell it in Pennsylvania, where the use of gas was increasing. He offered Godfrey a partnership in the business, and in November of 1886 they both headed south. Godfrey noted seeing through the early morning fog the statue of Liberty, which had just been dedicated. "Sam and I saw a number of insurance men today about this new gas regulator and were everywhere cordially received. . . . Gas is now coming into universal use for heating and cooking in Pittsburgh and I do not think there is a single large foundry or iron shop where it is not in use."

When Sam went back to Boston, Godfrey stayed in Worthington, improving the gas regulator and learning the gas business. On Christmas Day he noted that Sam had generously sought to perpetrate "a pious fraud" by himself absorbing some of the expenses he should have charged to the partnership. On New Year's Eve he noted in his Journal, ". . . I was making out my accounts when '86 passed into '87. Before I went to bed I thought over last year. It was not quite so bad a year as '85 and there is solid comfort in the thought that whatever my shortcomings, duty has been my chief purpose and occupation."

Back in Boston in January, Godfrey called on Frona Brooks, whose father had died. When Mrs. Brooks told Godfrey that there was no hope for him with Frona, he wrote in his Journal: "From this day I shall try to conquer my heart and I doubt not that I shall succeed. It is not the first time I have done it." In spite of his failure to win Frona, he agreed to be a bondsman for Mrs. Brooks, as executrix of her husband's will, in the sum of $30,000.

He bought ninety-nine volumes which he planned to give to Worthington as a nucleus of a public library. In his own reading he came across a book he found just to his taste, Frances Hodgson Burnett's *Little Lord Fauntleroy*.

For the first time he spoiled himself occasionally. "I slept until 11 this A.M. two hours later than I ever slept before in my life. . . . Went to a party at Aunt Lillie's in the ev'g, indulging in the, for me, unheard of luxury of a carriage thither and back. Frightful headache, shouldn't have gone except that I thought I should be wanted and I was.

"For the last six months I have been getting into the habit of sleeping a good deal more than I did for some years previous. I think I average now nearly nine hours in bed. Whether its laziness or what I don't know. I think the nervous and emotional excitement of the last two years has told upon me. I feel five years older than I did when I came back from abroad and have lost a little of my snap. I seem to have got lazy and indifferent. I go through the motions of being pretty busy, but I don't care enough about anything to throw myself into it as I ought to. I have been a little lenient with myself from the feeling that this depression would pass off and leave me stronger for the trial."

But on his twenty-sixth birthday he wrote in his Journal, "Today is my birth day and I mean to brace up and take a new grip of life, confident that there are better fish in the sea than have ever come out of it." Finally Godfrey reluctantly admitted to himself that his attack on the affections of Frona Brooks was a failure. He immediately chose another target, one Miss Leslie Hopkinson, but he first concentrated on building his fortune. He was much impressed by a visit to Sam's lampblack house, supposed to be the biggest in the world.

Back in Pennsylvania he continued his reading and the inevitable critique in the Journal. "I finished 'Ravenshoe' . . . think it quite clever and a good wholesome sort of book very optimistic . . . yet teaching the wholesome lesson that, Sunday school books to the contrary notwithstanding, goodness, wealth, the respect and admiration of others, are by no means guarantees of happiness in this world. Were children taught that they must be good for goodness sake we should see less people driven by misfortune to a drunkards grave."

Narrow himself, Godfrey was intolerant of narrowness in others. He accepted his own view of religion and morality, but was not inclined to grant others their right to a personal view—like Hobbes, who complained that "After the Bible was translated into English, every man, nay, every boy and wench that could read English, thought they spoke with God Almighty."

He visited local churches wherever he happened to be. "I went to church in the ev'g and came back in a state of wrath and indignation at the bigotry of the sermon old Schwartz gave us. . . . Read a book called 'One Commonplace Day' by Pansy, a bigoted temperence book. Went to a prayer meeting in the ev'g. Bigoted crowd there. . . .

"I have undertaken to give a course of free lectures on

Physics and Chemistry." His lectures were a great success; people were often turned away for lack of enough seating, even when the weather was bad. "I had a pretty good audience, better than a prayer meeting would and I talked to them for over an hour. I haven't enjoyed anything so for a month. At the close quite a group gathered round to ask questions and by good luck I succeeded in answering all.

". . . I seem to be popular with the girls for there were fully as many women as men and they were more attentive than some of the boys: The sexes sit separate in these lectures and in prayer meetings." When one of his lectures was interrupted by hecklers, he came down into the audience and faced them down. Later he got an apology from the ringleader, and confided to his Journal, "Despite his cubbishness, I couldn't help admiring his pluck."

"Thursday, April 21 [1887]. In the afternoon came a letter from Leslie Hopkinson announcing Miss Brooks' engagement to Morgan Brooks. I thought at first it didn't hurt much but before night-fall I knew it did. I am a queer piece nothing seems to hurt me at the time but I don't get over things. My first great sorrow was mother's death and I have not got over it to this day. I wrote a letter congratulating her on her engagement and returning her last letter. . . .

". . . As for me this ends it, nothing could ever bring us together again. Apropos, twice when I called last June I found Morgan Brooks there, quite by accident. She assured me, he rarely called on her. By which she meant to assure me as she was doubtless herself assured, that he was no suitor, (as he certainly once had been.) I wonder what she thinks now of what she said last November that she felt sure that when she met the man she could love she should know it. I have one consolation, it is not improbable that my pain has in a measure been the means of their happiness. Had she never known it might have taken her longer to know her own heart and that of her old lover. Dear soul how I loved her, and still love her and yet no longer wish she could be my wife."

Frona Brooks' marriage increased Godfrey's feelings of inadequacy as a suitor and his loneliness for his parents. "I was reminded by something in [Thackeray's] the Newcomes today of a little incident between myself and father that happened perhaps eight or nine years ago. He took me aside one day and told me I must try very hard indeed to be right and true in every way but come what might no matter how deeply I might sin I must never fear to come and confess it to him. I must never think that anything could ever come between me and his love and forgiveness. The one worst thing would be that there should ever be any estrangement between us. Thank God from my childhood up there never was for one hour a shadow between us. It is only in after life that one realizes the full import of such words. . . . How many young men and women are hurried along the downward track by the self-righteousness of their parents."

But the main result was an intensified pursuit of his business. "Feeling myself now the autocrat of the premises we occupy, I have stuck up a sign Danger! Smoking forbidden on these premises." Godfrey was demanding of his employees, firing those he found to be lazy, but raising the wages of his good workers to $1.50 a day. Increasingly he wanted things run his own way, and when Sam in Boston made some decisions contrary to Godfrey's advice, "I wrote him that if the business was to be run from both ends I would sell out cheap."

Godfrey worked hard, selling regulators, getting new customers for the extra gas he did not need to make into black, and repairing his lines. He used the cheapest secondhand pipe he could buy and, as a result, had constantly to repair leaks. Many of his gas lines were laid on the property of others from whom he had not obtained right of way and who threatened to sue him or tear up his lines. He was a dogged bargainer, settling claims by paying very small sums or preferably by giving the landowner a "light"—that is, a free supply of gas for light and cooking.

He came to know every farmer in the area and tried by means of his lectures, letters to the local newspapers, and gifts to the village to become a prominent local figure.

In September he received a letter from Sam offering to sell his interest in the business for $5000. This offer was so generous that Godfrey accepted immediately and became at last his own man in his own business.

In November he secured a charter for his gas utility business, calling it the Armstrong Gas Company. On Christmas Day he worked until two in the morning, repairing lines and blowing water out of his gas wells. A letter from his friend Will Putnam, announcing his engagement to Bessie Lowell, helped remind Godfrey of his own loneliness.

In his year-end analysis he pointed out that he entered 1888 poorer than he had entered 1887 but with better prospects and somewhat less blue. He was anxious to get back to Boston. Village society in Pennsylvania, where he was usually reduced to playing checkers instead of chess, he found dull.

In January of 1888 Godfrey returned to Boston, where he delighted in the company of his relatives and friends, in the theater, and in selling his first order of black since the company had become his own. He found the LeGay Heel Company bankrupt and his investment a total loss. He successfully led a fight against instituting free punches at the Puritan Club.

He went out to Harvard to see his cousin Professor Charles Jackson, who showed him the rebuilt chemistry laboratories at Boylston Hall. "I told Charley I thought they had practically built a new building round the same old smell."

On February 26 he took a walk with Leslie Hopkinson and noted in his Journal: "Twenty-seven years old today. How many changes have been crowded into the last six years. In this year I see myself fairly embarked in a business which bids fair to exile me from home and friends for the greater part of the time for years to come, and yet I am happier than I was a year ago."

At the end of March he headed south again. In Washington he called on a Miss Dodge. "She has cut off her hair and it is hardly longer than a boy's, she is a piquant and coquettish person very pretty and charming and rather flirtatious, just the kind of girl that makes me feel stumbly and awkward."

In Pittsburgh, Godfrey found "Everybody was on the streets and a large portion of the people drunk. I don't suppose I have ever been in a city where life and property are so insecure. The whole air is infected with trade unionism, drunkenness, vice, and crime. The hotel is the resort of drummers the most absolute set of cads it was ever my fate to be thrown among. There are three staple topics of conversation, business, drinking and whoring."

Back in Worthington, he went to work with a vengeance. "I sat up tonight and found Jim Semple who left work an hour early Saturday night was an hour late in beginning tonight. I shall have a new hand working night tour on Monday. . . . Had yesterday a long interview with Wm Falconer my chief competitor in the lamp black business. He is a huge and hideous Scotch man enormous hands, feet, and body, red nose, sunken cheeks, big jaw and beard, lack lustre eye and withal a most agreeable man whom everybody likes and speaks well of. I took him up and showed him my well. . . .

". . . They have struck gas in Graff's well but it is nothing like the well mine is. . . . Graff's well didn't seem as large as mine, but I have received the most positive assurances that it gauges as much. . . .

"My patent on lamp black process has been granted. . . . [Godfrey received a number of patents for inventions in the manufacture of lampblack, including one for a method of enriching black by the addition of oil. Although the addition was not important then, today nearly all black is made with some similar form of enrichment.] Got a scorching on my face and hand today in putting gas into the brick kiln. I put on some tallow and as soon as I could leave the kiln went up to Dr. Maxwell's and he bound it up with sweet oil and cotton batting. . . . I took off the bandages from my face last night . . . a good deal blistered. . . .

"I received word a day or two ago that the Craigsville well was a dry hole. This is as good as $2000 in my pocket."

As hard as he worked, Godfrey still had time on his hands and energy to spare. He read a book a night. "I finished a novel of R. L. Stevenson called Prince Otto. . . . The moral is that most of us are very lucky not to be born princes. I have often thanked my stars that I was not and yet I should think it would be enjoyable and interesting to be at the top of the ladder for a short time, say a single day. The trouble would be that afterwards every day life would seem 'flat stale and unprofitable.' On the other hand I should think to be a king would be the dreariest lot on earth. There must be moments when a king feels as if there were no such thing as sincerity and unselfishness."

Godfrey read a number of Thackeray's novels, which he found had "a sort of sparkle . . . like champagne (which, by the way, I have never tasted)."

But books did not satisfy his needs. "I read over all of Leslie's letters that I have here. . . . I had a curious dream last night of rescuing L.W.H. [Leslie Hopkinson] from a sort of 'Do the girls Hall' to paraphrase from Nicholas Nickleby." Godfrey decided to do more than dream about Leslie. He returned to Boston, where, on his arrival, "It pleased me to take my first refreshment at a fountain in P.O. Square given by me to the city. There are four others all with troughs to match, erected, and one not yet erected."

Every day he called on Leslie. Having failed in his two earlier courtships, Godfrey was resolved not to fail again for lack of wooing, and he wooed Leslie with Emerson.

"Sunday, Sept 2 [1888]. In the afternoon Leslie and I rowed out to Cranberry Island and read Emerson's essay on Heroism. Monday, Sept 3. . . . we rowed over to Green Island and read Emerson's Self-reliance. . . . Wednesday, Sept 5. Leslie and I rowed out to Sutton's and read Emerson together. We have read his Essays on Heroism, Self-reliance and Compensation. I like the third most." In view of Godfrey's later activities with the Watch and Ward Society, he must not have read carefully that part of the Essay on Compensation where Emerson wrote, "every burned book or house enlightens the world; every suppressed or expunged word reverberates through the earth from side to side."

It was not surprising that Godfrey admired some of Emerson's sayings and abhorred others, for half Boston thought the philosopher mad, while the other half revered him as a saint. Edward Everett Hale thought him half crazy after hearing "The American Scholar" lecture, whereas James Russell Lowell, who had wooed Godfrey's mother, characterized the speaker as a Yankee Abélard. Godfrey wholeheartedly agreed with Emerson's view that "Whoso would be a man, must be a nonconformist," and he must also have sympathized with Emerson, who had a brother who was a mental defective.

"Thursday, Sept 6. . . . Leslie and I went up Astican and read Emerson on Manners. . . . Saturday, Sept 8, [1888] . . . Took a walk with Leslie and played Hoppity in which I was defeated with great slaughter. . . .

"Monday, Sept 10. Leslie and I went out in the morning to the Outer Cranberry and walked the whole length of the island. . . . we sat down and she then and there promised to be my wife and I put my arm round her waist and kissed her and it seemed to me that that was a very comfortable place for my arm and I kept it there while we looked at the surf with unseeing eyes . . . I believe I have since collected all the arrears of toll that has been due since I have been plying so industriously to and from the Hopkinsons to the great amusement of the different observers . . . to my amazement I suddenly found myself within the gates of Happiness that I had so long laid siege to.

"Tuesday, Sept 11. I wrote Mme Emil Kopp and Lilla and then Leslie added postscripts and then she went to walk with me and took me to the spot where she had once said no to me and put her arms round me and told me she loved me and it seemed to me as if I should never despair of anything again."

Godfrey left his fiancée and returned briefly to Boston, where he told his friends and family of the engagement, which would not be official until November. He then returned to Pennsylvania.

"Friday, Sept 14 [1888], Had my first letter from my betrothed, what a glow it gave me. . . . Saturday, Sept 15 . . . Sent Leslie a diamond engagement ring. Had a second letter from her. . . . Saturday, Sept 22. Wrote Leslie. I had the sweetest letter from Leslie yesterday and I have been foolish enough to put it in my 'inside weskit pocket' on the left to keep my heart warm. We are having full harvest moon. Another letter from L. today such as make a man most humbly grateful. I spent the whole evening writing to her and indeed this delightful occupation absorbs a good portion of my time. Nor do I feel any compunction in this for once pleasure and duty go hand in hand.

"Sunday, Sept 23. Wrote Leslie. When I look back upon all the mistakes I have made and sadness I have passed through, it seems to me that if I could recall and alter the past I should not dare to change one day or lessen one pang for fear I might somehow lessen the perfect love that is mine, mine for life and, I hope, for eternity. A certain bashfulness and scrupulousness has ever made me a calm and reserved if not a backward suitor but never was there a more passionate and devoted lover or one whose measure of love was in return so heaped to overflowing. Now and again a great fear seizes me lest I may somehow fail to do my part; or that I have such a stake set upon a human life.

"Tuesday, Oct 2. . . . Among other things I went round to see a house that was to let. I also had my teeth polished and that was the first cent I ever spent on my very efficient grinding apparatus [and also the last]. Took night train for New York.

"Wednesday, Oct 3. Missed 9 A.M. train but got 10 A.M. train and telegraphed Leslie. . . . A blue streak might have been seen crossing Harvard square about 5:30 P.M. and shortly after I jumped off the front platform of a Mt. Auburn car and reached the door of 22 Craigie St. The house was full of flowers and luckily there were but few callers that evening. . . .

"Saturday, Oct 6. Lowering and threatening day. In the afternoon I went to see Leslie. She was pale and wretched; said she did not love me enough to be my wife. I took her hand and sat down by her side, she would not let me kiss her. I tried to sooth her, told her I was sure this feeling would pass off. She asked me for my reason, I could only say 'I love you.' I sat a good while by her side trying to think and then I took her over to see Nellie. She would not even take my arm; she seemed overwhelmed with remorse. I went up stairs and told Nellie and then I gave way and fled to my room.

"In a little while Nell came up and tried to comfort me. 'Is she gone' I gasped. 'Yes.' For a moment my muscles gave way beneath me and I fell to the ground.

"I took the 11:30 train P.M. for New York. On the train I met Evert Wendell just going home and he asked me to his house. . . . I accepted his congratulations as heartily as they were given and felt like a chap that has the rheumatis in a leg that has been cut off.

"Monday, Oct 8. Nellie has done her best for me in this pinch. She told me Saturday that she would give ten years of her life to have it otherwise; that if it were not for her children she would go with me to Worthington but somehow at the crisis my heart turned to Will Putnam I had an intense wish to clench his hand sure that his heart would leap to meet my mortal agony as no woman's could. I did some drumming today but could sell nothing. I had a letter from Nell. She gave me little hope but yet I think my heart is so strong and warm that this mist, the blackness that has arisen cannot stand before it. I sent Leslie a New Testament today. The marking ribbon was drawn and the lines marked were 'Blessed are they that mourn for they shall be comforted.' . . .

"Tuesday, Oct 9. Came to Phila. Spent the afternoon drumming and sold 1 bl. It is sick work drumming when you feel blue. . . . Wednesday, Oct 10. One month ago today I was happy for the first time since mother's death. How I wonder if she and father can see me now. . . . Thursday, Oct 11. Spent on business in Pittsburgh. I find business and sleep my best escapes from myself. I cannot read except newspapers a little. Took ev'g train to Kittanning.

"Friday Oct 12. Spent morning on business in Kittanning. Rec'd a number of letters of congratulation. To me fate has always been ironical, giving me what I cared less about instead of what I cared more and snatching from me the only deep happiness I have known. Reached Worthington.

"Monday, Oct 22. . . . Wrote Mrs. J. P. Hopkinson releasing Leslie from her engagement. This in answer from a letter I had from Leslie in the morning. Nasty rainy afternoon and ev'g. Awfully blue. Oddly enough Leslie's letter was the same day of the month as one last month containing the most positive assurance that ever mortal received of happiness. And upon the same day of the month Ellen Russell said no to me. Why should I be so scourged? Is there no end but in oblivion?"

CHAPTER VII

Marriage & Other Business

He knew it was his duty to marry some day, as it was his duty to go to college and to play football and to choose a profession. SANTAYANA, *The Last Puritan*, 236

The delight of its aspirations is flung up to the sky. The paths of its self-distrust and anguish of doubt is buried in the earth as its last secret. HENRY ADAMS, *Mont-Saint-Michel and Chartres*, 370

The oblivion Godfrey sought was in hard work. He traveled all over Pennsylvania, selling regulators and learning all he could about gas wells. He visited Rockefeller's Standard Oil drilling crew at Barnes and gas lines in the Tinesta valley. He visited dozens of factories of different kinds that were springing up all over the area and increasing the demand for gas—a glass works, a tannery, other carbon-black plants. At Kane gas sold for a dollar a year per "fire" (stove) and five cents a year per "light" (fixture). The rate in Sheffield was $2.50 per fire, in Barnes $.75 to $1. Godfrey decided to buy up all the cheap gas acreage he could get.

The first carbon black, made by the incomplete combustion of gas deposited by actual contact of flame upon a metallic plate, had sold in 1872 for $2.50 per pound. But with increasing production, the price rapidly decreased and fluctuated between fifteen cents and two and a half cents a pound.

Godfrey ran his business as a kind of parlay. He would find

cheap gas and build a black plant nearby. He would then go to another area, where there was little or no gas production, and buy mineral acreage. If he hit gas, he would use it to make black until he could profitably sell the gas to individual or business consumers, whereupon he would find new cheap gas and move his black plant again. He used his black plants to insure his use for the gas he discovered or bought until he could sell it more profitably for another purpose. He made between one and two pounds of carbon black from a thousand cubic feet of gas.

Everywhere he went, he sold his black—to ink makers, newspapers, paint manufacturers. He asked for samples of his competitors' black and studied their plants, resolved to make a blacker black. He toured the cities of the midwest, drumming in Buffalo, Cleveland, Toledo, Detroit, Chicago, Milwaukee, St. Paul, and Minneapolis. In some he sold ten pounds, in some none, but he met every possible user of carbon black. "I sold 10 lbs yesterday and 2 lbs today but have got the thin edge of a wedge in here [Cleveland]. . . . Canvassed for trade . . . tramped endlessly today. . . . Sold 10 lbs black to the only printing ink concern here [St. Louis]."

In spite of canvassing each city at a feverish rate and traveling all night he could not keep from brooding. "I'm afraid I looked back a little although my hand is at the plough."

When he could not sleep, he read. "One feature I dislike about most English novels is that the most interesting characters are very often idle men who seem to be absolutely incapable of getting ahead in the world until a 'deus ex machina' comes along in the shape of some adventitious circumstance like a legacy or a wealthy marriage, barring which they too often think it necessary to sit genteely on their tails and go to the devil, not to my mind a very heroic proceeding. The novel strangely stirred me and set my head and heart throbbing. As we rushed over some of the lofty trestles I pictured with delight to myself the possibility of a sudden crash, the cool air fanning my face and blowing back my coat and my hair as we fell, a moment of exaltation of exultant defiance of fear and then. . . ."

"As we passed Bellaire I thought of John Cabot as one

whose lot was harder than mine. Shortly after marriage his wife
became insane and died in about a year. . . .

"I fancy I am more of a success as a manufacturer than I
should be as a soldier. Come down to hard pan it is not death but
life I want. Constitutionally timid and shyish the habit of exer-
tion has become a second nature to me, and in my moments of
success I look back with something akin to regret to the ardor of
the fight. In fact my daily work and worry is the very breath of
my nostrils."

Godfrey had felt the tremendous self-doubts and painfulness
of making a choice which led so many rich young Boston men to
avoid action and decision by merely managing the family trust.
He had taken a long time to come to a decision, resisting pressures
from his father and his older brother. But he had finally entered
the lists because he knew, as a Harvard professor would say
nearly a century later. "A rich country, like a rich man, has the
luxury of choice. The only thing it lacks, much as we might wish
for it, is the privilege of avoiding choice."

"Wednesday, Nov. 14, [1888]. Indianapolis straggles all
over a plain on two sides of an unsightly stream. The state capitol
is large and ugly. Cheap natural gas has freed the city from soot.
Took the afternoon train from Cincinnati, the nastiest city in
America. Thursday, Nov 15. Ault and Wiborg showed me a black
blacker than mine delivered in this city at 6 cents per lb. . . . Sold
5 lbs. to Queen City Printing Ink Works.

". . . Called on the Mayor [of Pittsburgh], Wm McCallin,
an obsequious ordinary little man, spare, slight figure, no sign of
education or personal dignity. I had the greatest difficulty in
explaining to him that I had no private axe to grind in giving
nine troughs to the city of Pittsburgh. That any man should have
such a thing as public spirit seemed to him a new and inexplicable
phenomenon. Then he started to talk cant but I shut him off on
this by a stony glare."

Traveling from city to city, young and lonely, Cabot was
faced with temptations which frightened him. He was no less
susceptible than other young men to a pretty face. "Took night
train for Pa. In a compartment near mine, apparently travelling

with her husband and brother was one of the most beautiful girls I
ever saw. . . . Last night as I entered the hotel the parlor door
opened and a girl looked out and saw it was I and shut the door.
She was expecting somebody, not me. My heart gave a sickening
throb at the thought that I had hoped by this time there would be
someone waiting for me when I came home from my work at night.
. . . In the ev'g I went to the Opera House. . . . I thought all of
the female parts were pretty well taken nor was there an ugly
woman on the stage.

". . . Recent experience has brought to me with renewed
force the conviction that mere will-power and pluck are but bul-
warks of sand against the tide of temptation and that while the
habit of duty and self-control may for a long time curb and keep
in check the baser passions but the only permanent safety lies in
looking upward, in constant striving after the best things, so that
we have no time for the less good things."

In January 1889 Godfrey received from his brother Sam his
first order for a carload of black. His business was doing so well
that there was danger of a gas shortage; Godfrey asked the
village of Worthington to turn down a number of free streetlights
he had donated. When the village did not comply, Cabot cut the
gas off entirely, causing a scandal. When the villagers threatened
to band together and drill their own well, Cabot encouraged them
to do so and thereby to increase the cheap gas supply for his
factory. But he made peace with the village and offered it and the
town of Kittanning fountains and horse troughs of the same sort
he had given to Boston and Pittsburgh. He also offered the Kittanning Borough Council 200 shade trees on condition that the
Council set them out, just as his great-grandfather, Thomas
Handasyd Perkins, had given 437 trees to Quincy in 1826.

In his factory Godfrey was constantly experimenting with
new shapes of burners and new plates at different distances from
the burners in an effort to improve his production. Working and
living conditions were very difficult, particularly in the winter,
when his gas pipes frequently froze and Cabot had to thaw them
out. "We have nine fires now going along the line. Beastly muddy
roads . . . started back by moonlight. I lost my way three times

and finding I couldn't catch the night train to Kittanning I put up with a man named Gorman. All through this country people use but one sheet on their beds and wear no night gown."

In the spring of 1889 Cabot made another long drumming tour, this time to the South: Louisville, Nashville, Chattanooga, Atlanta, Augusta, Savannah, Charleston, Richmond, and Wilmington. At Nashville he was more fortunate than usual in curing his loneliness. "About sun-down a very pretty charming little girl of seven years old came and sat near me and I very soon made her acquaintance and had her on my knee telling her fairytales. Her name was Ethel Sullivan and she was the only daughter of a stone-mason. The next two hours which I had expected to be uncommonly tedious were on the contrary quite an oasis. I often think that children are the redeeming feature that makes this world tolerable."

While on the trip Godfrey wrote Nellie that he was wearing the engagement ring for which he had found no taker, and she answered: "But Godfrey—my dear unobserving brother, *don't* wear the ring. If you lived less in the clouds you would not need me to tell you that gentlemen of your social rank don't wear diamond rings in this part of the world. I cannot say how it may be in the South or in Europe. But in the Eastern States of America you seldom find even the 'gentlemen clerks' indulging in that sort of display (I wish it were equally true of 'salesladies'). It is confined mostly to second class actors, billiard 'sharps' & that sort. Another objection, if you want one, is that it is so essentially a lady's ring that it would be 'wearing your heart upon your sleeve' with a vengeance. Everyone would notice it, & guess its history. Keep it, my dear, & some day tell your *wife* the whole story & have it re-set for her."

Godfrey also received a letter at this time from his friend Will Putnam, which poignantly defined the problem suffered by so many Boston men. "I started to write to you a few days ago but like several similar efforts it was an unfinished failure & I tore it up. I have been reading the life of Emerson, and am much struck by his letters not merely by the poetic thoughts and language. . . . He writes what he really is thinking and caring about, writes without reserve not what he ought to be thinking, not what he has read that other people have thought under similar circumstances but his own thoughts. . . .

"Too much reserve may be better than too little, the English are preferable to the French, but the intense self-absorbed (not *selfish*) reserve so common in our New England stock causes much suffering. . . . I think I can speak out plainly enough in talk but in a letter I can say nothing . . . even to Bessie. I mean that I can not say even to her what I would like to her and to you. . . .

"I can not tell you how happy we are together, to her I can almost open myself & tell everything, and it is so blessed to have some one to whom you can rightly devote yourself wholly, for whom you can do everything without feeling that it looks queerly or hurts other people, or bores her. But who on the contrary rewards every little piece of thoughfulness for her, with unbounded gratitude, and in her turn gives up everything for what I want.

"I suppose there is a danger on the side of being too much absorbed in each other. We must, if only for the sake of our children, keep in touch with the outside world. But the family life is much more important to the children and in the many distractions of busy city life we get little enough time to ourselves. . . .

"I am still troubled by my strong love of money, I find that I even look at my profession mostly as means of money-making. I do not love it chiefly for itself. I am frequently worrying myself about investments or rather purchases of securities which to a person as ignorant of the interior facts as I am are little better than speculation. Of course I do need to earn and save money but I attach too much importance to it. I need a little of your generosity in that way. On the other hand you ought to make an effort to spend more on yourself. It is a trait of your family, which you have most strongly, to live too poorly. You ought if your digestion is bad to take great pains and not to hesitate to spend money to get the kind of food that suits you, and I believe that you ought for the sake of your character to get a good horse and make a companion of him & train him. A horse too who would carry you a thirty mile journey to see friends without trouble.

"Your first duty in this world is to take care of yourself. It is for him that you must answer at the final account. Physically and intellectually as well as morally and spiritually he must be given the best attention that you can afford and discover."

Godfrey's only note at the bottom of Will's letter is, "What % can you get me $2000?"

Although in Charleston Cabot had sold an order for a ton of black, he was always uncomfortable in the South and was delighted to get back North. In New York he went to the Metropolitan Museum and admired "the superb 'Horse fair' of Rosa Bonheur which I consider one of the greatest pictures ever painted." He was happy to be back where he could hear a Unitarian sermon, "delightful to hear some common-sense again after the pridebound orthodoxy I had heard at Bellaire, Augusta, and Richmond. . . . Finished a novel called Bryan Maurice describing the conversion of a Unitarian to Episcopalianism. The latter religion is like homeopathy, very attractive to the young and inexperienced because so exactly organized with a specific treatment prescribed for every case, a certain definite rigamarole for each several occasion. If spiritual comfort on this earth were the sole object of religion, Episcopalianism is far better but does not so well conduce to truth and unselfishness." Cabot attended church wherever he went and was as critical of religious services as he was of books. "Went [in Dayton] to services of Y.M.C.A. in the afternoon. They are too full of the Moody-Sankey and Salvation Army spirit for my taste. I hate this everlasting whining about Salvation. Did Christ ever talk about his own salvation. 'Others he saves himself he cannot save.' "

Much as he enjoyed getting back to Boston, Cabot came more and more to enjoy his "drumming trips." In Minneapolis in September 1889 he called on the now two-years-married Frona Brooks. "She looks exactly as she did the first day I laid eyes on her."

In Sandusky "I had a very whimsical dream which began with looking at a book of oil paintings over E.R.'s shoulder and ended with a fight with 3 burglars. Just as they were comfortably disposed of I was awakened by a most blood-curdling shriek in the next room. I jumped out of bed thinking murder sure. Then came a yell for water. I grabbed my pitcher and hurried into the room whence it proceeded to find an insignificant man with a full black beard just recovering from a nightmare. Suggesting that the water in his own pitcher might do just as well as mine I returned in triumph to my own room feeling like that valiant King of France of whom fable relates that with 15,000 men he marched up a hill and then marched down again.

"The bell-boy and a stranger then appeared on the scene to know what was the matter. My neighbor at table next evening told me that he occupied the room below and the bell-boy first stopped on his floor shouting what's the matter, what's the matter. When told to go up stairs he replied he wouldn't go another flight for a million dollars. It seems however that with sufficient reinforcement and the assurance that he was not the first on the scene he rose to the occasion and to the second floor. The gentlemen who told said it cost him two hours sleep. For myself I must have lain awake fully ten minutes."

In spite of his shyness, Cabot met and spoke to a wide variety of people on his trips. "Took the night train to Memphis. The most comfortable sleeper I ever was on. 14 sections, select library, improved water closet arrangements, etc. etc. . . . I had a very interesting chat with a mulatto clergyman the last part of the way . . . [from Little Rock to Pine Bluff] train occupied by a howling mob flourishing whiskey bottles spitting tobacco and all as happy as clowns and perfectly good-natured. At each station was a crowd of negroes in like condition. I understand this is the normal condition of the population on Saturday night. . . . Shortly after leaving Arkansas City a fire-eater got in, very drunk very dirty with a very dirty bag. He set his bag down and opened the ball by explaining in a loud voice what he would do if any ―――― nigger meddled with his bag. When he got out a revolver and began flourishing it to emphasize his remarks and came and sat down by me, the gentleman that was talking to me left the car. Presently the conductor came along and collected his fare and took away his revolver. Finally he refused to get off unless the conductor returned his revolver. I got up and said I'd lend a hand if need be but it wasn't needful. We lay a long while at Leland and he came back again and began worrying two negro women. This was the last straw and I told him to leave them alone and go about his business which he promptly did."

In December 1889 Godfrey went to Cuba, where he was shocked and fascinated. "Everywhere the air is fragrant, in the country with flowers, in the city every kind of stink. . . . If a Cuban wants to pump ship any place is good enough for him. If he blocks up the sidewalk as he stands, there is no law against people stepping into the muddy street to get around him. . . . At night . . . at each open door-way and window sit one two or more women some ugly, some beautiful all presumably for sale . . . saw a gang of convicts quarrying stone. They were mostly negroes and mulattoes, many of them stripped to the waist and such splendid fellows it was a pleasure to look at them. I did not pity them working in the open air with a glorious sea view before them, water to bathe in. . . . Prostitutes do not walk the streets as in northern cities and seldom speak unless spoken to but they are as plentiful as grasshoppers and shame seems to be a feeling unknown to most Cubans . . . the most obscene books and pamphlets are everywhere for sale."

For Christmas of 1889 Godfrey was in Augusta, Georgia, where he received his first invitation to help form a monopoly. "Had a letter from Nolan last night stating that black was being delivered @ 3½ cents and urging me to join a trust. I do not wish to lose control of my factory, nor to discharge my workmen, nor to milk the public. . . .

"Wednesday, Jan 1 [1890]. This last year has been one of travel for me. I have now been in 32 states of the Union have seen, in the Mississippi at New Orleans the largest of North American rivers, and have been for the first time within the tropics. I have doubled the size of my factory, in the face of a ruinous fall in prices have increased my outside investments, have paid off all money borrowed and given away about $1000. Such it is to be a bachelor with no expensive tastes and a comfortable income. I believe I stand at present fourth in the list of gas-black makers."

In January 1890 Godfrey sold in Atlanta his first carload to anyone other than his brother. Then, heading back to Boston, he stopped in New York, where he saw *Faust,* an opera he would later condemn as grossly immoral. At twenty-nine he only noted, "I saw the first really graceful ballet dancing I ever remember to have seen."

When he returned next to Boston, Godfrey began calling regularly on Maria Buckminster Moors, whom he had known for years, and who was the daughter of Joseph Benjamin Moors. Mr. Moors came from a farming family in Groton, Massachusetts. His great-grandfather, who had fought in the Revolutionary War and in the Siege of Louisburg, was the owner of much acreage in Groton in the days when farming in New England was profitable, before the Ohio Valley was opened up and the railroads came in. As farming declined, most of Joseph Moors' ancestors, excepting his father, had moved out to the Ohio Valley, taking their patrimony with them. Most of the land in Groton had had to be sold off to provide these funds.

The small farm that remained to Joseph Moors' father earned barely enough to send the oldest son to college, and he became a minister in the wheatfields of Massachusetts. Joseph, the younger son, having no money and no inclination to farm, had come to Boston to make his fortune. He had married a Miss Jones, who had a little money, and had gone into the drygoods business, in which he prospered, branching out into money lending and mortgages. Both Joseph Moors and his wife were socially as well as financially ambitious and had been doing quite well in both ambitions until the Boston Fire of '72 and the subsequent Panic of '73, which virtually wiped out their fortune. Godfrey later told his son that Joseph Moors had less money in a good year than Godfrey had in a bad month. When Moors' widow died in 1910, three years after her husband's death, her estate was bankrupt.

Maria Moors—or Minnie, as she was more often called—had hazel eyes, beautiful hair, and a handsome figure. She was even more socially ambitious than her parents. Because of her early background she was all her life frantically worried about money and was extremely parsimonious.

Godfrey's Journal reflected the progress of his suit for Min-

nie. "Sunday, February 23 [1890] . . . Supped with the Moors.
. . . Sunday Mar 2 . . . Spent my evening at the Moors. . . .
Sunday, March 9 . . . Supped at the Moors. . . . Thursday,
March 13 . . . Dined at the Moors. . . . Sunday, March 16 . . .
Took a walk with Miss Moors to the top of Carey's Hill and
supped at the Moors."

During a whole month of courtship the Journal makes no
mention of love or affection. Then, on March 20: "I walked home
from the conference of Ass. Charities Wd VI [Ward 6] with Miss
Moors yesterday, March 19, she is also of the visitors for this
Ward. I stayed to dinner and she promised to be my wife. I
walked down to her cooking school with her this A.M. Took a walk
with Minnie in the aft. and supped at the Moors."

Every day thereafter Godfrey saw Minnie. They visited his
relations and hers, had their photographs taken, went to the
opera and to church, received gifts, took tea, and visited their
paupers—but never a word in the Journal of love or happiness.
He noted on April 13 that his father had died five years earlier
and on April 22 that for the first time he spoke via long-distance
telephone to a Mr. Martins in Philadelphia, 300 miles away, at a
cost of $3 for five minutes; but no mention of love.

Minnie had three bachelor older brothers and two sisters.
According to her brothers, Godfrey the suitor shook his head
politely when Mr. Moors asked, "Did I ever tell you the joke
about . . ." but as soon as he married Minnie "he would yell
'Yes!' as loud as the rest of us."

Minnie's brothers were three of the most attractive and popular men in Boston, as gay and charming as Godfrey was serious.
Once their sister was married, they frequently joined together to
defeat Godfrey in the various competitions which he took so seriously; Godfrey nevertheless got on very well with his brothers-
in-law.

Before his wedding in Cohasset, Godfrey tried to buy some
life insurance, but was refused because, he was told, he had a bad
heart.

"Sunday, June 22. We put 500 cards into their envelopes
and after that Ernest Jackson and Arthur and Frank and I had a

game of base ball. In the evening we all took hold and shelled peas for the morrow.

"Monday, June 23. Weather threatening early in the morning but it cleared off later. We all worked like beavers decorating the house and before noon all was ready except clearing up the scraps. At four the guests came, over two hundred and at about half-past four Maria Buckminster Moors became my wife. I never was more calm and thoroughly self-possessed in my life and to my surprise I thoroughly enjoyed the ceremony, apart from the result. . . . I was so happy I thoroughly enjoyed receiving the subsequent congratulations which I had looked forward to as a tedious bore. We took boat to town and put up at U.S. Hotel.

"Tuesday, June 24. Went to Springfield where we took a row on the Connecticut and by later train to Pittsfield. I want to chronicle here one great essential fact that I am happier than I ever in the whole of my life expected to be."

Godfrey and Minnie took a one-week honeymoon to Saratoga and Lake George. Minnie later confided to her daughter that sexually the honeymoon was a horrifying disaster. When it was over, the couple went to live with the Moorses in their summer house in Cohasset, where Godfrey competed with his brothers-in-law, Arthur, Frank, and John Moors, at tennis, chess, Anagrams, and foot races, recording every victory and every defeat in his Journal.

Godfrey ran his business from Cohasset when he lived there with his in-laws during the next few summers. "I have made at Worthington in two months 457 bbls [or] 23,535 lbs, considerably more than in the whole of the first year, and at Fosters Mills [a smaller factory he had bought] about 140 bbls. in all over 30,000 lbs. . . . I am working now at the rate of 72 bbls. a week worth about 250 dollars. This is over double what I was making at this time last year and I expect to make over twice as much this year as I did last. In the first six months I have netted this year 2,271.87 on my investment of 13,254.79 in Worthington."

After two months in Cohasset, Godfrey took his bride to Pennsylvania early in September. Godfrey mistakenly assumed that Minnie had his own phenomenal energy and physical endurance. "We came to Kittanning last night and rode today to Fosters Mill and back 5½ hours in the saddle. . . . M. and I went to church in the A.M. took a walk in the aft. . . . Went out to Worthington with M. and back in a driving storm. . . .

"September 24. Minnie miscarried early this A.M. Feels better today and no fever." Minnie had had tuberculosis as a child and all her life had bad tonsils, which were never removed. In addition to her real health problems, however, she was a mild hypochondriac.

Minnie Cabot was miserably unhappy in Pennsylvania. The primitive apartment over a saloon, the rainy, cold weather, and the simple country people were not what she had expected when she married a Cabot. She made her unhappiness known to her mother, who came to visit Minnie and to enlighten Godfrey. Even Dr. Arthur Cabot, Godfrey's oldest brother, and his sister Nellie wrote him that he had better bring Minnie back to Boston.

On December 13 Godfrey took Minnie back home, and she never again lived with him "down South." While she was recovering, Godfrey read aloud to her, a practice which he was to continue for the rest of her life.

On her twenty-fifth birthday, April 21, 1891, Godfrey gave Minnie a watch. Two weeks later they moved to 15 Brewster Place in Cambridge, in a four-family frame house where Robert Frost would later live. After the couple had set up housekeeping, their first visitors were Minnie's parents. Godfrey tried to please his in-laws, particularly his wife's parents, but his mother-in-law was difficult. She was resolved that her daughter Minnie should enjoy fully all the joys of social prominence and money. Mrs. Moors was also very embarrassed by her insane daughter Ethel, whom Godfrey dutifully walked out to visit at Dr. Channing's in Brookline.

All spring and summer Godfrey stayed close to Minnie, going south only for short visits. "Thursday, Sept 24. Minnies girth last night was 42″ just after midnight water began to flow and pains set in soon after. At 6:10 finding she did not seem able to expel the child Dr. Taylor and Green assisting had ether administered and delivered by hand just about seven P.M. The child weighed 9½ lbs and was breech foremost which complicated matters. . . . Friday, Sept 25. M. and the baby both well. I spent most of the morning spreading the good news. Won three sets from Frank Dunbar, won 3 lost 2. . . . Saturday, Sept 26. Won two out of three sets against Mr. White."

Examples of Godfrey's own fierce competition now alternated in the Journal with reports on his firstborn son, James Jackson Cabot, who must not be a runt if Godfrey could help it. "M. has plenty of milk. . . . Dr. Preble beat me 4 sets of tennis. . . . Jim has gained 10 oz. this week and weighs 12½ lbs. . . . I won 4 sets of tennis from Frank Moors. He won at chess. . . . Jim weighs 14 lbs 1 oz net. He is weighed just before his bath."

Godfrey enrolled at Harvard as a graduate student in chemistry and geology, but his trips to Pennsylvania precluded his regular attendance.

In April 1892 he noted, "I went today to Benpew to see a black factory being put up to make black out of oil, by Welsh and Bamer of Butler, Pa. . . . The inventor Dietrich claims that he can make one pound of black to the gallon and that it is of very fine quality. . . . I do not believe the firm will ever live to make 10,000 lbs of black in all and sell it except at sheriffs sale." Godfrey had nothing but scorn for the notion of making black from expensive oil when gas was so cheap.

Cabot, deciding that he wanted to add wider distribution, took on European agents. "April 28 [1892], sent yesterday the most valuable ton of black I have yet shipped it went abroad and netted me 971.54." As his sales increased and he expanded his plants, he needed more and more gas. He spotted all his wells himself, disdaining to use geology, as he would all his life, and playing his hunches. "I had word of a good gas well my drillers have on the J. G. Smith farm, yield about 1,350,000 per day."

In spite of his full mustache and his success in business, his competitiveness increased. Often his Journal's only entries concerned the number of sets of tennis or games of chess he won or lost against his brothers-in-law. Godfrey was also constantly measuring himself against his business competitors. In 1892 he believed that he was producing from 16 to 17 per cent of all the carbon black made in America and that he was the third or fourth largest producer.

About half the carbon black produced was distributed by the New York firm Binney and Smith, who were constantly approaching Cabot to sell them his production, to be distributed under their trade names, or, if he insisted, under his own brands. Even though this move would have made his life easier, enabling him to concentrate on producing rather than also having to sell, Cabot refused. He wanted to create a demand for his own products under his own label and to be his own master, fearing to become dependent on others.

However, in October 1892 Cabot noted in his Journal, "Smith of Binney and Smith was in again today. Yesterday he talked about 6 solid hours trying to persuade me to sell thro' their firm. Finally we came to an arrangement by which I am to be guaranteed 1½ cent more on my black next year than I am now receiving. . . . I spent mostly with Mr. G. H. Smith and contracted for my '93 output at 6 cents f.o.b. Kittanning for Eclipse and 5½ cent f.o.b. East Brady for Keystone."

But giving Binney and Smith his production to distribute did not mean that Godfrey would now stay at home and relax. He still worked furiously, improving his black factories and buying gas land, every acre he thought might be productive, for from fifty cents to a dollar an acre. Every spare dollar went into this buying.

Cabot had drawn up a standard form of deed in buying mineral acreage which gave him seven eighths of the oil, the other eighth to be run free in the pipeline to the vendor, and which gave him a full eight eighths of the gas. He would select some low-priced small-town lawyer and tell him he would take any acreage on which the title was good for a dollar an acre. Godfrey let the lawyer make whatever profit he could on the deal by buying it from the farmer as much under a dollar as possible.

Godfrey was a shrewd buyer who bought as cheap as he could. He never thought about whether or not the price was fair, feeling no moral obligation to tell a seller the true worth of a property so long as it was not misrepresented. When Cabot sold acreage which he believed had no gas, he also refused to represent it as any better than he thought it was, but where price was concerned he believed, as had his New England ancestors, that business morality consisted in buying as cheap and selling as dear as possible. In addition to buying mineral rights, Godfrey made contracts to buy gas from producing wells, usually drilled by men looking for oil, who happily sold the gas for a cent per thousand cubic feet to recoup their costs.

He felt it was a sin to engage in a business which gave no service whatever, such as pure trading. Later he told his sons that he wanted always to make two blades of grass grow where one grew before.

Cabot's interests widened. He voted for the first time on November 8, 1892, noting, "Voted, mostly for the democratic candidates." For Cabot to vote Democratic, for the only time in his life, indicates that it was for him, as for most other Americans, an election based on personalities rather than principles. Cabot had not admired Cleveland in 1884, but he had abhorred Blaine, the "continental liar from the state of Maine," who had ended one of his "Mulligan letters" with the injunction "Burn this letter." For Cabot, who had refused to go into business with his own brother because he was not given a veto power on all moral questions, it would have been unthinkable to vote for a "plumed knight" who wrote letters that should be destroyed and who shouted as loudly for freedom for Ireland from British rule as though he were not a Republican at all but a Democrat in favor of "Rum, Romanism, and Rebellion." Not that Cabot had been unacquainted with the less than perfect sex record of Cleveland, but he had thought Blaine even more immoral. In 1884 Cabot had been on his way home from Europe, so he had not been able to vote for Cleveland, but he knew that his father had. While the votes of nearly five million other Americans were in the main votes against the inadequacy of the federal government, Dr. Cabot's was a vote against immorality. And thus Cleveland, the first Democratic President to be elected to that office since Buchanan, came to the White House. When Cabot in 1892 voted for the first time, he voted as his father had, and for the rest of his life he was able, on the basis of this single exception, to proclaim that he voted for principle and not for party. As have other Puritans before and since his time, Godfrey tended to make his view of moral character his only test of political fitness. Since politics is more frequently the art of compromise and reconciliation than it is a great crusade or moral beauty contest, this is a dangerous game.

Cabot appeared as an expert witness in an explosion case and so enjoyed his own performance in the box that he became less anxious to settle his own cases and more litigious. And he read and read and read. "M. and I finished Dan. Deronda. It is very interesting but I think D.D. was rather given to slopping over. There is a certain lack of virility in most of George Eliots men in fact in the heroes of most English novels. M. and I finished Thackeray's Shabby Genteel Story a coarse story of very vulgar people. . . . M. and I have finished Thackeray's 'Catherine' a horrid story of criminals."

Godfrey continued his sporadic graduate studies at Harvard. "3 hour exam in Engineering 5. I think I did pretty well but don't expect to score an 'A' as I did last year in Geology."

Results of competitive games and sports, as always, filled a good part of the Journal. "We went skating on the Charles River at Newton upper falls thence to Dedham and from Dedham to South Natick and back. I think I skated over 40 miles in all. . . . This is more than twice as far as I ever skated before and further than I have ever gone afoot but I could have gone 10 miles further with enjoyment I think. . . . Beat Mr. Marks giving him a castle. . . . Beat Hill at chess. Played in the ev'g with Dresel and he won."

Minnie and Godfrey went to lectures and concerts and theaters and gave teas and dinners of their own, but often the only Journal entry was "Quiet day with M."

"Sunday, Jan 1 [1893]. In the past year I have done more building made more black and had a larger gross income than in any previous year. . . . Looking back over the past year we have much to be thankful for and most especially that M.s health and little Jimmie's have improved so much."

Just after his thirty-second birthday in 1893, Godfrey went

down to see "a 4,000,000 cu ft per day gasser in the Duffy farm, the largest well I have yet owned. . . . After supper walked up to Fosters Mills to see W. C. Smith who has just lost a boy due to a horrible accident due to his own neglect of orders and the boys carelessness. . . . While walking into Kittanning . . . I was overtaken by S. F. Showalter in a buggy and he agreed to sell for $2000 a well and 2 leases for which he had asked $4000. . . . I have put Morris in charge at Foster's Mill in place of W. C. Smith."

At the Columbian Exposition in Chicago, Cabot was impressed with the just-invented Ferris wheel and visited the "Algerian theatre" and "Cairo street." On his way back to Boston he stopped in New York, where he sought to achieve some of the advantages of a trust, such as limiting competition, without the restrictions and loss of authority he would have suffered if he actually joined a trust. "I had an interview with B & S [Binney and Smith]. I think that thanks to my exertions great pressure will be brought on the American Carbon Black Co. the Bush Provision Co. and the Mt. Jewett Co. not to enlarge their output at the present very inopportune moment and on B. H. Blood not to inveigle any more people into the business on false pretenses."

The changes in America from Cabot's birth in 1861 to 1893 had been phenomenal. Henry Adams wrote of his family's return from London after the Civil War, "Had they been Tyrian traders of the year 1000 B.C., landing from a galley fresh from Gibraltar, they could hardly have been stranger on the shore of a world so changed from what it had been ten years before." These changes were wrought by the strength and wealth mobilized to win the Civil War, but they were only the beginnings. The next three decades saw America transformed from a society of individual farmers and artisans to an industrial nation in which masses of power and people counted for much and individuals for less and less. Not the least remarkable thing about Godfrey Cabot was his resiliency through drastic change.

Cabot always resented the fact that he had been too young to take part in the war. He was also too young to have been one of the first of the new breed of individual industrial giants, but he was one of the last, and the similarities and the differences between Cabot and his predecessors are significant. Many of the makers of great fortunes were from New England. J. P. Morgan and Collis Huntington were born in Connecticut; Jay Gould and Jay Cooke were of Connecticut extraction; Jim Fisk was the son of a Vermont peddler. Almost all these men were of Protestant-Puritan backgrounds, James J. Hill and Andrew Carnegie direct from Scotland's icy Calvinism. Many, though not all, were the sons of poor men, and even those who were not had early been taught the importance of thrift, self-denial, and sharp trading. According to John T. Flynn, Rockefeller's father, a quack medicine peddler, said, "I cheat my boys every chance I get. I want to make 'em sharp. I trade with the boys and skin 'em and I just beat 'em every time I can. I want to make 'em sharp."

These men made their fortunes not by inventing anything new, but by a ruthless ability to acquire power and to absorb or destroy competition. Carnegie, for example, was no pioneer in steel; indeed, he always maintained that "pioneering don't pay." The Bessemer process for making steel by decarbonizing iron had been used for over a decade when Carnegie finally reluctantly went into steel making. Nor was Carnegie a brilliant scientist or technician. Rather, he relied on others, particularly on William Coleman. But once he had stumbled reluctantly into steel making, he determined to become the biggest and the best and did so with a fearsome and brutal energy.

Similarly, although Cabot had trained in chemistry at Harvard, it was not any technological genius which made him successful. It had not been his own idea to make carbon black from natural gas, but his brother Sam's. Although Godfrey made some minor improvements in burners and received some patents, these were not substantial factors in his success.

In the myths surrounding great financial success in America, the factor of luck, good or bad, in the success or failure of businessmen is frequently overlooked. Two strokes of extraordinary good luck which Cabot could not possibly have foreseen were to a very large extent responsible for his amassing of a great fortune: the invention and widespread use of the automobile and the tremendous unforeseen demand for gas.

Before 1915 the preferred reinforcing agent for rubber was zinc oxide, and automobile tires, which lasted for less than 3000 miles, were usually white when they were new, although some were made black by the addition of minor amounts of carbon black. When zinc oxide became scarce as a result of the use of zinc in brass cartridges during World War I, the Goodrich Company, experimenting to find a suitable substitute, discovered carbon black to be far superior to zinc oxide; within a few months all the principal tire companies were using carbon black as the reinforcing agent, about five or six pounds per tire.

When Cabot decided to go into the carbon-black business, the only substantial use for black was in printer's ink. No one could have foretold the widespread use of the automobile, which, like Whitney's cotton gin, was to be one of the great enabling technological developments, with unimaginable effects not only in the steel and rubber industries but in the entire history of mankind. Ford brought out his Model T in 1908. In 1916 it sold over half a million and in 1923 two million. The price for the two-seat runabout had started at $825 but was down to $260 in 1925, and by 1927 Ford had sold over fifteen million cars.

Good luck, therefore, played a tremendous role in Cabot's life. He was in the proper place at the proper time, and with an inherited fortune. He was able to buy great reserves of gas at cheap prices because fortunately a lot of gas was available and no one saw any use for it.

But luck was not the only factor. If Cabot was extraordinarily unadaptable to certain of the social and moral changes which took place in his long life, he was nevertheless remarkably open to changes in technological processes. He demonstrated not clairvoyance, but that astounding swiftness of reaction to opportunity and the enormous animal aggressiveness which, far more often than inventive genius, have secured for a man success and power. Godfrey lived at a fortunate moment, when America's industrial production was growing rapidly. The production of steel in America was only 20,000 tons in 1867, when Godfrey was six. By 1895 it had passed the British output with six million tons, and before 1900 it reached ten million. However, it is at the very least probable that, had he been born earlier or later, he would have had a similar success.

A recognition of the importance of good fortune is not meant to underrate Cabot's or the other entrepreneurs' hard work, powers of organization, Puritan hatred of waste, and attention to detail, which are perhaps best symbolized by Rockefeller's note to his barrel factory: "Last month you reported on hand 1,119 bungs. 10,000 were sent you beginning this month. You have used 9,527 this month. You report 1,092 on hand. What has become of the other 500?" This anecdote is not dissimilar to one about Cabot's stopping his chauffeur, who was taking a pair of his employer's shoes to be resoled and reheeled; inspecting the shoes, he told the man to return them to the closet because the old soles and heels had several days' more wear in them. Like many of these millionaires, Cabot forgot or chose to ignore Emerson's definition, "Economy does not consist in saving the coal, but in using the time whilst it burns." Cabot did both.

There were, however, substantial differences between Cabot and some of the other industrial giants, and these are perhaps best symbolized by Morgan's yacht. Cabot never had a yacht, but even if he had, he could surely never have called it the *Corsair*. At the height of the panic caused by the Northern Pacific speculation, Morgan could say, "I owe the public nothing." William Vanderbilt could in a rage shout, "The public be damned." But Cabot, all his life, had a real concern for the welfare of others, shown early by his contribution of fountains and trees and later by tremendous gifts to education. All his life Cabot expressed a distrust of and contempt for New York bankers in general and Morgan in particular. Part of his attitude was certainly a disdain for the "palace cars," the yachts, and Vanderbilt's French chateau on Fifth Avenue. Nor did Boston aristocrats ever indulge in that first form of the Marshall Plan, the purchase of titles by rich American women, which by 1909, it has been estimated, had moved some $220,000,000 from America to Europe, the most famous example being the marriage of Consuelo Vanderbilt to the Duke of Marlborough.

Late in life Carnegie came to condemn the single-minded pursuit of wealth as the "worst species of idolatry" and to give away much of his fortune. Cabot was never an idolater and never practiced what the Adamses in their *Chapters of Erie* called "Caesarism in business." Carnegie could laugh at Gould for expecting him to deliver structural steel for the St. Louis Terminal Bridge at a contracted price when a shortage of steel caused a rise in price. Cabot, on the other hand, always believed in the sanctity of contracts.

Cabot had no awe of government and would later deliver himself of violent condemnations of Wilson, Roosevelt, and others in high office. But he never had the contempt for the federal government which, for example, Morgan displayed when he suggested to President Theodore Roosevelt in connection with the Attorney-General's investigation of his Northern Securities Corporation, "If we have done anything wrong, send your man [the Attorney General] to my man [one of Morgan's lawyers] and they can fix it up." Morgan also asked if the President planned "to attack my other interests," causing Roosevelt to comment when Morgan had left, "That is a most illuminating illustration of the Wall Street point of view. Mr. Morgan could not help regarding me as a big rival operator, who either intended to ruin all his interests or else could be induced to come to an agreement to ruin none."

Godfrey admired Teddy Roosevelt both for his imperialist, Mahan-inspired foreign policy and because Roosevelt was strong and preached strength. Godfrey believed that whatever was worth doing should be done full force, and he thought little of any man who, as Theodore Roosevelt said of Taft, "means well feebly."

This is not to imply that Cabot was a progressive. Though his business began in Pennsylvania, nowhere in his Journal or his correspondence is there any mention of the terrible Homestead Strike of 1892 or of the earlier Molly Maguires. Cabot was in favor of the mass importation of cheap labor, which reached its nineteenth-century peak in 1882 with 789,000 immigrants. He was not unlike Major Higginson, who, as Bliss Perry pointed out, enjoyed saying "the workmen ought to have a bigger share of pie," but who was "disinclined to pass the knife and ask the workman to help himself." But Godfrey was far less militantly conservative than many employers of his day. Cabot told his children that a mine owner had bragged to him about driving his men into the pits with clubs—"It made me wonder what he did that he *wouldn't* brag about."

When despite the election of Cleveland there was a Panic in 1893, Cabot felt that Morgan and the Rothschilds had taken advantage and overcharged the government for their gold. In the next year he was disappointed with the Wilson tariff, which pretended to the principles of free trade but was as protective as ever, but he would have been outraged at the 2-per-cent income tax on incomes above $4000 had it not been declared unconstitutional by the Supreme Court. From the enactment of the Sixteenth Amendment in 1913 until his death Cabot was second to no man in his hatred of the income tax.

Rockefeller pointed out that, unlike the steel business and some others, the oil business was simple and easy to get into, so that, unless there was monopoly and control, there would be excessive production and no profit. The carbon-black business, too, was simple to get into, and in the years after 1893 Cabot was increasingly pressured to follow the American pattern and help form a carbon trust.

If Godfrey differed from his business counterparts in New York and the West, he differed quite as markedly, but differently, from the Boston men who were his financial and social equals. Adventure and risk had left Boston, "the Brahmins were going into banking, retaining their titles as Brahmins and abjuring their function . . . trade of an earlier day had connected Boston with the history of Samarkand and Venice and given it some of the splendour of Lisbon and Antwerp, and the young men who sailed before the mast . . . had lived the sort of lives that were pictured in Homer. The days were passed forever when the Danas and the John Lowells roamed the world as argonauts or wrote their wills among the ruins of Thebes; and the young Boston men . . . were mostly to end their lives at desks in State Street, hugging their stocks and bonds and 'standing pat' . . . the city lost interest in the country except as a field of exploitation . . . immigration and factory problems replaced the older problems of good and evil, and men, immersed in money, ceased to read, and the 'feminization of literature' was a haunting question. One could foresee a New England turned in upon itself, while Boston, sulking in its tent, refused to play with Denver and San Francisco." Godfrey was to be the great exception to this withdrawal.

CHAPTER VIII

Rich at Last

Money answereth all things. *Ecclesiastes*, **X**, 19

Money brings honour, friends, conquest, and realms.
MILTON, *Paradise Regained*, Bk ii, line 422

Balzac was the first to perceive "that money was as necessary to a young man in the nineteenth century as a coat of mail was in the fifteenth." GEORGE MOORE, *Impressions and Opinions: Balzac*

Long before the advent of Jesus Christ, and no less ever since His time, it has been the business of business to make a profit—that is, to buy or manufacture as cheap and sell as dear as possible. In the last half of the nineteenth century and the early years of the twentieth in America (and in Europe as well) profit-minded men were increasingly vexed by competition. It was irksome in the extreme to the producers of oil and steel, the manufacturers of bathtubs, the slaughterers of beef to be undersold. And so there were formed in various industries what were called "trusts," whether they were trusts in the legal sense or merely gentlemen's agreements or holding companies, or whatever. These were set up to eliminate competition, to regulate production, and to fix prices.

Rockefeller's oil trust and Morgan's steel trust were the two models of how to form a trust despite tremendous difficulties. Seeing the initial success of the great trusts, smaller manufacturers in other fields decided to follow the pattern.

150

Again and again in the 1890's Godfrey Cabot was approached by his competitors to form some sort of trust; these approaches were noted by him in his Journal and also in his letters to Minnie. Godfrey wanted the advantages of a trust without the restrictions on himself. From Aberdeen, South Dakota, at a meeting of carbon-black manufacturers called for that purpose, on July 12, 1893, he wrote, "I wish in the first place to learn all I can with regard to the general business situation & the methods of manufacture of my competitors. Secondly to obtain if possible some general agreement by which all firms now in the business will receive immediate information of any new firm starting or proposing to start. Thirdly if possible to compel Binney & Smith to handle the different brands of carbon black under the brand names & to prevent their taking up any new brand."

In January 1895, at a series of industry meetings, Godfrey was sorely tempted to join in a trust. "January 5 . . . Great concessions have been made to induce me to enter a combination with the other makers of carbon black to prevent further cutting of prices. I am telephoning Sam tonight to induce him to come on [to New York] and talk things over. . . .

"Jan 9 . . . I have been worked and worried nearly to death but have postponed the whole business to Jan 24th when I expect to flatly refuse to have anything to do with the concern my gorge rises against the men who are in it. . . .

"Jan 13 . . . I do not think I should care to go in with these men unless I had absolute control. Sam did not go on to New York but we had a talk by telephone & he declined to advise me further than that he thought I ought to be treasurer of any such concern. . . .

"Jan 24 . . . Nine men representing four other carbon black making interests did their best to-day to persuade me to come into camp. They proposed 1. to buy my black for five years at 4¢ per lb. 2. to lease my factories 3. to buy my factories for cash 4. to buy my factories for 10% preferred stock on an appraisal 5. to buy my factories for 10% preferred stock & secure me by a mortgage on the plant all of which I declined giving some of my reasons but not all. . . . I tried to persuade them to form a combine without me but this they absolutely refused to do."

What all of Cabot's real reasons were it is impossible to know, and they were probably not known even to himself. He continued to be tempted to join and to increase his profits by eliminating price cutting and new competition. He sought advice from Will Putnam, who rather encouraged him to join. "Of course you are the best judge as to whether it [is] wise to go into a trust, but I don't fully agree with the objections on principle which you seem to feel. Large combinations do not seem to me to tend to increase prices permanently to the consumer. If successful they make prices more regular and prevent sales at a loss but on the whole I think they lead to lower prices & increase profits by cheapening the cost. All capital is under such strict supervision here that any attempt to increase the price beyond what prevailed under free competition is strictly watched, & if unreasonable will be prevented by law. Different businesses prosper under different conditions and some can be better carried on as small scale but more and more it appears that most work can be done better & cheaper on a very large scale this removes all the expense of fights & combines a good deal of work."

It is at least doubtful whether antitrust legislation, which was and would remain for many years a paper tiger, was what most affected Cabot in his actions. It is also doubtful whether principles, such as price protection for the consumer or job protection for his employees and agents, were the main influences on Cabot's decision, although he often gave them as reasons.

For example, he wrote Minnie in 1899, "They are trying to form a trust in the printing ink trade the first effect of which will be to throw a lot of men out of employment. I shall fight it tooth and nail." While expressing concern for the employees of the ink manufacturers, Godfrey failed to point out to his wife that an ink trust might be large enough either to dictate price to its carbon suppliers or to go into the carbon business itself. In a later letter he wrote, "They are trying to work up a printing ink trust in the interest of the carbon black trust & I am fighting it tooth and nail. I do not think it will affect me much whether it is a go or not but my position in the matter will greatly enhance my prestige and standing in the trade."

Godfrey had few moral compunctions against monopoly and near-monopoly, as was shown in a letter of a year later to Minnie explaining why he wanted a gas-utility franchise in the tiny village of Grantsville, West Virginia. "I am trying to get franchise & rights of way to allow me to bring gas into this town and obtain my share of the sale of gas which amounts to about $1000 a year. This does not amount to much the more important thing is to control the gas situation in this county, stop waste & have no competition in the purchase of gas rights." Godfrey was not as upset at the prospect of the farmers around Grantsville having no one to sell their gas to except himself and one other possible purchaser as he had been at the plight of potentially unemployed ink workers.

Some of the reasons which influenced Cabot not to join in a trust, at a time when they were so usual, were emotional and others were practical. He had come a long way, from being the "sat upon" runt of a large family to being the absolute autocrat of a successful business, and he enjoyed the power which he would lose as merely one of the owners of a large trust. "I do not intend to go into any carbon black combination unless I get practically my own terms. I do not think I shall ever go into such a combination unless I can control it." Another strong reason for Cabot's refusal to enter a trust, perhaps at least subconsciously the strongest, was his unwillingness to put his conscience in thrall to others. As a young man he had refused to be the partner of his brother Sam because he could not have an absolute veto over all moral questions; it was unthinkable that in later life he should merge a business he had built himself into a trust which would, in effect, give his former competitors the power to make moral judgments in his behalf. All his life he was to be a loner who viewed his competitors as "rascals," "liars," "drunks," and "thieves" and who had to see himself as a conscientious, moral man. It was simply not in his character to give others the power to make decisions which he might view as immoral, no matter how much such a merger might mean in increased profits.

Godfrey could never depend on "them" to justify his behavior. He had to be his own and only judge, a not uninteresting phenomenon, especially in our own time, when we are all more or less inclined, like insurance underwriters, to spread the risks of judgment. Cabot's feeling about his competitors was like that of the Adams family, as described by James Truslow Adams:

> A competitor is not merely a competitor; he is a malig-
> nant enemy, come from the Devil to destroy the noblest
> work of God. Circumstances that may oppose their
> plans are not accidents; they are damnable efforts on
> the part of society to thwart an Adams. . . . In reading
> innumerable entries in the *Diaries* of John and John
> Quincy, as well as the *Autobiography* of Charles Fran-
> cis and the *Education* of his brother Henry in the last
> generation, we are reminded of the *Diary* of Cotton
> Mather, whose vituperative vocabulary was even more
> copious, whose opponents were always 'vile fools,' 'tools
> of Satan,' and against whom the forces of society and of
> Hell itself were arrayed when anyone mildly disagreed
> with him. It is, indeed, an aspect of Puritanism, for if
> one is the elect of God what must, necessarily, one's
> enemies be? The inference to be made is of the simplest
> sort. To identify one's self with God is greatly to com-
> plicate one's social relations.

But there were also practical reasons which precluded his joining a trust not only in the 1890's but even in the early 1900's, when he was asked to be the head of the trust or, failing that, to set up informal price-fixing agreements on exactly his own terms.

Unlike many uninformed liberals, Cabot knew that monop-oly does not necessarily stifle competition and, indeed, may en-courage it. Morgan had put together his steel trust by paying high prices for steel mills and then watering the securities of the trust; but then, to show a profit for the security holders, he had to sell his steel for such high prices that in effect he held a price umbrella under which little companies could make a profit while underselling the giant and could eventually grow into large com-panies—for example, Bethlehem Steel. Since the giant simply could not afford to lower its prices when it controlled 80 per cent of the market, the pygmy grew, unmolested. Cabot was well aware that there were no real secrets to the carbon-black business and that, even if all the carbon makers formed a trust, others could make black wherever gas was cheap and plentiful.

In the next forty years he would often be asked to fix prices, but he did not want the business to be *too* profitable, lest it attract competition from small new carbon makers or, even more dangerously, from such a giant as Standard Oil, which could easily enter the black business if it appeared prosperous. "If there's too much sugar," he said, "you attract too many flies." Therefore, while sometimes joining his employees and competitors in complaining about the bloody price wars in his business, he was aware that they had their uses in warding off potential new competition.

Cabot was a Teddy Roosevelt–Mahan patriot and it is perhaps not unimportant to note that in America the struggle between the trusts and the increasing antitrust legislation has had a predominantly stimulating effect on the economy. In Europe, on the other hand, capitalism has suffered because of the extent to which cartels were successful in their restraint of trade. The evolution of capitalism in Europe and in America was concurrent, but by 1939 capitalism in Europe and capitalism in America were two different economic operations.

A further reason may later have induced Cabot to start price wars in the carbon-black industry. He owned all the stock of his own company, but his main competitors, United Carbon and Columbian Carbon, were publicly traded. A price war drove the price of his competitors' securities down where they could be bought cheap. When the price war ended and profits rose, the securities of the publicly held companies rose and could be sold dear. Until his death Cabot was an owner of shares of his competitors. In September 1905 he wrote Minnie, "I have just acquired a small interest in the Star Creek Oil & Gas Co. whereby the better to watch them."

Certainly not the least important reason Cabot would not fix prices was emotional. When his sons came into his business, he constantly told them, "Never make a gentleman's agreement, or you will find you are the only gentleman party to it. Only make agreements enforceable at law." He meant that if an informal and secret agreement were made fixing the price of black, a manufacturer willing secretly to undersell his co-conspirators could pick up much additional business. As moral as he thought himself, Cabot knew he would be sorely tempted to break any "gentlemen's agreement" to fix prices, and he assumed therefore that his competitors would surely not honor their word and would secretly undersell him and steal his customers.

Furthermore, Cabot enjoyed fighting for its own sake, and a trust would have taken away his chief fighting weapon, price cutting. In 1895 he wrote to Minnie about a title fight with his Kittanning, Pennsylvania, neighbors, the Graffs: "I shall carry the war into Africa by cutting the price of gas." Cabot always had what is often the deciding weapon in a long fight, a long pocketbook, and he was not afraid to use it.

Godfrey still spent a good deal of time with Minnie in Boston in the winter, and in the summer he rented a series of houses in Cohasset, Ponkapogue, and Beverly Farms. On September 24, 1893, they had a daughter, whom they named Eleanor, and on May 1, 1897, another son, who was named Thomas Dudley. With the beginning of the new century, on May 28, 1900, another boy was born and named William Putnam. On December 11, 1901, they welcomed their last child, John Moors Cabot.

But as his business grew, Cabot was more and more away from Boston, and since her miscarriage Minnie no longer went with him. But she wrote him constantly. Her reactions to his business plans were often negative and fearful. "I suppose you are very proud that you think you may be the largest producer of carbon black. . . . Don't buy any more factories. . . . I want you to think a good deal before investing too much out in Pennsylvania—Three thousand dollars is a lot of money. You must remember that we are getting on in years & your boys may not want to carry on the business, after your days are ended & will they be able to sell all of the property for what it is worth? I should dread having them take up the business, as it will keep them away from home too much. . . . I suppose 4,000,000 ft per day is very large but I am no wiser from those figures—when you return you must explain to me how to measure gas wells by the foot."

Many of her letters are lists of complaints, often about her treatment in society and by his family. "My days are not very amusing. People don't come here to call very much & I am not invited any where. Nellie never comes here. . . . I had my annual disappointment last evening at Nellie's—I do not think that Charlie and Nellie treat me right. I do wish that your relatives loved me." But she did not get on any better with her own relatives: "I haven't been in any other row except that Adelaide [her sister] says that I don't know how to bring up my children."

To her children, however, Minnie was a loving and interested mother, although she worried too much about trifles. Godfrey was often away, and when he was home he was autocratic and strict with them. He was not the least of those Boston patricians adept at "surrounding themselves with an ether of potential disapprobation in which they suffered strangers to gasp and perish." It was from Minnie, therefore, that the children received affection.

Like her mother, Minnie was a fearful snob, which made for real and imagined problems to write Godfrey about: "My mother was told that Mr. Storrow [a Boston Brahmin] has just married one of their servants—Mary Agnes Kelly. If it is true isn't it awful. If I should ever die—Don't you ever marry any one in a lower class in society than I have been. . . .

"I do feel more and more lately that you have made a mistake about immigration. [Like most businessmen, Cabot supported the importation of cheap labor, but he also felt that free immigration was a moral obligation of America.] The papers are full of robberies etc. every night now. I was particularly struck by the faces of the people going to and from East Boston on the 24th [Christmas Eve]. They seemed so hard and bad—I think that we have got to do something to prevent these Russian & Polish Jews coming here—Also many of the Italians."

Her most frequent problems concerned her health, her servants, and her constant fear of spending too much money. "I am much better, but I cannot speak out loud yet. I have not been out of the house, as it rains. It seems very strange but if I have an attack

of some thing like the grippe my friend always arrives to go with
it. . . ."

Money was always a source of worry to Minnie, despite the
fact that Godfrey sought to calm her fears. In 1903 he wrote her,
"I have yours of Friday the 9th stating you are the most miserable
woman in the world because the bank has credited no deposits in
your pass-book. . . . you can phone Will Putnam to draw a check
in my name for the amount. . . . There is no need at all to worry
about expenses.

"Your housekeeping expense last year was about $5500 to
$5600 our total expenses with what I gave away & everything
outside of business $8500–$9000. Income 30,000 or so net cash.
Let me know when you need more money."

Minnie had an endless variety of other worries. "I hope that
they will catch the slugger or sluggers soon. The girls are panicked about it. I am indulging in the family cold. . . . I expected
Adelaide and her friends but they did not turn up. I suppose
because I was dead tired & prepared some afternoon tea for them
that they did not come. I do not seem to get the house in order.
Every one is looking for servants. Amelia left today The new one
comes tomorrow afternoon. Why isn't an employment office like a
slave market? . . .

"The devil seems to be in things at home here. All my girls
are going to leave. Helda has had an offer of $7.00 a week in
Boston & no washing. Sophie has made things so very unpleasant
here that I certainly don't want to keep her. In fact I have turned
her off. I have a very strange girl as nursery maid now too. I am
sure I don't know if I can keep her. Nellie has just sent me up a
little Irish girl which I think that I shall engage. She isn't strong
& will be unable to do much work, but I like her looks. . . .

"I have sold 50 shares of N.P. at 120. I must have $200.00.
The bills are always more than I think that they are going to be. I
have engaged Miss Chamberlain. I can't bear it. I always feel that
if I ever have any great amount of pleasure [as she had just had
while away from Boston on a trip to Buffalo with Godfrey], I
must make up for it by being very unhappy afterwards."

Minnie's letters had errors of spelling, syntax, and careless-

ness, which Godfrey sometimes corrected: "Roger is getting to be
quite a wreckless young person. . . . [Charles Copeland's selections from Emerson] were very well chosen and he read beautiful
. . . several people have told me this last week that I was consider
the hardest worked woman in Cambridge." But although Godfrey
was inclined to point out to her that "a theatrical troupe is not
spelt troop," she never mentioned his chronic lack of punctuation
or his misspellings.

Most of Minnie's martyrdom, especially her feeling of pen-
ury, was imaginary and stemmed from her mother's concern about
Mr. Moors' up-and-down fortunes. In his letters Godfrey wrote
again and again, "let me know when you need more money. . . .
There is no need at all to worry about expenses. . . . I shall send
$100 to the Old Colony Trust Co. for you in a few days. Will this
be enough? . . . I enclose $300 will this do and if not how much
more do you want? I continue to think that you need someone to
help you & you need not worry about the expense. You would
better give a few lunch parties and get out and see your friends
and brighten up."

Not that Godfrey did not insist upon thrift. "Please mail my
shaving brush to % Greens Hotel, Phila Pa. One 2¢ stamp will
bring it. . . . One of the small buttons has come off the front of
my trousers. I mean the kind of a button that lives in a pigeon
hole & never shows its head when it is on duty. I wish you would
send one with a needle of thread to % Reynolds House Kittanning
with your next letter although I shall probably get one meanwhile." He could become livid over a lost pair of shoelaces or
whatever else seemed to him wasteful to the slightest degree.
Regardless of the service received, he never tipped more than a
dime.

On those rare occasions when Minnie decided on expensive
furniture or rugs, she would in the early years receive long
preachments from Godfrey: "I like the house first-rate that way
and do not wish to spend hard-earned money that I might give
away or use in buying factories, gas-wells or other bric-a-brac
that I can use, in crowding the house with things that we do not
need, simply to give your female friends a chance to say 'my isn't

that nice' when they come to call & then go home and pester their husbands to buy something equally useless. . . . I do not say these things in a spirit of complaint or criticism but in the spirit of cheerfulness & contentment that you may know how utterly satisfied I am & wish you to be with the simplicity & rational comfort which has hitherto been our aim. I do not in the least covet, far rather eschew, the luxury and extreme elegance which my brothers, or rather their wives, affect."

With rare exceptions, however, Minnie was extraordinarily thrifty; she not only dressed herself and her children as cheaply as she possibly could, but she constantly shopped for bargains, however odd or unusable. Her relatives and friends and even her children waited with amusement or horror each year to see what bargain Minnie would send for a birthday or Christmas gift. Her letters were often written on the very cheapest ruled paper, the unused part torn off for later use; they prompted even the thrifty Godfrey to write her, "Please eschew the pernicious habit of trying to crowd too much on a sheet of paper."

She was less than delighted when Godfrey wrote her about giving money away. "I think I can have cast iron signs made for almost the whole of Kittanning for about $50–$100 and they will be a great boon to the town. I find that my two fountains & horse troughs are an incalculable benefit in almost constant use by horse & man in hot weather & used every day of the year. The two hundred trees I gave them are also greatly appreciated." Minnie may have understood from another letter a week later that Godfrey's gifts were not always entirely altruistic. "It is a great satisfaction in the coming fight to know that the community is almost a unit in my favor." Godfrey was not displeased to advise his wife, "People are running after me here day and night to sell or lease gas & oil property etc. etc. When I am here I come pretty near being 'It.' . . . I am looking forward greedily to seeing you soon again although I enjoy the strenuous work & the feeling that I am becoming a rapidly increasing power in this community. Newark, Palestine, Reedy are clamoring for me to bring them gas and it is more and more generally known that I give the best gas service in this valley outside of Parkersburg."

He was particularly proud of his reputation as a great walker. "You could not throw a stick at a dog in Butler County without hitting three men that know me as the sine qua non, non plus ultra professional tramp." Godfrey enjoyed pointing out the physical hardships and his ability to withstand them; but he very rarely complained about problems such as the Little Kenawha River's freezing early or drying up in the summer, which stopped his shipping out black. He rather put a happy face on whatever he wrote Minnie. "Rain Rain blessed rain today. Not yet enough to open the river but some relief to the thirsty land."

Most of Godfrey's operations in West Virginia were at Grantsville in Calhoun County. Grantsville had no railroad and could only be reached by a boat trip up the Little Kenawha River if it was navigable. Otherwise Godfrey would walk the twenty-five miles from Creston, where the railroad ended, sometimes sending his suitcase by buggy. He always wore city clothes, never the work or camping clothes his sons later wore and his employees preferred.

Cabot was immensely proud of his reputation all through that country as a prodigious walker. The first time he had arrived in Grantsville, he had been walking and leading a worn-out horse, but as the years went by, the story spread that he had been carrying the horse.

He also loved to tell the story of having come upon a wagon load of pipe stuck in a mudhole. Deciding to play the Good Samaritan, he had helped the teamster pull the wagon out and then asked who the pipe was for, to be told, "Oh that goddam Boston millionaire, Godfrey Cabot."

And he always insisted on having clean white linen and a clean white starched collar every day, even when he was to spend the day wading in mud. This was no mean trick in a village which did not see its first bathtub until 1916, when one was proudly installed on the front porch of the local boarding house. The first inside plumbing came only in 1923.

Godfrey was fanatic about cleanliness, carrying with him all over the world a large sponge and taking a cold sponge bath whenever there was no tub. He even kept his hands clean, a minor miracle in an industry which today still blackens everything—grass, trees, and cattle—for miles around one of its channel-black plants. The problem of cleanliness was further aggravated by Cabot's insistence on walking not only crosscountry to check personally his miles of gas pipelines, but even on the roads, which for months on end were nothing but deep rivers of mud because of the frequent rains and the clay soil, which was constantly being churned by horse- or ox-drawn wagonloads of pipe and oil-well-drilling equipment. His tall proud figure in Boston Brahmin clothes, striding purposefully ahead, became a living legend among the farmers of West Virginia, as did the thrift of this man with only one suit who had to go to bed when it was being cleaned.

Walking through the back country to buy gas acreage or to visit wells he owned, Godfrey found that many of the people in West Virginia lived in hovels with dirt floors. They often had no shoes, even in winter, and both men and women smoked corncob pipes and lived on moonshine whiskey, sour-belly, and hominy. Sour-belly was pork, left sitting on the table between meals, accessible to flies, and cooked over and over again. Hominy was corn which had been treated with lye. There were often neither sheets nor blankets, only quilts on the beds which were shared by two or three occupants, who had often not bathed for months, and not infrequently the beds were infested with lice, fleas, and bedbugs. Occasionally Cabot could get fresh eggs or freshly baked bread, though it was not made with white flour, which had to be bought at a store, but rather with cornmeal. Even the stoic Godfrey was always delighted to return to the comparative luxury of a hotel.

But he loved this country and its mountains as no other in the world, and particularly the dogwood and redbud that bloomed every spring. Only occasionally did he allow himself the luxury of complaining. "I have been annoyed by varicose veins for the last four or five days but think it will soon pass off. . . . Tomorrow I must rise before dawn to go up the Little Kenawha river to spend the rest of the week. I feel like a school boy going to be whipped. . . . I do long for the delicious air of Beverly Farms & the sound of the many voiced ocean."

Minnie's letters, however, contained a never ending list of complaints. "Why shouldn't we come in for a share of Mrs. Paine's money? $200,000.00 to be given to the poor in our church. Did you ever hear of anything so crazy. We have hardly a poor person in the church. . . . I have turned off all the maids. . . . It is my birthday. I don't suppose any one will remember it. . . .

"I think that I shall take a sort of a German governess. I shall have to pay her five dollars a week & I don't think that she will do her own washing. I am tired of these cheap nursery girls such as Lizzie. I am sorry but I think Lizzie is likely to go right to the bad unless she can find a good place & yet I know that it isn't right towards myself & the children to keep her. . . . I wish I could have travelled more before I was married. I hope some day I shall be able to go off with you some where. . . .

"My maids here keep kicking. There is no use talking. We might as well have a chore man & be done with. The cook refuses to bring up the coal, Rose the wood. I feel sure the governess will not black Wm's shoes. I black Jackie's when he doesn't himself & my own Rose refuses to beat the rugs & so on. Every body else has a man so we have got to, that is the long and short of it. I know how fine it is to give away money to this and that thing & I know I feel selfish but I don't think there is a person in Massachusetts that needs money more than I. I have worked hard to save your money so far, but there is no use. I cannot go on any longer this way. I am tired out and weary. A little more would make me insane."

Godfrey tried to resolve Minnie's problems by letter. "If you wish you may give $6 or $7 a week for a cook but try to get value for your money. . . . I think you had better keep three girls this winter & get the best that money will hire. . . . I have yrs Wednesday with a lot of bills which I do not know about & therefore return. . . . Do you need some more money or why is it you send these bills to me. You worry yourself to much about trifles. I was out yesterday in a stiff breeze 19° below zero today it is 24° below zero & I have cut off most of my moustache as it gets very icy & uncomfortable. Don't worry. The first duty of men and women is to be cheerful. . . .

"You must settle the wages question yourself. $69 a month is of course a colossal sum but as my *net* income per day is nearly three times that we can probably still keep out of the poor house by rigid economy in other matters. I thoroughly believe in paying good wages & having good girls & if you like the girls I would not for an instant hesitate to pay them what was needful to keep them & I would not worry about it. . . . I wish you at all times to have money in the bank and to pay your bills promptly but do not care to have you carry a needlessly large balance in the bank on which we should lose interest as I am borrowing money at 5½%. . . .

"I think it is a needless expense to try to warm the whole house & the only way to avoid prodigious fuel bills is to go down cellar to or three times a day yourself & see that the drafts are right & if you need to open the cellar door I think it is enough to warm the rooms you actually use & not try to warm the hall & the front parlor nor the bedrooms. . . . There is no need of storm windows on the children's bathroom. I wish my children to grow up hardy."

Godfrey's attempts to solve Minnie's problems when he was away prompted a bit of advice from Nellie: "Don't telegraph Minnie any more instructions, dear old man. With children, the aspect of affairs changes so rapidly that when your advice arrives the emergency is over and Minnie has a worried & confused feeling that she ought to obey you in spite of her better judgement."

Despite his sister's good advice, Cabot continued to try to answer Minnie's flood of complaints. "I do not advise you to keep that ring on your finger if it is uncomfortable. Sentiment is a most excellent thing but it should not override common sense. . . . It is well to be a little careful what you write on postal cards and if you wish to criticise your husband's hotel on a postal card at least wait until he leaves it. . . .

"[In reply to Minnie's criticism of the man marrying his servant] I think probably Charlie Storrow knows what is best for him better than you do. A man needs a woman. It is the law of nature and it is better that he should have a wife than that he should indulge promiscuously which is the usual alternative. Yet the man who marries again is more often & openly criticised than the other. 'Judge not that you be not judged for with what measure ye mete it shall be meted unto you again.' Let us all strive to do our own duty and apply a much more severe test to our own shortcomings than to those of others. Charlie Storrow was a tender and devoted husband to a wife who was for many years a pitiful burden to him. I most ardently wish him joy in his new relation. . . .

"You are too fond of throwing stones my darling. Let us warmly wish every joy to Charlie Storrow and his wife. Let us reserve our censure for those men who seek the pleasures of sexual indulgence & yet are unwilling to bear the burdens and deprivations of matrimony."

In answer to Minnie's horror of immigrants, Godfrey wrote, "The older I grow the more I feel that abstract right in human affairs embodies the greatest practical wisdom as well as the most important moral considerations and my human sympathies are not confined to America. 'Homo sum et nihil humanum a me alienum puto.' Could it be shown that it was a bad thing for this country to permit this immigration it would still be needful to prove that it was a bad thing for the human race considered as a whole. It is however impossible to show that this human stream that has fed the bone and sinew of this land & been since time immemorial the very life blood by which this community has grown & thriven & demonstrated to mankind the magnificient success of free institutions has all of a sudden become poisoned & must be further filtered to avoid ruin and disaster."

In connection with the marriage of Minnie's sister, Godfrey wrote, "Now my dear love I want you to put a bridle not only on your tongue but also on your thoughts & strive to think no harm of Adelaide. If you deny yourself the luxury of sneering thoughts you will avoid sneering remarks. Put the best face you can on the whole business as if Adelaide were your daughter instead of your sister, bearing in mind that so far as the marriage relation is concerned nineteen years more experience places you almost in loco parentis and the day may shortly come in which you will be all the mother she has.

"Whatever Mr. Browns good qualities may be and I hope & *think* he is a good fellow & will make a loving faithful unselfish husband, it seems to be the general opinion that she will have to practise careful economy & forego many of the luxuries to which she has been accustomed & it will be your part so far as in you lies to make this easy for her not to needlessly refer to those things in which you may seem more fortunate than she and encourage her to face with absolute determination the new duties for which 20 years of comparative idleness have not been the best preparation & perform all the duties of a wife with entire devotion & concentration of purpose.

"Never speak slurringly of her husband or even think ill of him if you can help it. As for his kissing your mother I think it was rather nice of him. That is simply country manners which are often nicer than city manners and to me there is something pathetic in his efforts at conciliation so sneeringly referred to by you. Soften your heart my dear one & try to love all mankind whatever their faults & frailties not merely your husband and children. Thus you will be able to look without envy at the greater luxury of others so often, nay usually a great and growing injury to them even unto the third and fourth generation and, in searching your heart for nice things to say and think of, and for others, will find the best antidote for the blues that has yet been discovered. . . .

"I question whether George Eliot is good reading for you especially when I am away. She is a morbid introspective sort of writer & neither the world nor individual character does itself justice if turned inside out to look at it. Therefore shun that pet vice of yours and of George Eliots introspection. Do not be forever plucking your plants up by the roots to see if they are growing right & applying to yourself mentally & morally a stomach pump as it were to see if the mental & moral digestive functions are normal."

Godfrey was much concerned with what his wife should or should not read or see. "I do not think Tolstoi's books are very wholesome reading for you. . . . I wish you did not like Tristan & Isolde. It stinks to heaven with moral decay and fetid sentimental-

ity and fosters morbid self-pity and a weak indulgence in lacka-
daisical nerveless brooding." He had no fear, however, of being
corrupted himself.

"I have been reading that horrid book of Tolstoi's 'The
Kreutzer Sonata.' With all his genius his vivid power of description & his insight in certain directions he was a moral pervert
oscillating between bestial licentiousness on the one hand and a
gloomy and morbid asceticism on the other: hopelessly handicapped by a lack of imagination a narrowness of outlook which
made it impossible for him to realize the possibility of a sane and
normal life of a constant and unvarying flame of unselfish love
between man and wife, a relation in which the controlling motive
would be the common interest in the children & in the household;
mutual service and devotion the everyday occupation and under-
lying impulse."

Cabot's friend Will Putnam suggested the possibility of
other points of view on the subject. "Has Joe Lee written to you
since he came back. He is full of Tolstoi who he visited in the
centre of Russia and staid with for several days   He found him
very simple and childlike, full of enthusiasm and speaking of
improvements in his style & manner of writing which he purposes,
as if he were no nearer to thirty than he is to sixty. He says he has
always written carefully, pruning and cutting out from his manuscript and carefully revising it. But now he thinks this was a
mistake to be avoided in future and says he shall write straight on
just as ideas come to him & let it be printed without change. Then
people will see his thoughts as he thought them and those who care
for the ideas will not be troubled by any lack of arrangement."

Even Minnie was inclined, from time to time, to question her
husband's literary censorship. "I started to read today one of
Tolstoi's books, 'My Confessions.' I suppose that you will think
that I am very naughty. The literature in this house is very
scarce—that is why I did it."

But Cabot's literary obiter dicta continued nevertheless. "I
have been reading Guilderoy today by Ouida & may I be hanged
if I ever wish to see one of her books again for if ever authoress
served up to the public a dish of moral carrion it is one. She

assails the marriage relation on the ground that no man is faithful, it is against nature. She might as well arraign the laws of property on the score that all men are thieves. I could not help contrasting Lord Guilderoy, an absolutely worthless profligate marrying at a moments caprice then eagre to get away from his young & beautiful wife on all possible occasions with myself half sick with longing to return to your arms."

Considering their Victorian birthdates and Puritan upbringing, Godfrey and Minnie Cabot's early correspondence, full of expressions of intimate affection and desire, was extraordinary. Their desire for one another was private and well hidden—indeed, their children believed that Minnie was always appalled by intimacy.

With few exceptions, Godfrey began his letters "Dear Wife," and closed them "You lover, Godfrey L. Cabot." But in the letters themselves, he was less formal. "I lay awake longing for you last night. . . . I do long for you with an agony of desire my sweet heart. . . . It is raining again today & I am much bored with myself sitting here writing letters when I want to be speeding toward your arms (& your bed). . . . I do long for you and your soft arms this very moment. . . . I dreamt of you last night, such a naughty dream. . . . I have been dreaming of you a great deal then wake up & you are not there at my side where you belong. How I long to hold you in my arms again while you fall asleep on my bosom. . . . I was tormented with dreams about you last night. I was hunting for you & could not find you how I did long for you."

In fact, so strong were Godfrey's desire and his dreams that they could even lead him to write a letter with a naughty story in it. "Night before last I had a whimsical dream, I dreamt I was dining in mixed company and the following story was told of a young doctor in New York. He was asked if his practice did not lie chiefly in a very disreputable quarter of the city. Alas yes, I fear it is no idle dream that my services were required last night in an apartment where a young woman sat at a piano playing soulful melody with her right hand while [in] her left hand she held a pickled fish which she was eating; at which somebody related the following bon mot of your brother John's. Being asked if he recollected a certain place that he passed in the night on his return from San Francisco. 'Oh yes that is the station where all the ladies wake up to see if their nighties and hairpins are still clean.' "

Minnie's letters usually began "My darling husband" and ended "Your affectionate wife, Maria M. Cabot," but they too contained intimate expressions of affection. "Ich war allein gestern nacht. * The first night that I haven't had the dearest arms in the world about my neck for nearly ten months. . . . I miss you more and more each day my darling. I haven't had a letter for three days now. I should like to feel your great strong arms about me. . . . Last night I had such an awful dream—I dreamt that you were dead & I can't get it out of my head today. You will take care of yourself my dear won't you? . . . Godfrey darling how I wish that you could fold me in your arms. I feel as if I could hardly wait for you to return. I never missed you so much in my life as I have on this trip."

But after the first years of her married life, and increasingly after the unexpected birth of their last child in 1901, Minnie apparently grew less fond of intimacy. When her daughter Eleanor married, Minnie told her that she and Godfrey had never seen one another unclothed except by mistake. She gave her daughter the impression that intimacy was horrid, that when Godfrey came home from his trips he immediately took her to bed without waiting for dinner, and that although a woman must endure such attentions, she most certainly should not and did not enjoy them.

Godfrey's letters reflected his need for intimacy and affection and implied that they could be found elsewhere if not at home and that other women found him desirable if Minnie did not. "I understand Ed Graff has been neglecting his business for one or two years back travelling about with a woman named Wolf. (As he is in the wool business perhaps she wears sheep's clothing.) It looks as if I may be detained here [Kittanning, Pennsylvania,

* "I was alone last night."

May 31, 1895] till July & a wild idea has come into my head that perhaps my dear wife might like to come out here for a week or two to cosset me? . . .

"I think this [Oil City, Pennsylvania, February 14, 1896] is about the toughest place I ever was in. Last night as I was going to my room one of the waitresses here seized me by the arm and tried to strike up an acquaintance. I had to tell her twice very sharply that I had no use for her and wanted no fooling before she cleared out. . . .

". . . Platonic relations are a delusion and a snare for people whose hearts are mummified. . . . I do wish you were here [Pittsburgh, February 2, 1905] this very minute to cuddle and cosset. . . . Last night [September 7, 1913, Parkersburg, West Virginia] was excessively hot & I wanted you & could not sleep. . . . Louisville [April 9, 1916] seems to have three great industries whiskey, tobacco, prostitution. The third industry is on a more liberal basis than other institutions down south, *no color line*. I received urgent invitations both from white and black."

From 1893 to 1917 Cabot built his fortune, raised his family, and grew. His Journal in these twenty-four years reflected the fullness of his life, his adherence to duty, and the nurturing of his prejudices.

In 1899, the first year in which he produced over a million pounds of black, he drilled his first well in West Virginia, the Mathews No. 1, which was still producing gas in 1967. This event signaled the gradual movement of the biggest part of his business from Pennsylvania to West Virginia—a move, as he wrote Minnie, he now wished he had made years earlier. He bought all the acreage he could get in Wirt, Wood, Jackson, and Calhoun counties. After 1900 he paid an average of $1.50 an acre, and before the outbreak of World War I he had bought well over a hundred thousand acres. In addition to acquiring acreage he continued making contracts to buy millions of cubic feet of gas at a cent to a cent and a half per thousand cubic feet.

In the biographical sketch which he submitted to *The National Cyclopaedia of American Biography* in 1909 Godfrey pointed out that "in 1899 he built the Grantsville Carbon Works, which is considered the largest factory in the world employed in making carbon black. . . . Carbon black is a species of lamp black . . . and is the soot of natural gas. It is the most important basis for black printing ink, and is also largely used for giving a better color to stove polish; in fact, it is used wherever a strong, insoluble black pigment is required. It is manufactured by burning flames of natural gas beneath an iron surface, from which the black is automatically scraped and then automatically delivered to conveyers, which carry it to a bolt, where it is bolted, elevated and packed. All machinery at the Cabot works, excepting the packer, is automatic. There are over 100 large horizontal cast-iron plates for this purpose, twenty-four feet in diameter, under each of which revolve a system of pipes, a black box and scraper, and the other apparatus necessary to deposit, remove and deliver the black into a conveyer. This process is different from that in use in any other factory. The Grantsville factory has a capacity of 8,000 pounds a day, and requires upwards of 8,000,000 cubic feet of gas to supply it. It is run day and night from year's end to year's end, and is the nucleus of a system of natural gas mains over forty miles in extent. . . . The producing end of the business comprises about ninety gas and oil wells, about 120 miles of gas-mains."

Cabot tried various additional new businesses, all based on cheap gas. If they were not profitable, he ruthlessly closed them without regard to his pride. In 1904 in Saxonburg, Pennsylvania, he built a bronze factory which he closed after two years.

Foreseeing the future need for liquefied gas, he tried to bottle gas, but he was too far ahead of the demand and had not enough technological knowledge. He even predicted that someday coal, like gas, would be transported by pipeline, as turned out to be the case many years later.

His Journal reflected his continuing competitiveness. "Wednesday, Aug 8 [1894]. Beat Charley Wheelright in the finals of the tennis tournament at Cohasset. I played the best tennis I ever played in my life. . . . Monday, Aug 19 [1895]. I stopped a runaway horse last Saturday. I ran so fast to head him off that I feel a little stiff after it. A short sprint stiffens me up more than a 50 mile bicycle ride or a days tennis. . . . Tuesday, August 27 [1895] . . . I took a day off for the first time since my honeymoon and played 14 sets of tennis beating John 5 sets and C. Brocker 1 set (both giving 15) and Matt Luce 1 set. F. four sets and Arthur 2 out of three winning 13 sets out of the 14. . . . Friday, Jan 28, [1898] Played chess with Southerd the Harvard champion today and we each took a game. . . . I stopped a run away horse on Huron Ave yesterday ev'g."

When Godfrey tried to buy too cheap and missed getting what he wanted, he dutifully noted the failure in the Journal along with his successes. "I stopped by Nolens factory that cost $20,000 was sold for $600. I tried $550. . . .

"Just before I left the house this morning an automobile came past manned by two men standing upright and one of them wearing huge goggles and wind shield on his face. The apparation passed with the momentum and speed of a locomotive and carried with it a cloud of dust 15 ft high that completely concealed it from behind and lingered for half a mile in the rear. . . . It seems that the automobile I saw yesterday was owned and driven by Wm. K. Vanderbilt and reached a speed of 65 m an hour on Blue Hill Ave making the trip from Newport to Boston and back in 4 hours."

Cabot's competitors continued to try to bring him into a trust, but he continued to refuse to join on any formal or permanent basis. ". . . had further interviews with B. and S. Levey Ault and Murdock reiterating my determination not to sell or lease but offering to make a friendly arrangement as to prices, subject however to readjustment from time to time. This was not very favorably received but when they find they can do no better I think they will come to terms. Ownership of my business would enable them to swing the whip over the world and I believe they would give me twice the value but it is a question of principle with me I am willing to give them the legitimate advantage of a large buyer but not to give them an absolute monopoly and sacrifice my agents and outside customers." On October 22, 1906, he confided in a letter to Minnie, "Prices are better but this is only a matter

Dr. Samuel Cabot

annah Lowell Jackson Cabot

Godfrey as a Harvard undergraduate

Engaged

In the role of a maid, Hasty Pudding show

Maria Buckminster Moors Cabot, shortly after marriage to Godfrey in 1890 (In those days, only married women wore bonnets.)

Godfrey Cabot, rising industrialist, about 1900

Above: *Maria (Minnie) Cabot with three of her children, Eleanor, Thomas Dudley and James Jackson, about 1897* Below: *With Tom, Jim and John Moors (Jack) in 1912*

Godfrey Cabot in his personal Burgess-Dunn seaplane, The Lark

In flying gear, 1916

Lieutenant Cabot in Naval Reserve Flying Corps during World War I

Godfrey Cabot in Texas during the late 1930s, shown with two employees—
Edmund Billings, first head of sales, and Charles Wooley

Standing near his first produc
ing gas well (drilled in 189
West Virginia) about 194

Godfrey Cabot at age 97 in Boston

Members of the Cabot family on the occasion of Godfrey's 100th birthday
(The bust of Dr. Samuel Cabot in background was done by Daniel French.)

of agreement & doubtful whether the improvement will be permanent." (When Godfrey put profit reports or other information he
wanted to keep secret in his Journal, he cometimes wrote in German.)

Godfrey not only helped the villages and towns where he did
business, but also he not infrequently helped individuals when he
had thoroughly satisfied himself that they deserved it. "I heard
tonight of a young man [Fred Brook] crippled ugly deformed,
suffering from small-pox. After going without food for 24 hours
he left his house to obtain food and in his absence they burned his
house with all his belonging leaving him absolutely destitute unable to obtain shelter sick and suffering. . . . Did not sleep very
well last night and before breakfast this A.M. issued a notice that
I would pay $200 to whomever would take care of Fred Brook and
nurse him back to health. Biekel went with this notice to Brooks-
ville and immediately the woods were full of people that wanted to
take care of him."

He greatly admired the benefactions of Andrew Carnegie.
"Went to Unitarian church in A.M. and to an organ recital at
the Carnegie Library at Schenley Park [in Pittsburgh]. Truly
the people in the U.S. owe an incalculable debt to this public
spirited man who has filled the country with libraries and other
tangible evidence of his more than princely generosity."

Cabot cared individually for some of his employees when he
learned of their problems, but like Carnegie, he had less feeling for
his employees as a group, paying them as little and working them
as long as possible and becoming outraged at any notion that they
had a right to strike for better conditions. "There was a strike at
the works today but Smith rose equal to the occasion and they
were only shut down a few hours."

However, in 1902 he wrote Minnie, "I do think Roosevelt
deserves great credit for the judgment, temper, & tact with which
he had brought the coal strike to an end." Cabot greatly admired
and was in many ways not unlike the man Mark Hanna had called
"that damned cowboy."

Busy as he was making money, Godfrey interested himself in
politics as well. In 1896 he made a $10 contribution to the Demo-

crats, but he voted for McKinley, "the advance agent of prosperity," rather than for Bryan. He evidently believed, as have other businessmen before and since his time, that it was not inadvisable to support both parties. Cabot refused to support Woodrow Wilson, both because he felt Wilson's private life to be immoral and because he felt the President should already have brought America into the war on the side of the Allies. In October 1916 he wrote Minnie, "I am in the thick of the fight to elect Hughes."

Godfrey loved a fight, like God's horse in Job: "He paweth in the valley, and rejoiceth in his strength. . . . He swalloweth the ground with fierceness and rage. . . . He saith among the trumpets, Ha, ha! and he smelleth the battle afar off." But he hated to lose. He wrote Minnie about the great number of law suits in which his litigious and self-righteous nature involved him. "The jury brought in a most preposterous verdict against me $135 & costs in the trespass case & I have been feeling very sore over it all day."

By his own appraisal Cabot was a first-rate lawyer. "My lawyers floundered hopelessly through the forenoon & then we went down stairs. My chief attorney thought the judge intended to throw us down. I said not at all he merely wants us to do our work & not try to make him do it. I then sat down & put the case in shape myself. After dinner I presented it in about ten minutes called one witness & satisfied both judge and prosecuting attorney of the correctness of our contention. The court then granted us substantial relief.

"I am waiting and watching & planning & writing letters & chafing that I should be kept here doing routine business that I might as well or better do at home & yet I dare not go away for fear I might miss some chance. At the battle of Chickamauga, the only officer that brought material assistance to Gen Thomas was Gen Granger who laid his ear to the ground & located the heaviest cannonading & then led his troups thither. Well that is what I have done & right here is the heaviest cannonading the big important matters that no one can judge but myself & on which thousands may hang & I must stick right here till this business is finished. . . . With so many interests & so much happening all the time it is not always easy to know where the heaviest cannonading really is. . . .

". . . Where there is a will there is a way & can't is a word I have very little use for in my business except as a polite way of saying will not. . . .

"It is a curious fact that when I start out on one of these trips I very frequently fail in accomplishing the specific purpose with which I started but always accomplish a lot of other things that I had not in view.

"I do not think I shall be away more but less after this year [1899]. I shall try to get a pretty efficient man at this end [Pennsylvania] even if I have to pay a pretty high price for him. I do not think it is good for you and me to be separated so much and it is certainly not fun for me. It tends to work me deeper and deeper into the rut of business & withdraw me too much from you & from the cultivated world in which we are at home. Some diversity is a good thing but I think I am getting too much into the sordid push. . . . For you, on the other hand it would be a wholesome experience to see more of the lower crust & see how comfortable & happy people may be even in what you would regard as abject squalor. It would diminish the morbid & foolish dread you have of poverty for yourself & your children."

Cabot sometimes admitted frankly to Minnie when he was wrong or when business went otherwise than he had predicted or could understand. "Business is booming. The growth of the world's consumption of carbon black is a perpetually recurring miracle to me." Not unlike other wives, Minnie wrote Godfrey, "I like to hear about your business, but I should also like to hear more about you yourself."

Godfrey was not always frank about his purposes in business, as when he wrote in 1912, "I am taking steps toward getting franchises in this country with a view to putting gas in here." Although sometimes Cabot offered to go into the utility business to render service and make money, in this case he was merely threatening to go into the utility business so that Standard Oil would buy out his acreage and thereby preclude his competition.

Not unlike his ancestors, Cabot was quick to see money-making opportunities presented by war. In 1915 he wrote Minnie, "About this time next year it will probably be possible to buy English consols or French rentes [government securities] very low, not with the idea of a permanent investment but with the idea of selling them out at an advance in five or ten years."

By 1912 Godfrey had made a deal with the Standard Oil, leasing to their subsidiary, the Hope Natural Gas Company, at a rental of a dollar per acre per year tens of thousands of acres that he had bought for a dollar an acre. In addition to renting this acreage, he was selling them millions of cubic feet of gas at ten cents per thousand cubic feet for which he had paid a cent or a cent and a half. He had, therefore, an enormous income, far beyond anything he had ever dreamed of—so great that it financed all Cabot's tremendous expansion after World War I without any need for bank borrowing.

His letters to Minnie began to show that at last he felt rich. "I want you to buy yourself a HANDSOME cloak or coat suitable to wear at the opera. I am mortified every time we go to the opera because your cloak is not fit for such an occasion."

In 1914 he wrote her, "I have ordered violets to be sent you on the 21st as an earnest of a more substantial birthday present in the shape of another automobile later on. . . . Eleanor tells me you have your eye on a $2300 Detroit electric Limousine. . . . I think you will better buy it at once and send the bill to me."

But nothing could calm Minnie's fears of being poor and especially of being cheated. In 1916 Godfrey wrote her, "Answering your lugubrious letter not dated. It is silly to talk of being poor & eat 25¢ lunches and salt down from $5000 to $20,000 in a year. People know we are rich & subject us to annoyances to which all rich people are subjected. We can't expect to have the laws of human nature suspended for our benefit.

"If you are held up ten times a day I am held up twenty & Carnegie two thousand. Why worry? Meet the world with a smiling face & grow a thicker skin.

"A thick skin helps you to turn away the unworthy with an even voice and a smiling face, & not worry at what false things people may say against one."

In the years that followed, Canutelike he tried to calm her fears. "I am glad you are having a good time in New York & hope you will buy yourself an ample supply of nice clothes and a nice hat for Easter. . . . Mrs. Schuster ought to charge more for taking care of William. I am writing to tell her so. . . .

"I enclose $1000 toward the $5000 you are trying to raise. What is it for? . . .

"I hope you have got a handsome rug. Have you yet seen any tapestry you like? I am in favor of silk or cotton hangings. Woolen tapestry breeds moths. . . . You would better get yourself the nice furs you saw the other day. . . .

"Would you like me to put up $50,000 a year for the Symphony Orchestra on condition that I shall run it as Henry Higginson did which should really mean that you should run it? At the present time we could well afford it and if hard times come we could drop it. . . . My income last year was over $500,000 so you need not worry about expense."

CHAPTER IX

Paterfamilias

Pietas fundamentum est omnium virtutum. [The dutiful-
ness of children is the foundation of all virtue.]   CICERO, *Pro
Cnoeo Plancio,* Ch. xii, sec. 29

Even a child is known by his doings.   Proverbs xx: 11

He that spareth his rod hateth his son.   Proverbs xiii: 24

Most of the persons whom I see in my own house I see
across a gulf.   EMERSON, *Journals,* Vol. V, 324

Godfrey's upbringing having been Puritan, it was not unnatural
that he should raise his children with strict discipline, a demand
for absolute and immediate obedience, and a great concern for
duty. His letters to Minnie reflect this point of view. "Please
discourage the family from talking too much about Jim [aged 4]
in his presence & above all never show off any of his accomplishments. . . . I wish people would not buy so many things for Jim. I
do not think it is at all good for him. Do you give him a lesson
every day? I wish you would make a point of giving him a lesson
for fifteen minutes every day . . . is Jim learning to be obedient
polite and fearlessly & accurately truthful . . . ? . . . When Jim
is rough he had better be locked up in a dark closet or eat bread &
water for his next meal."

Being the oldest child, Jim was the most disciplined, and as he felt himself bullied throughout his childhood, he bullied his younger brothers and sister unmercifully. He regularly teased his brother Tom until he became like a cornered wild animal, and even his mother and sister were not exempt from his desire for revenge. Minnie wrote Godfrey, "Yesterday Jim locked Eleanor & me into the nursery, & I was afraid that we should have to have a lock smith to let us out, but I remembered that the cellar door key unlocked the nursery hall door so we came out safely. . . .

"Eleanor made a discovery yesterday. She looked at the baby's teapot, & said, Jim has one of those, but I haven't. I said nothing. . . . Jim does not seem well. . . . I had to go & see what was the matter with him two or three times last night. Nightmares I think."

Cabot was more often concerned with his children's duties than with their nightmares. "I think the scions of old families usually inherit talent but too often it lies dormant or is perverted to trivialities such as dress & polite conversation which are good things in themselves but should not monopolize our energy." When in 1898 Cabot built a new house for his family at 16 Highland Street in Cambridge, he refused to corrupt them with many of the luxuries Minnie wanted, such as electric lighting. Repeated pleas by Minnie, citing advantages of health, cleanliness, and safety, were to no avail. "With regard to electricity you will need matches for your fires & electricity introduces an entirely new element of danger so far as safety is concerned. . . . Gas with an incandescent burner makes nothing like as much heat as in the ordinary way & consumes much less air in proportion. I think it produces almost as much light in proportion to the heat as electricity." This letter was written from Copenhagen, where Godfrey was on a four-month trip which he characterized as a business trip but on which he did no substantial business. It had enabled him to be away when most of the house-building problems arose. The new house cost $16,000 including the lot; frame covered with gray shingles, it was of no architectural distinction.

After 1900 Godfrey had greater success in making Minnie come with him on his travels. In 1901 he took her to Cuba and Puerto Rico, in 1908 to Mexico, in 1909 to Egypt, and thereafter on most of his trips abroad, though not on his business trips in America.

Godfrey wrote often to Minnie discouraging her from purchasing new furniture and rugs for the new house, preferring to keep all the money he could in order to buy gas acreage and build carbon-black plants. "Don't worry because the house does not look furnished. I built that house to live in not to look at and I built it rather larger than our present needs. As you actually need a thing buy it but remember that every thing you buy is another thing to be looked after kept clean & in repair, an addition to your care & buy things that are not easily damaged for I wish the children to have their fun too & not be forever on tenterhook lest they should break something.

"The quintessence of style elegance and comfort can only be achieved at the expense of far more important considerations, among others real usefulness.

"This I leave to others without a pang of envy or regret. For myself and my children I choose, so far as the choice lies with me, the ardor of the combat, an active strenuous tenacious struggle not for existence merely, much less for pleasure & luxury & excellence in the outward display so dear to the vulgar & to the worldly but an effort for the higher achievement within their reach."

Periodically Cabot would urge his wife to attend church when he was away and to make the children attend. When he was home, he always took the children to church, insisting that they sit in the first pew. He was somehow able to ask each child a different question about the sermon even though he had appeared to sleep through it.

"I believe that there is a beneficent Intelligence that we call God & whose outward manifestation is the Universe, that this benign power has placed us here, not simply that we may amass wealth, still less that we should be in supine luxury on a bed of roses, but that we should build up character which we may rationally hope is of the things eternal that we may carry with us into another and a better world. All other things are but accessories to this deep purpose. How futile & foolish is it then for us to seek to dodge for ourselves & our descendents the shafts of wisdom that trial effort & adversity shoot into our souls and evade the necessity for strenuous & painful effort by which alone the sinews of intellect and character are developed.

". . . I am glad you have been to church & I wish you could contrive to go more. I sometimes think we lead a pretty heathenish life. I think to hear a good service and sermon is to the soul what a good bath is to the body it seems to rest you and open the spiritual pores & stimulate the moral nature. I think the present tendency among our circle is to let children follow their own bent altogether too much & escape wholesome discipline. The result is mental & moral flabbiness and inefficiency."

On December 5, 1899, Cabot noted in his Journal, "Some months ago little Tom [aged two and a half] doubtless noticing that the other children said their prayers every night begged to be allowed to do so too and has done so ever since. Twice within the last month it has happened that his mother has been prevented from hearing him and on each occasion he has waked up out of a sound sleep within ten minutes after his mother has gone to bed and asked to say his prayers to her. This strikes me as a very forcible instance of unconscious cerebration."

When he was sixty-nine years old, Tom Cabot had great difficulty remembering any word of encouragement or kindness he had ever received from his father, "except once when I was a kid, I had nightmares, terrible nightmares of chimeras and I used to wake up screaming and my father would come and hold my hand and recite psalms to me. He had an amazing memory and knew many psalms and hymns by heart and fairytales." Tom Cabot had no difficulty remembering other things from his childhood, however, such as being whipped for objecting to scum on his cocoa, and he remembered walking to and from school with his shoes in his hand to save shoe leather.

Jim Cabot continued small for his age and very shy. By way of remedy his father wrote him a few weeks after his tenth birthday: "I am sorry to hear that you are a cry-baby at school and afraid of the other boys. If you are always 'it' you will have all the more chance to run.

"You had better make two goals for foot-ball with the boards you have in the cellar & ask the three biggest boys in the school to help you set them up on the vacant field near the brick-yard on Vassal lane; then take your foot-ball to school for all to play with at recess & in the afternoon.

"You may be sure the boys will always tease you so long as you are a cry-baby."

On the same day Godfrey wrote his wife that she must insist that Jim follow his instructions. "Jim should learn to run and wrestle so that he can hold his own against any boys of his age. . . . I wish you would urge him to do this. I want him to learn to take the lead and keep it, by courage good nature and common sense."

Godfrey also wrote Minnie frequently about their daughter: ". . . glad to hear that Eleanor did well in her theatricals but I should be *very much more* pleased to hear that she was learning to dust to cook to wash dishes and make beds quickly neatly and well & was always cheerful & a comfort to you & a little mother to the younger children. . . .

"I think Faust is a very immoral play & totally unfit to take children to, especially Eleanor. Do you want to pave the way to seduction & unchastity? That is the logical lesson of a play in which the heroine is seduced and then goes to heaven and an inference which the child will not be slow in drawing or, if she does not fully appreciate it now she will later on with tenfold danger remembering that her own mother took her to see such an apotheosis of sexual complaisance. Please remember that those children are mine as well as yours. Let them risk life & limb if you will but do not take them to see what you know I disapprove of & endanger their ideals.

"If they must see vice let them see it as it is, not glorified & poeticised to make it attractive & dangerous to girls of pure instincts.

"Let them look upon the painted harlots in the streets, not upon Margheritas. . . . Is there any thing I can say or do my love to induce you to cooperate with me in these critical & formative years of the childrens lives to protect them so long as may be from all influences that tend to condone vice or even suggest it in any alluring guise.

"Soon enough the wicked old world will reach them in spite of us with a thousand siren voices. Let us postpone this time till their character is formed & they realize that fallen women of real life & the Margheritas of the stage do not look much alike." This attitude reflected a tremendous change in Cabot since he had first seen *Faust* as a young man in 1890 and been charmed by the beauty of the ballet.

Godfrey, concerned with Eleanor's safety and happiness, wanted Jim to share this concern. "I wish you would see to it that Jim always dances at least once with Eleanor when they are at a party together & makes it his business to see that she has a good time. Impress upon him that man carves his own destiny woman waits to be helped & it is his duty to help woman."

When Minnie panicked because Eleanor had at fifteen succumbed to puppy love, Godfrey tried to reassure her. "My dear love have you forgotten your youth? Have I not confessed my ardent affection for Lotta Lowell when I was 6 & she 3 & how jealous I was because she preferred Will Putnam to me?

"You have never confessed when you first felt the tender wound but it is not surprising that Eleanor & young Stover are susceptible."

But a year later Godfrey began to worry about Eleanor himself. "I think there would be no harm in your giving Eleanor more exact information as to cocks and hens than that percolating through at second hand from Charles Gulick & incidentally explain more particularly the human generative function. . . .

". . . sorry the children are so lazy but think . . . you coddle them too much especially Eleanor. The idea that she can not take a short stroll in the cool of the evening because she is menstruating is unwise & extreme. Later in life she will be doing much more strenuous & unwise things at this time unknown to you perhaps, or your remonstrances will have less effect because experience has shown her that your previous caution was extreme and unwarranted. . . .

". . . you might feel the advisability of saying a few words to Eleanor to put her on her guard. A very few words are enough, very simple words and as colorless as the nature of the case will permit. Girls of her age are sometimes kidnapped & sometimes ravished & I think that she should know something of this danger & in a general way its nature she will perhaps better learn it from you than from anyone else. . . .

"I have yours of the 2nd & wish you would tell Eleanor that I do not wish her to smoke & that any woman in this country who smokes thereby removes one of the barriers that separates her from the vilest of the vile & diminishes the respect in which every good woman wishes to be held by the opposite sex. . . ."

In his own dealings with Eleanor he showed affection and love which he never was able to show his sons. When she was little he held her on his lap and told her fairytales, he let her pull him over and roughhouse with him, and when she secretly tied a blue ribbon in his hair which he only discovered when adult guests arrived, he laughed. His letters to her were more loving and more full of jokes than those to her brothers. "Dear Puss . . . I congratulate you upon the heroic determination with which you put Fraulein to rout. Heroic determination (sometimes mistaken by ill-natured people for Cabot cussedness), is a very important winning card on certain occasions."

By the time Eleanor was a young woman Godfrey's letters reflected his growing concern about his daughter's personality. He wrote to Minnie, "I had a disagreeable dream this morning. I dreamt that you were in tears because some body had said that Eleanor was unpopular because she was so hard. I fear there is a little grain of truth in this. I fear Eleanor inherits from both of us a tendency to see the evil that is in people rather than the good. Let us try & see if we can not set her a better example hereafter."

With the boys there was no spoiling. Godfrey delivered spankings frequently and fiercely with his bare hands, and in the view of the recipients these were sometimes deserved and sometimes not. When Tom built a fire in the basement of the house, he felt he deserved the whipping he got, but on other occasions he felt unjustly punished and always resented the injustice.

All the children were forbidden to play cards or any game of chance on Sunday, just as their mother had had to put her dolls away on the Lord's Day until sundown. But they were allowed such games of skill as tennis and chess. The children were forbidden to bathe in other than cold water and forbidden to fill the tub more than a third full, any self-indulgence or waste being considered a sin. Many prohibitions led to many deceptions; thus, warm baths were taken, and the window in the bathroom was opened in order to avoid discovery. Prominent on Cabot's list of what his children were forbidden to read were parts of the Bible and poetry of Byron, a "lecherous person." The main result of his *Index Librorum Prohibitorum* was that all the books on it were thoroughly read by his children too early for any enjoyment or understanding.

Cabot's relationship with his sons was that of a European, or even an Oriental, father. He demanded obedience and reverence. The modern American notion that fathers and sons should be "pals" was as foreign to him as that of papa washing the dishes. He did not want to be called "Pa" or "Dad," but "Father."

He longed for his sons' love and confidences; and he wrote once to Tom, "Write me about whatever is interesting you my dear, whether it be your studies or the books you read or your day-dreams or your games. Whatever interests you will interest me." But communication from son to father was kept at an absolute minimum, since it almost invariably brought correction or criticism. And just as Godfrey's father had been too busy for him most of the time, so he was usually too busy for his family. When he was at home he made the children compete so fiercely for his time, approval, and affection that there grew between them a sense of rivalry and jealousy which was never to disappear.

Godfrey was unable to compliment his children when they did well in school, instead pointing out how much better he had done or displaying some feat of memory such as knowing the subheading of each volume of the Encyclopaedia Britannica, from "A to And," "And to Ans." "Ans to Bis," all the way to "Vet to Zym." Even Eleanor could only remember such limited compliments as her mother's once saying, "But there's no girl in the room that has the beautiful complexion you do" and her father's admission, "Well, you're not lacking in brains."

Cabot was able to note in his Journal or in letters to Minnie, "Very glad to see my little ones again" or "Jim is very lovable";

but he could not make his children feel loved. Even when he
taught them to bicycle or play tennis or took them to see the
fireworks on the Fourth of July or to the circus, his lectures and
criticisms frequently took the fun out of the event.

There were lectures on the greatness of his forebears and
especially on their physical heroism—swatting down eight or ten
Mexicans or winning boxing championships at Harvard. He
loved telling the story of his father's going out to Fort Dearman
when he was a Harvard freshman and chasing the wolves on the
ice on Lake Michigan, whom he could outmaneuver on his skates.
But family pride must not be passive; the lecture always ended,
"Don't be like a potato, the best part of you underground."

Minnie Cabot had never as a child been allowed to celebrate
Christmas, because it was a pagan holiday; and as Godfrey was so
strongly opposed to spoiling children, neither Christmas nor children's birthdays were lavish events. In a few things, however, the
children were given almost absolute freedom. The backyard was
theirs, and as a result it was an ever-changing mess of tunnels,
forts, lakes and moats, where the Russo-Japanese War was
fought, castles of tarpaper and dams of mud were built and
destroyed, and sections were flooded, to the intense annoyance of
the neighbors. A toboggan or shoot-the-shoot twenty feet high
was built, down which one slid into a great puddle of muddy
water, creating a tremendous splash and getting deliciously wet
and dirty.

All manner of pets were permitted, Minnie writing to Godfrey on one occasion, "Now we have left only the birds & two
kittens & we have been promised a great many more animals.
Guiney pigs that are not born & kittens that are just hatched, so
the children say. We have no puppy as yet." The dog shortage
was soon cured by a visit to the Animal Rescue League. Godfrey
permitted this very reluctantly, because he believed that animals
were carriers of disease; all livestock acquisitions were made when
he was away from home.

One of the animals caused Minnie embarrassment when it
proved that young Tom had a yen for profit. "Tom made five
cents on his turtle you will be ashamed to hear. He bought it of

Elizabeth Eliot for five cents & sold it to Harriet Lamb for ten cents." There is no indication that Godfrey was shamed by this profitable transaction. Profitable business was, in fact, the main tradition of the Cabots. Many later-generation members of other of Boston's First Families—the Adamses, the Lowells, and the Eliots, for example—when they inherited enough money to live in the style they wanted, chose to work in such unremunerative fields as politics, poetry, and teaching. One of Godfrey's sons, John, chose service in the State Department, and in the generation of Godfrey's grandchildren the taste for business is notably lacking in a few cases. But it is interesting to note, although impossible to explain, that while the Adams family produced presidents (and at least one president-manqué) and the Lowells and the Eliots produced professors and poets, the Cabots almost invariably chose business and business at a profit. Although these businessmen supported charities, arts, and education, in the main they spent their years building the Cabot fortunes.

Tricks were permitted to Eleanor, who tied her younger brothers to a neighbor's doorbell, pulled it, and then ran away. Her greatest triumph, however, came when she put toilet paper all along the hallway to her bedroom with LePage's glue on the upper side of the paper and then went to bed and yelled as if in great pain. When the two servant girls came running, their feet and legs became covered with gluey toilet paper.

When Godfrey was home, the children's lives were made up of impromptu quizzes, lectures on morality, and competitive sports. The encyclopedia and the dictionary were usually brought to the dinner table to settle arguments and facilitate quizzing, but the lectures required no outside source. Coffee, tea, and, of course, alcohol were sinful because they were stimulants; cocoa was not wicked, but any rich food and tobacco were; honesty was not the best policy—it was not a matter of policy, but a matter of principle; being of service was all that mattered, and if a man was of service, sooner or later he would be paid for it; courage was mandatory for Cabots—not only courage when the flag was waving and the charge was on, but also what Godfrey called "two o'clock in the morning courage," when the blood is cold and one is aware of all the possible unhappy consequences of the act of courage.

A life spent *pro bono publico* was the highest ideal, not unlike the attitude of John Quincy Adams, who went back to Washington as a mere Congressman after having served as President in spite of objections that the position was now beneath him. It is remarkable that the incessant lectures did not make "duty" and "service" stink in the nostrils of his sons as Horatio Alger had in those of a whole generation.

There was also no end to Cabot's warnings to his children, especially to the effect that a man should fear his friends because he could be more hurt by them, since he knew that his enemies might hurt him.

Minnie, on the other hand, although she worried too much about the children and interrogated them like a district attorney about every detail of where they went and what they did, seemed to them much more genuinely interested in their problems. When she was feeling well, Minnie even joined them in their practical jokes, which she loved as much as they, such as tying all the stockings from the clothes line together and then tying the front door to the back door. She allowed them to get up at four o'clock on Christmas morning to go down to open their presents, which usually included pocket money of $10 or $15, since they were not given regular allowances.

Minnie sometimes wrote Godfrey about her fun with the children. "I spend a good deal of time now writing stories. I suppose you will be surprised to hear it, as you never thought your wife literary. It seems to be Jim's delight now to make books out of paper & ask me to write stories in them. I suppose when you return you will be asked to contribute."

Sixty years later Minnie's daughter said: "She had a terrible inferiority complex. She had the kindest heart in the world, and yet my mother would say such tactless things and make herself and her family dreadfully unhappy.

"She cared frightfully about being at the center of things and craved sympathy terribly and constantly, so she stretched the truth—she exaggerated to get sympathy. She could make a terrible to-do about something little, and then she'd take a big thing on the chin without a whimper."

A great tragedy in the Cabot family occurred with William Putnam, the fourth child. For the first nine weeks of his life he was put in the charge of a trained nurse, Miss Anna C. Chamberlain. According to Minnie, "Miss Chamberlains methods of bringing up a baby is never to touch a baby except to have it brought to the mother to nurse & to be washed. She also believed that a baby should never hear a word spoken out loud. Miss Chamberlain has a very strong will & worked on my feelings so much that I carried out her ideas to the letter." Minnie and Godfrey went off on two trips leaving the children behind, and during the second, Minnie's mother was so shocked at Miss Chamberlain's brutal treatment that she took the three oldest away with her to Cohasset, leaving only William behind. Finally disturbed because William "would pound his head as hard as he could against the walls of the rooms chairs etc. so that his forhead was black & blue . . . ," Minnie called in a neurologist Dr. Charles Putnam, who was married to a cousin of Godfrey's.

"The doctors then told me that they thought I had made a mistake in the way in which he had been brought up. I then began playing with him a good deal. Strangely he improved rapidly that autumn & early winter in health & spirits."

When William was a year and a half old Godfrey noted in the Journal that the child's mind was not developing properly. His letters to Minnie contain his instructions on how to deal with the problem. "Do not worry so much about William. I think he will come out all right. Do not fuss over him too much and do not humor his whims too much; not at all in fact where they make unreasonable trouble. I think one or two good spankings would stimulate his mind & soul a good deal. He is now able to understand it [at age two and unable to speak] if judiciously timed & preceeded and followed by a moral lecture & proper amount of coaxing and cossetting so that the child shall appreciate that the discipline is not given with anger or an arbitrary use of power but with much regret and tenderness as the needful and natural result of disobedience to just and kind authority.

"I think the child is fully as intelligent as the average of his age though more self-contained and reticent. . . . William's mind has now reached a point where it is conscious of right and wrong & daily evolving. . . . Of course he has had a good deal of discipline, more than most children of his age receive &, in the first year of his life too much of a certain kind, but he is able now to understand direct punishment . . . in my judgement he is a very far from stupid child. . . . It is a very common error to bring up children to take themselves too seriously i. e. to expect to have their whims gratified, the greatest of all follies and the root of all evil.

"The old Puritan idea of self-abnegation, though pushed to a foolish extreme was a healthy and beneficial protest against this most enervating tendency in man & there is a lamentable lack of this strenuous and ennobling doctrine in these latter days."

Slowly and reluctantly Minnie began to admit to herself that William's mind was not normal. She consulted an increasing number of doctors, including Dr. Fernald, the head of a school for feeble-minded children in Waverly. Various doctors offered various treatments—rhubarb and calisaya, thyroid injections, gentian, hot salt baths, and a belly band. Only Godfrey's prescription stayed the same. "By all means spank William when he is naughty. There is no mental stimulus so wholesome and effective at the age [two years and nine months], to develop the moral sense.

"You must be particularly severe when he hurts Jackie & stimulate in every way his love & helpfulness toward his younger brother."

Minnie's distress over William increased her habitual tactlessness. She wrote Godfrey, "When Wm is well people always say that he looks like me, & when he is ill they say he looks like you." When it was suggested that perhaps his trouble had been caused by a touch of meningitis, she wrote Godfrey, "Your family are so subject to the disease."

Both Godfrey and Minnie continued to refuse to recognize that the child was permanently mentally retarded. His mother took him to New York, where a doctor who allegedly could effect cures by the laying on of hands was unable after many treatments to help William.

Minnie's letters reflected her love and increasing despair. She naturally magnified every small sign of normalcy. She wrote a long analysis trying to determine how his problem had begun and what she could do. "He seemed to be afraid of everything. He cried a good deal at night & made horrid throaty noises . . . he returned to his habit of pulling his hair . . . & began screaming again . . . the scream was awful almost unbearable. . . . When he was sixteen months old he was afraid of so many things. He was terribly afraid of water & going into some rooms in the house. Sometimes I would try taking him to drive, hoping to relieve the child but it would make him scream and cry."

Godfrey's recommendations continued the same, his remedies for all ills: discipline and exercise. "If William does not develope into a useful man we must simply bear our burden cheerfully . . . [but] I think William wanting to lie down is the lassitude due to the heat & I would insist on his having active exercise both morning & afternoon. . . . If there is one thing that our whole experience with William might teach us it is that your personal care is indispensable. Discipline plus love, perfect love, is most beneficial. Discipline without love & with ill temper is less desirable." Only once did Godfrey's letters reflect the terrible conclusion that William's problem had been the result of his ill treatment as a baby. "I lay awake an hour or so last night worrying about him and wondering if terror in early infancy had blighted his poor little soul. I don't suppose we shall ever know but it makes my very heart ache to think of it."

Godfrey never admitted to his own children that his brother Guy was mentally retarded, requiring that they treat him as though he were normal when he came to Sunday dinner. When Guy died, Dr. Stanley Cobb, a Boston neurologist who was the son-in-law of Nellie, Guy and Godfrey's sister, made an autopsy and sectioned Guy's brain. The family story had always been that Guy had had meningitis, but Dr. Cobb concluded this was not so, that Guy's brain was maldeveloped and defective. Godfrey was furious when he learned the results of the autopsy, which had been made without his knowledge.

Finally Minnie, convinced of the uselessness of hope, permitted William to be sent away to a home for such children. She wrote Godfrey, "I cannot help wishing for his death"; but in 1967 William Putnam Cabot was still living and still unable to speak.

Cabot's other children have no recollection that after the terrible experience with William, Godfrey's Puritan discipline diminished. Minnie continued short-tempered and confused but often affectionate and interested. "Jim loves to cook. Tom & Jackie are helping." She sometimes listened to their problems and sometimes interceded on their behalf with Godfrey. When Godfrey was traveling, she reminded him to save stamps and bring home little gifts.

But she continued to complain to Godfrey about the children's naughtinesses. "When you get back I am going to let you take Tom in hand & teach him not to say darn & darn fool. He has learnt these from Jim. I have my hands pretty full with him, he is what one would call fresh, at times. I suppose it is his age. It is hard for him to get down to breakfast on time too."

Godfrey wrote to Jim. "I am sorry to hear from your mother that you have been twice late to school lately & that you lost your dancing shoes & behaved in an unruly manner. The third commandment says, 'Take not the name of thy God in vain for the Lord will not hold him guiltless that taketh his name in vain.' "

From West Virginia and Pennsylvania, Godfrey continued to send Minnie instructions on child rearing. "If Sara Bernhardt comes to Boston I would like you to take Jim to see her if she plays Adrienne Lecouvreur or any play that is not immoral. I think he will in after life be glad to have seen this great actress. . . . Tosca is a vile filthy play. . . . Make Eleanor help you in the house work & call upon Jim whenever there is anything he can do for you. The present premier of England was very unpopular as a school boy & never interested in out of door sports. I don't in fact know that Jesus Christ was, so while I wish Jim to take more interest in outdoor sports I shall not be inconsolable, if he is nevertheless good & dutiful in other directions. The children have the country club to amuse their friends which is more than either you or I had at their age."

The instructions in Godfrey's letters were not limited to his children but frequently included Minnie. "Your mother loves style & fashion. I prefer that my children should never identify themselves with the fashionable set. Let us if possible bring up our children to be leaders of mankind. Leaders of fashion are very seldom leaders of mankind and not infrequently spend in the effort to lead in Society an amount of money, an amount of brains, energy and effort & opportunity that, if directed by a saner view would have made them leaders of mankind in far nobler fields. . . .

"Be rational my love and do not invite adverse criticism of yourself for an uncharitable attitude of mind. . . . Read your Bible my darling & soften your heart toward all. . . . I hope you will lose no opportunity to cheer up the old folks [her parents] & show them your love. . . . The testimony of love is the one pleasure that is common to both giver and receiver that is without alloy & of which the soul can never surfeit itself."

Only very occasionally did Cabot become so upset by Minnie's letters of complaint that he replied in kind. "Please remember darling that if you tell people I am away half the time and complain too much of my absence you will cause adverse comment upon me & possibly upon you behind your back. I am trying to be a power and influence for good in this world up to the limit of my ability and strength and yet you rather restrain my wish and effort for others when your approval and encouragement would help me much more to be unselfish & public spirited than that of any other person.

"My mind is tense with effort nearly every working hour would it not be nobler that you should seek to broaden rather than to narrow the purpose for good of my life?

"Remember my dearest that since our marriage I have not left your bed a single night except at what I conceived to be the call of duty nor have I ever had the desire to do so.

"The greatest deprivation of my life is my enforced absence from your side. I wish to bear this bravely and cheerfully. Pray do not make it a reproach against me among my dear ones at home. . . . My name is a tower of strength in two counties of W.Va. & two of Penna for those who are trying to raise the general welfare. Would you limit and confine this activity for good or would you encourage & share in it?

"Would you give all my friends and my children the feeling that I am simply striving and fighting for money and more money which is false and base or the truth that I am chiefly striving to use to good advantage such talent & opportunity as God has granted me which is true and may possibly inspire my children and others with a passion and an aspiration for usefulness. . . .

"I have yours of the 8th [of October 1915] & admit once and for all my indiscretion in buying you any electrical automobiles. At home my life has been made an increasing burden by my children. Away from home I no longer greet with joy your handwriting on the outside of an envelope knowing that it will probably chiefly consist of a list of complaints against things & innuendoes against people."

Not the least remarkable thing about Godfrey was that he could be completely unself-conscious when he criticized Minnie's intolerance and her constant criticizing; that he could, with no apparent embarrassment, adjure her to "soften your heart." It is only understandable in terms of the difference between the matters on which each of them was intolerant.

Minnie was intolerant about what Godfrey considered little niggling things, such as social slights. He directed his intolerance only at those objects which he felt substantially affected the health of society and the destiny of mankind. Cabot's great concerns were always with the loss or destruction of what he considered the kind of social cement which holds the world together, when from his point of view the dangers of its falling apart were great and constant.

As to the differences of method in showing intolerance, Minnie was a whiner. Intolerance which takes the form of complaining is terribly irritating even to a man whose own intolerance takes the form of righteous indignation and a determination to take action. Minnie suffered from her intolerances, and Godfrey tried to teach her not to complain about things she could not change or would not at least make an effort to change. She was a rather mean-spirited female, whereas there was a kind of breadth, almost a dignity, to Godfrey's Quixote-like attacks on sin and his tremendous personal commitment to the conquest of whatever he considered evil. A sniveler is not infrequently more difficult to abide than someone whose opinions are impossible but whose heartiness, whose constant willingness to put his money where his mouth is, to put his hand where his heart professes to be, inspires one, however reluctantly, at least to doff one's hat at his commitment and courage and energy. Poor Minnie's was a pinched heart. However horrifying many of Godfrey's opinions were, he had concerning them such a moral vigor and such an obvious integrity, and he was trying to *do* something, whereas Minnie merely complained.

And yet, in his marriage as in his business, Godfrey did not keep reviewing past errors or lost opportunities but rather made the most of what he found in wedlock as in West Virginia. Even on those few occasions when he was angry with Minnie's incessant whining, he never really considered seeking other feminine comfort or divorce. Surely one reason was his automatic and unconscious feeling for the sanctity of contract, an unconscious feeling that marriage was not only a legal contract between himself and Minnie, but also a moral contract among himself and Minnie and God, and not least a social contract. He would no more have welched on this than on a business deal in which his honor was at stake.

And here, as elsewhere in Godfrey's life, the moral thing seems to have been the most profitable thing. His courtship of Minnie had not been as romantic as his pursuit of the three other young women had been, and the marriage was perhaps on both sides a marriage of convenience, but in fact Minnie gave Godfrey what he really wanted and needed, and he did the same for her. His letters to her and to others demonstrated his love. "Dear Sweet Wife . . . I do remember right well what happened on the 19th of March four years ago and have thought of it a good deal since I have been away. It has certainly brought me more joy than anything else that ever happened to me. . . . Here is the kiss that you wanted [then a sketch of a mouth with a moustache]. I have put a moustache on this kiss because I know you like your kisses that way. . . . Did I write you that I have had a little cubby hole built in the sleeve of my new coat for a dear little hand?"

Godfrey also clearly felt love for his children. His Journal and letters to Minnie contain many bursts of it. "Dear boy, how I do love him. . . . I do miss my dear ones." But he was unable to communicate that feeling to the children. He was often sensitive to their feelings and understood their problems, but somehow he could never tell them so. "Having suffered as Jim is now a large part of my life (from nervousness, shyness, and eczema) I venture to make the following suggestions . . . abundant fresh air night and day . . . exercise. If walking is stupid for Jim & he shrinks from playing with other boys, bicycling is good fun alone. . . . He is too nice a boy not to help him all we can & it is pitiable that he should suffer so much in mind & body. . . . One reason for Jim's bashfulness is too much criticism of his personal appearance. Please be discrete in this & restrain impertinent personal remarks by the children."

Godfrey brought Jim to The Homestead at Hot Springs, Virginia, in the hopes of curing his eczema. There the boy developed measles. Godfrey wrote Minnie, "As you will doubtless remember I was much troubled at Jim's age, in fact from 16 to 22 or later by pimples large and small & little carbuncles."

Minnie was very anxious that her sons be elected to The Porcellian at Harvard; she urged Tom to learn to play the banjo in order to increase his popularity. But they were all stiff, nervous boys, repressed by their father's tirades and oddly dressed in their mother's bargains. It was not surprising that none were elected to The Porcellian. In fact, only Tom was elected to a "final" club, the D.U., although Jim was chosen by Pi Eta and Jack by the Hasty Pudding Club, both less exclusive "waiting" clubs.

Godfrey did not care about clubs, as he indicated in a letter to Minnie. "Tom is a good deal of a grouch & crybaby. The fact that he does not get into the fraternities does not worry me a bit. They distinctly tend toward the abuse of liquor & it is not unlikely that they have been injurious to Harry and Powell [Cabot cousins of Godfrey who were members of Porcellian].

"I would like Tom to have more time for sleep & study than he has. If he were in the fraternities he would have less. I would like to see him prominent in the non exclusive societies like the H.A.A. [Harvard Athletic Association] the Aeronautic Club, the Natural History Society & the debating club whatever it is now called. . . . Joe Gardner was made drunk the night he was initiated into the Δ.K.E. & it worried him a lot."

Godfrey continued to advise his children by mail on any subject he considered important. He wrote Eleanor, "Dear Puss . . . I caution you against taking long [horseback] rides or getting over heated for this may displace the uterus." But he constantly urged Minnie to worry less about the children and particularly not to badger them as they grew older about their affairs of the heart.

"I have yours of the 2nd [November 1918] and think you will best let Tom run his own love affairs. The girl seemed to me a well intentioned girl who would develop into a good unselfish woman.

"The less we say to our children about their sweethearts the more seriously we shall be listened to if strong ground should arise for our intervening. I do not advance this as an unfailing rule only as a frequent experience and whatever we say we should be VERY sure we are right and *very* careful not to say any thing unjust or to overstate any thing."

Eleanor Cabot had met and fallen in love with a young man, Ralph Bradley, who had been educated at Groton and was in the first graduating class of the Harvard Business School. His father, a minister, had died when Bradley was a child, however, and there was no fortune at all. Physically energetic and adventurous by nature, Bradley had after graduation ridden the rails as a hobo and then worked his way up from fireman on the Wabash to coal-purchasing agent of the Boston & Maine. A virile, handsome, and somewhat dashing figure, Bradley had reached an informal understanding with Eleanor before he went to Europe as a railroad officer in World War I.

Bradley stayed in Europe for some time after the war ended, and Minnie's constant worries about his social suitability and his reasons for staying in Europe grew daily. Godfrey not only correctly appraised young Bradley's manly qualities, but also seems to have doubted whether his daughter might do as well again if she succumbed to her mother's fears and broke off with Bradley. Cabot wrote to Minnie, "I am not sure that either you or she fully understand Ralph. Be not so quick to condemn. Let us get him home & then we can tell better what is trumps.

"He went abroad expecting to win promotion & hoping that this might make it easier to ask the hand of an heiress. He has not wholly given up the hope of winning promotion, he is ill in body & more ill in mind and it worries him.

"He fears Eleanor does not care enough for him & that he does not care enough for her. He finds that he is not impervious to the charms of other women & this worries him more than it would most men. I think he has had and is having a mighty hard lay and I feel sorry for him.

"Now don't you butt in and worry Eleanor with your gloomy talk. The next thing you know you'll worry her to death & then find you have made a mistake.

"Ralph knows he can not offer Eleanor the luxuries she is accustomed to. Let us get him home & I will talk with him and straighten things out. . . .

"You greatly need to build a comfortable & well warmed ell to your heart to accommodate sinners; then secondly you want to appreciate that we are all sinners & not entitled to any aseptic compartment of grace in anybody's heart or any where else.

"Lastly you want to focus your gaze on the good that is in people and thus & only thus can you hope to acquire more & more of the understanding heart without which we shall find life mere dust & ashes a long account of nothings dotted with a loss.

"If Eleanor thinks less of Ralphs duty to her & more of her duty to him and to you and to others it will be better for her. Now don't you go and make a mess of things. First get Ralph home and find out what we are talking about."

Minnie, however, continued to worry that her only daughter

was making a mistake. Before her debut Eleanor was always taken to parties either by a maid or one of her brothers, not by an escort, and even after her debut whenever she went with a young man to dinner or the theater the event had caused a fuss.

Again Godfrey, who recognized in Ralph Bradley a first-rate man, wrote a warning letter to Minnie: "It is possible he may have done things that he would find it difficult or improper to clearly explain to you or to Eleanor. I think however he will find it possible to explain & state every thing to me. I think I shall have no difficulty in learning every thing that is needful or advisable for me to know and in particular. First whether there is any other woman to whom he has obligations more binding than the very loose tie that binds him to Eleanor. Second whether there is any women that he prefers to Eleanor. Third whether there is any likelihood that if he marries Eleanor and she does her full duty to him he will be unfaithful to her. Fourth whether there is any physical reason why he should not marry her, that of course is a question of the best obtainable medical advice.

"I very distinctly think that he is a man who is likely to slip if she does not do her full duty to him & to such children as she may bear him.

"I think she is very much in love with him & that they are intellectually suited to each other and I shall not advise against it without strong cause. Now let us all do what we reasonably and consistently can to bring him home as soon as possible.

"I suggest that you have a heart to heart talk with his mother and draw her out as tactfully as you can. . . . She will very likely refer to his diffidence about money matters in which case you will tell her that if he is sound in mind and body and chuck full of days work it is immaterial whether he has $500 or $50,000.

"If he happened to have $50,000,000 I should prefer him to marry some one else's daughter for such a fortune would be a great temptation to worthlessness, to shameful luxury and sloth. . . . Did it ever occur to you my dear that one reason I have not given Eleanor more luxuries is that I did not want to scare away the most desirable suitors and attract the fortune hunters?

"When you see Mrs. Bradley you will of course avoid all reference to money matters unless she broaches the subject & then say what you have to say & *change the subject.*"

Fortunately Ralph Bradley was not scared away, and he and Eleanor were married on August 16, 1919, at Beverly Farms.

CHAPTER X

"First in the Air"

For the thing we long for, that we are
For one transcendent moment.   J. C. LOWELL, *Longing*

Hitch your wagon to a star. Let us not fag in paltry works which serve our pot and bag alone. Let us not lie and steal. No god will help. We shall find all their teams going the other way: every god will leave us. Work rather for those interests which the divinities honor and promote,—justice, love, freedom, knowledge, utility." EMERSON, *Society and Solitude: Civilization*

Man has mounted science, and is now run away with. I firmly believe that before many centuries more, science will be the master of man. The engines he will have invented will be beyond his strength to control. Some day science may have the existence of mankind in its power, and the human race commit suicide by blowing up the world.   HENRY ADAMS, in a letter to his brother Charles

At every possible opportunity of his adult life Godfrey quoted his father's words, "Man is going to fly and when he flies, he will fly farther and faster than the birds. Man is not a very fast runner but he learned to outrun all animals with his steam locomotive; he is a very slow swimmer, but he learned to outswim all cetaceans and all fish with his steamboat; by the same token he will outfly all the birds. I don't expect to see it, but you may."

"This prediction," wrote Godfrey, "was a part of my soul from that day until the confirmation came on the 17th of December, 1903."

Godfrey's Journal records that as a young man he dreamed about flying. Before the turn of the century he was writing Minnie, "I wish there were a flying machine able to take me back to your side in a twinkling, how happy I should be."

Godfrey and his brother Sam enthusiastically followed the gliding experiments of Otto and Gustav Lillienthal, and Sam tried unsuccessfully to build a glider. When news of the Wright brothers' work prior to their success reached Boston, Sam wrote them offering financial help, but he received no answer to what they considered a letter from some Boston crank. When word reached Boston of their success, Godfrey immediately wrote the brothers inquiring about the possibilities of moving his carbon black by air.

A few days later Godfrey wrote to his cousin.

December 31, 1903

Hon. Henry Cabot Lodge,
United States Senate,
Washington, D.C.

My dear Mr. Lodge:
    You will doubtless have noticed in the papers, an account of a successful trial of a flying machine made Dec. 17th in North Carolina by Wilbur and Orville Wright of the Wright Cycle Co., Dayton, O.

    In answer to an inquiry of mine, I have a letter from these gentlemen to the effect that they made four successful trials on that date, starting their machine with its own power and that it showed a sustaining capacity of over 100 lbs., in excess of the weight of the operator and motor.

    According to the newspaper accounts, they went as far as three miles through the air. It seems to me, that this may fairly be said to mark the beginning of successful flight through the air by men unaided by balloons. It has occurred to me that it would be eminently desirable for the United States Government to interest itself in this invention with a view to utilizing it for war-like purposes.

Whatever the difficulty of practical operations might be, the mere fact that such an invention was controlled by this Government, would have a perceptible moral effect and permit greater economy in other armaments.

I wish you a very happy New Year.

Yours very truly,
(signed) *Godfrey L. Cabot*

Despite Cabot's letter, it was not until 1909 that the United States government interested itself in the Wright brothers' work.

"I never thought seriously of learning to fly," Cabot wrote in 1953, "until the first World War. The heartless brutality with which, under the command of the last Emperor of Germany, the Germans invaded Belgium and France without a declaration of war, and in spite of a treaty in which Germany had solemnly covenanted with England not only never to invade Belgium, but to come to the rescue of Belgium in case it were invaded, profoundly impressed me. I was over twenty years over-age and Josephus Daniels [the Secretary of the Navy] would not allow me to go to any flying school for seaplanes and I could not build an airdrome or buy an airdrome and equip it, but the ocean was an airdrome available without challenge."

Outraged at his rejection by the Navy, Cabot at the age of fifty-four ordered his personal Burgess-Dunn seaplane, which he called The Lark, and learned to fly. "I built a hangar on Misery Island and put a little donkey engine in it to haul my plane on a car out of the water into the hangar." He then proceeded to patrol the coast looking for German submarines.

He continued to pull all available strings; finally, on March 20, 1917, he was appointed a lieutenant in the United States Naval Reserve Flying Corps. His commission was signed by Franklin Delano Roosevelt, then Assistant Secretary of the

Navy (who was born in 1882, the year Godfrey graduated from Harvard). This was a fact which Cabot never forgot and for which he continued to express his gratitude even in later years when he was criticizing the New Deal.

On April 14, 1917, Cabot was assigned two petty officers and given command of a small group of naval-aviation volunteers at the Eastern Yacht Club at Marblehead. When, because of the shortage, the Navy refused to give him live ammunition with which to train his men, he scoured Boston and found and bought his own. He continued daily to patrol Boston Harbor and the coast from Minot's Ledge Lighthouse to Gloucester, occasionally flying as far as the Isle of Shoals to the north and Plymouth to the south. Although he never spotted a submarine, he did see and report one whale, and he was once fired on by frightened citizens of Winthrop, Massachusetts.

Cabot became friendly with retired Rear-Admiral Bradley A. Fiske, who wanted to build a torpedo-carrying seaplane but who could get no support from the Navy Department. Convinced that such a plane, carrying a 2500-pound torpedo, was the only means of destroying the German fleet in Kiel and Wilhelmshaven, protected from other attack by mines and shore batteries, Cabot publicly offered $30,000 toward the development of such a plane.

To his great delight, Cabot's offer received wide publicity in the Boston and New York press, the New York *Sun* on September 8, 1917, running an editorial entitled "The Monitor and the Torpedoplane":

> Mr. Godfrey L. Cabot of Boston, the public spirited citizen who has agreed to furnish the funds necessary to build the torpedoplane designed by Admiral Fiske, as a weapon wherewith to attack the German fleet within its defense at Kiel, has an impressive precedent for his act.
>
> Only Americans far and away beyond draft age can recall the terror produced by the first day's performances of the Confederate ironclad Merrimac when on March 8, 1862, she destroyed at their moorings the ships of war Congress and Cumberland, and returned

unhurt to her station. Washington was frantic with apprehension of an invasion, and the Secretary of the Navy, Gideon Welles, tells in his diary how Cabinet Members interrupted a meeting to peer fearfully from the White House windows down the Potomac for the dreaded monster. New York feared that her harbor would be entered and her banks and treasure vaults laid under contribution. The whole country lamented that the blockade was certain to be broken, the ports of the South thrown open to the trade of the world, and the way prepared for Confederate recognition.

All the world knows how, a day later, these fears were quieted by the crushing defeat of the Merrimac by Ericsson's newly invented Monitor. But all the world does not know, though it should, that the little ship that battled for the nation was not the property of the nation, but was built by a private citizen, C. S. Bushnell of New Haven, at his own expense and against the solid opposition of the Navy Department of that day. It was not paid for until long after the action.

There is an easy parallel to be drawn between the official indifference to Ericsson's Monitor and that now manifested toward Fiske's torpedoplane. We hope the public spirited Bostonian, Mr. Cabot, who has come to the rescue today may lay his country under as deep obligations as did Bushnell of New Haven in 1862. New England, after all, is pretty good territory to count on in time of national need.

Still unhappy at having missed the Civil War, Godfrey was delighted to be compared to one of its heroes. Unlike those who merely complained about having been born too late for the War and the great reform movements, especially abolition, and who like Moorfield Storey grieved "that he was born to ignoble times, when the devil was handcuffed and muzzled," Godfrey satisfied his need to smite the Pharisees by taking part in whatever crusades were available.

He wrote the Bureau of Ordnance and Senator Lodge about the torpedo plane, but the project was blocked by the Navy, Josephus Daniels writing, "The possibility of obtaining satisfactory results from the proposed scheme is so slight as not to warrant the expenditure of time and talent required for its development." When the British developed just such a torpedo plane, Cabot was pleased that his faith in the project was well founded but furious that the Navy Department was not as anxious as he to make America "first in the air."

Cabot was convinced of the importance of developing a system for planes to pick up burdens in flight. He believed that only in this way could planes refuel in flight and go for long distances without stopping. With his own plane he experimented for months with an elasticized rope and a hook. Finally, on May 3, 1918, in full flight he picked up a six-pound oil can. By October of that year he was able to pick up a 155-pound load from a moving sea sled in Broad Sound near Shirley Gut in Boston Harbor.

Godfrey took out four patents for his invention and placed them at the disposal of the United States government at no charge. For a brief time his method was used in some areas for in-flight mail pickup, but as air transport progressed, the mail pickup was dropped. Cabot, however, would live long enough to see Crete captured during World War II by German troops transported in gliders picked up by much the same method as he had invented. Half a century ahead of his time, according to *Time*, he "established pioneering research into principles and mechanics of the ticklish art of mid-air refueling—which is today [1962] a commonplace technique used by pilots of the U.S. Strategic Air Command."

In March 1918 Cabot's Commanding Officer, Admiral Spencer S. Wood of the First Naval District, wanted to obtain joint seadromes in Canada as aviation bases available to both Canada and the United States. When Secretary Daniels refused to authorize traveling expenses, Cabot volunteered to go at his own expense to Canada and Nova Scotia. After an investigation he recommended Shelburne Harbor, Halifax Harbor, and Bedford Basin as joint air-patrol bases.

Cabot rigged up a rear-view mirror for his plane and offered to supply others free of charge to all United States military planes. He also made experiments in camouflage and flying in fog and reported them to Washington.

He sent both Jim and Tom to the Curtiss flying school and was so proud when they were both commissioned as Army flyers that he insisted on having their portraits painted in uniform and his own as well.

Transferred to the Naval Air Station at Hampton Roads in Norfolk, Virginia, Cabot conducted his business from there. He had drastically reduced his production of carbon black, despite the fact that it had risen from three cents a pound in 1913 to a high of twenty-five cents a pound in 1917, because he had sold most of his gas to Standard Oil, which was delivering it to the war-busy factories of Pittsburgh. From his less than Spartan headquarters at the Hotel Chamberlin in Old Point Comfort, he ran not only his own business and family affairs, but also the affairs of the Watch and Ward Society in Boston, of which he was now Treasurer, as well as an extraordinary campaign against corrupt politicians in Boston.

In addition he addressed himself to any other matter which seemed to Cabot his duty to take on. He wrote a letter published in the Boston *Herald* which showed the liberality of his heart and his concern for both practicality and justice. "To exclude children of this queer denomination [Jehovah's Witnesses] from school because they will not salute the United States flag is unjust and illogical; unjust, because they are simply obeying the orders of their parents; illogical, because such children are more than ordinarily in need of a common sense education under a normal environment.

"If given a reasonable chance, probably a majority of them will grow up to be normal, useful citizens and not have a needless injustice to brood over. If when they grow up, they are unwilling to take the oath of allegiance to the United States, they will under our present laws and court decisions thereby forfeit many opportunities and will incur the further penalty that many of their neighbors will look upon them as bumptious, unreasonable people, uncomfortable to have dealings with, and the evil that this custom is aimed against will be less likely to increase than where a desired end is pursued by unjust means."

Cabot also wrote a letter published in the Boston *Transcript* urging fair treatment of German sailors stranded in America. He was at this same time engaged in paying the expenses of a court test of a Florida statute forbidding white adults from teaching Negro children. He was not only willing to pay the bill, he even wanted to plan and direct the attack. ". . . if and when we win in Florida, the next step would be to attack the similar South Carolina statute. . . . In order to accomplish the greatest good it is desirable that you [Reverend Rufus P. Tobey] and I, slices of cold roast Boston, should study Southern psychology and the Southern viewpoint, and that we should use the best possible strategy as well as the most skillful and effective tactics.

"Nelson watched and waited many a long month for the opportunity that he so decisively utilized at Trafalgar, and had he pitched right in to the French Fleet, under the guns of a French fort, the result might have been different."

Cabot's letters to Minnie reflected his frustration in dealing with the government. "I have spent a large part of the day at the Navy Department and feel very much depressed. The closer I come to the actual administration of national affairs the more fervently do I pray to God to give eyes to the blind and show them that self-respecting conduct not verbose platitudes endlessly reiterated are required to make this country safe & that if the Navy waits for the Army to establish Coast Patrol & the Army waits for the Navy the net result is national unpreparedness." He was also unsuccessful in his attempts by personal persuasion to interest the Navy in working toward transatlantic flight.

Back in Cambridge, Minnie was doing her bit for the war effort by raising chickens in her backyard and through the newspapers advising the women of Boston that "Every single woman who has a plot 10 feet square in the vicinity of her home should raise hens thereon in the interests of wartime food conservation. . . . Ten or fifteen minutes a day is all I spend on my chickens yet everything is perfectly clean and nice. Once a week the chore man washes out the hen house and digs up the ground." She went on at length with directions for whitewashing the henhouse and for scrubbing it weekly with sulpho-napthol, and continued on the importance of planting sunflowers for their seeds. She was apparently unaware that not every woman in Boston had a chore man. Even with a chore man there were problems, and after a visit home Godfrey wrote suggesting an end to "that nasty stinking hen yard." Minnie also fed Godfrey whale meat, which thirty years later he remembered as tough but not salty.

When Godfrey came home on leave, which he managed to do not infrequently, he criticized his youngest son, Jack, for his poor marks at the Pomfret School, but was delighted at how tall the boy was growing, and he took him for a ride in his plane. He took Eleanor to the opera to hear Caruso, Scotti, and Geraldine Farrar; he flew over Salem, Cambridge, and Beverly Farms promoting the sale of Liberty Bonds; and he went down in a submarine. He had no qualms about flying down to Nahant in bad weather to pay a visit to Senator Lodge, but he refused, as he would all his life, to learn to drive an automobile.

He noted in the Journal that in 1918 he paid an income tax of "not quite $90,900." He referred to his contract with Standard Oil to take all the gas which he had been using to make black in Calhoun County at a minimum price of ten cents: "I think this will assure me an income of over $100,000 net a year from that county for many years; much less than this year, but more than I should average for black I think."

On October 25, 1918, while flying as an observer in an H-12 flying boat with two Liberty motors, he crashed. He calmly noted in the Journal that he suffered only two very slight bruises because he had "lessened the shock by rising to my feet and standing in a crouching position." Two days later he noted with pride at the age of fifty-seven, "My gold wings of a full fledged military aviator came today." He was also proud to learn on a visit to the Chemical Section of the army in Washington that his carbon black was being used in gas masks.

In December 1918 Tom was discharged after serving as a

flying instructor in San Antonio, Texas, and Jim came home from overseas in January 1919. Godfrey was discharged on March 23, 1919.

Although in the years to come he played a large role in making America "first in the air," he never again flew a plane. For him flying was not a sport; it was not a joy; it had been his duty to set an example, and he had done it.

CHAPTER XI

Watch and Ward

"My children," said an old man to his boys scared by a figure in the dark entry, "my children you will never see anything worse than yourselves." EMERSON, *Essays, First Series: Spiritual Laws,* 121

Fanaticism consists in redoubling your effort when you have forgotten your aim. SANTAYANA, *Life of Reason,* Vol. i, 13

A reformer is a guy who rides through a sewer in a glass-bottomed boat. JAMES J. WALKER

Censorship in America began with the advent of the first permanent European immigrants. Here, as elsewhere, it has taken three forms—religious censorship, political censorship, and the censorship of the arts, especially writing—in an effort to enforce particular views of morality. In the Massachusetts Bay Colony in 1650 an attack on orthodox religion, *The Meritorious Prince of Our Redemption* by William Pynchon, was burned in the market place in Boston after having been declared heretical, and various sedition laws early sought to effect political censorship in America.

The view that the early refugees to America's shores believed in intellectual and literary freedom is a grade-school myth. Massachusetts' settlers, for example, believed in free speech for themselves, but not for their critics. Indeed it was their duty, in their own view, to control the press and to stamp out heresy and sedition. Their repression was so severe that it caused Roger Williams and Cabot's ancestor Anne Hutchinson to leave Massachusetts and found Rhode Island.

The first prosecution of books on obscenity charges, however, did not come until 1815 in Pennsylvania. Once begun, censorship on grounds of obscenity grew rapidly in nineteenth-century America. It is hard in our own days of *Candy* and *Fanny Hill* to remember that only a hundred years ago Walt Whitman was fired when an Interior Department snooper found in his desk an annotated copy of *Leaves of Grass* and judged it obscene; that the Concord Library banned *Huckleberry Finn* because Louisa May Alcott said, "If Mr. Clemens cannot think of something better to tell our pure-minded lads and lassies, he had better stop writing for them"; and that Massachusetts' own Nathaniel Hawthorne was condemned as a broker of lust for his *Scarlet Letter* by a bishop who had evidently forgotten Paul's Epistle to Titus, "To the pure all things are pure; but to them that are defiled and unbelieving is nothing pure."

It would be foolish while reviewing literary censorship in Massachusetts to come to believe that it is a Protestant or Anglo-Saxon sport. In classical Greece, where freedom of philosophical speculation allegedly obtained, Socrates suffered the ultimate censorship, for as G. B. Shaw pointed out, the extreme form of censorship is assassination. The *Analects* of Confucius were destroyed in ancient China by the order of Emperor Chi Huang Ti.

After the invention of printing in the fifteenth century, the greater incidence of books made for a greater incidence of censorship. In 1557, under Pope Paul IV, the Inquisition drew up the first *Index Librorum Prohibitorum*, whose 1948 successor still enjoined good Catholics from damning themselves by reading *Decline and Fall of the Roman Empire;* John Stuart Mill's *Principles of Political Economy;* Pascal's *Pensées;* Richardson's *Pamela;* all the novels of Balzac, Dumas *père et fils*, Anatole France, Stendhal, and Zola; and all the works of David Hume and Voltaire. This situation obtained until the Vatican Council of 1965 rendered the *Index* relatively innocuous.

Censors have always been concerned only that their own particular oxen not be gored, and this has led to amusing anomalies. For example, although Boccaccio's *Decameron* was once on the *Index*, when an edition was brought out which eliminated none of the sins but transformed sinning priests and nuns into lay characters, it was allowed under the auspices of the Council of Trent in 1573.

"Banned in Boston" became a meaningful phrase because of the work of the New England Watch and Ward Society, to whose service Godfrey Lowell Cabot gave a large part of his total energies and substantial sums of money. Freudians will note with interest that the Society was originally called the Society for the Suppression of Vice, and its letterhead shows a male hand choking a writhing snake, with the injunction "Manu Forti" (with a strong hand).

The original Society for the Suppression of Vice was founded in New York, the outgrowth of a committee of the Y.M.C.A. set up by a former grocery clerk, Anthony Comstock, in 1872. Comstock was born in New Canaan, Connecticut, on March 7, 1844, and was the kind of fanatic who believed anything related to sex was obscene. In 1873 he guided through Congress an act tightening the federal laws on obscene publications which for the first time brought literature on contraception under the obscenity classification. Appointed a special agent of the Post Office for enforcing the act, he worked ferociously in that post until his death on September 21, 1915. Comstock was supported in his do-goodery by J. P. Morgan, who, like so many people, could not abide wickedness in others. Cabot always considered Morgan a scoundrel, in spite of their common attraction to the suppression of vice in others.

Comstock, like other rabid reformers including Godfrey Cabot, unconsciously proved the harmlessness of obscenity. Comstock, in his own words, for decades "stood at the mouth of the sewer," devouring filth for pay; and yet the service made him or kept him so pure that he could serve as the censor for less blessed millions. H. L. Mencken pointed up another unconscious service rendered by Comstock and his kind, whom he called "wowsers":

"The service that he performed, in his grandiose way, was no more than a magnification of the service that is performed every day by multitudes of humble Y.M.C.A. secretaries, evangelical clergymen, and other such lowly fauna. It is their function in the world to ruin their ideas by believing in them and living them. Striving sincerely to be patterns to the young, they suffer the ironical fate of becoming horrible examples. . . .

". . . He did more than any other man to ruin Puritanism in the United States. When he began his long brilliant career of unwitting sabotage, the essential principles of comstockery were believed in by practically every reputable American. Half a century later, when he went upon the shelf, comstockery enjoyed a degree of public esteem, at least in the big cities, half way between that enjoyed by phrenology and that enjoyed by homosexuality. It was, at best, laughable. It was, at worst, revolting."

As his Journals showed, Godfrey from his youth was an avid reader and viewer of plays and operas, always keeping a Pecksniffian eye for any obscenity or naughtiness, with the same single-minded reformer's zeal which his hero, Emerson, had condemned in men who "pull up lilies and plant skunk cabbages in their places." Had Godfrey had more interest in religion, he might have had less of an obsession with betting and bingo. Emerson also had noted in his Journal, "The unbelief of the age is attested by the loud condemnation of trifles" and "I hate goodies . . . We will almost sin to spite them." This contempt was later echoed by Mayor James Michael Curley's for the pious types in the Good Government groups in Boston, whom Curley christened "goo-goos."

Cabot's critiques often reflected boredom and disappointment when there was no naughtiness to condemn; on February 22, 1885, at the age of twenty-three he noted, "I finished to-day Wing and Wing by Cooper. I thought it unobjectionable but rather dull." At forty he still felt bilked on occasion. "Thursday, February 21 [1901], . . . Finished yesterday When Knighthood Was in Flower a much overrated book . . . rather coarse but harmless." And a few weeks later he again felt foiled at the inoffensiveness of a drama: "Went to Peaceful Valley at the

Grand, harmless but uninteresting play." This constant expecta-
tion of finding the worst in his fellowman was a part of Cabot's
Puritan inheritance. As Perry Miller has pointed out, "It is
impossible to conceive of a disillusioned Puritan; no matter what
misfortune befell him, no matter how often or how tragically his
fellowmen failed him, he would have been prepared for the worst,
and would have expected no better." If this point of view had
helped Cabot in the three rejections of his offers of marriage, it
played hell with the authors whose books he read in the hope of
being outraged.

If Godfrey was one of the most recent great Puritans to
project his private problems onto public affairs, the earliest Protestant to do so was Luther himself, of whom Dr. Friederich Heer
wrote: "We hear the characteristic tones of the salvationist, who
experiences his own demonic nature and all its emanations as the
work and will of God."

From his youth on, Godfrey was much happier when he
found something to condemn. At Harvard he had judged Dumas' *Les Trois Mousquetaires* "coarse and immoral" and was
even more outraged by Victor Hugo's *Les Misérables*. "I consider
it a great book . . . [but] by no means free from coarseness and
voluptuousness and far from artistic . . . The most pernicious
passage in the book is, I think, the one in which he speaks of love
as a resistless impulse, which will make or mar a man's life according as the object of it be worthy or unworthy. Love, as a passion,
attacks us on both our sensual and our emotional side, it can be
resisted, like every other temptation, and when it leads us into
error it is but cowardice and folly to assert that it is irresistible.
Every man ought to be able to say to the woman he loves,

'I could not love thee, dear, so much,
Loved I not honor more.' "

That a college boy was writing in his Journal to this effect
indicates the enormous moral burden passed early in life onto
Godfrey's shoulders from his ancestors. Nor did the college prude
relax once he graduated.

"Friday, June 12 [1885], I have just finished 'Lothair' by

Beaconsfield (then simply Hon Benj Disraeli) one of the most pernicious novels I ever read. The scene is laid in very high life. . . . One feels as if life must be an intolerable bore to people with nothing in particular to occupy them."

To be censorious one must feel superior to the common reader or playgoer. "Saturday, February 4 [1888]. Went to the theatre . . . to see Irving in Louis XI. . . . Irving is ultra-sensational and panders to the vulgar herd. . . . Tuesday, February 14 [1893] . . . went to 'A Masked Ball' at the Hollis. John Drew in the leading part. Play too Frenchy for my taste. Drew acts well but looks like a chief swell."

Amid Cabot's censorious complaints occasionally appears a depth of understanding that is surprising: ". . . went to the Lyceum to see Irving and Ellen Terry in Merchant of Venice. Irving grows more repulsive and Ellen Terry less attractive with each revolving year. . . . I hope before I die to see the title role filled by a great master of dramatic art. To my mind the Merchant of Venice himself is the noblest of all Shakespeare's characters and should be acted by a great genius and not treated as a minor part." But these insights were few, and most of Godfrey's comments were self-righteously condemnatory.

"Sunday, March 19 [1893], M. and I have finished Thackeray's 'Catherine' a horrid story of a lot of criminals. . . . Tuesday, July 4 [1893] . . . On my way here I read The Queen's Necklace by Dumas which is clever and amusing but full of the usual French nastiness. . . . Tuesday, July 24 [1894], I finished reading Trilby to M. a clever but pernicious book. Pernicious because totally false to nature and calculated to mislead the inexperienced and make them think it possible that a woman sexually impure can be absolutely perfect in all other respects."

A year later Cabot was still furious about Trilby. "Tuesday, June 4 [1895] . . . Finished Sapho by Alphonse Daudet. The most filthy story I ever read, and yet in my judgement much less likely to do harm than Trilby because more true to nature. It teaches the true lesson that a bad woman is a sink of filth no matter how much it may be begilded and that she is likely to deteriorate and drag down her companions in sin. Trilby advocates the utter falsehood that a woman leading a life of sin may be a good and loveable woman."

Godfrey was, in Coleridge's phrase, "a moral steam-engine," and the extraordinary degree of his reaction to what he viewed as immoral may perhaps best be suggested by a remark in his Journal: "We read an account of Abelard and Heloise. I think the former got no more than he deserved."

As Alan Simpson has pointed out, "The Puritan was always obsessed by his sense of sin. Taught to expect it everywhere, and to magnify it where he found it, he easily fell into the habit of inventing it." So Cabot, when he could not find particulars to condemn, often fell back on such general condemnation as "pernicious," "filthy," or "Frenchy." "Friday, April 3 [1896] Went to see Sarah Bernhardt in Adrienne Lecouvreur in which I saw her 16 years ago. I think her acting has improved in that time. It is full of the fire of genius. I picked this out as being the most decent in her repertoire the heroine at least being respectable but it is of the French Frenchy."

Cabot did not limit his critiques to matters moral but, as have many censors, volunteered as well strong opinions in matters of aesthetic judgment. He was almost an exact contemporary of Debussy and was born only six years before Bonnard, eight before Matisse and Gide, ten before Proust, and twelve before Colette. However, although in the sciences he was able to adjust to his time, in taste and morality he was not. "I finished *Vittoria* by George Meredith. . . . It is like a picture of the modern impressionist school gotten up for the benefit of artists with failing sight or too indolent or unskillful to draw correctly, leaving the chief burden to the imagination of the spectator . . . pictures that it is the fashion to admire and which I abominate . . . I fancy many art amateurs are nearsighted and nature looks to them as blurred as this monstrosity."

Cabot's sister Lilla was herself an artist and for a number of years a student and neighbor of Monet at Giverney. She and Monet once tried unsuccessfully to sell a painting by their then starving friend Pissarro to Mrs. Jack Gardner. With the benefit of hindsight, Cabot's heirs bemoan his distaste for the impressionists and his preference for chromos.

Although he had been a contributor since at least 1891, Godfrey's first reference to the Watch and Ward in his Journal appears on March 21, 1895, when, having made enough money in carbon black to pay off all his debts, he propitiated the jealous gods of morality by making a donation to the Society of $50.

He became a member of the Society in April 1900 and a member of the Board of Directors in 1908. Just as his Puritan ancestors had needed the Popes of Rome, the Stuarts, the witches of Salem, and slavery as objects of their hatred, so Cabot needed sin. Whereas Bishop Lawrence or Groton's Reverend Endicott Peabody could serve as Directors of the Watch and Ward without devoting too much time to the Society's business, Godfrey Cabot's interest was such that no detail of investigation or expense escaped his intense blue eyes. He had the awesome ardor of the elect, the untiring intensity of the demoniacally dedicated; in 1915 he was elected Treasurer, which post he filled until 1940.

The Society had been founded in Boston in 1878 by the Reverend Frederick B. Allen and employed a full time Secretary, one J. Frank Chase, both of whom were hyperactive sin chasers. But the greatest support for the Society, both financially and in energy, came from Cabot. Chase soon learned that no complaint was too small, no expense item too insignificant, to merit Cabot's attention. Cabot insisted that the Society rent office space and never own real estate, so that it could never be subject to punitive ad valorem tax valuations, as were the large landowners in Boston, who were therefore often reluctant to attack political corruption and vice. From the offices of the Society in the Equitable Building at 67 Milk Street (its later address was splendidly on Joy Street), Cabot sent out his first appeal for financial support under the headline "Lead Us Not into Temptation." He advised that "Weeds grow faster than flowers. To grow flowers, the weeds must be kept down. We keep down the weeds and give opportunity for the flower of youth to develop." There followed proof of the Society's weed-killing prowess—145 convictions in the preceding year for various crimes against the public chastity, health, and policy, ranging from the printing of dirty pictures to the selling of dope to the prisoners on Deer Island.

Cabot's job was to convince the members of the Society of the great danger and then to suggest that sufficient funds could deal with it. In his appeal of May 17, 1915, he wrote, "We are accustomed to thinking of France, and of Paris in particular, as the home of indecent drama and insidious suggestiveness. Permit us to call attention to the fact that in Paris the theatres are quite accurately classified and no decent woman or girl is in any danger of ever stepping inside of the theatres in which indecent suggestions form a part of the program. . . .

". . . It would be very shocking to a Frenchman to have his wife or daughter see some of the shows that are seen by the best society in Boston. . . .

". . . We hope then that you will not only support us with your purse this month but will give your advice."

In the Boston Puritan tradition of being shocked at the wickedness of French theater Abigail Adams had written to her sister from Auteuil on February 20, 1785, after seeing the ballet in Paris, "The dresses and beauty of the performers were enchanting; but, no sooner did the dance commence than I felt my delicacy wounded, and I was ashamed to be seen to look at them. Girls, clothed in the thinnest silk and gauze, with their petticoats short, springing two feet from the floor, poising themselves in the air, with their feet flying, and as perfectly showing their garters and drawers as though no petticoats had been worn, was a sight altogether new to me." Half a century later, Thomas Handasyd Perkins had been shocked to see the British waltzing at Chiltenham. And now Boston, in Godfrey's view, had become more debauched than Europe.

From 1915 on, Cabot's letter files contain communications from both professional sin chasers and amateurs. Cabot received a great deal of publicity for his Watch and Ward work, and as his fame as a vice killer grew, so did his correspondence from all over New England. A letter from Pittsfield, Massachusetts, urging the suppression of magazines such as *Snappy Stories* and *The Parisienne* is not untypical.

From as far away as Maine a Mrs. Mary S. Cobb wrote

seeking to have suppressed some moving pictures which she had not seen but which she understood were "in the interest of the Birth Control movement. . . . We all feel much sorrow for the misery of the thousands of little children who are born of diseased parents and into poverty and suffering, and who never should have come into the world . . . but two wrongs never make a right and birth control by any other means than self-control must inevitably mean the far greater prostitution of marriage and the deeper degradation of both men and women."

The Treasurer and his associates were constantly faced with the problem of how to conduct their dealings with sinners without themselves sinning or appearing to sin. In the "Private and confidential" Minutes of Meeting of the Directors of the Society on June 12, 1916, it was "voted that for the campaign in a city outside of Boston [New Bedford], agents of this Society be permitted to enter the general room of any suspected [whore] houses and if possible to purchase liquor therein and receive immoral tenders from the inmates, it being distinctly understood that the agents are not to place themselves in such relation to the inmates as would tend to compromise their character or reputation."

The subsequent Watch and Ward raid in New Bedford, led by the Rev. J. Frank Chase, brought headlines of the kind Cabot enjoyed.

50 PRISONERS IN SATURDAY NIGHT RAIDS
BIG CLEAN-UP MADE BY WATCH AND WARD

OFFICERS ARREST MEN AS WELL AS WOMEN CAUGHT IN ALLEGED DISORDERLY HOUSES—21 FOUND AT CRAP GAME—"ONLY THE BEGINNING" SAYS WATCH AND WARD SECRETARY

BIGGEST JOLT TENDERLOIN HAS HAD SINCE HUNTER CLUB RAID

J. Frank Chase, the Secretary of the Society, a muscular Methodist ex-minister, enjoyed leading the raids as much as Cabot enjoyed reading about them. Perhaps the only greater enjoyment he had was in talking to the press afterward.

When I was a boy in my native city of Chelsea I had a fight on my hands about every day and I was compelled to fight to protect myself. There was a time when I had licked every red-headed man in Chelsea. Some of the boys I fought with have since held high places in the state. I've got plenty of red blood and I like to fight.

Nowadays when I go into a raid, I always take my glasses off and fight with my fists first. Of course, I have other means of protection in case my fists fail, but I would rather fight with my hands than with weapons. . . .

Our enemies have made capital out of the fact that we employ college students in our work, by leading the public to believe that we engage boys in their "teens" to probe into the depths of immorality and iniquity. We do employ college students but they are students from the medical colleges who have seen enough to warn them of the effects of evil doing. They are not callow youths but men of 28 or 30 years of age.

There is only one way to get evidence against gambling houses and red light resorts and that is to go into them and mingle with the people who frequent them. If there were any cleaner way to investigate conditions we should adopt it. Our men do play the game when they are getting information about gambling houses; they also go into houses of prostitution when they find it necessary to get evidence against the proprietors. In visits to gambling places such as we have found in New Bedford, they have orders not to lose more than $2 at a time. Their losses are made good by the society and if they win anything they turn it in to the society treasury. Any man who attempted to go into a gambling place without getting into the game would not stand much chance of success.

In their visits to places of ill fame our agents travel in pairs and they have orders to go no farther than the general assembly room. We have no cases on record where our orders have been disobeyed. Our agents know that we do not want them to contaminate themselves in getting evidence.

If some people showed half the squeamishness regarding the existence of houses of assignation and other sinks of vice and immorality as they do regarding our methods of investigation, we wouldn't find much work to do.

Frank Chase's pugnacity was the cause of some criticism and complaint, but he was invariably supported by Cabot. The Puritan prophets of the New Israel were never sticklers for civil rights and never hampered themselves with procedural safeguards in their administration of the law. Like the old Jewish patriarchs, they were, at least in their own view, administering divine law and not elected responsible officials of a popular sovereignty, embarrassed by niggling constitutional restraints.

Indeed, the Watch and Ward Society did much of its work outside the law on a blackmail basis, threatening booksellers and politicians, magazine vendors and mayors with unfavorable publicity or economic boycott (as is still the practice with most self-appointed censors). Such extralegal censorship, sometimes with the unofficial cooperation of the police, post office, or customs inspectors, has always been both cheaper than the difficult and drawn-out appeals to the courts and less likely to awaken organized public protest.

The Watch and Ward Society's efforts, however, were not entirely limited to *sub rosa* arrangements with the Boston booksellers and to private deals with hotel and apartment-house owners. The Society devoted a good deal of effort to attempts to rewrite existing legislation or get new legislation passed in the Commonwealth. On January 4, 1917, for example, there appeared in the Boston *Transcript*, that bulwark of Boston Brahminism, a long letter signed by Frederick B. Allen, President of the New England Watch and Ward Society, urging that district attorneys be appointed by the governor of the Commonwealth rather than elected.

In *The Character of a Trimmer* Sir George Savile, Marquis of Halifax, wrote "Temporal things will have their weight in the World, and tho Zeal may prevail for a time, and get the better in a Skirmish, yet the War endeth generally on the side of Flesh and Blood, and will do so until Mankind is another thing than it is at present." Although Cabot would have considered this attitude pernicious moral defeatism, even he had some sense of balance in matters moral. In 1905, at the end of a cold Sunday in January, Godfrey wrote Minnie, "I hope there will be no attempts to close the theatres on Sunday. Let them first close the whorehouses and the liquor saloons on Sundays *at least* and not drive people into and thro' these gates of hell by depriving them of rational amusement."

Cabot's practical view of the Lord's day was in keeping with his family tradition. There had been a time in Massachusetts when one Captain Kemble, after a three-year voyage, arrived home on a Sunday and for kissing his wife on his front doorstep had been put in the stocks for profaning the Sabbath. With the rise of the merchant princes, however, the church had changed with the times. When Black Ben Forbes, Perkins' youngest captain in the China trade, returned on a Sunday after three years at sea with $30,000 in doubloons, he got Henry Higginson out of church to bank the money.

In writing to an acquaintance in Washington, D.C., on December 23, 1916, in regard to federal censorship of moving pictures, Cabot exhibited some awareness of the demands of the flesh and of differences of degree in wickedness. "I have seen a great many moving picture shows, chiefly in different parts of Florida and different parts of West Virginia and none among them that I would think could properly be suppressed by law. I have heard of moving picture shows exhibited in Havana, Cuba, and exhibited in a Lodge of the Elks, or some other secret order, and made for distribution in a State, which were distinctly obscene and liable to prosecution under existing law.

"We are all deeply interested in the diminution and suppression, if possible, of the sale of narcotic drugs and liquor, other than to those who need them in medical treatment, but we are so constituted that we must have our amusements. I think the moving picture business, on the whole, is a highly beneficial business, which places within the reach of the poor, an opportunity to see a much higher type of art and gain visual education as to many foreign countries, which would otherwise be out of their reach. I believe that they are very useful safety valves to the desire for amusement and the most successful competitor today existing to divert the people from saloons and low dives and I most earnestly deprecate being too censorious and striving to enforce by outside pressure, esthetic standards, which can only be effectively established by persuasion and suggestion.

"I was an eye-witness at the St. Louis Fair, to the incalculable harm done by the activities of the International Reform Bureau and the W.C.T.U., by shutting up the World's Fair on Sundays, by saddling this condition on a congressional appropriation and I fear the possibility that the measure you now propose may do even greater harm because one more widely diffused throughout the people. In 1904, on Sundays, the Saloons of St. Louis were jammed to the doors and I fear that a too rigid censorship of the moving picture industry may result in a great increase in the patronage of saloons and brothels throughout the length and breadth of this country."

Cabot insisted on signing every check of the Society himself; since he was off in West Virginia or "drumming" much of the time, and later was on duty as a Navy flier, difficulties arose in Boston. When he was away, Frank Chase sent him frequent and detailed reports, including one to Florida, on January 6, 1917, which said, "Owing to the delay in the check for my salary reaching you and being returned, I have had to secure from Miss Copeland two of the emergency checks which you so kindly signed, and I understand from her she is sending to you two more to replace them, also the payroll check for January 20th."

As no detail was too insignificant for Cabot, so no potential form of vice was too obscure for investigation by the Society. In the Minutes of the Directors Meeting at the Boston City Club on February 12, 1917, it was voted that "Doctor Boos and Doctor Cummings be elected a committee to report to the next meeting of the Directors on the evils of Coca Cola." There is also correspondence between Chase and Cabot on the dangers of Jamaica ginger, a medicine whose formula of 90 per cent alcohol and 10 per cent extract of ginger root inspired those made thirsty by the Volstead Act to apply to druggists for medicinal help.

One of Cabot's moral *bêtes noires* was any kind of lottery, and he fought them not only in Massachusetts but all over the country, in contrast to his ancestor, George Cabot, who had petitioned Alexander Hamilton to try to influence the Congress to institute a national lottery to help support his cotton mill.

World War I inspired Cabot and his cohorts at the Watch and Ward to a frenzy of activity. Cabot had been unable to admit to himself when his competitors suggested price-fixing agreements on carbon black that he might take advantage of such an agreement secretly to undersell his competitors and to woo away their customers. Instead, he projected such evil thoughts onto his competitors, telling his associates that he would not be a party to price-fixing agreements because "they," his competitors, would secretly undersell him. He was equally unable to admit to himself his passionate interest in dirty books and brothels, and by the same process of projection he instead attributed such interest to others and set himself up as the agent who would save them from their awful desires. When those to be saved were draftees for the Great War, patriotism could be wedded to prurience, a felicitous match.

In 1918 there was a protracted correspondence between the Watch and Ward Society and the War Department concerning a training film on the dangers of venereal disease entitled "Fit to Fight." In those pre-penicillin days the endless treatment for syphilis used various compounds of mercury and the War Department warned the doughboys that "An hour with Venus means a lifetime with Mercury." The Society objected to the "exhibition of a perfectly nude woman—Venus" in the film and various other aspects of "this delicate question of pedagogy." The representatives of the War Department explained at great length that the

alleged nude woman was obviously a statue, used for a particularly important purpose, but the pugilistic prude, Frank Chase,
who had no objection to the statue of Mercury, insisted that he
and Cabot wanted a more modest Venus. Chase said he was a
better judge of the pedagogy of sex hygiene than the film producer, Mr. Griffith, who failed to understand that passion was
more powerful than any "psychrosis" of fear.

Frank Chase's proselyting pugnacity reached an all-time
high during the war, as did his literary style during his raids on
various Massachusetts and Rhode Island whorehouses frequented
by "our boys." "He knew that more deadly enemies than Huns
were in that House, the spreaders of disease which maim as effec-
tually as German machine guns. . . . Ever since the war began,
the New England Watch and Ward Society has been fighting the
forces that fight the fighters, immoral houses, gambling dens,
narcotic drugs and obscene pictures. When it crossed the line into
Rhode Island it entered the State to stay until the promoters of
vice,—the powers that prey, the counterfeiters of pleasure, those
who coin character into tainted money and drop innocent heart
blood into dirty drachmas, the Huns of modern society heed the
challenge of decent public opinion and surrender, not alone because the President demands it but because God demands and the
public opinion demands it. And the surrender must be an unconditional one."

Unconditional surrenders are usually costly to achieve, and
wars are traditionally wasteful. But Cabot's war against wickedness was one of the most minutely audited attacks in history. He
constantly pressed Chase to reduce the payroll of the Society, to
hire as few free-lance detectives to investigate wickedness and as
few lawyers to help prosecute it as possible. In some years the
Society operated on as little as $15,000. By January 1919 Cabot
had squeezed Chase down to a staff of only three and himself. And
yet virtue was obviously its own reward since Chase could still say
that although few men envied his lot, he had a glorious time in
his job.

But as in other kinds of work, there were rewards other than
monetary. A form letter of October 23, 1919, invited the Directors to attend a meeting at which "Mr. Oberholtzer, Secretary of

the Pennsylvania State Board of Censors, will give a private exhibition of motion picture reels, incorporating the parts cut out of the pictures by his Board." Cabot's files also contain photographs of some of the naughty ladies involved in the sin of the city, and these perhaps provided some added incentive to the tedious business of trying to make Boston's apartments "vice proof, as they are now required to be fire proof."

Both the Board of Directors and the membership of the Watch and Ward Society was made up overwhelmingly of Protestants. Occasionally the Board was decorated with the name of a rabbi or a Roman Catholic, but these participants usually left before long and were hard to replace. No amount of hard work by Cabot or Frederick Allen could ever correct this problem, which enabled the victims of the Watch and Ward, particularly politicians, to charge the Society with religious bigotry.

Literary censorship was not unique to Boston. The same attitudes and activities were current throughout America in large towns and small in the first third of this century and, indeed, exist in many areas today. But the Watch and Ward's zeal gave Boston a greater notoriety as a center of book-burning than that of any other city. Henry James' novel *The Bostonians* gives a psychological picture of Boston in the 1870's as "a confused scene, slightly mad with neurotic repressions, provincialism and earnestness without intellectual seriousness." Henry Adams said "a simpler manner of life and thought could hardly exist, short of cave-dwelling": and Santayana characterized Boston as a "moral and intellectual nursery, always busy applying first principles to trifles." Even Ira Gershwin's lyrics took note of The Hub's prudery.

In spite of a brilliant defense by Clarence Darrow, the New York publisher of Theodore Dreiser's *An American Tragedy* was convicted on obscenity charges by a judge of the Massachusetts Supreme Court. This event inspired an anonymous wag to point out that the judge had missed another dirty book.

Your Honor, this book is a bucket of swill:
    It portrays a young couple alone on a hill,
And a woman who lived in a shoe as a house

With her brood, but not once does it mention her spouse.
I submit that this volume's obscene, lewd and loose
    And demand its suppression. Its name? Mother Goose.

It might be thought that Boston's antisex attitude reflected a weakness in her men, a thinning of the blood from too much intermarriage, or an inclination toward homosexuality. At least in Cabot's case such a conjecture could not be further from the truth. His letters to his wife indicate not only a strong and continuing appetite for sex, but also extraordinary sexual fantasies. These letters may give some insight into Cabot's tremendous concern with matters sexual.

At 4:12 in the morning from the Chancellor Hotel in Parkersburg, West Virginia, on May 8, 1904, Cabot wrote to his Minnie.

> *Dear Wife*
>
>   I have had a dream, I can't sleep for longing.
>
>   Ich träumte dass du in meinen Mund hineingeharnt hast, viel, sehr viel und dass ich deinen Harn begierig hinunter geschluckt. . . .
>
>   Ich liebe dich so. Ach dass du hier warst. *
>
>   It is very warm. I worked over my mail all yesterday I expect to finish it today.
>
>   I start for Grantsville early tomorrow morning. I called on the Episcopal rector Rev. Scollay Moore last night.
>
>   I do love you my treasure so so much.
>
> *Your lover*
Godfrey L. Cabot
>
> Ich sehne nach einem anderen Kinde
> Sollen wir es mal versuchen.†

Cabot often switched to German and occasionally to Latin or Greek when expressing affection or desire. That he was not other-

---

* I dreamed that you urinated into my mouth, much, very much, and that I greedily swallowed down your urine . . . I love you so much. Oh if only you were here.
    † I very much desire another child
    We should try again [*or* Should we try again?]

wise conscious of anything shocking in his words seems indicated by his matter-of-fact resumption of everyday topics.

From the Waldo Hotel in Clarksburg, West Virginia, on May 17, 1905, Cabot wrote another letter whose contents he might well have considered unfit for a lesser citizen of Boston to read.

Dear Wife

I saw "London Assurance" at the New National in Washington last night only passably acted. I took the 1245 train hither arriving here, one hour late, after 10 this forenoon.

After getting as far east as Washington I hate to have to return.

You do not know how I long for you. I was almost wild with desire as I came along hither in the train today.

Ich wollte dass deine Blase mit Harn bis zum platzen gefüllt würde und du könntest dich, um dein Leben zu retten, nur auf der Weise erledigen dass du in meinen Mund hinein harnen solltest bis du dich gänzlich entleert und ich mit deinem Harne ganz zum Platzen gefüllt wurde.

Oder wenn du eine grosse Riesin wärest, die sehr verhungert war und sehr danach sehnte einen Menschen zu fressen wie gerne wäre ich das Opfer, wenn du mich nur lebendig verschingen solltest, wenn du durch deine geliebten Lippen über deine schleimige Zunge erstens meine Füsse zunächst meine Beine meine Hüften meinen ganzen Leib meinen Kopf nacheinander dahin ziehen solltest durch deine schöne Kehle in deinen lieben Bauch wo ich deinen Herzensschlag und Athmen so lieblich und ruhig vernehmen konnte als ich in Wonne entschlafte und ich in dich durch Verdauung nach und nach dahinverschwand.*

* I wish that your bladder were full to bursting with urine and that you could save your life only by urinating into my mouth until you had

You would best destroy this silly letter or if you cannot understand it, with the help of a German dictionary, I will translate it to you when I return.

Your lover,
Godfrey L. Cabot

The injunction to destroy his letter conflicts with Godfrey's adamant position of twenty years earlier condemning Blaine, or any man, for writing letters that had to be destroyed.

In studying Cabot's progress from college prude to the chief keeper of New England's morals, it is perhaps useful to note not only that he read a great deal, but what he read in relation to what was being published. Although the period from the end of the Civil War to the end of World War I was characterized as New England's decline or Indian summer, it produced works by Henry Adams, Emily Dickinson, Henry and William James, Sarah Orne Jewett, Hugo Munsterberg, Charles Eliot Norton, George Herbert Palmer, Francis Parkman, Josiah Royce, Santayana, and Harriet Beecher Stowe. It is worth wondering why in Cabot's almost daily literary comment he never once mentioned having read anything by these first-rate authors and philosophers. His comments and, therefore, presumably his reading time were devoted mainly to hundreds of second- and third-rate American novelists, long since forgotten, and to British, French, and German novelists.

Cabot's century was the period when America changed from a primitive and agricultural country to an industrialized urban society, with the resultant problems and increasing leisure. But whereas at least a few men were addressing themselves to the large

---

entirely emptied yourself, and I was full to bursting with your urine.

Or if you were an utterly starved giantess who had a great craving to eat a human, how I'd love to be the victim if only you'd devour me alive, with your beloved lips, over your slime-slick tongue, drawing first my feet, then my legs, my hips, my whole trunk, my head—one after another—through your beautiful throat into your dear belly, where I could so joyously and quietly hear your heartbeat and your breathing as in ecstasy I fell asleep and through digestion little by little disappeared into you.

philosophical and social questions of the new society, Cabot usually did not.

Sigmund Freud, who was born in 1856 and whose work so tremendously affected American thought in the last half of Godfrey's life, was a man whose work he ignored, as were Carl Jung and Havelock Ellis. When Freud was so clearly the enemy of Cabot's point of view, it is noteworthy that Cabot ignored his existence, in spite of the fact that on Freud's only American visit, to Clark University in Worcester, his only American supporter was James Jackson Putnam, the Professor of Neuropathology at Harvard and a prominent Boston physician, whom Godfrey knew. Not only was Putnam himself related to Cabot, but his wife was Godfrey's cousin, Marian Cabot, the daughter of Francis Cabot and Louisa Higginson.

Cabot was able to ignore Putnam's book *Human Motives,* published in 1915, and even the fact that by 1916 there were 500 psychoanalysts in New York City, although Godfrey was not as frank about his blindness as was the great analyzer, Henry Adams, who had also refused to accept psychology. "He put psychology under lock and key; he insisted on maintaining his absolute standards; on aiming at ultimate Unity. The mania for handling all the sides of every question, looking into every window, and opening every door, was, as Bluebeard judiciously pointed out to his wives, fatal to their practical usefulness in society."

It is at the very least interesting that a man with so great an interest in sexuality as Cabot missed by so close a margin the man whose understanding of sexuality changed the world. Cabot's idea that sexuality is the dominant controlling biological force and must always be choked is very like Freud's idea that the id is insatiable and does not concern itself with the well-being of the ego or the psyche. Although the premise of Cabot and the premise of Freud are curiously alike, their conclusions were not.

Freud taught that man was inevitably sensual, as early Puritans had taught he was inherently wicked; both ideas were anathema to Godfrey. Difficult as it is today to believe in human perfectibility, to many in Cabot's time even science seemed to confirm

the Puritan dream. As Henry Adams wrote, "To other Darwinians except Darwin—Natural Selection seemed a dogma to be
put in the place of the Athanasian creed; it was a form of religious hope; a promise of ultimate perfection."

In Godfrey's letters or Journal there are no references to
Karl Marx. This ignorance of serious authors and this concentration upon novels may be only partially explained by a harassed
businessman's preference for amusement rather than education.

Cabot was typical as an aristocrat and as a businessman in
having been insulated from the really germinal ideas of his time
until their effects had become very general. He was well aware of
politics, diplomacy, tariffs, and such current events as had an
immediate effect on his business. He read the newspapers and
wrote letters to them about the annexation of Cuba and the
Philippines, the outrageousness of police strikes, and limitations
on the use of natural gas. But he did not read Marx or Freud.
While no psychoanalytical analysis of Cabot's selective inatten-
tion need be attempted, a historical analogy may perhaps be
useful. The aristocrats of Long Island's North Shore had no real
awareness of the importance of Franklin D. Roosevelt's ideas
until six years after his election, when one of their number,
George Whitney, was sentenced to jail as a result of the laws
produced by those ideas. So aristocrats almost always have been
shocked and outraged at the consequences of ideas whose births
they hardly noticed. Cabot was unaware of Marx and Freud until
their ideas were popularized and were reflected in the police strike
and the appearance of advertisements of women smoking ciga-
rettes. He failed to foresee the challenge and threat of the new
ideas and felt doubly shocked by the *faits accomplis.*

As to his reading of novels, he held the European view of
fiction as a mirror of society. He might never see or want to see
life in Montparnasse, but he could read Balzac. He most certainly
would never get or want an introduction to the likes of Fagin, but
he read Dickens. For him novels widened the horizons without
dirtying the fingers. Novels provided vicarious experience, and
vicarious experience was obviously a necessity for a man who
wanted to condemn and destroy brothels but could never enter

one. Thus novels were surrogates for real experience.

"In the ev'g I finished 'Smoke' by Ivan Turgenieff. His novels are not very pleasing to me, they take me into society in which I do not feel at home and do not wish to feel at home . . . finished in the ev'g 'Peregrine Pickle' by Smollet. This book is very clever and full of incident but is perhaps the smuttiest I ever [in 1884] read. I should not have begun it had I known how coarse and vulgar it was, nor shall I wittingly take up such books in future but I am not sorry I read it for I imagine it gives a pretty good idea of the taste of the last century, in novels."

On Saturday, June 4, 1898, Cabot noted in his Journal, "On the cars I finished Boccaccio's Decameron a most versatile and amusing collection much of it very coarse some of it very pretty, a German translation from the Italian. In spite of its immorality I think it a book worth reading at any rate for me and I regret that I did not read it years ago for it shows a very important side of human nature and one with which my life does not bring me into contact and God willing never shall, but yet which it is well to appreciate not wholly without sympathy."

Before criticizing the long list of novels Cabot read or criticizing the absence from it of many authors who are now admired, one would do well to look at book reviews of thirty years ago to see how many authors reviewed then are hardly known today. It is at least possible that fifty years hence those authors whose names now appear prominently will be as unknown as the authors whose names are in Cabot's Journal. He doubtless read what he found in the bookstores and what his friends mentioned at dinner parties, and apparently Howells and James were not included.

In view of the great numbers of books Cabot did read and on which he commented, however, and in view of the very large percentage of his waking hours which he spent on his work and also on his athletic and other interests, it is evident that even if he was a most extraordinarily rapid reader, he could not possibly have devoured that many pages. He must have done a great deal of scanning in the many books on which he reported, which seems to evidence his motive in reading. In his viewing of paintings he seems more often than not to have been seeking faults rather than artistic enjoyment. In his breathless progress through books, and in view of most of his reactions to books, it seems most likely that instead of savoring the book as a total artistic entity, he was looking for salacious parts to warn others about or for some kind of titillation or both. He was not really reading; he was practicing literary voyeurism.

What he read and what he did not read seem to confirm this view. He failed to read too great a percentage of the important books of his time, especially nonfiction books, whose titles evidenced no possibility of salacious content. Had he read the best books, he would have had to read them slowly enough to comprehend the total artistic performance. In his own view he simply did not have the time.

His older sister Nellie—Godfrey's favorite perhaps because she was the other Puritan of the family, though differently than Godfrey—wrote him frequently about his reluctance to read anything but novels and newspapers and his ignorance of important books and ideas. "You say in your last letter in answer to my request that you read Kerman's Russian articles that you 'have not sufficient surplus energy,' you 'lack the happy faculty to throw off the serious thoughts of life.' I read this sentence through twice before I could believe that you were referring to your Lamp Black, as claiming the 'serious thoughts of life,' in contradistinction to the Social Problem in Russia [in 1889]. Dear Goff, in the past two years I have preached you many a sermon, in my own mind, on this text. Yet now that the opportunity occurs, my eloquence fails, and I can only quote Romola to you. 'We can only have the highest happiness, such as goes along with being a great man, by having wide thoughts and much feeling for the rest of the world as well as ourselves.'

"Don't, my darling, let your absorption in business render you incapable of serious reading, as seems to have been the case hitherto. Let your thoughts and interests be so wide and earnest moreover that they shall *compel* you to read & inform yourself on the problems on which you are always so ready and eager to talk. You have excellent brains, my dear boy, but I doubt whether you realize to what a narrow field they have been turned for some time past, and how rusty they have already become. . . . I don't call newspapers, the ordinary magazine articles or light novels . . . *reading* at all. The servants in my kitchen do as much as that. . . . The old world keeps a-rolling pretty fast, and I don't want it to leave you behind, dear."

What Nellie did not realize, any more than did Godfrey himself, was that he really did not have time to do what she called reading. It was already remarkable that he was able to scan the hundreds of novels he criticized considering the long hours he spent working and at tennis and the many other activities he undertook.

Godfrey saw his role in the world as a reader who would protect the defenseless masses against the kind of titillations which he could handle but which they could not. He did not read inferior books and ignore superior books because his taste was such that he preferred mediocre literature to first-rate literature. He was not interested in literature as such.

As he saw it, his duty was to stop the use of literature to excite the desires of people, not as morally fortified as he, who might translate their excitement into some form of overt action. It was not that he was a bad literary critic; he was playing a quite different game. He was not a literator who read in order to achieve an exchange of existence between himself and the author and an entry into the author's world. He was policing the literary pharmacy for dope and for Spanish fly.

CHAPTER XII

Pelletier and Coakley

> If we had no faults, we should not find so much enjoyment in seeing faults in others. LA ROCHEFOUCAULD, *Maxims*, No. 31

> Who, then, is the invincible man? He whom nothing that is outside the sphere of his moral purpose can dismay. EPICTETUS, *Discourses*, Bk. i, ch. 18, sec. 21

Cabot's interest in brothels and dirty books not only made him a figure of fun, it also led him into the most dangerous fight of his life.

There lived with her parents in Boston in 1913 a lady of twenty-nine years, one hundred and fifteen pounds, and five feet three inches of height, whom we shall call Sarah Black. In an unsigned affidavit made before one of Cabot's lawyers, Miss Black swore to an extraordinary story.

Unmarried and virginal, Miss Black allegedly had a number of nervous complaints not totally unknown to other unmarried and virginal ladies in their twenties, thirties, and forties in other times and in other places. She was frequently unable to sleep; she was subject to tears and depression; she worried a great deal; and she had what she considered unfortunate dreams, both sleeping and awake.

When Miss Black confided her problems to a girl friend—an older and also unmarried lady, the leader of a ladies' literary club in Roxbury to which Miss Black belonged—her friend recommended that she see a doctor whom we shall call Cunningham, who had cured the literary lady of similar symptoms and had "saved so many she knew from disaster." So urgent was her desire that Miss Black see Dr. Cunningham that she offered to lend her $20, the sum which Dr. Cunningham required to be paid in advance.

"He said that the reason for the $20 in advance was that if a person went to him just once without any payment she would quickly and unfairly go away dissatisfied, but if she made a considerable payment she would give the doctor's treatment a fair trial, at least a month's trial."

Dr. Cunningham had a deep and soothing voice, strong but gentle hands, and a knowledge of the needs of worried and nervous unmarried ladies between the ages of twenty-five and forty. His knowledge of and skill in treating such ladies is perhaps not too surprising, since much of his practice was devoted only to them. He was five feet eight inches tall, of medium build, with white hair to inspire confidence and a close-cut white mustache to inspire romance. He was, at least by his own account, a graduate of Harvard College and an ex-Texas cowboy.

His treatment for all such patients differed sometimes in speed, but never in kind. According to Miss Black's affidavit, on her first few visits the doctor merely interrogated her as to her economic status and her sexual experience, expressing satisfaction with the former and horror at the total absence of the latter.

His apartment on Beacon Street also served as his office. As her visits there progressed, Dr. Cunningham's reiterated concern lest Miss Black's continued continence lead her to total madness impressed upon her his devotion and his interest in her well-being. He continually repeated to her that she must have absolute confidence in him and that his treatment was a medical necessity, also commenting frequently on the beauty of her hair, her skin, and her soul.

As her confidence in Dr. Cunningham grew, his treatment progressed from the gentle rubbing of her neck to a point when he convinced her to remove her shirtwaist and upper garments, to lie down upon a couch, and to allow him to massage her above the waist with a sweet-smelling ointment. At this stage her treatment came to a standstill for some weeks. Dr. Cunningham vehemently urged Miss Black to remove her skirt, petticoats, and other *impedimenti,* in order that he might increase the area of his massage. But Miss Black found herself unable to acquiesce to the expanding needs of medicine.

As this impasse continued, according to Miss Black's story, Dr. Cunningham interspersed his medical arguments with eloquent declamations of his increasing affection for her. Finally his declarations of love, combined with dire predictions of her rapidly approaching insanity if she did not follow his clinical advice, succeeded in convincing Miss Black to disrobe completely, but only after Dr. Cunningham had extinguished all of the electric lights. What then followed, Miss Black described in great detail and glowing wonder in her affidavit, but suffice it to say here that it constituted that treatment facetiously prescribed for hysteria by many Viennese doctors, which had outraged Freud and had set him off to his discovery, *penis erectus usus normalis.*

For a number of months Miss Black was quite satisfied with her treatment, and her confidence in and her affection for Dr. Cunningham increased with each visit. One afternoon, however, she found another young woman in the doctor's waiting room when she arrived, a circumstance which had never before arisen and perhaps might never have arisen but for the doctor's fatigue, which doubtless resulted from his intense and exhausting concern with the well-being of his patients. The doctor was rather a long time in arriving, which gave Miss Black an opportunity to chat with the other young woman, in the course of which conversation she discovered that the young woman had had symptoms distressingly similar to her own but was rapidly improving under a course of treatment practically identical to Miss Black's.

Thereupon Miss Black left the waiting room without seeing Dr. Cunningham, and in the next few days all her earlier nervous symptoms returned and in aggravated form. In addition she found herself the victim of a new symptom, more violent than any of her earlier ones—a terrible rage against Dr. Cunningham, combined with an increasing conviction that his medical treatment was not what it should have been.

When this last symptom became quite unbearable, Miss

Black took herself to the most prominent physician in Boston, Dr. Richard Cabot. After listening to her history, he determined that her problem was perhaps moral rather than medical and sent her to his cousin Godfrey. Upon hearing of Miss Black's unfortunate experience, Godfrey was, not surprisingly, outraged and decided that the whole story must forthwith be presented to the District Attorney of Suffolk County, one Joseph C. Pelletier.

District Attorney Pelletier had achieved his exalted position of power and not inconsiderable wealth by a felicitous combination of intelligence, cunning, and hard work. His background being French-Canadian and Irish rather than Boston Brahmin, his point of view was substantially different from Cabot's. When Pelletier was told the outrageous story of Miss Black and Dr. Cunningham, he laughed. Indeed, he expressed some admiration for and envy of Dr. Cunningham. Instead of prosecuting Cunningham, Pelletier called him in to his office, after which conference Cunningham disappeared from Boston. To Godfrey Lowell Cabot such a reaction was disgraceful, atrocious, infamous, and scandalous. Cabot thereupon decided that so opprobrious and ignoble a scoundrel as Pelletier must be removed.

To understand the immensity of such an undertaking as the destruction of Pelletier (at least for a hero without an enchanted sword) it is necessary to have some little knowledge of Boston politics at the beginning of the twentieth century. To say that Boston politics was more corrupt than that of New York or Chicago would be to reveal a kind of twisted and parochial chauvinism. But it would surely be easier to undertake proving that Boston was more corrupt than that it was less so.

Perhaps, however, it is not unfair to say that since they became important in Boston politics in the mid-nineteenth century, the Boston Irish have come to feel that if a politician is a son of a bitch, that is all right so long as he is "our son of a bitch." Indeed, chicanery, such as cheating on Civil Service or Harvard examinations, while not absolutely mandatory for success in Boston politics, has certainly not significantly hurt the careers of politicians from James Michael Curley to Teddy Kennedy.

One of the most important powers of a district attorney is

the power to nol pros (nolle prosequi) a case; that is, the power to
decide not to prosecute a case either before it has been presented
to the Grand Jury or even after a Grand Jury has found a True
Bill. Pelletier used his power to nol pros as a means of substantially augmenting his income. Although this practice was not
unknown to other district attorneys in other counties and other
states, Pelletier (and Nathan A. Tufts, the district attorney of
neighboring Middlesex County) developed the practice into a big
business. It was generally known in Boston that either Pelletier or
Tufts would nol pros virtually any case for a big enough bribe
and that the best conduit for such a bribe was an attorney named
Daniel H. Coakley.

Coakley was the *ne plus ultra* among Boston Irishmen of the
Jim Curley and "Honey Fitz" days who knew how to mulct the
last dime from a sucker, but he was also capable of the beau geste,
usually not at his own expense. In April 1906, when his horse and
rig were allegedly stolen by one W. A. Reynolds, a Cambridge
barber, Coakley announced to the reporters that he would not
prosecute the poor man, since he was not responsible at the time
on account of liquor. This gesture provided Coakley with free
publicity in the Boston press, and presumably few of the many
men who in the years to come were to sit in Reynolds' barber chair
escaped a panegyric on the darling Daniel Coakley and his great
heart.

"Dan" Coakley, as he was known to all of Boston, was a
small handsome man with wavy blue-black hair, a mobile and
expressive face, and a melodious, mellifluous voice with more stops
than the organ in the Cardinal's cathedral.

Born in Boston in 1865, he most commonly related that he
had been too poor to go further than parochial school and had
gone to work at fourteen as a teamster. At eighteen, while learning shorthand at night school, he worked as a streetcar conductor
but was fired when a strike he led against the transit company
failed.

He next went to New York, where he worked as a reporter on
the *Sun;* and then came back to Boston, where, at twenty-one, as a
sports reporter for the Boston *Herald,* he covered the John L.

Sullivan–Jake Kilrain fight in Mississippi, sending back a four-hour scoop on the "Boston Strong Boy's" victory. He beat his rivals in a thrilling burro-back race through the swamps to the only telegraph.

He next studied law with his brother and eventually won more tort cases against the Boston Elevated Railway Company, which had fired him, than any other "injury case" lawyer in Boston. He soon turned to criminal law and big civil cases, in which he made a fortune representing "Big Bill" Kelliher and also Miss Elizabeth ("Toodles") Ryan in a famous breach-of-promise suit, as well as Charles Ponzi, the "wizard of finance."

So profitable was the nol pros business that District Attorney Pelletier was not content merely to nol pros criminal cases which came as a natural result of the police apprehension of actual lawbreakers. Pelletier, Tufts, and their friend Coakley "created" nol pros business.

The most usual device for this was known as the "badger game." A man of some substance was led by a woman in Coakley's employ into taking her to a hotel bedroom. Some little time later, when the two were in a clearly compromising position, their room would be broken into, either by the police or by the husband or father of the lady. In those cases when the police broke in, the man would be formally charged with fornication, contributing to the delinquency of a minor, or any other appropriate criminal charge. Very soon thereafter the man or his attorney would come to know that Mr. Daniel Coakley felt he could get the charges nol prossed by the District Attorney (either Pelletier, if the charge was in Suffolk County, or Tufts, if it was in Middlesex County) for a fee which was carefully fixed so as to take the fullest possible advantage of the man's desire to avoid not only the possibility of a jail sentence but also the certainty of a great deal of unattractive publicity. In cases where the husband or father broke in, the man would be threatened not only with criminal actions, but also with civil actions, such as being named corespondent in the aggrieved husband's suit for divorce. He would soon learn, however, that a suitably substantial sum paid to Coakley could not only result in the plaintiff's civil suit being nol prossed, but, *mirabile dictu*, in reconciling the cuckolded man and his wife.

The permutations and variations of the badger game were endless, and its victims varied from big butter-and-egg types from all over New England to nationally known men who had been careless of the Seventh and possibly the Tenth Commandments.

The most famous example, known as the Mishawum Manor Case, is perhaps less luridly described in the words of the Opinion of the Supreme Judicial Court of Massachusetts in the Matter of *The Attorney General vs. Nathan A. Tufts* than it was in the press and has continued to be in various Sunday supplements. "Early in the morning of March 7, 1917, . . . about fifteen men, among whom were four residents of New York engaged in the moving picture business and reputed to be possessed of great wealth, went to the Mishawum Manor, a house of ill-fame. . . . Arrangements had been made in advance for their coming. Prostitutes were there to meet them. An orgy of drink and lust took place. Some of the men did not leave until daylight.

". . . the respondent [District Attorney Nathan Tufts] . . . and Daniel H. Coakley . . . and others . . . formed a conspiracy to extort money by threat of indictment, consummated by the extortion of $100,000 from . . . these moving picture men . . . participating in a debauch in a bawdy house .. . . . a stench in the nostrils of common decency."

The Opinion goes on to characterize the activities of District Attorney Tufts as "that which would have been adopted and followed by an astute and cunning district attorney, who was an accomplice in a conspiracy designed to separate this great sum of money from men of wealth, timid about notoriety concerning their participation in a disreputable affair."

The Court also ably described the problems involved in nol prossing. "The powers of a district attorney under our laws are very extensive. They affect to a high degree the liberty of the individual, the good order of society and safety of the community. His natural influence with the grand jury, and the confidence commonly reposed in his recommendations by judges afford to the unscrupulous, the weak or the wicked incumbent of the office vast opportunity to oppress the innocent and shield the guilty, to trouble his enemies and to protect his friends, and to make the interest of the public subservient to his personal desires, his individual ambitions and his private advantage."

Journals as disparate as *The Nation* and the St. Louis *Post-Dispatch* were much given to articles on "Blackmail à la Boston." The latter in a two-page spread with thrilling illustrations described another badger game involving Coakley; the headlines were more colorful than the words of the Massachusetts Justice:

WHITE HAIRED ROMEO PAYS $387,000 TO HUSH SCANDAL, THEN TELLS ALL ABOUT IT IN COURT

Elderly Puritan, a Pretty Girl, a "Petting Party" and Two Peepers at Transom Figure in Remarkable Blackmail Case

"I Was Just Embracing Her, and That Was All, Your Honor," Edmund D. Barbour Told the Court, "When A Voice Said 'Ah Now We've Got You' and There Looking Over the Transom Were the Eyes of Two Men"—83 Year-Old Millionaire Totters to Witness Chair and Describes Woes that Followed His Indiscretion With "Little May" who Sent Him a Bill for $287,000 Just When He Thought Attorney Had Bought Him Silence

Once Cabot had determined to destroy Pelletier, he proceeded with the vigor and thoroughness which typified all his undertakings. He not only used the detectives and staff of the Watch and Ward Society, but also hired attorneys and private detectives of his own. A number of attorneys who would happily have represented Cabot in other matters refused to take part in his campaign to disbar and impeach Pelletier. This fact impressed on Cabot the great power of Pelletier and the fear of that power general in Boston, but it merely moved him to fight harder, rather than deterring him.

From 1914 on, hundreds of reports from private detectives came to Cabot, some signed by the name of the detective, some, more mysteriously, with the detective's secret number. These detectives reported on Pelletier's activities in Boston and also followed him to New York and Chicago.

When it became known that Godfrey Lowell Cabot was "after" Pelletier, numbers of unsolicited letters about Pelletier, some signed and some anonymous, came to his office.

Every detail of every report was studied by Cabot as carefully as every expense item on every bill submitted by his private detectives. When Operative Number 32 reported that Pelletier and a lady, after dining together on the night boat from New York to Boston, both retired to cabin Number 440 and the operative ceased watching the door of the cabin at eleven at night, Cabot wrote in the margin of the report, "ought to have watched that door all night."

One of his detectives, disguised as an electrician, succeeded in putting a "dictagraph" in Pelletier's office, and thereafter Cabot received a flood of eavesdropping reports. Justice Holmes was a cousin of both Godfrey and Minnie and their neighbor at Beverly Farms. The two men occasionally walked together on the beach, but Godfrey did not share the Justice's view that wire tapping was "a dirty business."

In Cabot's files were also photographs of a number of the ladies used by Pelletier and Coakley in their badger games. The ladies are dressed in the long bathing suits of that day.

Pelletier and Coakley sought to trap Cabot with a prostitute who had alleged by phone that she would give him "the goods" on Pelletier if he would visit her. Agents and double-agents were working for both sides.

Cabot's attacks on Pelletier took a variety of forms. In 1917 he had introduced into the Senate of Massachusetts a bill calling for an investigation of the District Attorney's office by a commission to be appointed by the Governor. The bill, filed by Thomas Henry Bates and Nils T. Kjellstrom, pointed out the high number of nol prosses given and the low number of bail bonds collected under Pelletier. "This monument of extreme clemency extends to criminals of highest and lowest degree," said Bates, and he and Kjellstrom also pointed out the large percentage of Pelletier's nol prosses which concerned cases in which a certain few criminal lawyers were defending the accused. Pelletier, in defending himself, pointed out that Kjellstrom was a defender of the Birth Control League, "who advocated the rights of his clients to teach the public, even young girls, how to use contraceptive devices. The same man introduced legislation for the inspection of convents." Pelletier pointed out that his office had ruthlessly prosecuted both "the birth control and illegal surgery propaganda that involved the chastity of maidenhood of this city."

When the attack on Pelletier through the Senate came to nothing, on December 13, 1917, Cabot filed with the clerk of the Supreme Judicial Court a petition for the impeachment of Pelletier. The petition, signed by Reverend Frederick D. Allen, President of the Watch and Ward Society, and by Cabot, its Treasurer, charged the District Attorney with negligence in prosecutions and failure to collect bonds of defaulters.

Pelletier's answer to this new attack was to characterize it as politically inspired. "This is the Watch and Ward Society; it is the Fitzgerald-Gallivan, Peters-for-mayor game; it is an attempt to discredit Mr. Curley." Pelletier went on to point out that the petition was filed by Reverend Allen. "Mr. Allen has justified the use of the most outrageous methods that would bring a blush of shame to any decent man and leave available of employment by him only the dregs of society."

He reminded his listeners that the Reverend Mr. Allen had engaged a number of Harvard and Tufts students to solicit women in an effort to prove them prostitutes. "Cabot first came to dislike me when the Watch and Ward got college boys to go out and get lewd women to solicit them openly and accompany them to hotel rooms. . . . When I first heard of this . . . I said, 'My God, are our young men being used in this fashion.' It filled me with horror to think our young college students would do any such work at a dollar per assignation."

Pelletier went on to characterize Godfrey Cabot as "a peeping Tom" and to decry attempts "to govern Boston by a self-chosen few." "Cabot came to see me once about two girls who he said were being abused by a doctor. The girls denied it to me. Investigation proved that they were respectable, and they begged me to let the matter drop—that they had no complaint.

"Physicians stated that the girls' ailment might have been the result of many causes besides the one Cabot had in mind. And so I refused to take action against the doctor. I merely told him to get out of town and he went. I took no action against the girls.

"Cabot was outraged at that. He couldn't see why I didn't pursue the case. But I didn't. Now one of those girls is married and very happy. I might have wrecked her life had I taken action against her without proof.

"So I have incurred the displeasure of this man. Now the district attorney's office is a confessional for stranger things than one could ever imagine—stuff that would make Oppenheim give up. This is private. If there is any place that a person will lay his or her cards on the table it is in my office."

When Cabot's attack through the Supreme Court came to nothing too, he then worked with the Boston Bar Association, which, after Cabot had fought the fight virtually alone for years, could no longer hide its head.

Cabot was so sure that his fight with Pelletier would be a long one and that his life was in danger that he wrote to the two executors of his will instructing them to carry on the fight after his death.

> 940 Old South Building
> Boston, Mass., December 14th, 1917.

Messrs. William Lowell Putnam
and Henry Lee Shattuck

Gentlemen:—

In case of my death, before my petition for ousting Mr. Pelletier has been answered, I desire that the needful and reasonable expense for prosecuting this case to an ultimate decision, should be paid by my Estate.

My chief impelling motive is as stated by me before the Legislature,—that both the deeds and the

words of Mr. Pelletier have clearly indicated an unwillingness on his part to prosecute ravishers of women and
a greater sympathy with the assailant than with the
victim.

Other grounds are set forth in my petition.

Very truly yours,
Godfrey Lowell Cabot

When Pelletier appeared before the Kiwanis Club of Belle-
vue in 1920, some weeks after Cabot had addressed that body, he
characterized Cabot's attack as a personal vendetta, which, indeed, it had become. "This man Cabot has left $30,000 in his will,
the income to be used to chase me. I don't mind the living, but it
makes one uneasy to be up against the dead. I sent word to him
that if he would give me $25,000 in cash, I'd quit now."

Pelletier also pointed out the unfortunate means which
Cabot and the Watch and Ward Society employed in their fight
against him, including the secret installation of a dictograph
machine in his office, ". . . if any of you gentlemen came there
and confided in me, it would be just as inviolate as though anyone
else came there. . . . I'd go through hell rather than say a word of
it. . . . And this man planted a dictagraph in my office and paid
attendants to listen to the private talks that went on in my
office—to get something on me. He had it there for 19 months. He
had detectives at the front and back door of my home and I used
to pity the poor fellows standing out there in the cold while I sat
in the house comfortably reading. We got to know each other
quite well those detectives and I."

Although he was nearly sixty, Cabot was fighting harder
than he had ever before in his life, and indeed this time he had
gone too far in his pursuit of the sinner. As a result, to the great
amusement of all Boston, Cabot himself was brought to trial for
the crime of larceny.

In the course of his trial it was proven that Cabot, with the
help of an attorney, Hector M. Holmes, had planted a detective,
one Michael J. Hayes, in the office of Daniel H. Coakley, and that
Hayes had stolen from Coakley various papers, letters, and pho-

tographs. During the trial Hayes, a former policeman, admitted that beginning in November 1919 he had got himself hired at $30 a week in Coakley's office and that he was paid an additional $70 a week by Cabot. He confessed that he stole various documents for Cabot until he was found out and fired in July 1920.

It was alleged that the conspiracy was revealed to Pelletier and Coakley by Oswain T. Bourdon, who originally was part of Cabot's conspiracy but who allegedly defected to the other side and was a Commonwealth's witness in the Cabot trial. It was thought by some, although never proved, that Bourden was actually hired by Coakley to get himself hired by Cabot and pretend to spy for Cabot while actually under the direction of Coakley. At his trial Cabot's delight in the cloak-and-dagger aspects of the operation was revealed in detail. This included his hiring a room at 400 Boylston Street for secret meetings at which Cabot spoke of the necessity "to fight fire with fire."

The trial amused and fascinated the citizens of Boston at all levels of society, with the righteous Cabot cast in the role of the thief and the larcenous Coakley relishing the role of the aggrieved party. When Cabot's lawyers tried to prove that there was no larceny because the stolen pieces of paper had no intrinsic monetary value, they asked Coakley to estimate the value of the papers. "Some of the papers were of the value that my reputation is to me," Coakley answered grandly, "my life's value. They were of the value that my reputation is worth to me. . . . The market value of the Hunnewell letters was in the hundreds of thousands of dollars."

Indeed, the so-called Hunnewell letters, which had been stolen for Cabot from Coakley's office, were of great value to Coakley and illustrated the backbone of his law business. The papers included an unsigned affidavit. "I, Mabel Adamson of Boston . . . met Holles H. Hunnewell . . . the said Hunnewell induced me to leave my husband and live with him as his mistress . . . maintained me as his mistress and payed all my expenses in a luxurious manner of living . . . the said Hunnewell notified me that our relations had become known to his wife and family and that he could no longer continue to keep me as his mistress; . . . he said that he still loved me . . . that in consideration of the fact that he had taken me away from my husband and ruined my life and in consideration of my promise and agreement not to become the mistress of some other man and to live a virtuous life thereafter, he promised to pay me the sum of five thousand ($5000.) dollars annually as long as he should live." Also among the stolen papers were love letters to Mabel from Holles written from the Knickerbocker Club, Newport Reading Room, The Homestead in Hot Springs, and that bastion of Boston propriety, the Somerset Club.

Cabot's counsel clearly intended to prove that Coakley's retention of these papers after he had obtained a settlement for Mabel and had agreed to return all such papers to Hunnewell was for the purpose of later blackmailing Hunnewell again. Coakley was so infuriated by this allegation that on November 15, 1920, he ran an advertisement on the front pages of the Boston *Herald*, the Boston *Traveler*, the Boston *American*, the Boston *Post*, the Boston *Record*, the Boston *Evening Globe*, and the Boston *Morning Globe*, under the headline: HUNNEWELL MYTH EXPLODED.

> Lying sick in bed . . . I have been reading . . . the current gossip of the gutter . . . that I spend most of my time in the criminal courts. This gossip has been invented and diligently cultivated by ex-convicts, crooks, dope fiends and "pimps" (I have their names), who have been and are on the payroll of the archfanatic.
>
> . . . What have these hirelings been doing for their money? . . . They merely plant rumors, innuendoes, and systematically circulate stories of blackmail, by the District Attorney and myself, of this rich artist, or that statesman, or merchant, or banker, or big lawyer, taking pains always to mention a large sum of money. . . .
>
> Starting thus in the underworld these yarns have by dint of persistent repetition, . . . penetrated the circles of decent society . . . and whenever people gather who do not know the high character and integ-

rity of Joseph C. Pelletier. . . .

My praise can add not a cubit to his stature.

The honors and decorations which he has won not only in our own country but also abroad, distinguish him as the leading Catholic layman of Massachusetts. Despite this (or should one say because of it), Mr. Godfrey L. Cabot, of the Watch and Ward Society, boasts that he has spent $100,000 in his campaign, and had arranged by will after his death to perpetuate his pursuit of the District Attorney.

As for me, the sum of my offending seems to be that in a minor way I am going up. As a car conductor, as a teamster, as a bartender, as a reporter, I seem to have escaped these cultured antagonisms which of late beset me. Perhaps it was a mistake, to have moved onward from these humble but honorable occupations. In the canons of my antagonists it is in such callings that I and such as I belong.

Even as a lawyer, arriving somewhat late in life, my career occasioned no alarm to anyone, until I got my head far enough above water to look horizontally at some of those on whom Fortune had pinned the blue ribbon. I, too, dared to ask and to receive large fees.

My clients were satisfied—not so the bigoted pack now yelping at my heels. They disapprove. I am practising "out of my set." . . .

DANIEL H. COAKLEY

The result of this tirade, appealing to class and religious hatreds, was that on December 23, 1920, the Court was of the opinion that a fair trial of Cabot and his codefendants could not be had before jurymen who knew the contents of Coakley's letter. The Court then ordered the cases taken from the jury.

Cabot's defense was brilliantly handled by Edward F. McClennen. His most effective move was somehow to convince Cabot not to take the stand himself. McClennen obtained a directed verdict for Cabot of not guilty by reason of a variance.

Only on two minor indictments were two of Cabot's employees found guilty and fined $300 each.

As a result of Cabot's fight Pelletier, Tufts, and Coakley were disbarred, and Coakley was later sent to jail. "Darling Dan," however, was undefeatable. He later won election five times as an executive councilor and was eventually impeached by the Legislature. Once, when he applied for reinstatement to the Bar before Justice Fred T. Field of the Supreme Judicial Court, he served as his own advocate and the magic of his own defense grew on him. Midway through his speech he suddenly started to describe how he had been framed in the first place. Less enchanted by Coakley's oratory than the orator, Justice Field interrupted, "Just a minute, Mr. Coakley. You will really have to make up your mind, A. whether you are repentant, or, B. whether you were framed."

"Well," answered Coakley, "I guess I'm repentant."

After returning from a trip around the world with his wife, Cabot told reporters that his activities in connection with Pelletier really began as a result of a doctor who "had been guilty of wrongs to young women patients for which they hang men in some States. I said in the hearing of those in the room that Mr. Pelletier's remark to me indicated he had more sympathy with the methods of the doctor who shortly thereafter disappeared from Boston than he had for the doctor's innocent victims. It was Mr. Pelletier's remark which really started me after him. I dared him then to sue me civilly or criminally for libel. . . . I have no personal feeling against Mr. Pelletier. I pity him."

All the rest of his life Cabot was more proud of his part in the disbarment of Pelletier, Tufts, and Coakley than of any of his other accomplishments. That he had undertaken the task at all when no one else in Boston dared to attack these powerful men would have been remarkable enough. But to have undertaken it while at the same time conducting his business, serving as a Navy flyer, raising his family, and supervising personally all the other work of the Watch and Ward Society gives some indication of the energy which came to him when he was in the joyful pursuit of "duty."

CHAPTER XIII

The Middle Years—Sixty to Ninety

> Yet puritan he was conscious of being, and determined to remain, if this meant being self-directed and inflexibly himself. . . . There might be no depth, no inside to anything, only a homely, hurried, mechanical life; but that conventional routine was what his heart needed: a sort of protection for it against itself, a means of banking the fires and living sanely meantime among indifferent things. What a relief to be innocently, foolishly, perpetually busy! SANTAYANA, *The Last Puritan*, 326, 329

After he and his sons were discharged, Godfrey had concentrated on winning the fight with Pelletier and Coakley and on becoming one of America's chief civilian spokesmen in all matters concerning aviation. He therefore left the running of his business more and more to Jim and Tom, paying them initially $125 a month each, giving them more and more responsibility but little authority.

Despite his extraordinary shyness, Jim had in 1919 married Katherine Rush, the gay and worldly daughter of a Navy captain, William Rees Rush, who had received the Congressional Medal of Honor for extraordinary bravery in action at Vera Cruz in 1914. Katherine had been all over the world with her father and had very different ideas on how life should be lived than had her ascetic father-in-law or his penurious wife. An irrepressible and sophisticated hedonist, she delighted in shocking her in-laws by spending money on her pleasures and expressing her preference for Europe over New England. When Jim died in 1930, his widow took their only child, Jane, and moved to Europe, never to return, much to the wonderment and annoyance of Godfrey.

Tom at least had married a Massachusetts girl, Virginia Wellington of Medford, but his rapport with his father was, if possible, even worse than Jim's. Much as Godfrey had written to his wife and in his Journal about his affection for his sons, he had never been able to express it. They all considered their father a martinet and throughout their lives resented his autocratic ways and the almost total absence of his praise or overt affection.

Godfrey's behavior had a different effect on each. Jim became so shy that it was impossible for him to have normal exchanges even with his contemporaries. He could not deal with farmers for gas rights or rights of way or with his father's customers; he could not even converse easily with his father's employees.

The effect on Tom was to make him at least as driving and ambitious as his father in order to prove his worth. It was Tom who transformed his father's profitable business into an international enterprise. Besides his success as a businessman, Tom served in a number of important posts to which he was appointed by the Federal government and has led a full and wide-ranging life.

Jack suffered terrible headaches for many years. After he finished his schooling, he escaped to New York, where for two years in psychoanalysis he traced the headaches to sexual repression caused by the fact that he was terrified of his father and felt that he must be perfectly virtuous and never do anything of which his father disapproved. Despite his early unhappiness, Jack had a very successful career in the Foreign Service, in posts from South America to China to Europe, serving as United States Ambassador in a number of important capitals.

Although it is obvious that both Tom and Jack Cabot have

lived lives of considerable distinction, Jack has said they could have achieved far more had they been encouraged or shown some human understanding by their father.

What Godfrey's effect on William was can only be a matter of speculation.

Typical of the sons' relationship with their father had been Tom's announcement of his engagement, which he had wanted to make under the best possible circumstances. He had waited until Godfrey was in a good mood and had then accompanied him on one of his beloved walks along the beach at Beverly Farms. At great length he described to his father the multiple virtues of Miss Wellington and finally brought himself to say that he was planning to marry her. Godfrey's only comment was, "Well, it's no surprise."

Despite their common difficulties with their father, Jim and Tom were not allies. The terrible competition of their childhood had made them permanently jealous and mistrustful of each other. It was fortunate, therefore, that they were little together. While one son worked in the Boston office in the Old South Building at 294 Washington Street, the other was out in Charleston, West Virginia, supervising field operations, and they took turns in each place.

Jim was never very interested in the business, but Tom, who had only managed to graduate *cum laude* as compared to his father's *magna*, early resolved to prove his worth in business. His first job he requested himself. He had studied engineering at Harvard and he became convinced on his first trip to Pennsylvania that the regulators measuring the gas his father sold to Standard Oil were faulty; he requested permission to prove his belief. After considerable effort he demonstrated as much not only to Godfrey, but also to the Standard Oil; the larger company paid Cabot $100,000 to compensate for its errors. Although Godfrey was delighted, he was unable to say so to his son.

Tom next convinced his father to change the business from a sole proprietorship to a corporation—Godfrey L. Cabot, Inc.— and to form an accounting department and hire a national auditing firm to set up books on the standard double-entry basis.

Godfrey's books, which he had set up to his own taste, constituted no more than a blotter—that is, a check book which showed
all receipts and all expenditures but made no differentiation between current expenses and capital expenditures and such other
nuances so dear to the hearts of tax collectors. Godfrey had for all
of his life a princely contempt for all forms of taxation, but Tom
was more in touch with and afraid of the fiscal realities of the
twentieth century. Godfrey was impatient with bookkeeping and
inventory systems, relying on his many friends in Pennsylvania
and West Virginia to keep tabs on his underpaid managers. The
method was not very successful. One superintendent sold several
carloads of pipe before he was caught; in another case, when a
bargeload of pipe was sunk by accident on the way from Creston
to Parkersburg, the barge operator paid off the superintendent
and no report was made of the lost pipe. Slowly, however, Tom
was able to introduce new business procedures as the company
grew.

Tom was less successful in his attempts to clean up and
modernize his father's Dickensian offices, which consisted of two
rooms with bare floors, filled with old worn furniture and a single
coat rack and reached by a tubercular cage elevator. In one room
a bookkeeper with a green eyeshade sat at his desk on a high stool.
Also in the room was a male clerk-stenographer, who went to
answer the wall telephone in the vestibule whenever it rang and
then went into the other office to advise Mr. Cabot, who came out
and spoke. Both rooms were littered with samples of black, boxes
of correspondence, and piles of copybooks.

Godfrey believed in a permanent, unalterable record of all
letters and invoices which left the office; this was accomplished by
means of a letterpress and copybooks. These latter were folio-size,
permanently bound books of a thousand numbered tissue-paper
pages each. Everything that went out of the office was written or
typewritten with special soluble ink, put between the leaves of the
copybook with pieces of damp blotting paper above and below,
and set in the letterpress, where it was squeezed by means of a
wheel and screw until a copy was made on the tissue page.

All incoming correspondence was filed by month in boxes, so

that it was necessary to remember what month a letter had been received in order to find it. This feat presented no problem to Godfrey, who had a phenomenal memory and who was one of the best chess players in New England. Once Tom had brought home eleven college friends and they had played twelve boards of chess simultaneously against Godfrey, who won ten and drew two. Forty years later Godfrey accused Tom of being impetuous in a business decision. "I'll give you another example of your being impetuous." he said. "You remember when you moved your knight to bishop's fifth in that game you played me a Ruy Lopez opening . . . ?" Tom could not remember the opening, he hardly remembered the event; his father then told him that he could remember every move of every chess game he had ever played seriously.

Jim Cabot in an act of unparalleled courage once threw out an old roll-top desk of his father's while Godfrey was out of town. The old man was furious when he returned, and he never forgave Jim.

Even in 1934, when Cabot moved the company offices to 77 Franklin Street, they were still hungry offices. Tom and Ralph Bradley managed a bit of carpeting for their offices in Franklin Street and even a bit of painting. When a visitor remarked to Godfrey that his office was the least pretentious of any in the company, the old man suggested, "Perhaps it's because I'm the least pretentious man in the office."

Leaving his business in the hands of his sons, on October 1, 1921, Godfrey began a trip around the world, taking with him his reluctant Minnie. On the trip Godfrey started writing a novel which he called *The Chess Player*, the scene of which was laid in the future, 1959. He described one of his characters, a Mr. Brodrib, as "very narrow, very bigoted, very domineering, very prejudiced, but fearless, honest and dependable, tenacious of purpose but always stumbling and falling headlong over his own lack of tact and the obstacles it raises in his path." After writing some 7000 words, Godfrey stopped and never finished this work.

Godfrey was now sixty, and for the first time he spoiled

himself, staying at the most expensive hotels. His critical view of nearly everything, however, had not softened. "I regret that Velasquez should have wasted his valuable time in painting royalty at its climax of worthlessness. Not only the faces but the figures, the clothes, the entourage . . . of many of his pictures of Philip IV, his wives, brother & relatives suggest intellectual vacuity, the quintessence of selfishness, of pride in absolutely vicarious merit such as wealth, clothes, family, of physical feebleness, of moral turpitude, of bigotry, and of consanguinity savoring of incest and of the imbecility therefrom resulting. . . . The usually coarse & sometimes revolting Goya seems to be a fad in Spain at present. . . . I wonder what Rubens might or might not have accomplished had he not been handicapped by the desire of his second wife to have the world plastered with portraits of her somewhat ample form in a state of nature."

Perhaps nothing differentiated Godfrey from the typical reticent Boston Brahmin more than his insatiable desire for travel and adventure, and especially his insistence on meeting people at all different social levels. When viewed from the Olympian heights of the last third of the twentieth century, Godfrey appears sometimes the ultimate provincial prig, but compared to his contemporaries he was not, and his travels accounted for much of what breadth he had. Even Adams had written, "I care a great deal to prevent myself from becoming what of all things I despise, a Boston prig (the intellectual prig is the most odious of all). . . . Anything which takes a man out of Beacon Street, Nahant and Beverly Farms, Harvard College and the Boston press, must be in itself good."

Godfrey's youthful willingness to go West, to take a chance rather than merely manage conservatively the family trust, was a kind of courage which had virtually disappeared from Boston.

Godfrey showed not only an extraordinary spirit of adventure, but also considerable open-mindedness, considering the lack of these found in many Boston men of his class and time—men such as Harvard President Abbott Lawrence Lowell, who had found against Sacco and Vanzetti and had opposed the appointment of Louis D. Brandeis to the United States Supreme Court, causing Walter Lippmann ironically to describe Brandeis as a "rebellious and troublesome member of the most homogeneous, self-centered and self-complacent community in the United States."

After his appointment was finally confirmed, Brandeis characterized Lowell and the men like him as "blinded by privilege, who have no evil purpose, and many of whom have distinct public spirit, but whose environment or innate narrowness—has obscured all vision and sympathy with the masses."

It is hardly surprising that, considering his environment, Godfrey was basically conservative, but on many individual issues he, as well as other Brahmins, showed surprising open-mindedness. Godfrey, like his cousin Henry Cabot Lodge and like Bishop Lawrence, opposed the League of Nations. On the other hand, President Abbott Lawrence Lowell of Harvard supported the League.

Even Godfrey's refusal to smoke or drink was less extraordinary in his own milieu and time than it seems today, Charles Francis Adams and Bishop Lawrence being but two of his contemporaries who also abstained. Smoking by women was frowned on in Boston Society long after it had been accepted elsewhere. It was forbidden for so long at the best women's club in Boston, the Mayflower Club, that smoking members finally resigned and founded their own club, the Chilton.

In Spain Godfrey attended an International Air Conference, and he and Minnie were informally received by the King and Queen. "This king business gets on my nerves. At these functions it takes from three to seven men to take your hat, ergo unless you pursue it with relentless and acute vigilance a la Sherlock Holmes they will surely exchange it for somebody else's. It takes from five to ten men to open a door. It is great sport to rush through suddenly and rout them in platoons."

Minnie, on the other hand, was delighted at the opportunity to meet the great and famous, and she encouraged Godfrey in his work with the Fédération Aeronautique Internationale in order to meet more celebrities. In the period between the two world wars, Cabot was quite influential in building up the F.A.I. and its American counterpart, the National Aeronautic Association.

This was important work because governments had not then attempted to make agreements with one another as to laws of overflights, arrangements for landing privileges, safety standards, and the like. It was therefore necessary for a private organization to concern itself with many matters later taken over by government negotiations.

In dealing with foreigners, Cabot learned to hide but never lost his distrust, especially of the "wicked" French. Minnie, however, was not a little pleased when in 1931, in recognition of his work for the F.A.I., Godfrey was decorated with the Commander Star of Rumania by King Carol.

Although on his trip Godfrey was staying at the Ritz and dining at Prunier, he saved pennies where he could, carefully changing his currency with sidewalk money changers to pick up an extra five per cent and insisting on a hundred-peseta refund from Cook's on an unfilled contract, later giving a thousand francs toward repairing some of the war damage done to Rheims.

One of Godfrey's great joys throughout his life was seeing flowers in bloom, and his Journal is full of descriptions of bougainvillaea in Port Said, anemones at Tiberias, tamarind trees in India, and azaleas in Japan.

His strongest comments, as always, were on the treatment of women and all matters relating to sex and the natural functions of the body. "One of the most disgusting traits in the Arab is his habit of loafing and leaving the heaviest labor to his women and little girls. . . . I have heard of Port Said as the wickedest place on earth and was dreadfully disappointed to find no indication of turpitude during our stay here . . . [but] the beach was crowded with people many of them bathing 'au natural.' . . .

". . . The son [of an Indian Maharajah] is more civilized and has given his father's widows the choice of freedom or of a pension and has contented himself with the legal wives allowed in the harem and no concubines. . . . The caves [east of Bombay] are shrines to Siva and other gods & goddesses. There are three phalli in three small shrines which were worshipped by sterile women and others desirous of offspring. They are simply small stone cylinders with rounded tops. . . .

"[At Ahmedabad] On the east bank was a very interesting camp of a sect stark naked except for a very meagre suspensory partially concealing their genital organs. The rest of their costume is simply a whitish smear of ashes. They live on what they can beg or steal and they are celibates. Some of them wore clothes but many did not and among them were the physically best men I have seen among the natives of India. . . . The seed of manly sport sown by the English seems to be taking root and will help to lift the apathy that obsesses the dark skinned population of India."

Minnie, who could not keep up with Godfrey's extraordinary pace, became ill in February 1922. Godfrey reluctantly slowed down and cut Java and the Philippines out of the tour. But Godfrey remained in high spirits, as he usually did while traveling, writing little jokes in his Journal. "I would not advise a steady diet of this brand of milk [sap from a rubber tree] for it makes your lips sticky and you might get stuck on yourself. . . . The streets [in the Chinese section of Rangoon] in the older quarters average perhaps 10′ wide and have zigzags, presumably to prevent evil spirits using them for evil spirits have a predilection for straight roads in China. (N.B. I am an evil spirit.)"

In Japan, Godfrey was delighted with the three earthquakes he experienced and with "the only good part of the entertainment . . . the pretty girls that flirted with us and afterwards gave us a little dramatic pictorial dance." He noted, however, that "The Japs are very casual about relieving the necessities of nature, even more so than the Germans: If a Jap wants to relieve his bladder any old place is good enough. It does not embarrass him or her, meanwhile, to carry on a conversation with a lady friend standing close at hand in a crowded street. If European ladies approach when he feels the call, he does not wait for them to pass or turn his back on them."

On the way home Godfrey visited Hawaii and the western and southern states of America, returning to Boston on June 20, 1922, in time for Commencement and his fortieth-reunion dinner.

* * *

Before World War I the carbon-black business had been a small one, the only large use for black having been for printer's ink. At that time Cabot had produced about 25 per cent of all the black made in America. During and immediately after the war, as the production of automobile tires in America and in Europe increased, the demand for black grew tremendously. In 1887 about a million pounds of black were produced in America; by 1900 it had increased to seven million, and by 1915 to twenty million; but by 1926 it had reached 180 million. During the war and the immediate postwar period Cabot's own production had fallen because he had sold most of his gas to Standard Oil at a tremendous profit rather than manufacturing it into black. Cabot's percentage of the black business had, therefore, dropped to about one per cent.

With the increased demand for black the price had risen rapidly, and more and more people had gone into the black business, especially in Louisiana, where there was a great surplus of gas. Cabot, whose European agents were clamoring for larger quantities of black, made sales-agency agreements with a number of the new small factories in Louisiana and in Montana. By 1923 it was evident that the building of new factories had exceeded the growing demand, and many of them were in financial difficulties. A number of these were merged into the United Carbon Company, in which Cabot became a substantial minority stockholder as a result of the money owed him by some of the smaller plants taken into United. He was also sales agent for 25 per cent of the production of United.

While Godfrey and Minnie were on a visit to Europe in 1927, Tom had one business experience which he never forgot. One of the small carbon companies which had not done well in Louisiana was the Standard Carbon Company, which had exchanged its plant for 17,000 shares of United Carbon common and some preferred shares. Cabot owned 95 per cent of Standard Carbon's common stock, and all of its notes. He decided to liquidate Standard, whose only assets now were its shares of United, which Cabot preferred to own in his own name. It was therefore announced that there would be an auction with a professional auctioneer. Cabot expected the affair to be entirely routine, as he was virtually buying from himself. In order to be fair, however, to the 5-per-cent minority interest in Standard Carbon, Cabot not only announced a public auction for the assets, but declared that he would bid $15 a share for the common stock, which until the announcement had been selling over the counter at $7 or $8 a share and which then rose to about $11.

On the morning of May 1, Godfrey was out of the country and Tom and his brother-in-law, Ralph Bradley, represented Godfrey at the auction which was held in their offices, a small red flag proclaiming the auction having been put outside the office. On their arrival they were not a little surprised to find two directors of United Carbon, Osman Schwartz and William P. Willetts, already there. These two had brought along a three-inch bundle of certified checks on Boston's Shawmut Bank and asked Tom whether in the upcoming bidding certified checks would be acceptable, or whether they should obtain cash. Tom, noting with amazement that the topmost check was for a million dollars, agreed to the use of certified checks and opened the bidding at $15. Schwartz and Willetts raised an eighth. After a quick conference with Bradley, Tom raised his bid an eighth. So it continued until Tom had bid $17½ and his opponents, $17⅝. After another conference with Bradley, Tom decided that since they really had no authority other than Godfrey's instruction to pay $15, they had better stop. Having sold the common, they then agreed to sell Schwartz and Willetts the $100 par preferred at $65 since it had missed several dividends.

Tom later concluded that Willetts and Schwartz were part of a pool which controlled United and had determined to list it on the New York Stock Exchange and with that inside knowledge were buying up shares as cheaply as they could, planning to unload them on the market at a far higher price. Some months later United was listed on the Curb and later on the New York Stock Exchange, where it rose to a high of $111 in the fall of 1929, before the crash.

When Godfrey returned he was furious with his son. In his view, Tom had been outsmarted and should have consulted him.

No protests that the matter had had to be settled there and then at the auction and that it would have been impossible to reach him satisfied Godfrey. Nearly half a century later Tom Cabot's anger and hurt at having been unjustly blamed and taxed with having no judgment were still evident.

For many years Tom Cabot, embarrassed by his father's serving on the Board of Directors of the United Carbon Company because of the obvious conflict of interest, unsuccessfully urged his father to resign. Godfrey felt no such embarrassment. Never a house divided on any point, Godfrey did not care at all how his actions impressed others, so long as he was satisfied that he was doing the moral thing.

Tom was frequently embarrassed by his father's complete lack of self-consciousness. When Godfrey was the chairman of an industry meeting and was against a motion which had been made, even if everyone else voted "Aye," he would rule that the "Nays" had it. When he made a speech, he would read it, correcting his secretary's spelling and punctuation aloud as he went along and totally oblivious to the effect on his audience. When he spoke extemporaneously, Godfrey spoke as though dictating to a secretary, with long silences as he searched for just the word he wanted. Not the least evident difference between Cabot and his wife and sons was that he was virtually unembarrassable.

It was not understandable to him that his wife or his sons could concern themselves with the opinions of others. During the height of the corruption fight, when Coakley and Pelletier were daily accusing him of all kinds of wickedness in the press and Minnie was concerned with what later would be called "image," Godfrey said, "My friends know I am not a liar; Pelletier's friends know he is a liar; and who else gives a damn?"

A year after United Carbon was formed, the going price for black was a weak five cents a pound, and yet United advised Cabot and its other agents that its price would thereafter be eight cents. It soon became evident that the two major producers, United and Columbian, had agreed to fix the price at eight cents. Cabot immediately decided to increase his own production, knowing that he could undersell the big two and still make a large profit, and increase his percentage of the market while they held the price umbrella over him.

Tom Cabot was sent to Texas, where there was an unbelievable excess of gas—so much so that much of it was simply flared or even vented into the sky, night and day, the year around. Tom arranged to build two plants, one in partnership with Phillips Petroleum and the other in partnership with Humble Oil; he then had a far more difficult time selling his father the deals than he had with the outsiders.

Cabot did not believe in partners, automatically assuming that any partner would steal from him. He trusted only his own flesh and blood, and then only as to honesty, not judgment. Tom was somehow able to persuade his father to allow him to go ahead. When in 1926 one of the plants proved tremendously profitable, earning 100 per cent on the invested capital in the first year, he convinced his father that he should build more Texas plants; and between 1925 and 1930 he started nine in all. By selling this carbon black just under the prices maintained by Columbian and United, Cabot raised his share of the total carbon-black business to about 15 per cent by the time of the Depression. During this period Cabot was described by one of his competitors as "slick as snot on a doorknob."

The infrequent meetings between Godfrey Lowell Cabot and Frank Phillips were to become legendary in the oil business. Frank Phillips was an ex-barber, a drinker and a gambler, a bully, and as uneducated and profane as any fictional stereotype of an Oklahoman who had struck it rich in oil. When he was with Phillips, Cabot became even stiffer, colder, and more correct than usual; as a result, Phillips was even more profane and loud, which further stiffened Cabot. Exciting as this clash of personalities was to the onlookers, it was fortunate for both autocrats that most of their negotiations were conducted by others.

Even during the Depression, Phillips wanted to maintain the price of the carbon black made by their partnership company, the Texas Elf Carbon Company, and to continue getting a high price for his gas. When Phillips' representatives met with Cabot in Boston, he asked them, "Do you wish to crowd the mourners' bench?"—a clear threat that the company would go bankrupt if they had their way; but they refused to allow him to lower the price.

When Cabot lowered the price of his carbon black made in other plants not owned with Phillips, the sales of Texas Elf black fell, and Phillips threatened lawsuits, alleging that Cabot owned a greater percentage of the stock in these other plants than he did in Texas Elf and that this was the real reason he sold more of their product and less of Texas Elf's. The fight was eventually settled by Cabot's buying out Phillips' interest, although Godfrey disliked ending a fight in any way other than by winning it.

In 1927 a Cabot subsidiary had made a contract with Skelly Oil Company to buy gas beginning at two cents per thousand cubic feet and going up a quarter of a cent a year. By 1931, when Cabot was paying three cents, the effect of the Depression had so lowered the price of black that to have continued to pay three cents would have bankrupted the company. One of Cabot's executives negotiated with Skelly and induced the company to tear up the old contract and to sell Cabot gas at the then going rate of half a cent. When this move was reported to Godfrey, tears came to his eyes and, putting his hand to his chest, he kept repeating, "But, my God, they had my name on the contract." He was almost unable to believe that Skelly would not hold his feet to the fire, and Cabot's associates doubted whether, had the positions been reversed, Godfrey would have been as generous. Skelly's decision, as is the case with most good deeds in business, also had a practical reason: Skelly would rather sell gas for which it had no use and no other market at half a cent for a long period of time than to sell it for three cents for the short period it would have taken to bankrupt Cabot's subsidiary.

Cabot's love of a fight sometimes led him into highly unprofitable business undertakings. In 1934 Cabot had acquired some gas wells in southern New York State and northern Pennsylvania which he could not use in making carbon black, having no plant nearby, and which he could not sell directly to consumers. He therefore decided to sell the gas wholesale, at the well head, to Cities Service, Northern Penn, Sinclair, and Hope Natural Gas, who would buy it, he thought, because they would not want Cabot laying pipeline in their country and competing with them.

This deal was all arranged verbally, but then the oil companies held a meeting in Pittsburgh and decided that they need not buy Cabot's gas at full price. They believed that if all refused to buy or offered a ridiculously low price, Cabot could be frozen out until he acquiesced to their terms. They each therefore wired Cabot, alleging that for different reasons they could not buy his gas or offering him four or five cents per thousand cubic feet when the going price was about twenty-five cents. It was not lost on Cabot that all the wires were sent on the same day.

Godfrey immediately rushed out to New York, resolved to build his own pipeline down to Williamsport, Pennsylvania, where industrial users were paying a high price for gas. Tom Cabot felt that since there was already a pipeline to Williamsport, building a second one would be unprofitable, but he knew that once his father got into a fight, it was difficult to stop him. Deciding that the only way to meet his father's idea was with a better idea, Tom suggested laying a pipeline to Rochester, New York.

Godfrey Cabot had known the Chairman of Eastman Kodak, a Mr. F. W. Lovejoy, because they were both members of the Corporation of M.I.T. On hearing Tom's suggestion, Godfrey sent his son to Rochester with instructions not to return until he had made a contract with Kodak, which was then using coal as fuel for its steam plant. Tom drew up a three-year contract with Kodak guaranteeing a saving of $100,000 per year, based on the prevailing price of coal, if the company would change over to gas.

Tom and a number of Godfrey's associates urged Godfrey not to sign the contract because after further research they concluded that the gas reserves were insufficient. But Godfrey had begun to fight and did not propose to stop. When Tom saw that the project would cost $10 or $12 million and that it would very probably be unsuccessful, he induced the company's counsel, Fred Fernald, to call Godfrey with the message that a number of the company's officers thought they should not go ahead. Godfrey asked Fernald how recently he had read the corporation's by-laws, and quoted the section, paragraph, and subparagraph which gave the president the right to buy, sell, or do anything he saw fit. "Now you tell the boys," Godfrey concluded, "that if they don't like it, I'll call a stockholders' meeting as soon as I hit Boston." Since Godfrey owned or controlled virtually all the stock, his meaning was clear.

Shortly the fight grew dramatically when Cabot announced he was building a pipeline to Rochester. The coal companies; the railroads, which would lose their freight business on coal; and the Rochester Gas and Electric Company, which feared Cabot might seek to become a utility if ever he got to Rochester with natural gas—all combined forces to oppose Cabot. And the greater the opposition, the more resolved Cabot became to reach Rochester, regardless of profitability and regardless of gas reserves.

Godfrey ordered air maps made, although this was not yet a common practice, and he sent a corps of right-of-way men into the field, all on the same day and all optioning farms for alternate routes. He optioned several alternate rights of way all the way to Rochester, but he could not get rights of way across the nine different railroads with sixteen different tracks which had to be crossed.

The railroads had clubbed together after a meeting called by the president of the Baltimore & Ohio, Mr. Daniel Willard. Under the leadership of Frederick E. Williamson, the president of the New York Central, they fought Cabot all the way. Eastman Kodak became so angry that for a number of years the company took its freight business away from the New York Central.

Every imaginable trick was employed by each side. Cabot found that where a trail or a road antedated the railroad, he could get a right of way from the local town or county to lay the pipeline. Where the railroad got its right of way under the state's power of eminent domain rather than by buying it in fee, he could not be legally stopped from tunneling under the railroad. Cabot had instructed his men not to pay off any politicians, but this order was ignored. Having no power of eminent domain, his men had to deal with officials of over thirty villages and counties, and they had caught Godfrey's fever to win the fight at all costs.

In one place Cabot found that a railroad had abandoned its right of way and that its rights ended fifteen years after the abandonment. The railroad, refusing to produce any records of its cessation of use of the right of way, claimed that the date was less than fifteen years before. Cabot's men cut down a tree in the center of the right of way and proved by its rings that the tree was more than fifteen years old.

In another place Cabot's men found an old Indian woman who swore in her deposition that, long prior to the railroad, there had at the same place been an Indian trail from the east side to the west side of the Genesee River where the Indians had gone to mine salt.

Often Cabot would send his crews to lay pipeline across a railroad on Sunday, when no injunction could be obtained to stop him. There was, remarkably, no violence between Cabot's crews and the railroad police and railroad work gangs hired to tear up Cabot's pipeline.

Cabot needed the permission of the New York State Public Service Commission. In the hearings before the Commission on his application to build the pipeline to Rochester, Cabot arrived wearing such a seedy coat that one of his own executives asked him, "Chief, is this the best coat you've got?" and Godfrey replied with a smile, "No, but I don't want to be in any position of displaying a surplus of wealth."

The lawyers for both sides were brutal in their examinations. Herman Russell, who was then president of the Rochester Gas and Electric and later president of the American Gas Association, was so upset by Cabot's lawyers that he broke down in the witness stand and was taken weeping from the hearing. Godfrey, however, thrived on the contest and remained unflappable throughout.

The opposition, seeking to prove Cabot's gas reserves inadequate, were convinced that Godfrey would not lie if put on the stand. They therefore qualified him as *their* expert witness, so that they could ask him both real and hypothetical questions, hoping to prove that the reserves could not fill Kodak's needs. They were not aware of how tricky a witness he would prove, nor that he had told other employees of his who were to be called as witnesses, "I never want you to lie, but you don't need to tell everything you know." This attitude represented a change since the day, half a century earlier, when Godfrey had criticized his brother Sam for not dealing completely openly and honestly with competitors.

The opposition lawyers had been informed by their geologists that no gas field in America with the same geological conditions as Cabot's Oriskany Sands field in Tioga County, Pennsylvania, ever had gas reserves in the quantities needed by Kodak. When they called Cabot to the stand, they asked him a series of questions on his qualifications as a geologist and his many years of study and of actual experience in the gas business. Cabot answered at length and with pride. They then asked him to describe the geological conditions in Tioga County, which he did.

Then, having set the trap, they asked Cabot if ever in his long experience he had seen a field with the same geological conditions that existed in Tioga County which was a long-lived producer.

"Yes," answered Cabot.

"And where was that, Mr. Cabot?"

"In Georgia," Cabot replied.

Thoroughly nonplussed, the opposition lawyers called for an adjournment. Assured that afternoon by their geologists that no gas fields of any kind had ever been found in the State of Georgia, they were in high good spirits the next morning as they prepared to prove Cabot a liar or a fool.

"Now can you please continue, Mr. Cabot, where you left off yesterday and tell us where and when in Georgia you saw such a gas field."

"It was about halfway between Tiflis and Baku on my trip to Russia in 1898," Godfrey answered with obvious delight, "and it is still producing to the best of my knowledge."

"But, Mr. Cabot," objected the dazed and disappointed attorney, "I have been asking about the State of Georgia."

"No," replied Cabot, "you have been asking about geology."

Cabot was thereupon excused as a witness, and his application was approved by the Commission.

As a number of Godfrey's associates had predicted, the whole Rochester venture turned out to be very unprofitable because Cabot ran out of gas and had to settle with Kodak on his unfulfilled contract. He eventually sold the pipeline at salvage prices to Rochester Gas and Electric and Consolidated Gas and Electric. Years later it was used to bring natural gas from the southwest to Rochester. But he had delighted in winning the fight, even though he lost the war.

There were three great price wars in the carbon-black industry. The first was in 1923, when the oversupply, caused by overbuilding to meet the postwar demand, dropped the price from thirty cents a pound to about five cents, resulting in the failure of many small plants and the creation of United Carbon.

There was relative price stability from 1925 to 1930, the two giants, Columbian and United, selling their black at about eight cents while Cabot was growing by selling his increasing production for seven and a half cents. But with the onset of the Depression in 1930, price cutting dropped the price to two and three quarter cents. In the years following, until 1937, the price slowly crept back up to about four cents.

Since a channel-black plant must be run twenty-four hours a day to be economically feasible, the carbon-black industry during the Depression could not, as some other industries did, work on a three- or four-day week. Cabot decided not to close down any of his plants entirely during the Depression because he was under contract to buy so much gas per day and would have had to pay for it whether he used it or not. The other big cost in the carbon-black business, the capital cost of plant construction, was already paid, and the cost of labor, which was all Cabot could have saved by closing a plant, was so small a part of total cost that he kept running the plants and building warehouses for the black he could not sell. He was convinced that someday he would sell it at a profit, and he was right.

In May 1937 came the worst price war of all. Cabot's company had invented a method for the bulk handling of carbon black—pelletizing it and shipping it in covered hopper cars, rather than bagging it. In order to induce its customers to put in the necessary facilities for handling black in bulk, which required an expensive investment in new equipment, Cabot had promised a price differential of a quarter of a cent.

Two large Cabot customers, Firestone and Goodrich, put in bulk handling equipment, but two others, Goodyear and United States Rubber Company, refused. Firestone and Goodrich insisted that Cabot live up to its promise, and finally in May 1937 Cabot announced that, as of the end of the year, it would inaugurate a price differential of one quarter of a cent per pound on bulk shipments.

Shortly it became apparent in the industry that Binney and Smith had assured its customers that it would meet Cabot's bulk price with its bag price. Now the dog was chasing its tail. Every two weeks or so, Cabot would drop its price another quarter of a cent, only to have Binney and Smith meet the drop, until finally by winter the price had fallen to two cents a pound—well below the cost of production, even below the cash cost for labor and materials without counting interest, overhead, or depreciation.

Finally, to everyone's surprise, Godfrey L. Cabot Inc. backed down, pointing out in advertisements that it had tried to effect the differential but could not bankrupt itself in the effort. The tire companies, which had profited from the price war, knew it could not go on forever.

There was in truth no real market price because during the Depression period secret deals were made between some of the tire companies and certain black manufacturers. One carbon producer had a secret arrangement to provide a major tire maker with black at a price halfway between actual cost and the going market rate; another tire company had a half-interest in a carbon plant, which in effect lowered its price. Cabot never felt, therefore, that he had to deal equally with all customers by giving the same price to each. The recovery from this price war was so slow that the price at the outbreak of the World War II was only about three cents a pound, where it was frozen by the Office of Price Administration.

While the tire companies were promoting price wars, which were to their advantage, the big oil companies, who supplied most of the gas to the carbon-black industry, were trying to stabilize black prices to allow the black companies to pay a good price for gas. An early and totally unsuccessful effort had been made by Judge Amos L. Beatty, who had been Chairman of the Board of the Texas Company. He had invited all the important carbon-black manufacturers to a luncheon meeting at his New York club and delivered a speech on how unfortunate it was for the black makers to be fighting one another; he suggested the mutual benefits of "stabilization," a euphemism for reducing production and fixing prices. When the speech was over, Godfrey asked Judge Beatty whether what he was suggesting was legal, which broke up the meeting, because it was apparent that Cabot would enter into no agreement not enforceable at law.

In the 1920's the Congress passed a bill which came to be known as the Webb-Pomerene Act. Its purpose was to allow United States manufacturers to band together as a cartel in dealing with foreign competition in foreign markets. American competitors were allowed to form an association to fix prices for the export market only, after approval by the Federal Trade Commission in Washington.

Although there was no foreign competition because all the carbon black in the world was made in America, it occurred to Phillips Petroleum that if a Webb-Pomerene association could be put together to fix the export prices of carbon black, prices in the American market might also be stabilized. There were only five carbon-black makers—Columbian, United, J. M. Huber, R. I. Wishnick, and Cabot—and it seemed inconceivable to Phillips, which wanted to get more than half a cent per thousand cubic feet for its gas, that in so simple an industry no price-fixing agreements could be made.

Under the sponsorship of Phillips, and after two years of negotiation, such a Webb-Pomerene association was formed on

May 16, 1933, after two years of haggling. It was called Carbon
Black Export Inc., or Carbexport, and it was run by Carl Kayser, a friend of Phillips Vice-President Clyde Alexander. A quiet,
scholarly man, the son of a Columbia University German professor, Kayser gradually gained the confidence of the distrustful
carbon-black manufacturers and set up machinery which precluded any member's cheating another. Quotas were set up so that
each American firm got the same percentage of the foreign market as it had had prior to the forming of the association. Since
each company had considerably exaggerated its foreign business,
it was required of each company in setting its quota to prove by
paid invoices its actual foreign sales.

Strict penalties were set up and enforced for any black
maker who sold to any foreign market directly or even through an
American exporter. Kayser carefully played no favorites as his
five employers maneuvered to cheat one another, having pointed
out at the first meeting of Carbexport, after each maker had
complained of the dishonesty of his competitors, "Gentlemen, we
are all the same color and the color is black."

Cabot frequently spoke to his sons about "tainted money"
and lectured them to the effect that they should only take money
for rendering a real service. He was, however, sometimes more
elastic in his definition of what constituted service when he was
appraising his own operations than when he was appraising those
of others. He would quote sections of Ida Tarbell's attack on
Rockefeller and compare Rockefeller unfavorably to Carnegie.
Cabot much admired Carnegie, not only because he gave so much
money toward the building of free public libraries all over America, but also because of Carnegie's hatred of waste and his mania
for efficiency. He repeatedly told his sons how Carnegie whipped
up competition between his steel mills to increase production and
profits and to eliminate waste by tying a broom to the smokestack
of the mill with the biggest output at the end of each month.
Cabot never commented on Carnegie's allowing Frick to brutalize
his employees in the great Homestead Strike.

In the famous Police Strike in Boston, Godfrey and Tom
had immediately volunteered and served as policemen, Godfrey

erect in his old Navy cape with a pair of pistols strapped on, marching up and down Washington Street, where for thirty blocks every store window had been broken. The family's views on labor organization were made clear in a letter from Jim in Charleston, West Virginia, to his mother in Boston. "I'm sorry the police strike worries you so much. However I trust pa & Tommy understand how to take care of themselves. He has at least a good chance to kill at least one Bolshevik. I wish he could shoot Sam Gompers."

Godfrey agreed with Coolidge's dictum that there was "no right to strike against the public safety, by anybody, anywhere, anytime." He knew that Coolidge had considered his action against the police strike political suicide and admired the Vermonter's willingness to put principle above expedience. He also agreed with Coolidge's New England view on collecting foreign nations' debts to America—"They hired the money, didn't they?"

Cabot's horror of waste was one motive that had brought him into the carbon-black business. When he first went to Pennsylvania, he had been horrified at seeing gas flared uselessly into the sky by drillers who were seeking oil and had no use for gas. He was proud of having created a use for this gas and of "making two blades of grass grow where only one had grown before," a maxim he constantly preached to his sons. It was a major tenet of Cabot's business morality that a man must not merely trade but must perform a service. His morality had paid off handsomely, because being the only user of this gas, he was able to buy up cheaply great reserves of it, which he used not only in making carbon black, but also sold to home owners and eventually to large commercial users.

When the carbon-black business began to be attacked in the middle 1920's by members of various state legislatures as a wasteful industry, because the manufacture of black until after World War II was able to convert into carbon black only about 1 to 3 per cent of the carbon in the natural gas, Cabot's reply was that the process was at least less wasteful than flaring or venting gas into the air, and that he benefited the areas into which he came by

providing employment. At the same time Tom pointed out in an
article that "an incandescent electric bulb obtains as light only
about 5% of the energy imparted; a hen produces in eggs only
about 10% of the nutritive value of the feed."

Like Carnegie, Cabot did not much concern himself with the
working conditions of his employees. A cousin of Godfrey,
Charles Moors Cabot, a partner of Godfrey's brother-in-law
John Moors in the stock-brokering firm of Moors and Cabot,
spent much of his life fighting against the eighty-four-hour week
in the steel industry, leaving a fund of $50,000 in his will to
continue the fight. Godfrey also worked his employees eighty-four
hours a week, but he pointed out that the work was far easier than
in the steel mills.

In the last twenty years of Godfrey's life, from 1942 to
1962, when his sons and grandsons had substantially taken over
the running of the business, all the modern employee benefits were
put in: shorter hours, insurance programs, pension programs,
profit-sharing schemes, and the inevitable hortatory employee
magazine. But the old employees looked back at the past as somehow better. The difference was one of climate and size. When
Cabot's business became so big that it was run by committees
rather than by Godfrey, the old satisfaction of pleasing "the old
man" disappeared. Demanding as Godfrey had been, once an
employee gained his confidence, that employee was given a great
deal of authority, and he felt a personal commitment to live up to
Cabot's confidence and a justified pride and sense of real achievement in doing so.

In 1966 one of the major officers of Cabot Corporation, as it
had come to be called, said, "There was more humanity in the
business then than now. Now it's a cold business, like most businesses. You're responsible to a committee. The Chief was a suspi-
cious man to begin with, but once he got faith in you, you knew it
and it inspired you to perform for him, not to let him down
because he believed in you.

"Now we're better rewarded with stock options and so forth,
but psychologically it's not as rewarding. He was a better man to
work for than Tom or Louis [Tom's son] because he created in

you a desire to please him. He was like a king or a duke, a difficult, demanding man, but you could be at ease with him more than with Tom or Louis because he was pleasable. You knew that it was within you to do what he wanted and although it was physically impossible for The Chief to compliment you, you knew when he was pleased. But with Tom and Louis, no matter what you do, it's not enough, you feel driven, but with the old man you felt obligated; you felt inspired.

"Particularly when he was away from Boston, he was great. If you drilled a dry hole he'd never be discouraged. He'd just say, 'Well, if at first you don't succeed, try, try, try again,' or 'If you got a well every time you drilled a hole there wouldn't be any fun in this business.' And if you failed to do something one way, he'd say, 'There's more ways than one of skinning this cat.' "

Away from Boston, especially in West Virginia without his family, Cabot was a different person—happy, relaxed, and often joking with his employees. He made fun of Cabot snobbery, pointing out how much of his family's money had been made in slaving and opium. "They were pirates," he said. "But now we're so refined we call them 'traders.' "

He told his staff that the real basis of the Cabot fortunes was that his grandfather had "married the boss' daughter." He laughed at Cabot prejudices, saying that another ancestor who had married for money was an Irishman, one Patrick Tracy, who had come to Newburyport from Wexford in 1735.

He even told jokes bordering on the salacious, pointing out that Philadelphia, the City of Brotherly Love, referred to the incestuous love between the royal brothers and sisters of ancient Egypt and wondering whether William Penn was aware of that fact. He told about a stay in Paris, when a hotel maid had stared at his hot water bottle, which was in the shape of a long, thick rubber tube; and he said, "She must have had an exaggerated opinion of my manly powers." Once when the sun was shining brightly on some papers he was trying to read, he told an employee, "I am not able to make the sun stop shining, but if there were a man in Boston who could, it would be me." When after Godfrey had told a joke, one of his employees said, "That's not the way I heard it," Godfrey replied, "I plan to have put on my tomb-stone, 'Here lies Godfrey L. Cabot who never took anything from a story but always added something to it.' "

In Boston, Cabot allowed neither tea nor coffee in his home, but when he occasionally found a favorite executive in West Virginia drunk, he told his friends, "Take Buck to bed, can't you see he's tired out from working so hard?" He smilingly confessed to a friend in New York, "The amount of alcohol I've drunk you could put in your eye and it wouldn't hurt you, but I hate to think of all the alcohol my money has paid for." He knew his sons and employees entertained customers and friends at cocktail parties, but the bills for these were kept hidden from him, and he pretended not to know.

He had strict rules, however, against his executives' giving kickbacks to the purchasing agents of the big tire companies or bribes or favors to state or national legislators or regulatory commission members. Cabot made it plain that he would instantly fire anyone who did so. This kind of illegality was so common in the oil and gas business that his executives admired the old man's stand and were very careful that anything they did of this kind appeared as a contribution to an industry association or came out of their own pockets, so that there would be no record in the company files.

In the field Cabot was also a far more generous and understanding employer than he was in Boston. Long before the days of mandatory workmen's compensation, if his men were injured, he kept them on the payroll. Employees who got in trouble in West Virginia received from him quiet help of a sort he would have left to Ralph Bradley in Boston. Even when money was stolen by employees, Cabot was unwilling to fire them until he satisfied himself that he could not reform them; he quietly arranged for medical treatment for a female employee who had contracted syphilis.

In the early days Cabot had taken every short cut imaginable to make what money he had go as far as possible in his business. He had made agreements with county courts to supply the county courthouses with free gas if they would allow him to lay his pipelines above ground on the edge of the county roads at no charge for right of way, and he bought great amounts of second-hand pipe of varying sizes, much of which was leaky and dangerous, but he got more pipe than if he had bought it new, and gas was cheap enough to waste. After he had made his fortune, he ordered his men to buy the best obtainable pipe and was much concerned that his employees be protected from accidents and that "Safety must be the first consideration in everything we do."

Godfrey was more at ease with people he met away from home, and he made friends with men of social and economic backgrounds very different from his own. Many of them were dirty, chewed tobacco, and even cursed or drank, but if they played a good game of chess or had good brains or did their jobs well, Godfrey managed to ignore their sins.

When he showed off his learning, quoting Shakespeare by the page or using the Latin name for skunk, speaking slowly and distinctly as he always did, his employees were flattered that he would take the time, and curiosity stimulated a number of them to read more about what they had heard from Cabot. Some developed a real hero worship for the tough old man. They knew that however hard he was on them, he was harder on his sons and still harder on himself. They knew Cabot had been told that two plants which he built during World War II, one for making gun barrels and the other for making carotene, a source of vitamins, would be unprofitable; but that he had built them anyway, against the objections of his associates, because he said these would be his contribution to his country. They learned that Jack Cabot had tired of being supported by his father and planned to resign from the Foreign Service and go into business, but that his father had written him that he considered his support to be a contribution to America and successfully urged him not to resign.

When Godfrey invited employees to stay at his house, they were flattered at his attention. He saw them to their bedrooms at night, inquired after their needs, and was a most gracious host—except at the dinner table, where he served himself first,

grabbing whatever he wanted that was near him and reaching for
what was not, shoveling in food at a rate they had never before
seen. Even his bad manners pleased many of them, when they got
over the shock, because they thought the display so
un-Cabotlike.

During the last thirty active years of his life, Godfrey directed only the West Virginia operations, leaving the running of
all the rest, which was now the biggest part of his business, to
Tom. Even in the West Virginia operation his executives often
listened to Cabot's detailed instructions, but then, with Tom's
approval, secretly did otherwise. Cabot had always demanded of
his employees, as he had of his children, absolute and immediate
obedience. He objected strongly to being called "The Boss" because he thought the term was not respectful, but he was delighted when one of his executives began referring to him as "The
Chief," which soon became common throughout the company.
Unknown to any of them, Godfrey, Tom, and Ralph Bradley were
also referred to behind their backs as "Father, Son and Holy
Ghost." Many of the things which terribly embarrassed Tom,
such as his visceral geology, merely amused his associates, and
they enjoyed his sometimes violent exchanges with his sons.

More and more his employees had very carefully to learn to
deceive him, because Godfrey directed in detail from his Boston
office where, when, and how deep a well was to be dug in West
Virginia, and even how to set the packer, which his executives
considered "practicing surgery by telephone."

On a visit to West Virginia, Godfrey saw the remains of an
illegal liquor still on one of his lines; he immediately ordered all
moonshiners routed from his land by fire and sword. His West
Virginia executives had spent years working out a *modus vivendi*
with the bootleggers. These were old or unemployed coal miners
who were delighted with having gas to run their stills because it
was smokeless, which made it more difficult for federal agents to
find them. They needed fire to cook their corn mash until it was
sour and then to boil it, running their copper pipes through cool
water and catching the distilled moonshine which they sold. If
they were approached by Cabot's men walking the gas lines, they

shot at them. They would punch holes in Cabot's lines, and when they moved on they never stopped them up. One of Cabot's executives made a deal with all the bootleggers in the area that he would provide them with stop cocks and a mixer, so that they would get more heat and no light, if they would stop punching holes indiscriminately in the lines and would turn off the cocks when they moved. He agreed when Cabot told him to run off the bootleggers, but he knew he would be unable to, and he did nothing to try.

Cabot's own method of computing his profit was merely to see how much more cash he had in the banks at the end of the year than at the beginning, and he had promised bonuses to Tom and to Ralph Bradley based on increased profit which was really only an increased cash flow. His executives could have taken advantage of Godfrey's singular bookkeeping and stopped drilling wells and thereby built up the cash reserves and their bonuses. But they did not.

Cabot was usually unable to accept that anyone knew more than he in any field in which he had any knowledge. Having studied geology at Harvard and in Zurich, he refused to recognize the tremendous advancements in oil and gas geology made in the twentieth century and forbade the use of trained geologists by his sons. The primary cause of Godfrey's dislike for "experts" was probably his lifelong compulsion to be second or inferior to no one, to be the biggest and the best himself. Perhaps part of it, too, was the traditional anti-intellectualism of the Puritan: "the picture of the Puritan as an intellectual has been overdrawn, to the extent that Puritanism was always more an affair of the heart than of the head." Godfrey's demands for absolute obedience and no questioning of his orders or his reasons were equally in that tradition of rigorous Puritan theocracy. Godfrey wanted simplicity, not subtlety—absolutes, not shades of gray, like "the Puritan scholastics—the last representatives of the medieval ambition to synthesize all experience."

For Godfrey, as for his Puritan ancestors, it was "necessary to bury difficult questions in a wise silence . . . or to shunt them aside." Puritans and their descendants were less and less intellectually respectable as they refused to face the difficult and complex

questions raised by man's intellectual and scientific discoveries,
but they continued to impart their ethical convictions "to almost
all classes of society, so that even the high aristocrat in Victorian
England cultivates a sense of duty and the agnostic himself is a
very earnest moralist." Henry Adams pointed out that "The idea
that one has actually met a real genius dawns slowly on a Boston
mind." This was even more true of Godfrey than of his fellow
Bostonians because of his additional burden of moral righteous-
ness. For example, he refused to consider Albert Einstein a genius, because he smoked cigars.

This prejudice against expert geologists was one of the reasons Cabot's company did not go into the tremendously profitable
drilling of oil wells in the early days in Texas. The other reason
was the fact that so much of the oil prospecting and drilling was
done on a partnership basis, and it was extremely difficult to
induce Godfrey to enter a partnership. Having himself drilled for
gas on small city lots and school lots, where he was taking gas that
belonged to his neighbors, he was convinced that he would be
cheated by his partners if he took any.

Similarly, he was afraid others would steal his gas in the
ground. Therefore, when he got an extremely high-pressure field
in northern Pennsylvania near Wharton, where he could have
made more by selling his gas in the winter only, he nevertheless insisted that his customers take the gas out at a fast constant rate,
even though they were storing it in another field. He predicted
that someday gas would be piped all the way from the Southwest,
and when it was, he sold this exhausted field for $2 million dollars
to one of the Texas pipeline companies to use as a storage pool.

In regard to geologists and seismologists as in other matters,
his subordinates in the later years hired these experts against his
orders and without informing him.

Particularly when he was away from Boston, Godfrey loved
to go to the movies. His favorite movie, which he saw twelve
different times, was *King Kong;* given the slightest opportunity,
he would tell and act out the whole scenario, playing the part of
the great ape with relish and invariably turning over tables and

chairs and pulling up the rug.

From 1922 to 1929 Godfrey was on the Board of Governors of the National Aeronautics Association and spent more and more time on aviation matters, and less and less on his growing business. In 1925 and 1926 he served as president of the Association and lived in Washington, D.C., where he and Minnie moved in the society of senators, ambassadors, generals, and admirals. These were the two happiest years of Minnie's life, spent leaving her calling cards with the appropriate corner turned down and attending teas, receptions, and balls. Even after other Proper Bostonian matrons had ceased dog-earing their calling cards, Minnie meticulously continued the practice, turning down the upper righthand corner for a personal visit; the upper left for congratulations; the lower left for condolences; the lower right for adieu; and the whole left end for a call on the entire family.

In spite of her happiness at her social activity and success, Minnie still worried about money. She wrote to Ralph Bradley from Washington: "Washington is a terribly expensive place to live & I do not entertain either. I have had a couple of very small teas & an informal dinner of ten for those English people to my sorrow. Monday & the Monday after I have my two at homes in the afternoon—A very easy way of entertaining. All one does is to tell the newspapers that one is going to be at home & then people come, so they say. No invitations sent out. I have never in my life imagined there could be so much entertaining as here. We were invited to four large dinners for next Tuesday & we can't but one. We have had to refuse a great many. . . . Many houses here are like palaces. I lunched today with Mrs. Marshall Field. I have never seen so many beautiful things together. I especially like the men here. They are most interesting and a different crowd at each dinner. . . . I just live for Society."

Minnie sat on the advisory council of the National Woman's Country Club, where she happily hobnobbed with the Princesse de Ligne, Viscountess d'Alte, Lady Isabella Howard, and various other members of Washington diplomatic society.

Godfrey was delighted to see his Minnie finally blooming, and he urged her not to worry about expense. From Ft. Worth he wrote her: "I enclose $1000. Get yourself some gowns." At sixty-seven he still sent love letters to his wife, including on February 14, 1928, a poem:

> There was an old fossil from Mass.
> Who loved a superlative lass
> For lack of a fine
> picturesque Valentine
> He hopes that this tribute will pass.

Godfrey, too, blossomed in Washington society as he never had in Boston, and he was thought of in the capital as a distinguished and even courtly old gentleman. As much as Minnie enjoyed meeting social bigwigs, he enjoyed intimacy with Eddie Rickenbacker, Howard Hughes, Charles Lindbergh, Glenn L. Martin, and Igor Sikorsky. He knew General "Billy" Mitchell and in principle agreed with his views, but he disapproved of Mitchell's breaches of military discipline. He was an enthusiastic supporter of Richard E. Byrd, who in 1936 sent him in gratitude an autographed piece of insulation from the wall of Advance Meteorological Base, the southernmost habitation ever occupied by man.

In 1930, however, a series of disasters in addition to the Depression brought Cabot briefly back to full-time concern with his business. Jim suddenly died as the result of a strep brain infection, after having been operated on four times for a nonexistent brain tumor. He recited Kipling's "Recessional" on his deathbed, and Godfrey insisted that he be given a military funeral.

A few months later Tom, too, was gravely ill fom a strep infection and was for months not expected to live. When he recovered, he was told he could never work again, but after a year of convalescence he was able to go back to work. It was Tom who built Cabot Corporation from a profitable little enterprise into the largest carbon-black company in the world, but Godfrey, while giving his son authority to operate, tenaciously refused to relinquish substantial stock control, which was later to cost his heirs millions in taxes. Having come this far from being a runt,

Godfrey was not going to be deposed and not infrequently reminded Tom who was the owner.

Not only do the chief executives of large businesses have a pleasing and reassuring power over their own employees; but if their firms carry large bank deposits or place substantial advertising or make contributions or build branch plants and hire substantial numbers of workers, they also usually have instant communication and a respectful audience for their views among bank presidents, editors, real-estate owners, and politicians, who seem to seek them out and value their opinions in all matters of business, art, international affairs, and education. These executives know or at least feel subconsciously that their appeal to college presidents, publishers, and senators may lie not so much in their person or in their wisdom as in their office. They are therefore loath to give it up.

Although Cabot gave his children generous salaries or allowances, he would not give them nor their children any substantial blocks of capital, saying that he did not want to corrupt them, although he sold them a little stock in his company every year at very low prices and allowed them to invest in some of his subsidiaries in the Southwest. They were not a little resentful, therefore, when he loaned his friend Will Putnam $250,000 to put into Putnam's son's brokerage firm to save it from bankruptcy.

In the years from the early 1920's to the early 1950's—that is, from the age of sixty to the age of ninety—Cabot was expanding his interests at a time of life when most men are limiting them. He walked to work every day when he was in Boston, including Saturday when the office was closed, but after the early 1930's he worked at the office only until noon, spending the afternoon pursuing his other interests. In that period, in addition to supervising his company's growth from sales of under $2 million to sales of over $40 million, and in addition to his work in aviation and with the Watch and Ward, Cabot undertook a wide variety of new work.

In 1923, for example, he decided to run for Mayor of Cambridge as an Independent (that is, Republican), hoping to smite sin and corruption again, as he had in the cases of Coakley and

Pelletier. Had his name been Kennedy or O'Brien, Cabot would have had an uphill battle winning on any ticket but the Democratic. With his name and party, the chance of victory was virtually nonexistent. But Godfrey, like the hero of his fairytale, was undismayed. He challenged his opponent, the popular Mayor Edward H. Quinn, who was running for his fourth term, to debate with him, but Quinn refused. Cabot promised the citizens of Cambridge that if he were elected, he would effect what would then have been and today would still be a series of miracles— city contracts awarded according to the letter and the spirit of the law, without evasion of the requirements for competitive bids; appointments based upon qualifications for office and not upon political indebtedness; protection of the city's funds; a reduction of administrative expenses; and an end to corruption.

To no one's surprise except Godfrey's, the citizens of Cambridge re-elected Mayor Quinn with the largest vote ever cast in a Cambridge election, 16,897 voting for Quinn and 9,861 for Cabot. In the spring of 1924 Attorney-General J. R. Benton threatened to investigate Cabot for having failed to file a report of receipts and expenditures after his race, as required by state law. (Cambridge election laws allowed a candidate for mayor to spend $40 for every thousand voters in the city, which would have permitted Cabot legally to spend $1400.) Even those newspapers which had opposed Cabot, however, editorialized that it would be too ironic for Cabot, a reform candidate, to be the first ever to be prosecuted under this law so long ignored, and the investigation was not pursued.

As Cabot left his business almost entirely in the hands of his son Tom and hired managers, he was able to devote even more time to the Watch and Ward, which in the late 1920's reached the zenith of its book-burning activities. In the year 1927 the Society banned nearly a hundred books, and its angry anathema fell, like the rain, on the just and the unjust, on the talented and the trashy. Among the authors whose books were banned were Conrad Aiken, Sherwood Anderson, Michael Arlen, John Dos Passos, Theodore Dreiser, John Erskine, William Faulkner, Lion

Feuchtwanger, Ernest Hemingway, Aldous Huxley, Sinclair Lewis, Bertrand Russell, Upton Sinclair, Carl Van Vechten, and H. G. Wells. The wide variety of banned books included *Ulysses*, *Elmer Gantry*, *Antic Hay*, *An American Tragedy*, and *The Sun Also Rises*.

There were amusing aspects to this book burning. The first United States Senator from Utah, Reed Smoot, said about American literature of the day, "I would rather a child of mine take opium than read one of those books." Perhaps the Senator's anxiety to display his love of virtue and horror of vice was not totally unrelated to the fact that he was very nearly not allowed to take his seat in the Senate because of his constituents' predilection for polygamy; and he was only finally seated when another Senator ended the debate with the comment, "I'd rather have a polygamist who doesn't polyg than a monogamist who doesn't monog."

In New York, a counterattack against censorship was launched by Heywood Broun, Dorothy Parker, Jim Tully, William Allen White, Alexander Woollcott, and others. Their Committee for the Suppression of Irresponsible Censorship and a book called *Nonsenseorship* poked fun at Comstockery, with Heywood Broun pointing out that "A censor is a man who has read about Joshua and forgotten Canute. He believes that he can hold back the mighty traffic of life with a tin whistle and a raised right hand. For after all it is life with which he quarrels."

As do most books against censorship, *Nonsenseorship*, while remembering Canute, forgot Plato, who suggested in *The Republic*, Book ii, section 377: "The first thing will be to have a censorship of the writers of fiction, to accept the good and reject the bad."

When H. L. Mencken went to Boston in 1926 to sell copies of his *American Mercury* on the Boston Common after it had been banned because of "Hatrack," a short story about a prostitute, he was charged; but the case was dismissed.

The courts in America have reflected the country's varying moods on the subject of censorship. The best definition of obscenity was Judge Learned Hand's in the 1913 case of *United States v. Kennerly*: "should not the word 'obscene' be allowed to indicate the present critical point in the compromise between candor and shame at which the community may have arrived here and now?"

Time makes a difference in ideas of what constitutes obscenity, as New York Magistrate Henry Curran pointed out in 1937 when James T. Farrell's *A World I Never Made* was brought before him. "I don't think this book is pornographic. I think it is photographic . . . consider the young ladies in their bathing suits nowadays, how they toil not neither do they spin, but the Gibson girl in all her glory was not arrayed like one of these. If one of these lovely creatures of the far away nineties had really appeared in one of the little forget-me-not-suits of today, I fancy there would have been a commotion on the beach—and the rockers on the summer hotel piazzas would have rocked hard and long."

In 1948 Philadelphia's Judge Curtis Bok in *Commonwealth v. Gordon* dismissed obscenity charges against seven books, pointing out, in effect, that all looks yellow to the jaundiced eye and that it is virtually impossible to define the average modern reader. "It is impossible to say just what his reactions to a book actually are. . . . If he reads an obscene book when his sensuality is low, he will yawn over it. . . . If he reads the Mechanic's Lien Act while his sensuality is high, things will stand between him and the page that have no business there."

Throughout his life much appeared between Cabot and the pages he read that outraged him, and he watched the increasingly liberal decisions of the courts with contempt. It would be interesting to know what Godfrey Cabot was reading when as a youth he studied Greek; surely not Aristotle's theory of catharsis. Cabot throughout his life felt that a man left a theater or opera house full of unfulfilled stimuli, in contrast to Aristotle's theory that he was there cleansed by pity and fear. It never seems to have occurred to Cabot, as St. Thomas said, "That belongs to the nature of the beautiful which being seen or known, brings the appetite to rest," or, as Walter Kerr wrote, "Beauty may, after all, be less a temptress than a tamer."

In 1966, only four years after Cabot's death, the pendulum as reflected in at least one decision of the United States Supreme

Court seemed finally to be swinging back in the direction of Cabot's view—or, in any event, against the view that there should be no censorship of any kind.

Mr. Justice Brennan's language, in his March 22, 1966, opinion in the Ginzburg case, sounds not unlike Cabot's. Brennan condemned "commercial exploitation of erotica solely for the sake of their prurient appeal . . . the sordid business of pandering, . . . 'the leer of the sensualist,' " and "efforts to sell their publications on the basis of salacious appeal."

On that same date Mr. Justice Douglas dissented. "This new exception condemns an advertising technique as old as history. The advertisements of our best magazines are chock-full of thighs, ankles, calves, bosoms, eyes and hair, to draw the potential buyers' attention to lotions, tires, food, liquor, clothing, autos, and even insurance policies. . . . I cannot imagine any promotional effort that would make chapters 7 and 8 of the Song of Solomon any the less or any more worthy of First Amendment protection than does its unostentatious inclusion in the average edition of the Bible."

Nevertheless, Justice Brennan's view obtained, that there should be censorship of obscenity. For his definition of obscenity (in the *Fanny Hill* case of the same date), he took terms of the *Roth v. United States* decision of 1957: "Whether to the average persons, applying contemporary community standards, the dominant theme of the material taken as a whole appeals to prurient interest." In addition, obscenity, in Mr. Justice Brennan's view, must be "utterly without redeeming social value."

Books can be used to condone evil, as assuredly as Cabot's ancestors had justified their burning of witches and trading in human slaves by passages in the Holy Bible. But Cabot's view that books corrupt individuals who would not otherwise be corrupted is at least subject to doubt.

Just as the pendulum of literary censorship seems to be swinging back in Cabot's direction, so the day may not be too distant when the present feeling that the courts of the country can cure all of its ills will be reversed; again, if not to Godfrey's degree of conservatism, at least in that direction. Today's judicial activists have deified Judge Learned Hand while ignoring his counsel of self-restraint to judges: "Nor is it desirable for a lower court to embrace the exhilarating opportunity of anticipating a doctrine which may be in the womb of time, but whose birth is distant."

The Watch and Ward Society was, however, but one source of those fights which made Godfrey know he was alive and which provided an outlet for his phenomenal energy.

Between 1920 and 1950, besides actively participating in this wide variety of endeavors outside his business, the very least that Cabot did concerning other matters which interested him was to express his views in letters to newspapers and magazines, his favorite forum being the Boston *Herald,* whose readers he instructed on subjects ranging from how to right a capsized dory to his predictions of coming events in aviation, which included: "The discontinuance of heavier-than-air transatlantic flights and needless loss of lives. . . . Man-made islands in mid-ocean with arched foundations towering high over lashing seas—havens of safety for transoceanic [dirigible] flights . . . landing fields on sky-scrapers hundreds of feet above sea level, with huge catapults hurling into space planes headed for distant ports."

All of his adult life Cabot had deluged a variety of publications and their readers with his views. In July 1913 in the Parkersburg, West Virginia, *News* he excoriated the wickedness of Wilson and Bryan. In 1914 in the *Oil Paint and Drug Reporter* he pointed out inequities in our patent laws and suggested cures.

In April 1915 in the Parkersburg, West Virginia, *News* Cabot recommended the thrifty spending of tax dollars, apparently in response to an editorial in the same journal which had read in full, "Notwithstanding the fact that Godfrey L. Cabot, the Boston millionaire, has a number of gas wells, a large carbon factory, and several miles of pipe lines in Roane County, he paid only about $300 taxes into the county treasury last year. Wonder who swears to his assessment?"

Before 1920 Cabot had had numerous letters published in various West Virginia and Boston papers, the *Army and Navy*

Journal, Flying magazine, and the *Harvard Alumni Bulletin*, supporting the Allies, supporting Hughes for president, condemning the proposed League of Nations, favoring women's suffrage, and urging the adoption of the metric system.

On January 26, 1933, in the Boston *Transcript* Godfrey criticized the Germans for not paying their war reparations to the French and the French for not paying their just debts, and on April 27 in the Boston *Herald,* in spite of his strong pro-Negro feeling, he criticized his friend Judge Lowell's refusal to permit extradition of a Negro, one George Crawford, back to the state of Virginia.

What shocked members of Cabot's family and his conservative friends was the frequency with which his letters to the newspapers reflected admiration for certain acts of men whose general policies Cabot despised. On November 1, 1934, he wrote to the Boston *Herald,* "President Roosevelt is personally known to me, first, as a naval officer under his command in the world war, and last, as his guest this month at a White House reception. Although one of many critics of Mr. Roosevelt's financial policies, I affirm without fear of contradiction that he is a gentleman in the highest sense of the word—a man of the most exquisite courtesy to every one he meets or with whom he has relations. I am convinced that this is not merely surface polish; that it has been instinctive in him from his youth up and is the natural outgrowth of a gentle heart."

Even more surprising to many was Godfrey's letter in March 1951 to the *Christian Science Monitor,* in which he commended Truman and supported his action in Korea. No one should have been surprised, for often, unlike many of his business contemporaries and most of his ancestors, Cabot had written and spoken out on public matters expressing a view against his financial interest if he thought it in America's interest. He had, for example, very early urged America's entry into World War II and was contemptuous of the many American businessmen who said, "You can do business with Hitler."

As he grew older, Cabot's letters occasionally were not in anger but in fun.

To the Editor of The Herald:

I notice something in your issue today about stale eggs offered for sale at $5000 apiece. They are obviously absurdly cheap at this price. If a frugal dinosaur had sold one of these eggs when fresh at one cent and put the money in the bank at 4 per cent, compound interest, his heirs-at-law would now own all the money there is in the world and a whole lot more.

Please call this financial proposition to the attention of any dinosaurs of your acquaintance so that the error may not be repeated.

Godfrey L. Cabot

After years of having rented different summer houses on the North Shore, in 1908 Godfrey had delighted Minnie by buying a fine estate at fashionable Beverly Farms. As the years went by both he and Minnie had become increasingly proud and fond of it. It is difficult to explain the attraction of the Massachusetts seacoast at Nahant, at Beverly, at Pride's Crossing. There is none of the lush growth of the tropic seashore, nor even the beautiful sand beaches found elsewhere along the Atlantic Coast. No natural beauty instantly greets the eye, though diligent search may produce the geometric delight of a sand dollar. The appeal may be the visceral pleasure of a congenitally seafaring people for the sea itself. Perhaps the appeal lies in nothing more than the absence of people, the restful respite from city crowds and their individual worries which compound into group tensions. Perhaps it also involves the intimate contact with the elements—the sun (or storm) and especially the immensity and mystery of the sea.

In 1928 Cabot made one of Minnie's dreams come true by buying her a house in the most fashionable location in Boston, on the water side of Beacon Street, at number 242. Here she would happily have spent all her time between visiting grandchildren and her favorite chow, Ming, but Godfrey insisted that she accompany him on his trips all over the world, saying that she had no excuse not to, since her children were grown. But Minnie now did have good reason not to travel; clearly her health was too

poor. When she died of emphysema on November 5, 1934, her
sons felt that her end had been hastened by Godfrey's insistence
that she join him on his arduous junkets.

Godfrey had been a loving husband, putting up with Minnie's incessant fears and complaints, tucking a blanket around her
as he read to her from some favorite book of his, and buying her
those things which made her feel a little more secure in society.
But he was clumsy in showing kindness, and in most matters he
insisted on having his own way absolutely. Minnie once confided to
her sister-in-law, Lilla, that the greatest unfulfilled desire of her
life was a bedroom, or even a bed, of her own, where she could
escape from Godfrey's sexual demands and the freezing cold
which resulted from his insistence that all bedroom windows always be kept wide open, even in winter.

On Minnie's death Godfrey, broken-hearted, asked his
daughter and her family to move into 242 Beacon Street. His
son-in-law, Ralph Bradley, had by now come to work for Cabot
Corporation, but he was very nearly the opposite of his father-
in-law and his brothers-in-law. Relaxed and gay, he was not upset
by Godfrey's manner, choosing instead to laugh at the old man or
to ignore him.

Bradley played an avuncular role in the Cabot Corporation,
listening to and often solving the problems of employees whom
Godfrey and Tom were too busy to notice. There grew up a real
affection between the old man and Bradley because they were so
different and did not compete. Bradley, a man of great physical
courage, had been awarded the gold medal of the Massachusetts
Humane Society for jumping overboard and saving the life of the
department store tycoon Bamberger on a Mediterranean cruise.
Godfrey admired both his courage and his kindness.

Before Christmas, 1884, in spite of his fears about entering
business, young Cabot had nevertheless sent his usual $50 check
for support of Negro schools in the South. His public philanthropies, beginning with gifts to Boston in his twenties, had continued
in a small way wherever he did business or traveled. Minnie had
objected to any sizable gifts, but after her death Godfrey was free
to do as he chose. He told his daughter, "You ought to give money

away when you're alive, when it costs you something. If you give it away when you're dead, you're giving other people's money away. If you have too much money you have a lonely life."

On June 10, 1935, Godfrey Cabot was given an Honorary Doctorate of Laws by Norwich University in Northfield, Vermont, at the same time that honorary degrees were given to General Douglas MacArthur, then Chief of Staff, and David Sarnoff, president of Radio Corporation of America. Cabot was also elected a Trustee of the University.

In August of the same year Cabot gave $144,000 to endow a Professorship in Aviation at Norwich, in memory of his son Jim. He hoped Norwich might develop an air safety code for the world comparable to the British safety rules at sea. In later years Cabot made further donations, in the hope that Norwich might eventually become the West Point of the air, which was permanently precluded by the creation of the Air Force Academy.

For years in his dinner conversation Cabot predicted that before long the whole world was going to run out of fossil fuels. He also pointed out that in the 6,000 years since the days of the early Egyptians, the productivity of small grains had probably increased only fiftyfold. He believed that in the long run man was going to be dependent on solar energy and that trees were the best way to store it. Selective breeding of trees to increase their productivity would certainly take longer than breeding of small grains, because there is a new generation of corn every year but a new generation of trees takes longer; it was therefore high time to get on with the job.

"In the last hundred and fifty years," Cabot once told a friend, "mankind has been utilizing solar energy stored up over millions of years in the form of coal and oil and gas and some day these must come to an end. I have made money from this and it seems to me I should put some of my money to work so that men may learn to live on their daily or their annual income of solar energy."

In 1935, when Cabot was visiting Gifford Pinchot, then Governor of Pennsylvania, in an effort to secure his help in obtaining permission to lay a pipeline, he expressed these views at great length to the father of conservation in America. Pinchot, a Yale graduate, told Cabot that Yale had the best school of forestry in the world and that if Cabot would give Yale a million dollars, the university might use it very effectively toward better ways to breed trees and thus work on solving the problem of solar energy. When Tom learned that his father was considering such a gift to Yale, he immediately called Harvard's President, James B. Conant, who asked Godfrey to lunch. Some time later Godfrey gave Harvard what he believed to be a million dollars worth of his own stock, which Harvard set up on the basis of its book value at $615,733 and which in 1966 was worth over seven million dollars.

These funds created the Maria Moors Cabot Foundation for Botanical Research to provide for a long-range research program in artificial selection and hybridization of trees, soil science, tree physiology, and forest genetics at the Harvard Forest in Petersham and at the Arnold Arboretum. Cabot did not foresee that man's future energy needs would someday be solved by nuclear fission, but he provided that after fifty years Harvard, at its discretion, could employ these funds for any suitable purpose, and he made similar provisions in all his other gifts.

A few days after Cabot's gifts to Harvard became known, Karl Compton, the president of M.I.T., called on Godfrey, who was a Life Member of the Corporation, and told him of the work M.I.T. was doing on the problems of the direct use of solar energy by physical means. Cabot then gave M.I.T. the same number of shares in his company as he had given Harvard, to be used for harnessing the energy of the sun.

Cabot's youngest son, John Moors Cabot, after graduating *magna cum laude* from Harvard and taking another degree at Oxford, had gone into the State Department. Much of his diplomatic career was spent in Latin America. In 1938 he convinced his father to endow a series of annual journalism prizes at Columbia University. Known as the Maria Moors Cabot prizes and consisting of a gold medal, a silver and ebony plaque, and a thousand-dollar honorarium, they are annually awarded by Columbia to Latin American journalists for advancing sympathetic understanding and strengthening friendly relations among the peoples of South, Central, and North America.

Cabot also received honorary doctorates from Northeastern University in Boston and from Morris Harvey College in Charleston, West Virginia, and he made substantial contributions to both schools.

After receiving his honorary degrees, Cabot seriously advised his friends in Boston that he expected to be addressed as **Dr.** Cabot.

In 1927 Cabot had established a prize fund of $10,000 for the creation of a device by means of which a pilot could see through a hundred feet of fog. In 1948 this was changed to the Wright Brothers Memorial Trophy, presented annually by the National Aeronautics Association to the person contributing the most to aviation. Among the recipients have been Charles A. Lindbergh, Jimmy Doolittle, and Stuart Symington.

All his life Godfrey believed in sea serpents, having read Thomas Handasyd Perkins' report of seeing one in Gloucester harbor. He studied all he could find on the subject of whales and therefore was fond of bringing the conversation around to the subject in order first to show off his erudition and then to expound on this theory that sea serpents thought to be prehistoric still lived in the ocean's depths. He became furious if his views were belittled, and he once stopped speaking to Jim for a week when his son suggested that there might be a correlation between Perkins' having seen a sea serpent and the seven silver champagne buckets mentioned in his will.

Alfred Romer, Director of the Museum of American Zoology at Harvard (which is more often called the Agassiz Museum in memory of Louis Agassiz), heard of Cabot's interest in sea serpents. He went to see Godfrey and told him he had a collection of bones in the basement of the museum which might be those of a sea serpent, but that he needed $10,000 to have them put together into an exhibit. Cabot immediately gave him a check, and the Kronosaurus skeleton now attracts more people to the museum than anything except its famous glass flowers.

By the end of the 1930's various colleges and charities were the major stockholders of Cabot's company, of which he had given away over 25 per cent. Harvard and M.I.T. were larger stockholders than any of Cabot's children, and both universities had representatives on the Cabot Board of Directors, having been precluded from selling the shares during Cabot's lifetime.

Directors' meetings of the company were often tense and sometimes embarrassingly boisterous because of exchanges between Godfrey and Tom. Godfrey, in touch only with the West Virginia operation, wanted to speak of the latest well drilled, its depth, its production, how he had located it, and such details as how many nipples on the Christmas tree and how tight the pipe was screwed, all of which he thought he had directed. Tom, embarrassed by this display when he wanted to discuss major matters of policy, sometimes became so frustrated and enraged that he screamed at his father, to the considerable discomfort of the outside directors. Old Godfrey, however, was never embarrassed; having kept the power in his own hands, he could quietly insist on having his way.

Money gave Cabot his only constant sense of security. His endurance as a walker and as a multiple-set tennis player compensated sometimes for the old feelings of the sickly runt which remained in the nearly-six-foot adult. Winning at chess or quoting at length from Shakespeare or the Britannica gave occasional moments of superiority or relief from the old feelings of inadequacy. Banning books and imprisoning bookies temporarily relieved any guilty feelings of the little boy who had been frightened and fascinated by the Carver Street whores. But money, with its power to impress and frighten, was the real relief giver. It made him a big man in Boston and even New York, let alone in the cities he visited all over the world or the villages of West Virginia. And it kept his employees and his family in his power.

He took no pleasure in beautiful objects, such as his relatives collected and showed with pride. He never wanted to eat from Lowestoft plates or collect Hester Bateman silver. Chippendale furniture gave him neither the pleasure of beauty nor the pleasure of snobbery. He therefore never bought beautiful objects but enjoyed instead the power of his money, well-invested and increasing so rapidly that he never really knew how rich he was. But he knew that he was safely, powerfully, beyond any possibility of losing the great fortune he had built—gratifyingly, comfortingly, satisfyingly rich.

CHAPTER XIV

Grand Old Man

It is time to be old, To take in sail.
EMERSON, *Terminus*

And if I should live to be
The last leaf upon the tree
    In the spring,
Let them smile, as I do now,
At the old forsaken bough
    Where I cling.
OLIVER WENDELL HOLMES, *The Last Leaf*

In the early 1950's Cabot was still busy with a variety of activities, walking to his office every morning until 1954, writing as many as twenty letters a day, and traveling all over the country.

It would never have occurred to Godfrey to retire, once and for all to give up the tremendous power he had acquired. Not only would it have been psychologically difficult, but in Boston it would have appeared slothful and immoral. Justice Holmes had refused to retire from the United States Supreme Court until he was past ninety and as Cleveland Amory pointed out, "Retiring from business is like giving in to the Boston winter; it reflects on a man's character." Godfrey in his eighties and early nineties thought himself at his peak, just as his sister Lilla as she approached ninety still continued to paint five hours a day and was sure her work was improving. "To retire from business is, in Boston First Family Society, a suspect action. The Proper Bostonian of advanced years may not be fortunate enough to have any more business, but if he doesn't he pretends he has and whiles away his mornings at least at directors' meetings, in the Family trust office, or at some other place where he is still an active part of the world. Failing all these, he takes up a hobby in a stern business-like manner."

Godfrey knew and was proud of the fact that people in Boston said you could set your watch by his morning walk to the office; that even the Irish and Italian citizens of the city repeated real and apocryphal tales of eccentricity and success attached to his name to their children; and that these tales had become part of American mythology.

Not until 1954, when he was ninety-three, did Godfrey finally become Chairman of the Board of Cabot Corporation, allowing Tom to become president at fifty-seven. Resolved not to do to his son Louis what Godfrey had done to him, Tom, six years later, made Louis president at the age of thirty-nine.

Godfrey had wanted to serve on a number of boards in Boston, but he was known to be such a stubborn and prickly character that he was never asked. As one of his lawyers put it, "He was the opposite of a clubbable man." Godfrey had once bought 10,000 shares of New York, New Haven and Hartford Railroad stock, hoping to be asked on the board, but he was not invited.

Tom Cabot felt so oppressed until his father retired that he was constantly trying to prove his worth not only in his father's business but also in mountain climbing, in sailing, as an Overseer of Harvard, and in serving in the State Department. Another method was by serving as a director of other companies, for he had proved himself a very knowledgeable businessman and far less difficult than his father, and he was invited onto the boards of various Boston businesses, banks, insurance companies, and mutual funds.

One of these was the United Fruit Company; after serving on its Board, he was invited to become President in 1948. It being a far bigger and more important company than his father's, Tom accepted, this being quite a salve to his long bruised self-esteem. Tom, like his father, was much concerned with duty and being of service, and he felt "It might enable me to make a profound difference in the social development of tropical America." Unfortunately, however, he soon found that he was unable to change the "gunboat diplomacy" attitude of Samuel Zemurray, who controlled United Fruit, and in a year Tom resigned, returning to Cabot Corporation on a full-time basis.

Over Godfrey's increasingly less forceful objections the Cabot Corporation in the 1950's was building carbon-black plants all over the world. Before World War II all the black in the world had been made in America, but during the war other countries, including Nazi Germany, had had to develop methods of black manufacture to keep their truck transport rolling. After the war more and more countries wanted carbon-black plants within their own borders.

Competition in America was growing too, particularly by major oil companies, as Godfrey had predicted would happen if there were "too much sugar." Cities Service took over Columbian Carbon, Ashland Oil and Refining took over United Carbon. Continental, Phillips, and even such comparatively small independents as Sid Richardson in Texas went into the carbon-black business on their own.

In order to keep its leadership, Cabot Corporation built plants in England, Argentina, Italy, Canada, Australia, and even "immoral" France; it also built partnership plants or made manufacturing agreements in Holland, Japan, and Germany.

Wherever his employees and his grandchildren went, Godfrey's questions and suggestions followed, often based on experiences of nearly a century earlier. Like Franklin, Godfrey in his old age remained curious and interested. "It would take me hours to describe the things that have been dug up since I was first in Rome in 1884, for instance the neolithic graves on the Via Sacra which show that Rome was inhabited centuries before the A.U.C. from which Roman history is usually dated. Pray tell me if you have seen the remains of the Egyptian temple they dug up since I was last there beneath the floor of St. Peter's. I flew vertically in a zeppelin over the dome of St. Peter's in 1926 . . .

"How does the death rate from automobile accidents in Norway and in Sweden compare with that in the U.S.A.? Did you see cows being milked by machinery in Sweden? Did you see the opera either in Sweden or Norway? . . .

"Is it not possible that the brand new German ship which was loading for the Black Sea might have gone to Trebizand or Sansum or Asiatic Turkey? Is there still a steamboat building yard at Zurich? . . .

". . . I am very glad indeed to know that the factory [in England] is now in operation, although the yield is not quite as high as the yield of lamp black at my elder brother Sam's factory seventy years ago . . . if England becomes engaged in war, you will have a loud speaker somewhere in the factory equipped with radio to operate during lunch time and keep the operatives supplied with the latest war news . . . it is one of our most important duties to impress the situation on those who are working for us and make them feel that the highest possible co-operation between employer and employed is an important factor in human well being throughout the world.

". . . I have been reading your report and will be glad to know if the contractor, Simon-Carves, are any relation of Simon-Carves T. Side Collieries at Newcastle on Thames which I visited in 1883 or 1884 and saw one of the first retort coke oven plants that was ever erected in England, although at that time there were plenty of them in Germany. Do the English bricklayer unions still limit the number of bricks a workman is permitted to lay in a day?

"When I was in Chester in 1883 there was still part of the old Roman wall . . . there was marked off on the walls of Chester the length of the *Great Eastern* which at that time was incomparably the greatest ship in the world. I think it was 667 feet long or thereabout—a mere dwarf beside the Queen Mary or the Queen Elizabeth. . . .

". . . Our crocuses are just shoving some little green needles above the surface of the ground. . . . Please don't forget to make

Louis plant some trees around the factory and it would not be a
bad idea to have some ivy clinging to the building—particularly
the office building . . . they will be growing while you sleep and
before you know it will be some pumpkins and add to the beauty
of the surroundings."

Half a century earlier, when Cabot had been about to inspect a compressor station on one of his gas lines, he had instead
spent his time admiring a flower garden planted in front of it,
telling his superintendent, "If your man keeps his garden this
well, I don't have to worry how he keeps the station."

". . . a dramatic illustration of the most important scientific fact known to man: that every living thing from the lowest
bacterium to homo sapiens rises in the scale of evolution under
adequate stimulus and falls in the scale of evolution if adequate
stimulus is lacking. In the case of bacterium, if you plant in a rich
nitrogenous soup the bacteria that live in the roots of clover and
make their living by tearing nitrogen from the air and converting
it into protein, they degenerate because they get great supplies of
nitrogenous material in the rich soup. If, on the other hand, you
put them into a pure syrup of sugar they have to tear every
particle of nitrogen that they need to live out of the air and
become exceptionally proficient in the art and industry. . . . On
the other hand, we have the lizard that has degenerated first to the
skink and then to the snake for lack of adequate stimulus through
unknown thousands of years, and the rich men's sons who with
good ability and character fail to achieve as great usefulness as
their forebears for lack of stimulus.

"I have read with much pleasure the clipping you sent me
under date of April 26th. The Channel tunnel, the construction
of which was begun in 1882, and promptly quashed by Parliament due to the frantic opposition of Sir Garnet Wolseley and
some fools in Parliament, would of course have been worth billions
of dollars to the English during either of the two great wars and I
certainly hope that they will at long last get busy and build it. I
also hope they will build a tunnel under the Straits of Gibraltar if
it is technically feasible. . . . Frankly, I wouldn't much like
to be digging with this weight of water above my head, but

there are lots of men who would be willing to take a chance under competent technical surveyance.

"The imbecile opposition of Sir Garnet Wolseley reminds me of a remark made by Moltke when asked if he had any plan for an invasion of England across the channel; 'twenty' he said, 'but I haven't been able to make any plan by which I could get back.' Obviously any such tunnel could be mined and connected by wires with numerous different points in both countries from which it could be blown up by pressing a button and all the people in the tunnel drowned. Catch any German commander being fool enough to put troops into such a trap."

Cabot's correspondence all over the world so excited his desire to travel again that in 1954 he wrote Thomas Cook & Son requesting information on a round-the-world cruise of the *Caronia*, but not forgetting to chide the agency for a failure now a third of a century past. "I have travelled a good deal with various branches of your Company and have never got a severe throwdown but once, and that was in Spain in the fall of 1921, where the men and the machine with which I went with my wife from Barcelona to Montserrat were wholly unsatisfactory." Convinced by his children he should not at ninety-three travel alone around the world, Cabot threatened to learn Chinese from his son Jack who had served in Shanghai, "so that I can do all the tall swearing that is necessary for the health of a Cabot and still escape detection in the circles in which I move."

He still traveled every spring to West Virginia to see the redbud, and he went to Tulsa, Oklahoma, in 1953 to be honored along with seven others as a Grand Old Man of the Natural Gas Industry and then proceeded to inspect in three days all his operations in New Mexico, Texas, and Louisiana and some operations of Shell Oil, as well as a performance of *Call Me Madam*, "which consisted chiefly of an enormous amount of dancing mostly by the female sex . . . their skill was simply supernatural."

In November 1955, Godfrey L. Cabot, along with a number of other pioneers in aviation including Glenn L. Martin, was elected an Elder Statesman of Aviation by the National Aeronautic Association, which he had so long and so joyfully served. He thoroughly relished his role as sage when he was sought out by newspapermen and questioned on various subjects.

Especially to young people Godfrey Cabot in the last few decades of his life seemed *sui generis*. But the truth was that he had only lived too long. Until 1930 there had always been men like him in America, and such men had been those most responsible for the growth of the Republic.

Godfrey enjoyed his reputation as an eccentric and his eccentricity was not unlike that found in Britain on which Henry Adams had remarked, "Americans needed and used their whole energy, and applied it with close economy; but English society was eccentric by law and for the sake of eccentricity itself. . . . Often this eccentricity bore all the marks of strength; perhaps it was actual exuberance of force, a birthmark of genius. Boston thought so. The Bostonian called it national character—national vigor—robustness—honesty—courage. He respected and feared it. British self-assertion, bluff, brutal, blunt as it was, seemed to him a better and nobler thing than the acuteness of the Yankee or the polish of the Parisian."

He still carefully studied with Patrick J. Malloy, his gardener at Beverly Farms, how best to exterminate the cabbage maggot destroyers, and he checked various bills ranging in amount from $2.02 to $8.98.

Godfrey continued to read with relish, especially paperbacked novels with bare-bosomed ladies on the covers, declaring them "Absolutely outrageous!" He also read newspapers and scientific journals, trying to stay abreast of everything new. He wrote to a niece, "I concur with you in your understatement that the days of miracles are not yet past; quite the contrary. Since I was born more fairytales have come true than Grimm ever wrote, greatest of all being man flight, in which I have taken an honorable part."

When one of his grandsons expressed the desire to become a lawyer, Godfrey told him, "Well, I suppose it's an honorable career, but I'm disappointed. My experience is, and I know all the best lawyers, that their lives are consumed in looking at the worst aspects of human relations rather than the best."

At the end as at the beginning, his attitude toward life was nearly opposite to that of Henry Adams, who viewed America in the new century with contempt and despair: "A traveller in the highways of history looked out of the club window on the turmoil of Fifth Avenue, and felt himself in Rome under Diocletian, witnessing the anarchy, conscious of the compulsion. . . . The two-thousand-years failure of Christianity roared upward from Broadway, and no Constantine the Great was in sight." Unlike Adams, Cabot had never expressed a hope for "a world that sensitive and timid natures could regard without a shudder."

In writing to his then fourteen grandchildren and twenty-one great-grandchildren, as well as to his numberless cousins, grandnieces, and grandnephews, he could not always keep them straight. "I feel greatly disgraced that I know so little about them and plead in extenuation that for 44 years, 4 months and 14 days I was spoiled by Minnie who remembered everybody—my own relatives as well as hers—far better than I did and I forgot to remember people under her mild and devoted regime."

During most of his life Cabot was absolute in his dicta but in his last years he became less absolute, even writing to Tom in a letter objecting to the building of foreign plants, "However, God knows I have guessed wrong a good many times, and particularly after the close of the first World War, when I thought that it would be something like one hundred years or more until the next World War, and that it would be unlikely that the Germans would start the next World War."

He recommended increasing the company's oil and gas business by underwater drilling in the Gulf of Mexico. But he questioned Tom's and Louis' determination to diversify into entirely new businesses in a big way. "I deprecate very large new enterprises where we take up something that we have not demonstrated to have been profitable elsewhere. I think we should begin on a small scale and get our experience cheaply, but I think we may be bolder in new enterprises in gas, oil and carbon black where we have long experience. . . . I hope you will keep this letter where you can lay your hand on it. At my age [ninety-three] I can't expect to last much longer and I want, so far as possible, to leave with you some of the advantages of my experience."

Some of the major diversification efforts taken by Cabot Corporation have proven unfortunate and carbon black, gas, and oil are still its most profitable businesses.

"Last and most important of all," Godfrey wrote his grandson Louis, "we should at all times have before us the profitable interests of those with whom we bargain and not try to lure them into any bargain that we think they would subsequently regret."

This feeling that business should be mutually advantageous is as close as Godfrey ever came to the possibly irreconcilable conflict between business and Christianity. It cannot very well be argued that Christianity is irrelevant to business, but in nearly two thousand years there has never been written an acceptable Code, and this in societies such as our own which have written numberless Codes, Good Practice in Law, Good Practice in Medicine, Good Practice in Insurance Huckstering or Plumbing or Broadcasting; so that malpractice could be defined thereby.

Cabot continued by frequent letters and memoranda to try to keep a spirit of service in what had now become a tremendous company, with profits in the millions of dollars a year and sales rapidly approaching a hundred million: ". . . incomparably the most important factor in the conduct of our West Virginia business is that there is an unwritten law that has so far as I know never been questioned or disobeyed in our territory; that when domestic consumers are pinched, the industrial consumers and the public service corporations are shut back enough to make up the deficit." Cabot's attitude so permeated his company that his chief company counsel could remark with no evident self-consciousness that he had chosen the law after considering the ministry because he felt he could accomplish more good in business than in the church.

Godfrey regularly sent checks to a number of his poor relatives, usually deprecating the gift with the sentence, "I enclose a scrap of paper." And in most of his letters now he put some humor. "On one of the 47 times I crossed the Atlantic I happened upon a very affable Southerner. He asked me my name and I told him and he said: 'What business have you addressing me? I thought Cabots spoke only to God.' I threw into my august countenance the most absolutely imbecilic expression (I'm good at that) and opening my mouth wide said in a cracked voice, 'Why, I thought you were God.'

". . . This well known saying had a new version of it printed in the Harvard Lampoon ten or twenty years ago when a gentleman named 'Kabotsky' got a bill through the legislature to change his name to 'Kabot.' Various people urged me to intervene to prevent him, but in as much as I did not think I should be getting his mail nor that he would be getting mine, I did nothing about it. The Lampoon version is as follows:

> A toast to dear old Boston
> Home of the Sacred Cod
> Where the Lowells have no one to talk to
> Since the Cabots talk Yiddish to God.

". . . I had quite a chat with Tom yesterday and he is very much disturbed about atom bombs and the threatened extinction of civilization, but as for me, I don't worry about a little trifle like that."

In addition to showing more humor, Godfrey occasionally returned to the brief efforts at self-analysis which he had abandoned with his youth. He told both his daughter and an executive of his company, "If I had my life to live over again I'd spend far less time with books and far more time with people."

He spent as much time as he was allowed with his grandchildren and great-grandchildren, kissing them, swinging them between his legs, and telling them all the fairytales he knew by heart. He had always enjoyed reading the comics aloud with great feeling to his grandchildren, especially "Mutt and Jeff" and "The Gumps," which ranked almost with Lewis Carroll in his affection. Whenever children kissed him or when he told them of kindnesses done to him, he had tears in his eyes.

Godfrey still enjoyed fighting on the side of the angels. Joining with Charles Francis Adams as Vice Chairman of an

attack on pari-mutuel betting, bookmakers, numbers, and all organized gambling, he compared the racketeers to the Barbary
Coast pirates to whom Americans had refused to pay tribute
nearly two centuries earlier, and he wrote, "Gambling is a school
of avarice productive of every crime traceable to avarice."

In 1955 he offered $3000 to help fight a plan to build a
parking garage under the Common. "My guess is that James
Michael Curley is behind this plan and figures on getting a big
rake-off from some contractor." Cabot's chronic suspicions of
skulduggery were not limited to his own times. He told a friend
that he was sure that the money changers and dove sellers in the
Temple at Jerusalem had been paying off the Pharisees and
Sadducees. His friend's reaction of "honi soit qui mal y pense" he
kept to himself.

Requested to join in the fight against the building of Storrow Drive, which eventually separated his house from the Espla-
nade and the Charles River, he responded enthusiastically, promising, "We will fight them until hell freezes over and then we will
fight on the ice." Godfrey's whole life was not unlike a fight on the
ice.

Today we tend to doubt or even to make fun not only of the
Puritan idea of Hell, but even of the value of the Puritan promise
of Heaven.

> Burning at first no doubt would be worst,
> But time the impression would soften;
> While those who are bored with praising the Lord,
> Would be more bored with praising him often.

Godfrey did not believe in Hell and was not at all sure of the
existence of Heaven; indeed, he might be considered an Existentialist, but an Existentialist with a highly developed and active
sense of duty and of right and wrong.

In his nineties Cabot was still intensely interested in politics,
making substantial contributions to the Republican Party.
"When I was born I think this country was in an even more
puzzling situation than it is today and God sent us a rail splitter,
whose infinite patience and miraculous judgement in hitting the

happy mean and using only right means to accomplish only right ends, left a monument to guide future generations in statesmanship and human relations generally. I think we have in Eisenhower a similar man . . . and I am doing what little I can think of to help his supporters."

Like his ancestors who had furiously denounced Thomas Jefferson as Machiavellian when that president's policies adversely affected their business, Godfrey was terrible in his outrage against Franklin Delano Roosevelt, whom he equated with Woodrow Wilson as "unfit to run a peanut stand."

Besides what Cabot considered the immorality of Wilson's private life, he faulted the President for waiting too long to enter the war. He always "wished that we should go into it immediately when the Lusitania was sunk and have never ceased to regret that we did not enter the world war at that time, which might perhaps have saved the Russian empire."

Roosevelt's sins had been too numerous to list, although Godfrey could spend a tempestuous hour in the attempt. First of all, he came from New York, the new Babylon where Morgan was Baal. Roosevelt's greatest sin was taxes, which to Cabot's dying day he believed would eventually be rescinded.

Roosevelt and Truman were too concerned with luxuries for the common man. Cabot was proud of his own ability to get along with common people, whether they were farmers or oil-field roughnecks, but he had no patience with the view that they should be provided, out of his pocket, with what Roosevelt and Truman considered necessities but which Cabot viewed as the corrupting luxuries he had denied to his own children. Cabot saw himself as steward of his great fortune, and if he refused to spend it frivolously on his own, his rage at seeing it wasted on lazy unknowns was terrible.

He wrote letters to all the employees of his company and its subsidiaries expressing his political views but stating, "if there are any of you who feel differently about this, I beg you to forgive me on the ground that 'out of the fullness of the heart, the mouth speaketh.' " He criticized the New Deal and the Fair Deal for building up such an immense national debt and for tending "to diminish the desire to render service and to practice self-denial and thereby accumulate savings against a rainy day."

Cabot tried to be fair, pointing out in the same letter that "President Roosevelt is deserving of the highest respect for his boldness and wisdom on the conduct of our foreign affairs, although, of course, he made many important mistakes as would certainly have been done by any human being in his position. . . . With regard to Truman, I think he deserves great credit for doing perhaps more than any other president since Lincoln to protect and secure the constitutional rights of the colored people."

Godfrey wrote to his niece, "I have throughout my life cultivated an unusually large crop of very violent prejudices and I have the utmost faith that you have the like and will show up on the 4th of November with a vote for General Eisenhower." Godfrey had not only reached the point where he could joke about his prejudices, but where they were softening. He not only began writing again to Katherine, the widow of his son Jim, whom he had long ostracized, but admitted to her some of his past errors of judgment. "Mussolini made a very good start when he came into power and conditions were incomparably better when I was in Italy in 1936 than when I was there in 1921. . . . He certainly proved himself a good deal of a humbug, and your Aunt Minnie and I were among those who were humbugged. . . . I met him in Palazzo Chigi . . . and was very favorably impressed by him; but I didn't see far beneath the surface."

He wrote to Percy W. Bidwell of the Council on Foreign Relations: "When the McKinley bill was up, I was in general opposed to it and so was Harry Lamb, President of the Free Trade Association, but in a very few years we discovered that in that particular case we were entirely wrong: that that very well-conceived piece of legislation had produced a great industry and converted the United States from being the largest importer of tin and terneplate to becoming large exporters . . . showing our ability, once we were started to compete with the world in that branch. So please let me counsel you in the first place to judge every bill affecting tariff not only on general principles but also on the particular circumstances preceding that particular case."

A frequent recipient of Cabot's advice was Joseph C. Grew, who had married a daughter of Godfrey's sister Lilla. As World War II ended, Godfrey had written him, "I am heartily in favor of . . . treating the Germans as bad children—but I do not believe in trying to starve them, as Clemenceau did" and he had urged that the Japanese be allowed to keep their emperor.

After nearly a century of unsuccessfully trying to wipe out sin, Cabot was still not discouraged about the human race, as he pointed out in another letter to Grew: "We hear a great deal of pessimistic talk . . . in attempts to prove that mankind is recently growing worse rather than better so far as character is concerned . . . which could be confuted by a visit to Egypt and the inspection of the contemporary records of what the Pharaohs did, or by a study of Herodotus' history. . . .

"That there is a great deal of loose living and other evils is a summons to all of us to fight with all our power and soul against these evils; but in doing so let us not forget that international generosity and charity have been shown on a scale never before approached, and do our best in the eternal struggle of right against wrong. It is helpful to study intensely and carefully both sides of the picture that we may view the whole situation in reasonably correct proportion, and not emulate Cassandra's shrieking prophecies of future evil."

In his letters to Grew, to Christian Herter, to most of the great figures in politics and education he knew, Cabot preached the same sermon against unenforceable "gentlemen's" agreements in political and international affairs as he had preached to his sons in regard to price fixing. ". . . next to the spirit of greed, it seems to me that nothing has contributed more to encourage international aggression than the treaties made by many of our presidents with foreign countries pledging abstention from certain weapons of war, for instance, poison gas. I do not believe the Germans would have used poison gas at Ypres if they had not previously been parties to a treaty most solemnly forbidding the use of poison gas. I do not believe that the Germans would have invaded Belgium in 1914, if they had not previously bound them-

selves by most solemn treaties not only not to attack Belgium but
to protect Belgium from foreign attack, so that they had less
resistance to these new forms of attack by reason of more effective
surprise. I don't doubt that you can find in history hundreds of
instances in support of this opinion, for instance: the third Punic
war where the Carthaginians disarmed themselves on the solemn
covenant of the Romans that they would not be attacked, and then
the Romans immediately attacked them and destroyed the city."

This same suspiciousness had also led Cabot on his long
crusade against dirty books and brothels. He knew how hard it
was for himself to resist temptation, and he believed that most
men—weaker, lesser men—had not his strength and had to be
forcibly deprived of the opportunity to sin. The terrible temptation he would have felt to cheat on an unenforceable agreement he
projected onto all mankind, but not his power to resist. For this
same reason he had grave doubts about the United Nations, just
as he had agreed with his cousin, Henry Cabot Lodge, about the
League of Nations.

Those who knew Cabot only as the sin stalker of the Watch
and Ward Society were surprised at his frequent and public
pronouncements on free speech during the McCarthy days. Actually Godfrey in his own crusty and highly individualistic way
had always been concerned with civil liberties. During World
War II, when one Max Stephan of Detroit was condemned to
death for harboring an escaped Nazi German pilot, Godfrey via
Senator David I. Walsh of Massachusetts sent a private petition
urging commutation of the sentence to President Roosevelt. "I
have no doubt of the guilt of the accused. I do not question the
wisdom of the law or the correctness of the conduct of every court
and official of the United States in connection with the case, but I
do think that if Edith Cavell, the latchet of whose shoes I am
unworthy to unlace, were alive, she would join in this petition."
Stephan's sentence was commuted the day before his execution
had been scheduled.

In 1945 Cabot signed a statement of the National Federa-
tion for Constitutional Liberties which took the position, with
regard to the eligibility of Communists and Communist sympa-
thizers for Army commissions, that "the basic consideration is not

the propriety of the individual's opinions; but his loyalty to the United States." In his letter of support, Cabot wrote, "In this connection it is interesting to note that the early Christians were Communists and that the Pilgrim Fathers who landed at Plymouth in 1620 founded a commune and during the two years that this commune endured they lost a very large percentage of their people by starvation and disease which taught them that Communism simply didn't work." Godfrey was but one of a number of very strange bedfellows among the signers, including Michael J. Quill, President of the Transport Workers Union, Paul Robeson, Thomas Mann, William Zorach, and Exeter Headmaster Lewis Perry.

Godfrey wrote Harvard President James B. Conant in 1947, "I saw with pleasure in today's paper that permission has been given to 26 young men at Harvard to organize a Communist Society." He urged that they be supplied with a clear history of Communism's many failures and its evils, and he expressed his outrage that Stalin, whom he habitually called Joseph Vissarionovich Djugashvili, be called a Communist, when in fact he was really a despot, a bandit, and a murderer.

In 1949 Godfrey wrote to President James Killian of M.I.T. concerning a professor accused of being a Communist, saying that "he should stand or fall by the broad question as a whole is he desirable as an instructor or not?" In defense of a similarly attacked Harvard professor and against Tom's advice, Cabot wrote a long letter to the Boston *Herald*, marshaling all the same arguments including the probability that Jesus Christ was a Communist.

Cabot considered McCarthy a bad joke, writing in 1954 to various people, "As for McCarthy, it is a great misfortune for the U.S. that I am not the autocrat that orders everything for I would win untold wealth for our beloved country by setting him to blow a windmill and generate all the electricity in this country 'Free, gratis and For Nothing.' "

The virtues of the father, however, were visited on his son. Tom Cabot had been sent by the Truman Administration to Egypt to study that country and its new leaders. When the Eisenhower Administration took over, Tom sent his report to the new Secretary of State, John Foster Dulles, recommending that the United States support the building of the Aswan dam.

When he returned home, he found that he had lost his security clearance from the State Department. The alleged reasons for this withdrawal were hidden in the desk of Scott MacLeod, the ridiculous State Department Security Officer whom Eisenhower had appointed. Eventually a security officer from the State Department was sent to question Tom, asking him first about his relationship with his father and whether or not he usually agreed with him, and then specifically if he agreed that Jesus Christ and the Pilgrim Fathers were Communists. Tom was not only furious, but also alarmed that he might lose his Defense Department, Atomic Energy Commission, and Central Intelligence Agency clearances and as a result not be allowed to continue on the Corporation and Executive Committee of M.I.T. Finally Tom reported his problem to M.I.T. President James Killian, who called the White House. Within twenty-four hours Tom had his clearance back.

Despite Godfrey's one year spent at M.I.T. and his pride at being a Life Member of its Corporation, his first love was for Harvard. Like most Boston Brahmins, he had a greater feeling for Harvard College than for any other institution, not excepting any church.

Much of the business of Harvard is run by its Board of Overseers, a group including thirty men elected by the alumni. A number of Godfrey's antecedents and contemporary relatives, including his son Tom, served as Overseers, though Godfrey himself never did. But the real control of Harvard is in a nondemocratic self-perpetuating group of seven men, the Harvard Corporation, made up of five Fellows of Harvard College and the President and the Treasurer. The Fellows run Harvard and are accountable to no one. A number of Godfrey's ancestors and his older brother Arthur had been Fellows, and his cousin Paul Cabot was the Treasurer of Harvard who from 1950 to 1966 helped raise the University's endowment from $217 million to over a billion dollars.

It was natural that Godfrey would become a part of the

strong town-and-gown relationship between Boston and Harvard
which has existed since the College was founded in 1636 and
which always somehow secured from Boston for the College men
of intellect and men with money, sometimes in the same person.
Unlike some universities, Harvard has not often "built its endowment 'by degrees,' " by giving an honorary degree in recognition
of a large donation. There was, therefore, some criticism when in
1951 Godfrey Lowell Cabot was given an honorary LL.D., it
being felt that if he deserved an honorary degree at ninety, he had
deserved it at seventy or eighty, and that the late bestowal was a
bid for more contributions. Godfrey, however, was unaware of or
unconcerned with any such speculations and proudly accepted the
degree, going to and departing Cambridge by subway.

In 1954 Godfrey wrote to a niece "I went this week to a
luncheon at which I had a brief chat with President Pusey of
Harvard, and I think he is well worthy of that important office.
He has a wise head and a wise heart, and if there is anything more
important than the first it not infrequently is the second." A year
later, however, Cabot was less enchanted, writing to Pusey and to
the *Alumni Bulletin* criticizing Harvard's dropping classical lan-
guages as a requirement for entrance. "When I entered Harvard
in 1878, I had to have passed four examinations in Greek; four
examinations in Latin; one examination in Ancient History and
Geography, out of a total of sixteen examinations. . . . I appreciate very fully the enormous value of the natural sciences to
which I have given a great deal of attention. . . ." This step of
President Pusey's was the logical continuation of the policy of
"practical" education and a skeptical scientific outlook begun
nearly a century earlier by President Charles Eliot, which had
caused Godfrey to compare Eliot unfavorably to the Cabot cook.

After dictating this letter, Godfrey confided to his secretary,
"I might be able to bribe Doctor Pusey in this connection. You
know he wants a million or a million and a half dollars for a
building at Harvard to be paid for by me. I think this business of
classical education very important and I might be able to bribe
Doctor Pusey by offering—not to him, of course, but to Harvard—my United Carbon Company stock, which is worth some-

thing over $800,000."

Cabot's bribe attempt, however, was not successful; in fact, Harvard soon thereafter even ceased writing its diplomas in Latin. Cabot was concerned, as others have been since, that Harvard not become merely a highly specialized trade school. Within Godfrey's lifetime he had seen an unbelievable change in Cambridge. He was a boy when M.I.T. was founded and a real chemistry department begun at Harvard, and as an old man he saw along Route 128 great corporations such as Polaroid, Raytheon, and Sylvania, whose existence was based on the new technology. Indeed, the real estate firm of Cabot, Cabot and Forbes (founded by cousins of Godfrey) had made so great a fortune by leading all others in this wedding of university and industry that it had come to be known by jealous competitors as "Cabot, Cabot, and Grabit."

Since Godfrey's time others have become concerned with the triple play of government to education to business; with the propriety of a university doing "classified" research in peacetime; with a research program itself becoming little more than a "boondoggle"; and with the ethical problems involved in a man's being at the same time a professor, a government employee, and a businessman.

Others too have come to worry, as Godfrey's cousin A. Lawrence Lowell had in 1931 when he wrote: "The idea that going to college is one of the inherent rights of man seems to have obtained a baseless foothold in the minds of many of our people."

One of the problems of Cabot's last years was the disposal of his money, but it was a problem which concerned his heirs far more than himself. In 1957 *Fortune* magazine published a list of the seventy-six richest Americans, those with fortunes of between seventy-five million and a billion dollars; Godfrey L. Cabot was listed in the group worth between seventy-five and one hundred million dollars.

Year after year Tom had sought to interest his father in some estate planning which would give his heirs a maximum inheritance with a minimum of taxes, but the old man refused to be interested.

In 1939 before writing a will, Godfrey, then seventy-eight, wrote his son Jack, "I feel that there is no urgency in this matter." Year after year in response to Tom's efforts, Godfrey repeated the same answers: no need to take into account estate taxes which would be removed once a Republican administration was elected; there should be less thought given to corrupting children into folly and extravagance by possession of too much money and more concern with "The best heritage that we can leave to our children [which] is the habit of industry and the earnest, poignant desire to render service to others."

Cabot regularly gave a set of the Encyclopedia Britannica to each grandchild as a wedding present, but when, contrary to his wishes, the debut and subsequent wedding of one of his granddaughters were in his view too ostentatious and elaborate, he pointedly gave her a secondhand set.

As Godfrey progressed through his eighties, evidencing no interest in the inheritance problems of his heirs, it was clear that he had power and did not intend to give it up.

After trying to sell Godfrey on a plan, one of Boston's prominent attorneys said, "He was perfectly prepared to pay death taxes if that was the price of keeping absolute control. He feared any trust arrangement might enable Tom to get in the thin edge of the wedge."

Cabot had made it known that he did not want to be cremated, what hymns he wanted played at his funeral, and that he wanted some evidence of his military service in his funeral; but except for small annual gifts to his descendants, he stoutly refused to make plans about the disposition of his fortune.

Finally, when he was over ninety and saw that President Eisenhower had not eliminated or even lowered taxes, he paid attention to the many memoranda Tom had sent him about his money going "to a profligate Government" for "its handouts" rather than to his grandchildren and great-grandchildren and that outsiders would be running the business he had built.

But rather than using any of the elaborate plans worked out over the years by the leading law offices and accounting firms in Boston, Godfrey one Saturday told Fred Fernald, his house counsel, that he wanted to make equal gifts of most of his stock to each of his descendants and descendants' spouses. When Fernald started to explain that this was not the most propitious way to proceed and that the plan would cost his heirs millions in taxes, Cabot cut him off and fixing him with his blue eyes, he said he wanted his wishes carried out that very day.

The result was a much more favorable distribution to Godfrey's older children, who had more children and grandchildren. Godfrey was later convinced by his grandson Louis Cabot that he should make compensating gifts to correct some of the inequities. The new arrangement was not only more just, but also tended to avoid stockholders' fights in what was still a family-controlled business.

When he was reminded by his lawyers that the stature of probate judges has not shown much tendency to increase, Cabot put the balance of his fortune into an *inter vivos* trust, which would avoid the legalized chicaneries of probate court and save considerable expense after his death. He also agreed to the purchase of real estate in Bermuda and Nassau because it would not be subject to estate taxes.

Because of Cabot's advanced age the danger existed that if he died within three years after these arrangements had been made, the Internal Revenue Service would conclude that much of what he had done was "in contemplation of death." Three years later Godfrey told one of his attorneys, "Tom told me then, 'Father, you can't afford to die now,' and I said, 'Well then, I won't,' and I kept my word."

Although Godfrey's stubbornness and arbitrary method cost the family millions in taxes which might have been avoided, his heirs nevertheless inherited substantial fortunes. Not the least remarkable thing about the Cabot family members has been that they survive not only in name but in wealth and social prominence when so many other prominent Boston families, as Cleveland Amory pointed out in *The Proper Bostonians*, have not.

Thomas Boylston, the richest man in Colonial Massachusetts, who was worth $400,000 at the time of the

Revolution, has left his name on Boston's chief uptown
commercial thoroughfare, but there are no Boylston
descendants in Boston's *Social Register* of today. Paul
Revere is a striking case. He was rich, lived to be eighty-
three, joined a dozen clubs, organized the first Scottish Rite Masonic Lodge in Massachusetts, married
twice and had eight children by each wife—yet not one
of his many descendants today cuts a social swath in
keeping with the aspirations the famed midnight rider
and silversmith had for his Family.

Hutchinsons and Gores, Royalls and Vassalls,
Dudleys and Pinchons, Brimmers and Bromfields, once
names to conjure with in Boston Society circles, have all
fallen by the wayside. Some of these early-day Families
died out from natural causes. Other whole family
groups were among the thousand Loyalists who left for
Halifax, and did not return, when the British evacuated
Boston in the Revolution. But these facts alone do not
explain so many fade-outs. Many a Family, rising
early, lived too well to last. They spent their money
instead of leaving it for their descendants. The Han-
cocks did this, or rather one Hancock, John, did it all
by himself. His Uncle Thomas had made all the money
before the Revolution, and John spent it, half a million
dollars—a huge fortune for those times—in just ten
years after the Revolution. In that period, as King of
Boston Society, he lived on a social scale that included
the wearing of solid gold buttons and the snubbing of
George Washington. But when he died in 1793 he left
no will at all, and even his house, Beacon Hill's famed
Hancock House, once the pride of Yankee Society, was
unable to ride the storm. It was torn down for taxes in
1863, Boston thereby losing what has been called the
finest example of Colonial architecture in all the thirteen colonies . . . and generations of Proper Bostonians were thus provided with a lasting textbook example of the wisdom of stern wills, trust funds, and other

ways of nipping extravagant heirs in the bud. . . .
There is scarcely a Family that does not owe its position
in the city's Society to the money he [its founder] made
and saved and left in the spendthrift-proof trusts.

Godfrey himself demanded of his children an Oriental sense of
family—that is, not just respect and obedience in the immediate
family circle, but also knowledge of and pride in the whole clan,
living and dead. He could and did himself make fun of some of his
family's peculiarities and warned his children against the false
pride and ancestor worship not uncommon in Boston, telling
them they must not be "like potatoes, with the best part underground."

Once, when a Western brokerage firm had written to the
Boston investment bankers Lee, Higginson, asking about the
qualifications of a young Bostonian who was applying for a job,
the venerable Boston house had sent a genealogy showing the
youth's connections with the first families of Boston. The Western
firm had thanked Lee, Higginson but pointed out that this was
not the kind of information they were seeking, since they were not
planning to use him for breeding purposes. Godfrey demanded of
himself and his sons that each prove himself, but he was also
proud of his family's history and even of Cabot idiosyncrasies. An
insistence on accomplishment has led to the inclusion of nine
Cabots in the 1966–67 *Who's Who in America,* four of them
Godfrey's direct descendants. A greater number appear in the
Social Register.

Not the least interesting appraisals of Godfrey were his
children's. Eleanor, a not untypical product of Miss Winsor's
School, the Vincent Club, the 1913 Sewing Circle, and some
training in landscape architecture, viewed him as a great man. He
only shocked her badly once, when after his older brother Arthur's death, Eleanor discovered her father weeping in back of
their house while Minnie comforted him.

William's view of his father was never known, for though
still alive in 1966, he had never learned to speak. When Jim died
at thirty-eight, his only known feeling for his father was anger.

At sixty-nine, speaking of his father, Tom clearly admired much about Godfrey, while still hurt by his lack of affection and approval. "He was a non-conformist in the sense that he wanted to do things differently and better than anyone else had done them. Even the silly, show-off, learning of facts or Latin names by heart was evidence of his consuming ambition and determination to whet his intellect. The purpose to which he whet his intellect was to try to improve the world, to improve the lot of mankind.

"You can call it vanity, but if it was creative, if his terrible competitiveness to be better than whomever, to have a better idea himself than whatever was suggested, if that meant something worthwhile for the public, then it was good.

"I think this determination that he was going to find a better way than anyone else in everything, even in trivial things, and his desire to bring even trival things to public attention, is both extraordinary and of some benefit to mankind, which is becoming far too conformist.

"He had a terribly strong feeling of duty toward the world and we need more people with feelings of duty. The man in Kansas City owes much of his America to the Puritans and my father was the last example of a real Puritan, a good example of what made New England great and what spread to the rest of the United States and made them great.

"My father never worshipped money *per se*, he only worshipped the power that money could bring him, the power to enforce Right with a capital R. He never lived conspicuously. He lived a very frugal, a very simple life.

"Despite the fact that his business had long since grown incomparably larger and more profitable than Sam's paint and shingle stain plant, my father always somehow felt he lived in Sam's shadow.

"Sam had built a mansion and he and his family revelled, at least for Bostonians, in the rich things of life. Dr. Arthur Cabot, childless and carefree, had, even while serving as a Fellow of Harvard, lived the life of a bon vivant by any standard in the world. But my father continued all his life to be the family's only real Puritan, carefully counting out change from his mesh purse and on guard against the slightest sign of hedonism in any member of his branch of the Cabot clan.

"I did not admire him particularly as a businessman nor in some other areas, but as a man I admired him. I admire the fact that my father was not cut to the ordinary mold, that he was unique, and that he had in him elements of greatness. I too am a Puritan, not a good one. He was a real Puritan. I admire his concern for duty, for doing what was right, not simply right in the passive sense, but right in the active sense."

Ambassador John Moors Cabot's view of his father was less admiring. He attributed his father's coldness and cruelty to Godfrey's own childhood, to his having been too strictly brought up and bullied by his own parents and his older brothers and sisters. He believed that Godfrey's own parents recognized this and that the reason he was sent as a boy every year for ten years to his uncle Walter Cabot's house in Manchester was to get him out from under his family.

Jack thought his father cruel to Minnie, as well as to his children; he believed that what little affection his father showed was put on, and he could not remember that his father had ever told him he loved him. "After Jim died and after they moved to Washington he softened a bit and was perhaps a bit less of an autocrat and a martinet. He may even have begun to realize that sin was endemic in this world and that his lone efforts could not eradicate it once and for all. He began to evidence a slight tolerance for grace or elegance in other people.

"But he was always a lone eagle. He never flew in a flock, but always above and lonely."

Godfrey's daughters-in-law had a less critical view of him and were less embarrassed by his idiosyncrasies. Jack, whose careful tailoring matched his careful Groton accent, was appalled at his father's cheap ready-made suits which he never had pressed and at his heavy policeman's shoes. Jack's wife, however, saw Godfrey as the usual "genteel Boston shabby." She thought him a charming and even courtly theater companion. She said that away from Boston he was so relaxed that he could become profane, for example, in Guatemala cursing a caddy who pretended

Godfrey's golf ball was lost when in fact he had hidden it. She was amused that the few cents the golf ball was worth meant as much to Godfrey as to the boy and that he faced him down and got it back.

Cabot's son-in-law, Ralph Bradley, could also be less emotional in his appraisal, and he admired and liked the old gentleman except for his "disgusting point of view on sex that even a married woman who enjoyed sex was wicked and that a man and wife should never see one another naked. What he practiced was legalized rape. Hell's bells, he must have been starved sexually and he suffered from an awful mother complex. If there had never been a Freud, you'd have had to invent one to explain Godfrey Cabot."

There were a number of people who hated Cabot, including some of his employees who were thought by the Cabot family to adore the old man but who secretly despised him as a bigoted, penny-pinching, evil-tempered despot. Some of his relatives thought that "Godfrey killed his wife by requiring her to walk and to travel when she was sick and by his mania for fresh air, when it was freezing. She did not love him, nor did his children, which is a sad life no matter how rich you are. Godfrey missed the whole adventure of living because he was so concerned with himself."

A number of his chief executives, however, had more admiring views.

"I guess he was the last of his breed around Boston, stubborn, shrewd, completely individualistic. I'm not sure he was more than others of his time, maybe he just lived so long his world died before him.

"He had such a marvelous way of using English. I remember once Fred [Fernald] was explaining to the Chief the terrible alternatives if we lost a suit Huber had brought against us, and he stopped Fred, who was well along in his fifties, saying, 'Young man, in this long life I have learned the unexpected always happens, the impossible frequently, but the worst never.'

"I was proud of him and proud to work for him. I was a kid who grew up around poolrooms and he made me want to go to

libraries. And he took other guys, some of them uncouth, uneducated hillbillies and made them not just rich but smarter and more
moral, more like him. He spoke slowly so people could think and
could keep up with him, but he made it clear this was no place for
dumbbells and he made you want to learn.

"Way back in the thirties he made it damn clear that he
wanted no discrimination anywhere in the company including at
the executive level, not on any basis of race, color, or religion and
anybody he caught at it would be fired on the spot. There's not
many companies this size even today where that's true.

"Sure it was an industrial autocracy and thank God there
was Ralph to mediate between the Chief and Tom and between
them and the rest of the employees. But he was a helluva man,
especially away from Boston, and he wasn't the prude he was
made out. He loved a good joke, even a dirty one, not about
infidelity, but say about the unreasonableness of women and he
loved to tell about Johnny the Orangeman shouting, 'To hell with
Yale.' And he knew how to cuss himself too.

"I think particularly when he was older he enjoyed being
thought of as an eccentric. When Avery [Cabot's secretary-
clerk] came to the office one day smelling of Bay Rum, the Chief
told him 'Go home and sleep it off. Every man's entitled to one
mistake.' I think he knew it wasn't liquor, it was his kind of joke
on himself. I know when Owen Brown [the sales manager] ordered fifteen cases of booze from S. S. Pierce, the bill was sent by
mistake to the old man, but by the time he got it there had been a
twenty-five per cent price increase and the Chief called in Brown
and congratulated him on his vision. He was never fooled by those
big expense vouchers for 'tea' in Akron.

"He liked young women and he sparkled when they were
around. He charmed the wives of his employees like Rhett Butler.
But he always said what a great lady his wife was. I guess we were
proud of the moral standards he set, which were unique for any
business but especially the oil and gas business.

"But what impressed you most was the courage, the energy
and the courage. He used to tell how no first-rate law firm in
Boston had the guts to go after Coakley and Pelletier and he'd

say, 'You know, it's a funny thing. You can go out to kill a lion and get lots of people to help you, but when you go out to kill a skunk you've got to do it yourself.'

"I guess what made him different from most men today was that he wasn't afraid of his customers. One Saturday in 1937 when he was the only one in the office he got a call from a vice-president of one of the major tire companies who wanted to place a big order but told the Chief he wanted him to stop the bulk differential price war. The Chief was sore at him anyway because his company had made a deal with one of Cabot's competitors and was in effect in the carbon manufacturing business. So the Chief interrupted him and said, 'I am not, sir, accustomed to taking instruction from my competitors' and hung up. And for years afterward we couldn't sell a pound of black to them, but the Chief never gave a damn."

In his last years, Godfrey's interest in religion increased. In his youth Godfrey's religion was a simple, dutiful, Boston Unitarianism. He once wrote his wife, "I think Unitarianism is greatly needed all over the world. At first, perhaps, not for the many but most certainly for the few, the intellectual leaders in every clime, in whose hands lies the welfare & the guidance of the many. Unitarianism can best teach them how to well discharge this sacred trust."

Godfrey remained a Unitarian all his life, resisting with no apparent effort the charms of handsome Phillips Brooks, who had come to Boston in 1869 and led so many, especially ladies, up (or down) the Christian path he had taken from Unitarianism to Episcopalianism. Although Episcopalianism was to become in a very few years as fashionable among First Families as had Unitarianism over many decades, Godfrey would probably have agreed with Emerson's definition of Boston Episcopalianism as the best diagonal line that could be drawn between the life of Jesus Christ and that of Boston merchant Abbott Lawrence. Godfrey was practical enough, however, to write Minnie about Jim, "I would much rather that he would go to an Episcopal church every Sunday than stay away from a Unitarian church."

All his life Godfrey felt that he was obligated to an active search for duty and whatever was difficult, not unlike his view in business. It was reminiscent of what Daniel Webster wrote to Henry Cabot from Sandwich, where he had gone fishing. "I got these by following your advice; that is, by careful and thorough fishing of the difficult places, where others do not fish."

During Godfrey's lifetime thousands of white Protestant Americans had sought the syrupy, soothing solace of passive religions as preached by various doubtless sincere salesmen of salvation-cum-sympathy from Emile Coué to Norman Vincent Peale. Not for Cabot, however, were these tranquilizing therapies. For him there was no alternative to active service for others and struggle against evil. He wrote Minnie, "I am deeply interested by your charitable work & so sure as the sun rises it will bring its blessing upon you. It will help you to learn what is the most important lesson here below that the deepest highest & most fundamental truths are beyond the grasp of the intellect & make themselves known only through the intuitions of the heart.

"The wider and deeper our sympathy the more will our heart attune itself to vibrate with the divine harmony or with those few notes of it that are within human ken."

In another letter to Minnie, Godfrey had made clear the source of his dutiful religion. "I have your postal card of the 19th in which you say you shall go crazy if you do not hear from me by tomorrow morning. [Cabot had written her six letters in the preceding nine days] . . . Beware of a complaining petulant disposition my darling. Jim has a tendency that way, so has Tom & I want you to set them a good example.

"When I was a little boy nine years old, in the winter of 1870 mother and I made a visit at Aunt Lizzie Cabots in Brookline. We slept together, & in the morning while we were waiting for the girl to come in and make our fire mother taught me two hymns either of which might be considered a psalm of life.

"The first is by Miss Coleridge I believe

> One by one the sands are flowing
> One by one the moments fall
> Some are coming some are going
> Do not strive to grasp them all

One by one thy duties wait thee
Let thy whole strength go to each
Let no future dreams elate thee
Learn though first what these can teach

One by one thy griefs shall meet thee
Shadows passing through the land
Some shall fade while others greet thee
Do not fear an armed band.

One by one bright gifts from heaven
Joys shall meet thee here below
Take them readily when given
Ready too to let them go.

Every hour that fleets so slowly
Hath its task to do or bear
Luminous the crown and holy
If each gem be set with care.

"The other is by Longfellow

Tell me not, in mournful numbers,
Life is but an empty dream
For the soul is dead that slumbers
And things are not what they seem

Art is long and time is fleeting
And our hearts, though stout and brave,
Still, like muffled drums, are beating
Funeral marches to the grave.

Life is real life is earnest
And the grave is not the goal.
"Dust thou art, to dust returnest,"
Was not spoken of the soul.

In the world's broad field of battle
In the bivouac of life
Be not like dumb pastured cattle
Be a hero in the strife.

Trust no future howe'er pleasant
Let the dead past bury its dead
Act, Act, in the living present
Heart within the God o'erhead.

Lives of great men all remind us
We can make our lives sublime
And departing leave behind us
Footprints in the sands of time

Footprints that, perhaps, another
Sailing o'er life's solemn main,
Some forlorn and shipwrecked brother,
Seeing, may take heart again.

Not enjoyment and not sorrow
Is our destined end or way
But to act, that each tomorrow
Find us farther than today

Let us then be up and doing
With a heart for any fate
Still achieving, still pursuing,
Learn to labor and to wait.

"These two inspiring poems have been my talismans through life, talismans that I have worn not next to my heart but in it to keep it warm, strong, unconquerable by any trial or fear, calm in every exigency, firm against every shock.

"Learn these yourself & let your children learn them at your knee and remember that there is One whose ear is ever open to us, who stands ever ready to 'hold the cross before our closing eyes. Shine thro the gloom and point us to the skies.' "

To his sons, to friends, and to prominent scholars and politicians, Godfrey wrote: "David Harum's remark 'A reasonable amount of fleas is good for a dog; keeps him from broodin' too much on bein' a dog,' embodies in very homely phraseology what is by far the most important scientific fact that . . . the basis of all evolution in organic things from the lowest bacterium up to

homo sapiens is the need of stimulus; need of the practice of over-
coming every kind of competition; physical, mental and perhaps
most of all, moral.' "

Godfrey was also fond of quoting both in Greek and in
English,

ἢ ὁδὸν εὑρήσω ἢ ποιήσω
"I shall find a way or I shall create one."

Godfrey's real religion was an instrumental concept of duty,
for limited as he was by "Thou shalt nots," he was even more
affected by "Thou shalt." His idea of freedom was not "freedom
from," but rather "freedom to." His morality was not exclusively
negative, but mainly a positive morality of aspiration, a Greek
morality of excellence and the fullest realization of human powers.

Godfrey's greatest admirers were the trained nurses who
were with him for the last six years of his life. In the summer of
1956, at the age of ninety-five, Godfrey had his appendix removed, and after that he no longer walked to work. At the end of
1956 he stopped coming to work at all, staying at home, going
out only for drives or very short walks.

His confinement made him lonely and in his continuing flood
of letters he wrote, ". . . stop in at 242 Beacon Street and give
me a hug and kiss and take a meal with us, or with me if I happen
to be alone, as is often the case. . . . I am spontaneously and
automatically in love with all very little girls. . . . I confess
myself to a love of stroking stray cats that come near me and look
up with mournful eyes as if wishing to be cosseted."

Godfrey himself more and more needed cosseting, especially
in the last years, when increasingly he lived in his own childhood.
His children visited him less frequently than his nurses thought
they should. "Tom Cabot came and talked and talked and talked
about Australia or West Virginia or Timbucktoo so fast and
furiously that Mr. Cabot got nothing out of it.

"Mrs. Bradley didn't stay with him much and when she did
she was cold. But one of the other nurses said, 'Whatever she is, he
did it to her.' He made her what she is. She was his daughter and

she couldn't be any different, because that's the way he treated
her. It was easy for us to love him and be sweet to him. We had
him only six years. But she had had him all her life.

"Mr. Bradley was the member of the family who visited him
most often and was always sweet and affectionate."

Godfrey seemed to his nurses a great man from another age.
He used language they had never heard—not only Greek and
Latin and German, but old-fashioned terms; he called his rice
pudding "hasty pudding" and his oatmeal "porridge." But what
appealed to them even more was the little boy who wanted every
morning a whole pint of thick cream and bananas on his "porridge." They were very moved by Godfrey's terrible loneliness
and his obvious desire for affection. Whenever one of them entered
the room, he held up his lips to be kissed and a hand to be held.

His nurses were flattered by his compliments. "He did me the
honor to tell me I read beautifully. At first I read him *Ivanhoe*
and *Great Expectations* and biographies of Lincoln and parts of
the encyclopedia. But later he wanted *Alice in Wonderland* and
poetry, *The Vision of Sir Launfal, A Visit from St. Nicholas, The
Wreck of the Hesperus, Abou Ben Adhem, You Are Old Father
William, The Walrus and the Carpenter* and the poems of James
Russell Lowell. His favorite was *Mr. Hosea Biglow to the Editor
of the Atlantic* and *My Love* which Lowell had written to Mr.
Cabot's mother. And he knew them all by heart and recited with
us as we read to him.

"We read the Bible clear through to him and sometimes
when I tried to skip a few verses of the Old Testament when they
were not interesting he invariably interrupted with 'Read it all.'
His favorites were the Twenty-Third Psalm and the story of
Ruth, but especially the story of the Prodigal Son.

"If any of us played the piano, he sang, old songs like
'Seeing Nellie Home' or German songs, 'Tannenbaum' or 'Lorelei'
and once, when he was ninety-nine—it was when Mrs. Skinner was
on duty—I played a waltz, *The Blue Danube,* and he danced with
one of the nurses. My, he loved to dance.

"You know he'd been a very stiff and proper man all his life
and now finally the defenses were down. Sometimes he not only

wanted us to kiss him, but he'd ask us to marry him or to get into
his bed or to make a baby. But you couldn't be angry, he was like
a sad lost boy."

More and more Godfrey lived in his boyhood and told stories
of his youth. He particularly remembered his first walk with his
mother, when he was three or four years old. It was to a home for
destitute children, and his mother had put some money for the
poor children in his hand to give to the woman who ran the home
so that he would remember to share what he had. Godfrey recalled
not sleeping that night, thinking about the children who had no
mothers. He constantly pointed to the picture of his mother by his
bed and said how beautiful and good she was. He rarely spoke of
his wife or children but often of his adored mother, that she was
such a good Christian woman and had taught him to be honest
and truthful.

Godfrey's nurses noted, however, that his face was happier
when he spoke of his grandmother. "When I was on night duty, he
loved to talk at night, he told me that as a child he was much
troubled by what God thought about him. It was his grandmother
who told him, 'He loves you and He will take care of you.' And he
said he would be happy to see his grandmother again. He was a
lost little boy who needed affection and taking care of and to be
made to feel important. My God, how he wanted love!"

Godfrey spoke often, too, of another occasion, when he had
seen a man with no legs pushing himself along on a board on
rollers in Park Square. He had run crying home to tell his father,
who had given him some money for the cripple; but when Godfrey
rushed out again the man was gone, and again he had not slept,
worrying about the man and if he had a home.

He recalled to his nurses the day he had gone in 1876 to the
hundredth-anniversary celebration of the Battle of Lexington
and had been too shy to go up and shake the hand of President
Grant. Godfrey said he had regretted it all his life because he was
a great admirer of Grant—as indeed he must have been to have
ignored Grant's predilection for what Godfrey considered vice.
He told the nurses that as a boy he had had a picture of Tad
Lincoln in his room and that his greatest hero was Lincoln, whose

wife was a burden rather than a help. Godfrey said Robert E. Lee was a traitor and argued fiercely with the nurses who held Lee to be a great man.

Some of his recollections of childhood were happy. He remembered that when one of his father's horses was sick, Joe Lee, a cousin who was a genius with horses, had made a diagnosis of appendicitis, and his father had then successfully removed the horse's appendix. He remembered happy summer days at Ponkapoag, where he was paid half a cent for every hundred flies he caught around the house, and he was quite pleased with his earnings. He laughed when he recalled some of his mischief at the Brimmer School and later at Boston Latin and at Mr. Hopkinson's school.

"He said that when he went to the engagement party of his friend, Will Putnam, they were having a fine time until the father of the fiancée took Mr. Cabot into the library and said, 'You know, Godfrey, I have another daughter.' Mr. Cabot laughed and said, 'I got my hat and stick and got out of there as fast as I could because the other daughter was Amy Lowell.' "

But mostly he told the nurses of his regrets. He said he had wanted to be a doctor like his father and that having honorary doctorates was not the same. He said he had loved his cousin Ruth Cabot, but that his sister Lilla had said he could never marry her because it was wrong to marry a cousin. He told how sad he had been when he finally realized that his brother Guy was mentally retarded and that his father had never explained the facts to him; he also spoke of how sad it was that his son William could not uphold the family name.

"He said how shy he had been as a boy and that he had not been able to show affection or make friends easily and had retired into himself. He overcame it somewhat in college, but he was always shy with girls. 'I hope you were kind to your mother,' he would say to me, and he would then tell how every day he came home and read aloud to his mother.

"He often had terrible nightmares in the last years. He would dream that he was the captain of a ship, taking it through a very dangerous rocky channel and he shouted, 'Turn her aft!

Fend her off! Pull that rope!' He kept it up for hours and it was very exciting, because he was terribly strong, you know, until the very end and we had difficulty keeping him in bed. Once he had a dream that he and Tom were in a shell on the river and Tom fell overboard in all his clothes and Mr. Cabot *ordered* Tom to swim ashore and run home as fast as possible and change his clothes. There was no question but that Tom *must* obey."

The childhood recollection of which Godfrey spoke most feelingly, however, concerned his experiences with the girls who lived and worked in the brothel on Carver Street directly behind his father's house at 11 Park Square. "They were not good women. They were wicked. They washed their long hair right there in the back yard and they stroked it and brushed it and dried it in the sun."

Godfrey became very wrought up when he told how terribly upset he had been when the girls would sit on the back fence and laugh at him and invite him to come over the fence, and he said they made obscene gestures and said wicked things to him and the men who were always coming and going made fun of him too.

"They were not like women I knew, they looked common and bedraggled. I was very angry at them and I wished God would punish them or that somehow I could get enough money together to buy that house and turn them all out."

One night, when he was 101 years old, he said to his nurse, "You know there is something I would like very much to do."

"I asked him what it was and he said he would like to go to his grandmother's house for Thanksgiving. I assured him that his grandmother would welcome him with open arms. He said he would like to stay with her overnight and asked if I thought it would be presumptuous to ask her about it. I told him I was sure that she would prefer him to any other member of the family and you should have seen how happy he was believing that. He turned over and went right to sleep."

He never again recovered consciousness, and two days later, on November 2, 1962, Godfrey Lowell Cabot died.

On November 5, 1962, at the First Church in Boston, at Godfrey Lowell Cabot's funeral service, which was so simple that some found it stark, there were sung the two hymns he had requested.

> We praise thee, God, for harvests earned
> The fruits of labor garnered in;
> But praise thee more for soil unturned
> From which the yield is yet to win!

> We praise thee for the harbor's lee,
> And moorings safe in waters still;
> But more for leagues of open sea,
> Where favoring gales our canvas fill.

> We praise thee for the journey's end,
> The inn, all warmth and light and cheer;
> But more for lengthening roads that wend
> Through dust and heat to hilltop clear.

> We praise thee for the conflicts won,
> For captured strongholds of the foe;
> But more for fields whereon the sun
> Lights us when we to battle go.

> We praise thee for life's gathered gains,
> The blessings that our cup o'erbrim;
> But more for pledge of what remains
> Past the horizon's utmost rim!

Lead, kindly Light, amid the encircling gloom,
Lead Thou me on!
The night is dark and I am far from home—
Lead Thou me on!
Keep Thou my feet; I do not ask to see
The distant scene,—one step enough for me.

So long Thy power hath blest me, sure it still
Will lead me on,
O'er moor and fen, o'er crag and torrent, till
The night is gone;
And with the morn those angel faces smile
Which I have loved long since, and lost awhile.

NOTES, BIBLIOGRAPHY
AND INDEX

Notes

The page numbers cited in the works of others in these Notes refer to the editions listed in the Bibliography.

Page Number

x   "Yankee passion": Brooks, *Indian Summer*, 85.

x   "pours righteous indignation": G. K. Chesterton in an interview in *The New York Times*, November 21, 1930.

x   "suspect that it would have required much more heroism": Santayana, *Last Puritan*, 46.

x   "It's a popular error to suppose that puritanism": *ibid*, 8–9.

xi   "We are no longer sure": James Truslow Adams' 1931 Introduction to *The Education of Henry Adams*.

xii   "never got to the point": Henry Adams, *ibid*, 4.

xiii   "not exempt from the passion": *ibid.*, 502

CHAPTER I   *Earlier Cabots*

Page Number

4   "to be hanged": This quotation and most information on Cabot genealogy comes from *History and Genealogy of the Cabot Family 1475–1927*, in two volumes by L. Vernon Briggs, privately printed in Boston in 1927. All quotations and letters in Chapter I not otherwise identified are from Briggs' work.

13   "renders most of those" and "gradually brings a numbness upon the heart": qtd. in Mannix and Cowley, *Black Cargoes*, ix and 145. I am particularly indebted to Mannix and Cowley, not only for information on the history, the economics, and the politics of the slave trade, but also for their clear and moving picture of slavery in all its aspects, which I have tried briefly to reflect in this chapter.

13   "the distinguishing feature of the trade": qtd. in *ibid.*, ix–x.

13   The distinction made between white and black slaves was small, as may be seen by their joint appearance in an advertisement in the *Boston News Letter*, May 3, 1714: "Several Irish Maid Servants time most of them for Five Years and one Irish man Servant who is a good Barber and Wiggmaker, also Four or Five Likely Negro Boys," qtd. in *ibid*.

14   The quotations from Leviticus and Genesis are cited in *ibid.*, 60.

14   "creatures of another species": qtd. in *ibid.*, 60

14   "domestic animals" and "I will remember": qtd. in *ibid.*, 64

14   "England had formerly": *ibid.*, 51.

15   "By 1750, there were sixty-three distilleries": *ibid.*, 160.

15   "Before that time": *ibid.*, 187.

15   Figures on slave population and cotton: *ibid.*, 68.

15   "The interior is drained" and "Africa is bleeding" and "the slave trade will die": qtd. in *ibid.*, 243.

15   "upon pain of the highest displeasure": qtd. in *ibid.*, 173.

16   "He has waged cruel war": qtd. in *ibid.*, 174.

16   "in complaisance to South Carolina": qtd. in *ibid.*, 174.

16   "I am drawn along": qtd. in *ibid.*, 174.

16   "It cost me thousands": qtd. in *ibid.*, 174.

27   "Certainly not": qtd. in Amory, *Proper Bostonians*, 93.

27   "I am about as good": *ibid.*, 93–4.

Chapter II   *Godfrey's Parents*

28   "The end is to improve our lives": John Winthrop, "A Model of Christian Charity," written in 1630 on board the *Arabella* on his way to the Massachusetts Bay Colony, where he was for many years Governor. Qtd. in Handlin, *American Principles*, 33–4.

30   "knew each other well": John T. Morse, Jr., *Memoir of Colonel Henry Lee*, qtd. in Amory, *Proper Bostonians*, 20.

30   "Oh! to be born in Boston": qtd. in Morison, *One Boy's Boston*, 24–5.

32   "I'm getting rather worried": qtd. in Amory, *Proper Bostonians*, 43–4 and 70.

32   "It is no derogation": qtd. in *ibid.*, 5.

Chapter III   *A Bumptious Boyhood*

Page Number

36   "the boy Henry": Henry Adams, *Education*, 41–2.

39   The history of boys on the Common and Boston boyhood games comes from Morison, *One Boy's Boston*, 31–5.

40   "more in the dread of damnation": Santayana, *Last Puritan*, 4.
40   "with nothing in it": *ibid.*, 19.
40   Re the Stamp Act atmosphere, see Henry Adams, *Education*, 43.
42   "I pride myself": qtd. in *ibid.*, 29.
42   "to hate the sin": Benét, *John Brown's Body*, 162.
42   "hated bear baiting": Macaulay, *History of England*, Vol. I, ch. 2.
46   "Resistance to something": Henry Adams, *Education*, 7.
47   "Town was winter": *ibid.*, 7–9.
53   "From women the boy got": *ibid.*, 41.
53   "To balance this virtue": *ibid.*, 40–1.

CHAPTER V   *Wanderjahr*

Page Number
76   Stubbornness like Cabot's was a leading characteristic of the early
      New England settlers, many of whom were sent to America as
      indentured servants. A number of these were Scottish prisoners
      who had been too stubborn to heed Oliver Cromwell's plea for
      compromise before the Battle of Dunbar: "I beseech ye in the
      bowels of Christ, think that ye may be mistaken."
80   "Goethe was raised to the rank of Shakespeare": Henry Adams,
      Education, 62.
80   "Emerson served up Goethe's philosophy": Santayana, *Last Puri-
      tan*, 126.
88   "carries his own inch rule of taste": Henry Adams, *Education*,
      182.

CHAPTER VI   *Cabot in Love*

Page Number
90   "one could learn nothing but": Henry Adams, *Education*, 100.
91   "the president of Harvard college": Godfrey was referring to
      Charles William Eliot, whose revolutionary changes at Harvard
      were less appreciated when he introduced them than later.
95   "It is quite possible that some other person than myself": Cabot
      was much concerned about future readers of his Journals. When
      he built his house at 16 Highland Street in Cambridge, he had a
      safe put in the basement, and nothing was ever kept in the safe
      except his Journals. His wife said that any burglar who broke
      into the safe would be sadly disappointed.

115   "The boy went to church": Henry Adams, *Education*, 34.
115   "The Universalists believe": qtd. in Morison, *One Boy's Boston*, 66.
117   "After the Bible was translated": Hobbes, qtd. in Muller, *Uses of the Past*, 271.

CHAPTER VII   *Marriage and Other Business*

Page Number

128   "A rich country": Galbraith, *Affluent Society*, 307.
143   "Had they been Tyrian traders": Henry Adams, *Education*, 237.
144   "I cheat my boys": qtd. in Josephson, *Robber Barons*, 46.
145   The figures on Ford are from Morison, *Oxford History*, 889.
145   Steel production figures, *ibid.*, 761.
146   "Last month you reported on hand": qtd. in Josephson, *Robber Barons*, 270.
146   "Economy does not consist": Emerson, *Journals*, Bk. IV, 225.
146   The figure of $220,000,000 to purchase titles is found in Josephson, *Robber Barons*, 342.
148   "the Brahmins were going into banking": Brooks, *Indian Summer*, 15–16.

CHAPTER VIII   *Rich at Last*

Page Number

154   "A competitor is not merely a competitor": James Truslow Adams, *Adams Family*.
157   "surrounding themselves with an ether": Brooks, *Indian Summer*, 38.
174   "He paweth in the valley": Job 39: 21–5.

CHAPTER IX   *Paterfamilias*

Page Number

195   Cabot's feelings about divorce were not unlike those of his fellow director of the Watch and Ward Society who viewed divorce as the "natural climax of self-indulgence." Peabody had once written a forty-five-year-old Groton graduate who married a divorcee: "The step is directly contrary to the teachings of Christ and strikes at the very foundations of family life. . . . To me it is not a question of error but of actual wrong." Frank D. Ashburn, *Peabody of Groton*, qtd. in Amory, *Proper Bostonians*, 325–6.

CHAPTER X   *First in the Air*

Page Number

205   "born to ignoble times": qtd. in Brooks, *Indian Summer,* 123.

206   "Established pioneering research": from Cabot's obituary in *Time,*
       November 9, 1962, 25.

CHAPTER XI   *Watch and Ward*

Page Number

212   On *Huckleberry Finn* and *Scarlet Letter* see Blanshard, *Right
       to Read,* 141.

214   "The service that he performed": Mencken, *Prejudices: A Selec-
       tion,* 238–9.

214   "The unbelief of the age": Emerson, *Journals,* Bk. IV, 479.

214   "I hate goodies": *ibid.,* Bk. IV, 491–2.

215   "It is impossible to conceive of a disillusioned Puritan": Miller
       and Johnson, *The Puritans,* 60.

215   "We hear the characteristic tones": Heer, *Intellectual History
       of Europe.*

217   "The Puritan was always obsessed": Simpson, *Puritanism in Old
       and New England,* 91.

219   "The dresses and beauty": qtd. in *Familar Letters of John Adams
       and His Wife Abigail Adams.*

221   "When I was a boy": J. Frank Chase, qtd. in New Bedford *Sun-
       day Standard,* July 16, 1916, 21.

223   The changes in attitude about the Sabbath are noted by Amory,
       Proper Bostonians, 45.

227   These quotations from Henry James and Henry Adams and
       Santayana are qtd. from Hardwick, *A View of My Own,* 146–7.
       Irwin Edman called Santayana's *The Last Puritan* "the com-
       mentary of a philosopher . . . upon the blind, tortured confusions
       of modernity. It is a comment also on the self-destruction in
       America of so much hope and beauty by moral conventions and
       material idols." There were in the heredity and the environment
       of Godfrey Cabot the same possibilities for self-destruction as
       existed in Santayana's hero or in Captain Ahab. There were the
       same possibilities for bitterness as in Henry Adams. And yet Cabot
       somehow made of his life a success—that is to say, on balance, in
       his career, in his marriage, in his children, in his business, and in
       most of his fields of interest, he built more than he destroyed.

227   "Your Honor, this book is a bucket of swill": qtd. in Amory,

Proper Bostonians, 329.

230 For a fuller view of New England's intellectual non-decline see Howard Mumford Jones in *Harvard Alumni Bulletin,* February, 1966, 426.

231 "He put psychology under lock and key": Henry Adams, *Education,* 232.

232 "To other Darwinians": *ibid.,* 231. Interestingly, many of the newer, non-Freudian ideas in psychology are close to Godfrey's ideas. Dr. Viktor E. Frankl of Vienna believes that most neuroses today are caused not by sexual frustration but by a lack of "will-to-meaning," a lack of adequate purpose, as Godfrey preached to Minnie. O. H. Mowrer at Illinois says that what is the matter with most people is not a false sense of sexual guilt but a feeling of real guilt. There is increasingly expressed the view that unless the human organism inhibits its own impulses, it cripples the possibility of optimum response in the total overall range of excitation and response, and an increasing number of psychiatrists now believe that the chief problem in education, psychology, and morals is the acquiring of freely accepted self-inhibitions about appetites, tastes, and use of time, sexuality being only one of the dimensions of this problem. Even modern sociologists and economists are expressing views surprisingly close to some of Cabot's. David Riesman has written about these same two problems: modern man's unwillingness to do what is difficult, which he calls "the cult of effortlessness," and the lack of direction and meaning in the lives of many moderns. Even such a modern professor of "the Dismal Science" as John Kenneth Galbraith points out that "Men must see a purpose in their efforts" (*Affluent Society,* 281).

CHAPTER XIII *The Middle Years—Sixty to Ninety.*

Page Number

257 "I care a great deal": a letter of Henry Adams, 1875, qtd. in Brooks, *Indian Summer,* 8.

258 "rebellious and troublesome" and "blinded by privilege": qtd. in Amory, *Proper Bostonians,* 323–4.

275 "an incandescent electric bulb": from an article in *American Ink Maker,* September, 1927.

280 "the picture of the Puritan as an intellectual": Simpson, *Puritanism in Old and New England,* 106.

280 "the Puritan scholastics": *ibid.,* 107.

280 "necessary to bury difficult questions": *ibid.,* 107.

281 "to almost all classes of society": *ibid.,* 107.

281 "The idea that one has actually met a real genius": Henry Adams, *Education,* 141.

286   "I'd rather have a polygamist": qtd. in Harris, *Political Wit,* 234.

286   "A censor is a man": Broun qtd. in Roeburt, *Wicked and the Banned,* 30–1.

287   "Beauty may, after all": Kerr, *Criticism and Censorship,* 75.

289   "Nor is it desirable": Hand's opinion in Spector Motor Service, Inc. v. Walsh, 1944, qtd. in Hand, *Spirit of Liberty,* xix.

CHAPTER XIV   *Grand Old Man*

Page Number

298   "Retiring from business" and "To retire from business": Amory, *Proper Bostonians,* 90–1.

304   "Americans needed and used": Henry Adams, *Education,* 181.

305   "A traveller in the highways": *ibid.,* 499–500.

305   "a world that sensitive and timid natures": *ibid.,* 505.

308   "Burning at first": qtd. in Hand, *Spirit of Liberty,* 61.

318   "Thomas Boylston, the richest man": Amory, *Proper Bostonians,* 37–9.

325   For a description of Episcopalianism's progress in Boston, see *ibid.,* 105.

329   "freedom to" see Lon L. Fuller, "Freedom—A Suggested Analysis" and *Morality of Law.*

Bibliography

Adams, Charles Francis, *An Autobiography*. Boston, Houghton Mifflin, 1916.

——, and others, *A Cycle of Adams Letters*. Boston, Houghton Mifflin, 1920.

Adams, Henry, *Chapters of Erie*, new edition. New York, Henry Holt, 1886.

——, *The Education of Henry Adams*, New York, Modern Library, 1931.

——, *Letters of Henry Adams*, 2 volumes, edited by Worthington Chauncey Ford. Boston, Houghton Mifflin, 1930–38.

——, *Mont-Saint-Michel and Chartres*. New York, Mentor Books, 1961.

Adams, James Truslow, *The Adams Family*. Boston, Little, Brown, 1930.

Adams, John, *Diary and Autobiography*, 4 volumes, edited by Lyman H. Butterfield and others. New York, Atheneum, 1964.

——, and Abigail Adams, *Familiar Letters of John Adams and His Wife Abigail Adams*. New York, Hurd & Houghton, 1876.

Adams Family Correspondence, December 1761–March 1778, 2 volumes, edited by Lyman H. Butterfield and others. New York, Atheneum, 1965.

Amory, Cleveland, *The Proper Bostonians*. New York, E. P. Dutton, 1947.

——, *Who Killed Society?* New York, Harper & Brothers, 1960.

Barron, C. W., *They Told Barron: Notes of the Late Clarence W. Barron*. New York, Harper & Brothers, 1920.

——, *More They Told Barron*. New York, Harper & Brothers, 1931.

Beard, C. A., and M. R. Beard, *The Rise of American Civilization*, 2 volumes. New York, Macmillan, 1927.

Benét, Stephen Vincent, *John Brown's Body*. Garden City, Doubleday, Doran and Company, 1929.

Blanshard, Paul, *The Right to Read: The Battle Against Censorship*. Boston, Beacon Press, 1955.

Bowen, Catherine Drinker, *Yankee from Olympus*. Boston, Atlantic–Little, Brown, 1944.

Brandeis, L. D., *Other People's Money and How the Bankers Used It*. New York, Frederick A. Stokes, 1932.

Briggs, L. Vernon, *History and Genealogy of the Cabot Family 1475–1927*, 2 volumes. Boston, Charles E. Goodspeed & Co., 1927.

Brooks, Van Wyck, *The Flowering of New England*. New York, E. P. Dutton, 1936.

——, *New England: Indian Summer*. New York, E. P. Dutton: Everyman Library, 1940.

Broun, Heywood, and Margaret Leech, *Anthony Comstock: Roundsman of the Lord*. New York, Albert & Charles Boni, 1927.

Carnegie, Andrew, *Autobiography*. Boston, Houghton Mifflin, 1920.

Cary, Thomas G., *Memoir of Thomas Handasyd Perkins*. Boston, Little, Brown, 1856.

Clews, Henry, *Fifty Years in Wall Street*. Irving Publishing Company, 1908.

Corey, Lewis, *The House of Morgan*. G. Howard Watt, 1930.

Craig, Alec, *Above All Liberties*. New York, W. W. Norton, 1942.

——, *Suppressed Books*. Cleveland, World Publishing Company, 1963.

Davis, Elmer, "Boston," *Harper's Magazine*, Vol. 156 (January, 1928), 140–152.

——, *But We Were Born Free*. Indianapolis, Bobbs-Merrill, 1954.

DeConde, Alexander, *The Quasi War*. New York, Charles Scribner's Sons, 1966.

Duniway, Clyde A., *The Development of Freedom of the Press in Massachusetts*. New York, Longmans, Green, 1960.

Emerson, Ralph Waldo, *Essays*. Boston, James Munroe, 1841.

——, *Essays, Second Series*. Boston, James Munroe, 1844.

——, *Journals of Ralph Waldo Emerson*, edited by Edward Waldo Emerson and Waldo Emerson Forbes. Boston, Houghton Mifflin, 1909.

——, *Basic Selections from Emerson*. New York, Mentor Books, 1954.

Ernst, Morris L., and Alan U. Schwartz, *Censorship—The Search for the Obscene*. New York, Macmillan, 1964.

Flynn, J. T., *God's Gold: John D. Rockefeller and His Times*. New York, Harcourt, Brace, 1932.

Forbes, Allan, *Early Myopia*. Boston, privately printed, 1942.

Forbes, Esther, *Paul Revere and the World He Lived In*. Boston, Houghton Mifflin, 1942.

Frankl, Viktor E., *Man's Search for Meaning*. New York, Washington Square Press, 1963.

Freidel, Frank, and Norman Pollack, *Builders of American Institutions*. Chicago, Rand McNally, 1963.

Freidel, Frank, T. Harry Williams, and Richard N. Current, *A History of the United States to 1876*. New York, Alfred A. Knopf, 1965.

Freidel, Frank, T. Harry Williams, and Richard N. Current, *A History of the United States Since 1865*. New York, Alfred A. Knopf, 1965.

Fuller, Lon L., "Freedom—A Suggested Analysis," *Harvard Law Review*, Vol. 68, No. 8 (June, 1955).

——, *The Morality of Law*. New Haven, Yale University Press, 1964.

Galbraith, John Kenneth, *The Affluent Society*. Boston, Houghton Mifflin, 1958.

——, *The Liberal Hour*. Boston, Houghton Mifflin, 1960.

Green, Martin, *The Problem of Boston*. New York, W. W. Norton, 1966.

Greenslet, Ferris, *The Lowells and their Seven Worlds*. Boston, Houghton Mifflin, 1946.

Hale, Nancy, *New England Discovery*. New York, Coward-McCann, 1963.

Hand, Learned, *The Spirit of Liberty*. New York, Alfred A. Knopf, 1953.

Handlin, Oscar, *Boston's Immigrants*. Cambridge, Harvard University Press, 1959.

——, *American Principles and Issues*. New York, Holt, Rinehart & Winston, 1961.

Hardwick, Elizabeth, *A View of My Own*. New York, Farrar, Straus, 1962.

Harris, Leon, *The Fine Art of Political Wit*. New York, E. P. Dutton, 1964.

Heer, Friederich, *The Intellectual History of Europe*. London, Weidenfeld & Nicolson, 1966.

Hoffer, Eric, *The True Believer*. New York, Harper & Brothers, 1951.

——, *The Ordeal of Change*. New York, Harper Colophon Books, 1964.

——, *The Temper of Our Time*. New York, Harper & Row, 1966.

Howe, Helen, *The Gentle Americans*. New York, Harper & Row, 1965.

Josephson, Matthew, *The Robber Barons*. New York, a Harvest Book, Harcourt, Brace & World, 1962.

Kerr, Walter, *Criticism and Censorship*. Milwaukee, Bruce Publishing Company, 1954.

Kronhausen, Drs. Eberhard and Phyllis, *Pornography and the Law*. New York, Ballantine Books, 1959–64.

Lawrence, William, *Memories of a Happy Life*. Boston, Houghton Mifflin, 1926.

Linscott, Robert N., ed., *State of Mind*. New York, Farrar, Straus, 1948.

Lodge, Henry Cabot, *Early Memories*. New York, Charles Scribner's Sons, 1913.

Lowell, A. Lawrence, *What a University President Has Learned*. New York, Macmillan, 1938.

Mannix, Daniel P., and Malcolm Cowley, *Black Cargoes*. New York, Viking Press, 1962.

Marquand, John P., *The Late George Apley*. Boston, Little, Brown, 1936.

Mason, Alpheus Thomas, *Brandeis*. New York, Viking Press, 1946.

McAllister, Ward, *Society as I Have Found It*. Cassell, 1890.

Mencken, H. L., *Prejudices: A Selection*, edited by James T. Farrell. New York, Vintage Books, 1958.

Meyer, Donald, *The Positive Thinkers*. New York, Doubleday, 1965.

Miller, Perry, *Orthodoxy in Massachusetts, 1630–1650*. Cambridge, Harvard University Press, 1933.

——, *The New England Mind: The Seventeenth Century*. New York, Macmillan, 1939.

——, *The New England Mind: From Colony to Province*. Cambridge, Harvard University Press, 1953.

——, *Roger Williams: His Contributions to the American Tradition*. New York, Bobbs-Merrill, 1953.

——, and T. H. Johnson, *The Puritans*. New York, American Book Company, 1938.

Morison, Samuel Eliot, *Builders of the Bay Colony*. Boston, Houghton Mifflin, 1930.

——, *Three Centuries of Harvard*. Cambridge, Harvard University Press, 1936.

——, *One Boy's Boston*. Boston, Houghton Mifflin, 1962.

——, *The Oxford History of the American People*. New York, Oxford University Press, 1965.

Muller, Herbert J., *The Uses of the Past*. New York, A Galaxy Book, Oxford University Press, 1957.

Parrington, V. L., *Main Currents in American Thought*. New York, Harcourt, Brace, 1927.

Perry, Bliss, *Life and Letters of Henry Lee Higginson*. Boston, Atlantic Monthly Press, 1921.

Putnam, James Jackson, *Human Motives*. Boston, Little, Brown, 1915.

Rand, Christopher, *Cambridge, U.S.A.* New York, Oxford University Press, 1964.

Reinfeld, Fred, *The Great Dissenters*. New York, Bantam Books, 1964.

Riesman, David, with Nathan Glazer and Reuel Denny, *The Lonely Crowd*. New Haven, Yale University Press, 1950.

Roeburt, John, *The Wicked and the Banned*. New York, Macfadden Books, 1963.

Russell, Bertrand, *The Conquest of Happiness*. London, Allen & Unwin, 1930.

——, *Why I Am Not a Christian*. New York, Simon & Schuster, 1957.

St. Louis *Post-Dispatch*, June 22, 1924, 18–19.

Santayana, George, *The Last Puritan*. New York, Charles Scribner's Sons, 1936.

——, *Persons and Places*. New York, Charles Scribner's Sons, 1944.

Simpson, Alan, *Puritanism in Old and New England*. Chicago, Phoenix Books, University of Chicago Press, 1961.

Smith, Homer W., *Man and His Gods*. New York, Grosset's Universal Library, 1952.

Smith, Richard Austin, "Fifteen-Million-Dollar Man," *Fortune,* Vol. 56 (November, 1957), 176.

Talese, Gay, *The Overreachers.* New York, Harper & Row, 1965.

Tarbell, Ida, *History of the Standard Oil Company,* 2 volumes. New York, Macmillan, 1925.

Teilhard de Chardin, Pierre, *The Phenomenon of Man.* London, Collins, 1959.

Tharp, Louise Hall, *Mrs. Jack: A Biography of Isabella Stewart Gardner.* Boston, Little, Brown, 1965.

Time, November 9, 1962, 25.

Veblen, Thorstein, *Theory of the Leisure Class.* New York, Viking Press, 1924.

Warner, Arthur, "Blackmail à la Boston." *The Nation,* November 2, 1921.

Index

349